# Random House
# Compact Atlas
## of
# World History

# Random House
# Compact Atlas
## of
# World History

**Random House
New York**

# Random House
# Compact Atlas of World History

Copyright ©1997, 1995 by Times Books

All rights reserved. No part of this book may be reproduced, in any form or by any means, without the written permission of the publisher.

All inquiries should be addressed to Reference and Information Publishing, Random House, Inc., 201 East 50th Street, New York, NY 10022.

Published in the United States by Random House, Inc., New York and simultaneously in Canada by Random House of Canada Limited, Toronto.

Originally published in Great Britain by Times Books, London in 1997.

The Random House compact Atlas of world History/edited by Geoffrey Parker
        p.        cm.
ISBN 0-375-70505-8
1. Historical geography--Maps. I. Parker, Geoffrey, 1933--.
G1030 .R39  1998  <G&M>
911--DC21                                  98-31173
                                  CIP
                                 Maps

Random House website address:
www.randomhouse.com

0 9 8 7 6 5 4 3 2 1
February 1999

ISBN 0-375-70505-8

New York   Toronto   London   Sydney   Auckland

# CONTENTS

**INTRODUCTION** *page* 9

## PART ONE

# The Ancient World

**HUMAN ORIGINS** *page* 10
1 Traces of human origins

**THE ICE AGE** 12
1 Hunters colonize the world
2 The colonization of the Americas

**THE ORIGINS OF AGRICULTURE** 14
1 Centres of animal and plant domestication
2 The decline of hunting and gathering

**THE FIRST FARMERS OF ASIA** 16
1 The agricultural revolution in the Near East
2 Early Chinese agriculture
3 Early farming in South Asia

**THE RISE OF CIVILIZATION** 18
1 The rise of civilization

**THE NEAR EAST 3000-605 BC** 20
1 Early empires of Mesopotamia
2 Old Kingdom Egypt c.3000-2000 BC
3 The growth of the Assyrian empire

**THE AMERICAS TO AD 800** 22
1 American peoples and cultures, c.AD 500
2 The Classic period in Mesoamerica AD 300-800

**PREHISTORIC AFRICA AND AUSTRALASIA** *page* 24
1 Africa: the Stone Age to the Iron Age
2 Early settlement in the South Seas

**SOUTH AND SOUTH-EAST ASIA TO AD 500** 26
1 India's first empires, 297 BC-AD 150
2 Prehistoric sites in South-East Asia
3 Gupta India

**EARLY EUROPE 6000-1000 BC** 28
1 The spread of agricultural settlement
2 The Aegean 2500-1200 BC

**THE GREEK WORLD 750-300 BC** 30
1 Greek colonization, 750-550 BC
2 The Peloponnesian War
3 The campaigns of Alexander

**WORLD RELIGIONS** 32
1 The diffusion of world religions

**ROME 264 BC TO AD 565** 34
1 The Roman Empire, AD 14-284
2 The later Empire, AD 284-565

**CHINA: THE FIRST EMPIRES** 36
1 The expansion of the Han Empire
2 Han China in AD 2

**THE COLLAPSE OF THE ANCIENT WORLD** 38
1 The collapse of the ancient world

## PART TWO

# The World Fragmented

**THE SPREAD OF CHRISTIANITY TO AD 1500** *page* 40
1 Christianity in Europe
2 The spread of Christianity

**CHINA 581-1279** 42
1 T'ang China
2 Sung China

**THE BYZANTINE WORLD 610-1453** 44
1 The Byzantine Empire, 628-1143
2 The Crusades and the decline of Byzantium

**THE ISLAMIC WORLD 632-1517** 46
1 The expansion of Islam
2 The Middle East and North Africa, 786-1260

**FRANKS AND ANGLO-SAXONS 714-814** 48
1 The Frankish Empire, 714-814
2 Anglo-Saxon England c. AD 800

**EUROPE 814-1250** 50
1 Viking, Magyar and Saracen invasions
2 The Hohenstaufen Empire 1152-1250

**EARLY RUSSIA 862-1242** 52
1 Varangian Russia, 862-1054
2 Kievan Russia, 1054-1242

**AFRICAN STATES AND EMPIRES 900-1800** 54
1 Africa, 900-1500
2 Africa, 1500-1800

## THE MONGOL EMPIRE
**1206-1696**  *page 56*
1 The Mongol Empire
2 The conquests of Timur, 1370-1405

## THE MUSLIM EMPIRES OF INDIA AND PERSIA
**1206-1707**  *58*
1 The Safavid and Mughal Empires

## SOUTH-EAST ASIA TO 1511
*60*
1 South-East Asia, AD 500-1500
2 Cultural divisions of South-East Asia in 1500

## EUROPE 1250-1500
*62*
1 Europe at the time of the Black Death
2 Eastern Europe 1278-1389

## CHINA AND JAPAN 1279-1644
*64*
1 The Ming dynasty, 1368-1644
2 Civil War in Japan 1467-1590

## THE OTTOMAN EMPIRE 1300-1699
*66*
1 The rise of the Ottoman Empire 1300-1520
2 The Ottoman Empire 1520-1639

## PRECOLUMBIAN AMERICA
*68*
1 Archaeological sites in North America, from AD 1000
2 The Aztec Empire in Mexico
3 The Inca Empire in Peru

## THE WORLD c.1492
*70*
1 Dominant economies and major civilizations 1492
2a Distribution of races, 1492
2b Diffusion of races after 1492

---

## PART THREE
# The Rise of the West

## THE GREAT DISCOVERIES
**1480-1616**  *page 72*
1 Voyages of discovery, 1480-1630

## EUROPEAN OVERSEAS EXPANSION 1492-1713
*74*
1 Spanish and Portuguese trade and settlement by c.1600
2 Commercial expansion to the East, 1600-1700

## THE EXPANSION OF FRANCE 1440-1789
*76*
1 The reunification of France 1440-1589
2 France under Louis XIV
3 The War of the Spanish Succession 1701-1713

## THE EXPANSION OF RUSSIA 1462-1815
*78*
1 Muscovy and the Russian Empire, 1462-1815
2 Russian expansion in Siberia, 1581-1800

## COLONIAL AMERICA 1519-1783
*80*
1 The development of colonial America
2 European settlement in North America

## SOUTH-EAST ASIA AND JAPAN 1511-1830
*82*
1 Japan in isolation
2 Trade and politics

## THE REFORMATION 1517-1660
*84*
1 Religious divisions in 1560

---

## THE HABSBURG ASCENDANCY IN EUROPE
**1519-1659**  *page 86*
1 The Habsburg Empire in Europe
2 Dutch Revolt, 1572-1648
3 The Thirty Years' War in Germany 1618-48

## CHINA UNDER THE CH'ING DYNASTY 1644-1911
*88*
1 Imperial expansion, 1644-1760
2 The dismemberment of the Chinese Empire, 1842-1911

## INDIA 1707-1947
*90*
1 The growth of British power in India to 1805
2 India, 1805-57
3 The Indian Empire in 1931

## THE AGE OF REVOLUTION 1755-1815
*92*
1 Revolts and revolutions in Europe and America
2 The Empire of Napoleon

## THE INDUSTRIAL REVOLUTION IN EUROPE
**c.1750-1914**  *94*
1 The beginning of the Industrial Revolution: Great Britain c. 1750-1820
2 The Industrial Revolution in Europe, 1850-1914

## THE EMERGING GLOBAL ECONOMY c.1775
*96*
1 The Atlantic economy
2 Trade in Africa and Asia

## THE UNITED STATES 1775-1865
*98*
1 The American War of Independence, 1775-1783
2 Territorial Expansion, 1803-1853
3 Union and Confederate states, 1861-1865

## AUSTRALIA AND NEW ZEALAND FROM 1788 page 100
1 The settlement and development of Australia
2 The settlement and development of New Zealand

## THE DECLINE OF THE OTTOMAN EMPIRE 1798-1923 102
1 The decline of the Ottoman Empire, 1798-1923

## AFRICA IN THE 19TH CENTURY 104
1 European penetration after 1880
2 Africa after partition, 1914

## LATIN AMERICA, 1808-1929 106
1 Political development in Latin America

## THE EXPANSION OF THE RUSSIAN EMPIRE 1815-1917 108
1 Russia in Asia, 1815-1900
2 The first Russian revolution, 1905

## NATIONALISM IN EUROPE 1815-1914 110
1 The unification of Italy, 1859-70
2 The unification of Germany, 1815-71

## IMPERIALISM 1830-1914 112
1 Colonial expansion, 1815-70
2 The colonial empires in 1914

## NORTH AMERICA 1865-1929 114
1 Urban and industrial growth, 1860-1929
2 The development of Canada, 1867-1929
3 Population density in 1900

## JAPAN 1868-1941 page 116
1 Industrialization and economic growth, c.1880-1922
2 Japanese expansion, 1931-41

## THE EUROPEAN POWERS 1878-1914 118
1 The Balkans, 1878-1913
2 European alliances

## THE WORLD ECONOMY ON THE EVE OF THE GREAT WAR 120
1 The development of the world economy
2 Foreign investment in 1914
3 The share of world trade

PART FOUR
# The Modern World

## THE CHINESE REPUBLIC 1911-1949 122
1 China under the Kuomintang, 1928-37
2 The Chinese Communist movement to 1945

## THE FIRST WORLD WAR 1914-1918 124
1 The Great War in Europe, 1914-18
2 The Western Front, 1914-18

## THE RUSSIAN REVOLUTION 1917-1945 126
1 Russia in war and revolution
2 Collectivization and population movements, 1923-39

## EUROPEAN POLITICAL PROBLEMS 1919-39 page 128
1 National conflicts and frontier disputes, 1919-34
2 German and Italian expansion, 1935-39

## THE GREAT DEPRESSION 1929-39 130
1 The World economy, 1929-39
2 The Depression in the United States

## THE SECOND WORLD WAR: THE WEST 1939-45 132
1 The German advance, 1939-43
2 The defeat of Germany, 1943-45

## THE SECOND WORLD WAR: ASIA AND THE PACIFIC 1941-45 134
1 The Japanese advance 1941-1942
2 The Allied counter-offensive against Japan 1941-45

## THE UNITED STATES SINCE 1945 136
1 Growth of metropolitan areas 1940-75
2 Civil rights and urban unrest, 1960-68

## EUROPE 1945-73 138
1 Post-war population movements
2 Post-war Germany 1945-90
3 Military and economic blocs, 1947-73

## THE SOVIET UNION 1945 TO 1991 140
1 The nationalities of the Soviet Union, 1989
2 Soviet armed forces deployment: military districts and bases

## EAST ASIA SINCE 1945  142
1 The Korean War
2 The Chinese economy, 1979-92
3 Japanese industrial production and exports, 1945-90

## RETREAT FROM EMPIRE AFTER 1947  144
1 The post-colonial world, 1947-90

## THE MIDDLE EAST SINCE 1917  *page 146*
1 The Iran-Iraq war, 1980-88
2 Israel and Palestine, 1947-94
3 The Gulf War, 1990-91

## LATIN AMERICA SINCE 1930  148
1 Social and political movements, 1930-94
2 Economic development

## AFRICA SINCE 1945  150
1 Africa: post-independence wars and revolutions

## SOUTH AND SOUTH-EAST ASIA SINCE 1945  152
1 Post-independence wars and revolutions
2 Vietnam, 1966-68
3 Japan, Australia and Asia to 1989

## THE COLD WAR 1947-89  154
1 The Soviet and American blocs, 1949-59
2 The Cuban crisis, 1962
3 The nuclear balance, 1955-80

## EUROPE SINCE 1973  156
1 The expansion of the European Union, 1981-96
2 Changes in economic structure, 1960-93
3 European GDP growth, 1950-92

## THE COLLAPSE OF COMMUNISM IN EUROPE SINCE 1989  158
1 The collapse of communism, 1985-91
2 The Yugoslav Civil War, 1991-95

## THE WORLD IN THE 1990s  *page 160*
1 World population 1995
2 Infant mortality and life expectancy
3 The world in the 1990s
4 Ozone depletion

## INDEX  162

# INTRODUCTION

This volume, like *The Times Atlas of World History*, first published in 1978 and now in its fourth edition (and available in 16 languages), attempts to cover the whole story of humankind from its origins, when our ancestors first emerged from the tropical forests of Africa, to the complex, highly articulated world in which we now live.

It differs, however, from the original *Atlas of World History*, and also from *The Times Concise Atlas of World History*, first published in 1982, in three important ways. First, as its name makes clear, it presents the data in a more compact form. Although it includes 76 spreads – one more than the *Concise* – each contains fewer, simpler maps and (proportionately) more text. Second, every map has been reviewed in order to highlight the salient trends and facts it features. Third, the topics selected for treatment include far more material from the modern period: 20 spreads concentrate on the period since 1914 (as against 16 in the *Concise*) and no less than 13 of them cover the half-century since 1945.

Nevertheless, although the present volume incorporates new material and differs in other important ways from its two predecessors, it rests upon the same principles. Above all, it tries to break away from a concentration on Europe and to offer instead a view of history that is world-wide in conception and presentation and which does justice, without prejudice or favour, to the achievements of all peoples, in all ages and in all quarters of the globe. It thus remains true to the vision of Geoffrey Barraclough, who planned and edited both the *Atlas* and the *Concise Atlas*:

"When we say this is an atlas of world history, we mean that it is not simply a series of national histories loosely strung together. In other words, it is concerned less with particular events in the history of particular countries than with broad movements – for example the spread of the great world religions spanning whole continents... In singling out topics for inclusion we have adhered to the principle of selecting what was important then rather than what seems important now."

The essence of history, as Geoffrey Barraclough realized, is change and movement over time; and the historian's principal mission is therefore to discern the static from the dynamic, the aberration from the trend, and the contingent from the constant. So instead of presenting a series of individual snapshots, *The Times Compact Atlas of World History* seeks to emphasize change, expansion and contraction. It aims to convey a sense of the past as a continuing process and thus to provide a fresh perspective on today's world which will meet the requirements and interests of present-day readers in all parts of the globe.

This revised edition incorporates several new features. First, all the later spreads – both maps and text – have been updated to cover events since the original edition went to press. Second, several other maps have been revised and improved and physical bases added. Third, errors brought to our attention by readers have been corrected.

GEOFFREY PARKER
October 1996

# Human origins

All major developments in the evolution of the human species took place in tropical Africa. Although life on earth, in the form of single-celled organisms, can be traced back some 4,600 million years, ape-like species only emerged 15 million years ago. Despite obvious physical differences, the great apes of Africa (chimpanzees and gorillas) are genetically almost identical to humans. The divergence of the human line occurred there between 5 and 8 million years ago (diagram 1).

Remains of the earliest hominids, *Australopithecus* or 'southern ape', dating from about 4 million BC have been found in both the limestone caves of southern Africa and in the Great Rift Valley. About four feet tall, they lived almost exclusively on fruit and nuts, with a brain size of about 700 cubic centimetres (not much different from a modern ape); but they walked on two feet and had complex social lives which stimulated the development of a larger brain. They already operated in nuclear family groups. Around 2.5 million years ago a new species appeared in east Africa known as *Homo habilis* or 'handy man', with a rounder skull. These were the first hominids to make and use tools (chipped stones and flakes), and perhaps also the first to scavenge for meat as a regular part of their diet. Their brain size was still only 800 cubic centimetres, but with *Homo erectus* ('upright man'), who developed around 1.7 million years ago, this increased to 1000 cc and sometimes more. These creatures made more sophisticated tools (above all stone handaxes and cleavers worked on both faces), used shelters (both caves and simple houses) and clothes, and learned to make and control fire – three developments that, between 1.5 million and 500,000 years ago, enabled their descendants, known as *Homo sapiens* ('thinking man'), to spread beyond their original tropical homeland and colonize less hospitable environments in Europe and Asia (map 1).

The spread of human groups beyond Africa was a gradual process – halting or even reversing as the glaciers advanced, more rapid in interglacial periods. *Homo erectus* was already in Java by at least 1.3 million years ago. The first fossils in Europe, some 500,000 years old, are of an archaic type of *Homo sapiens*, but the dominant form in Europe and western Asia was, by around 100,000 BC, a specialized form of *Homo sapiens* known as Neanderthal Man. Their brain size approached 1500 cubic centimetres, but their cold-adapted bodies were heavily built and so their brain as a proportion of body weight was less than that of modern man. Several of their settlements include careful burial sites in which some male skeletons lie with animal remains, unusually well-made stone tools, and even flowers (implying belief in an after-life), while others bear marks of previous disabling injury or disease (so the men must have been supported by other group members). They also hunted in groups and there is evidence they may have employed some form of speech, although this is disputed.

The earliest anatomically modern humans, *homo sapiens sapiens*, date from around 100,000 BC and also originated in east and south Africa. They co-existed with Neanderthal Man for tens of thousands of years, but eventually prevailed. They too spread to other parts of the Old World, bringing with them composite tools which combined the use of stone for the cutting edge and organic materials for the rest, such as spear-throwers and (probably) arrows, making it possible to kill animals some distance away. This enabled human groups to hunt more efficiently, following particular herds on their annual migrations and even perhaps taming a few horses and reindeer. By 30,000 BC, of the many species of hominid which had walked the earth during the past 5 million years, only one – *homo sapiens sapiens* – remained.

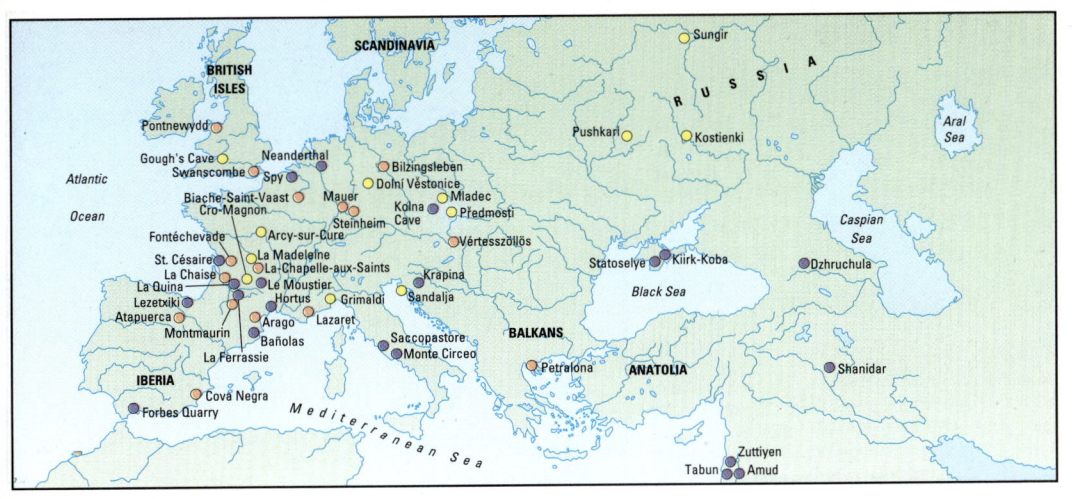

1 Traces of human origins
- Australopithecus
- Homo habilis
- Homo erectus
- Homo sapiens (archaic)
- Homo sapiens (neanderthal)
- Homo sapiens (modern)

11

# The Ice Age

The first Ice Age began some 1,500,000 years ago, and the pattern of alternating glacial advance and retreat has been the dominant feature of the global environment ever since. At intervals of around 90,000 years, temperatures on earth fell by up to 15°C and ice-sheets covered the northern parts of the Asian, American and European continents – almost one-quarter of the earth's present land surface lay under glaciers – preventing human settlement. Further south, however, the tropical regions remained warm, although much drier than today: about half the land between the tropics of Capricorn and Cancer became arid desert. In between the glaciations came warmer periods characterized by temperatures similar to those of the present day; but whenever the ice advanced, the animals suited to temperate conditions – such as humans, a species of tropical origin – had to move southwards.

The last Ice Age began some 80,000 years ago. As the ice advanced and more water became frozen at the poles, sea levels fell and caused the appearance of land bridges which linked most of the major land areas and many present-day islands (including the British Isles) into one vast continent (map 1). In the midst of this period a new species of human, *Homo sapiens*, began to spread from Africa, replacing or interbreeding with existing hominid populations in Europe and Asia (page 10). These modern humans, using an extensive range of bone, antler, and stone tools, and capable of creating imaginative art in several media (cave paintings, carvings, sculptures), spread throughout the habitable world. They took advantage of the shorter sea crossings caused by falling sea levels to colonize Australasia in about 50,000 BC. A little later, perhaps as early as 40,000 BC, they also reached Japan, across a land bridge from Korea. At about the same time they began to populate the Americas, either by crossing the land bridge which joined the two sides of the Bering Strait or by using boats. Within a few thousand years groups of hunters and gatherers had traversed the entire continent, reaching New England in the east and Chile in the south by 9000 BC (map 2).

Humankind's development of the skills, equipment and behavioural patterns to permit survival in such inhospitable environments constitutes a remarkable achievement. The mastery of fire and the invention of clothing and shelter, as well as new social and communication skills, all stem from this period. The human species is the product of the long process of adaptation to the harsh conditions of the Ice Age. The onset of warmer conditions around 10,000 BC, ushering in the interglacial period in which we now live, caused sea levels to rise and cut off America from further contact with Eurasia. Henceforth, these regions and their people pursued their own independent lines of development. By then, however, a total of perhaps 10 million humans engaged in hunting and gathering almost everywhere and had already become the world's most widespread and successful mammal.

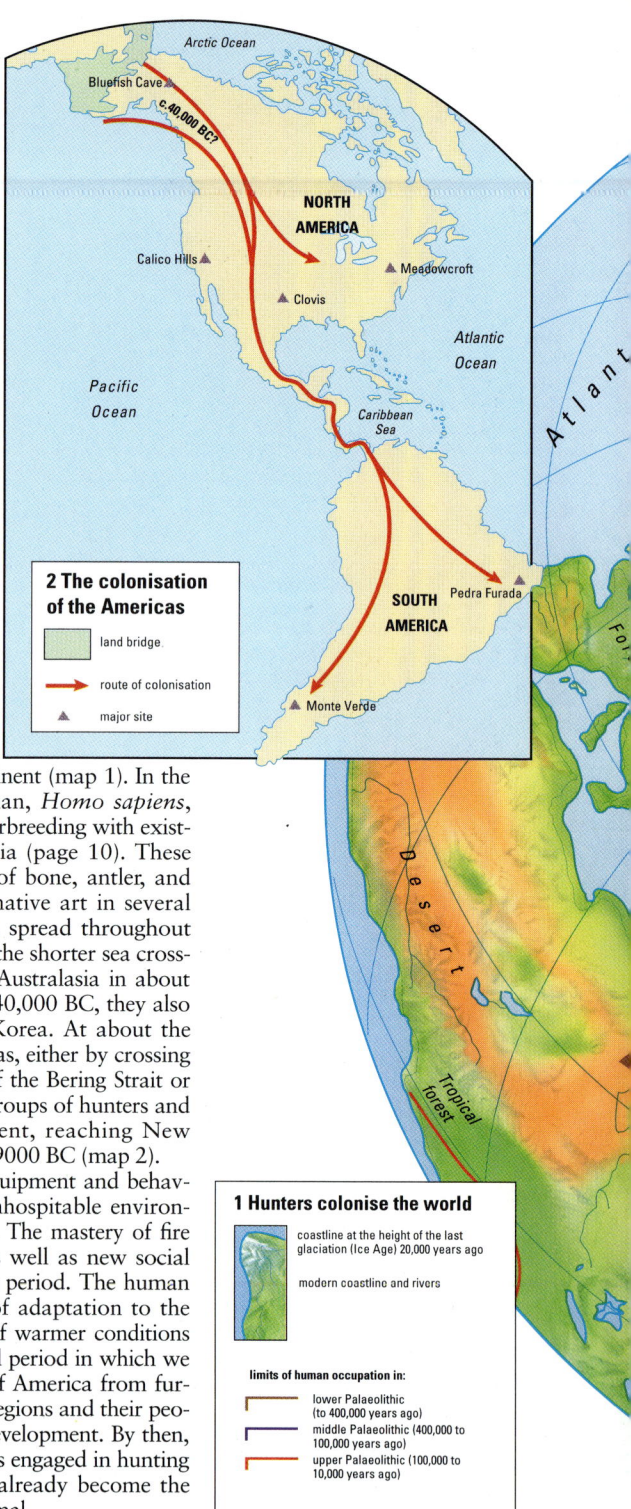

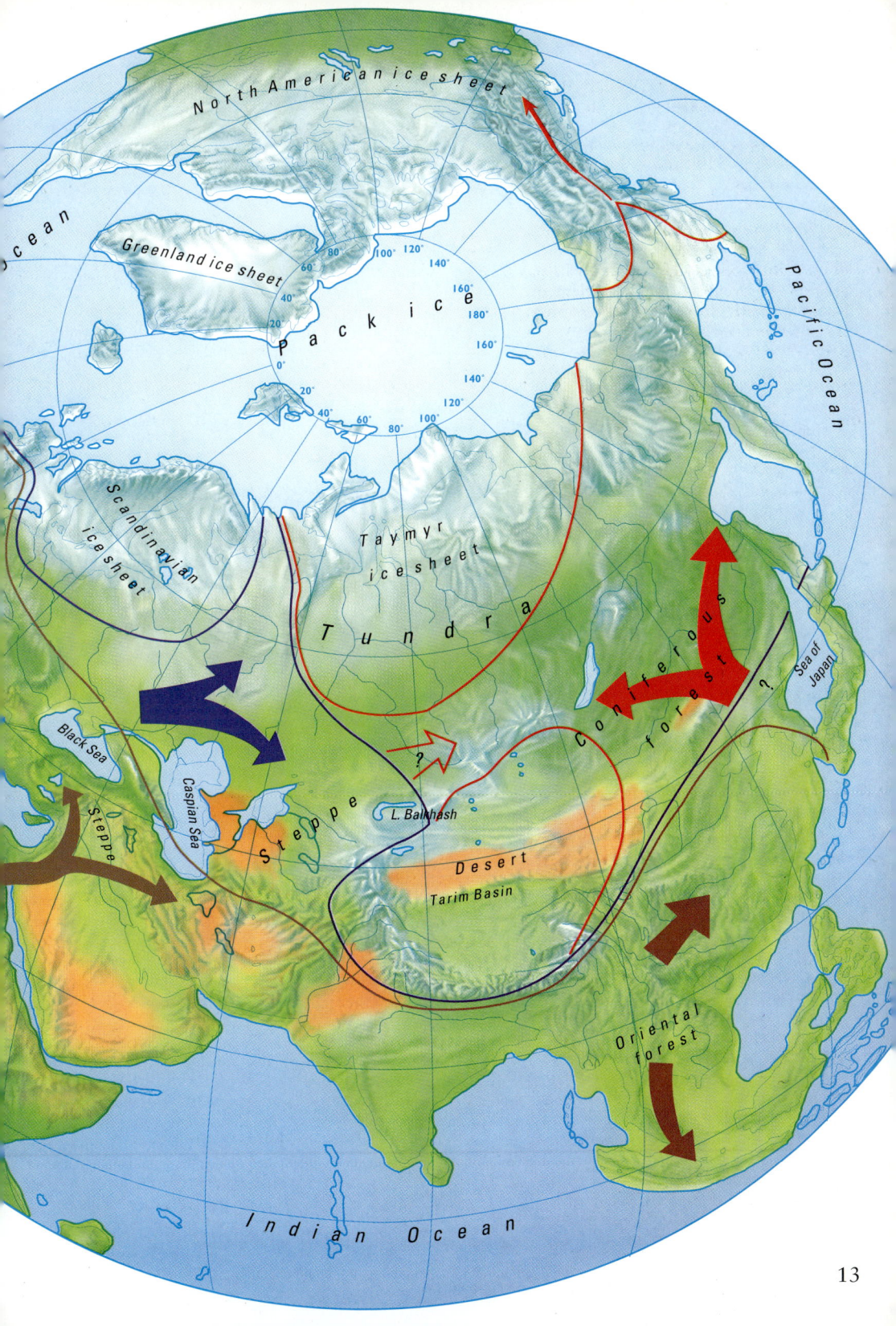

# The origins of agriculture

By 8000 BC, when present-day climatic conditions began to prevail, humankind consisted of bands of hunters and gatherers who, although more numerous than ever before, pursued a lifestyle that differed little from that of their predecessors up to 100,000 years before. But within the next 2,000 years substantial villages appeared in certain regions; and in another 3,000 years there were towns and cities.

This decisive quickening in the pace of human development can be attributed largely to the beginning of agriculture: the deliberate alteration of natural systems to promote the abundance of an exploited species or set of species. Many parts of the globe, especially those between latitude 10° South and 50° North, have contributed to the present-day repertory of domesticated plants and animals (map 1). Among the earliest and most important centres of cereal cultivation were the Near East, where the wild ancestors of wheat and barley grew; China and South-East Asia, where millet and rice thrived; and Mesoamerica, which developed maize as a staple crop. In Africa, people in the lands south of the Sahara and in the high grasslands of North-East Africa domesticated a wide variety of native plant species. On the whole, cereal cultivation characterized temperate regions and root crop cultivation – potatoes, yams, bananas – predominated in tropical zones.

At the same time, useful local animal species were domesticated to provide meat, milk, hides or wool, and (except in the Americas, which lacked suitable animals) an important source of power for ploughing and other agricultural tasks. On the dry steppe-lands of central Eurasia, animal-keeping was more important than plant cultivation and the domestication of the horse gave rise to a specialized life-style based on nomadic herding.

The exact origins of agriculture remain unknown. The end of the Ice Age was certainly accompanied by an abundance of plant and animal food. This may have encouraged hunting and gathering communities to grow until their numbers made it necessary to find another subsistence strategy. Once chosen, however, farming developed a momentum of its own: once adopted, there was no easy turning back,

and the very success of the new lifestyle induced other fundamental changes. The increase in food resources which followed made possible a spectacular growth of human population, which may have multiplied several times between 8000 and 4000 BC. It also required cooperative effort, particularly after the introduction of irrigation led to the establishment of settled organized societies, at first in villages and later in towns and cities, and the development of new technologies, social systems and ideologies.

The transformation from hunting and gathering to agriculture, from a migratory to a sedentary life, was a decisive event in world history. Hunting and gathering peoples survived but, as farming spread, they became increasingly confined to the marginal world environments where agriculture could not secure a foothold (map 2). Both absolutely and relatively, their numbers declined until today their representatives survive only in hot deserts such as the Kalahari and central Australia, in the dense rain forests of the Amazon basin, central Africa and South-East Asia, and in the frozen wastes of the Arctic. Even there traditional lifestyles – followed by mankind for millennia – now face the threat of extinction.

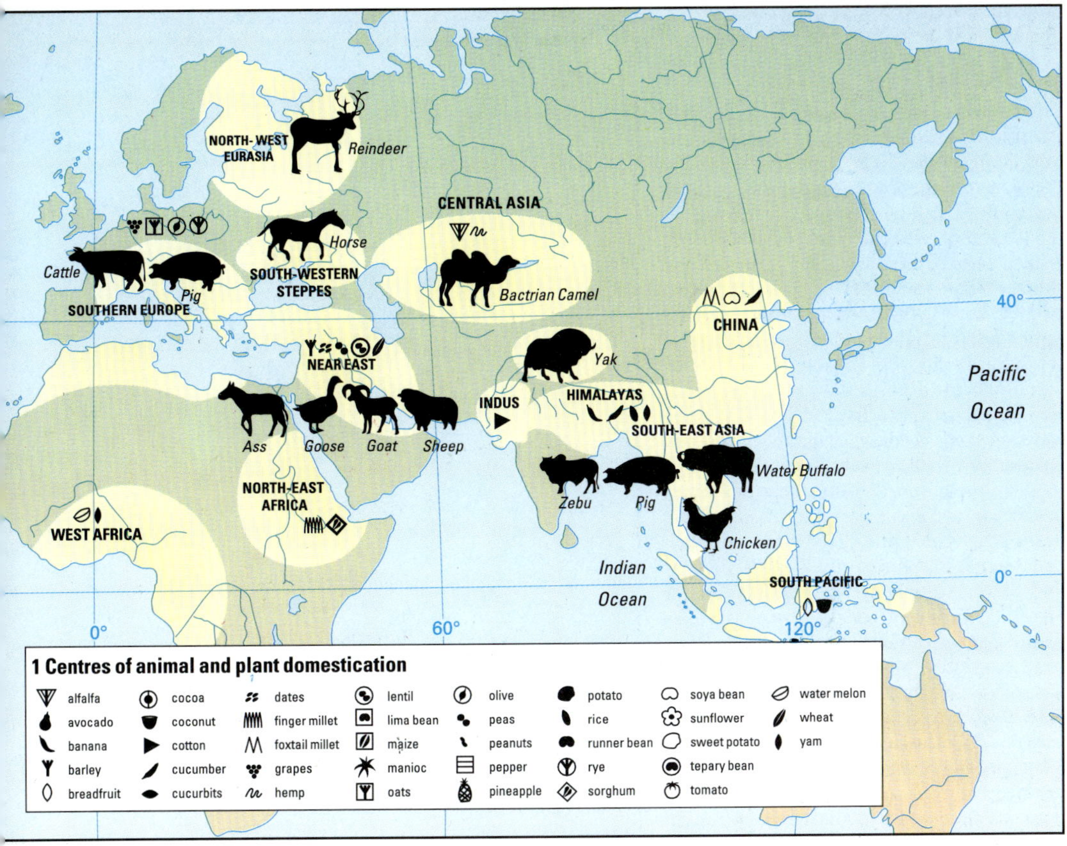

## 1 Centres of animal and plant domestication

| | | | | | | | | |
|---|---|---|---|---|---|---|---|---|
| alfalfa | cocoa | dates | lentil | olive | potato | soya bean | water melon |
| avocado | coconut | finger millet | lima bean | peas | rice | sunflower | wheat |
| banana | cotton | foxtail millet | maize | peanuts | runner bean | sweet potato | yam |
| barley | cucumber | grapes | manioc | pepper | rye | tepary bean | |
| breadfruit | cucurbits | hemp | oats | pineapple | sorghum | tomato | |

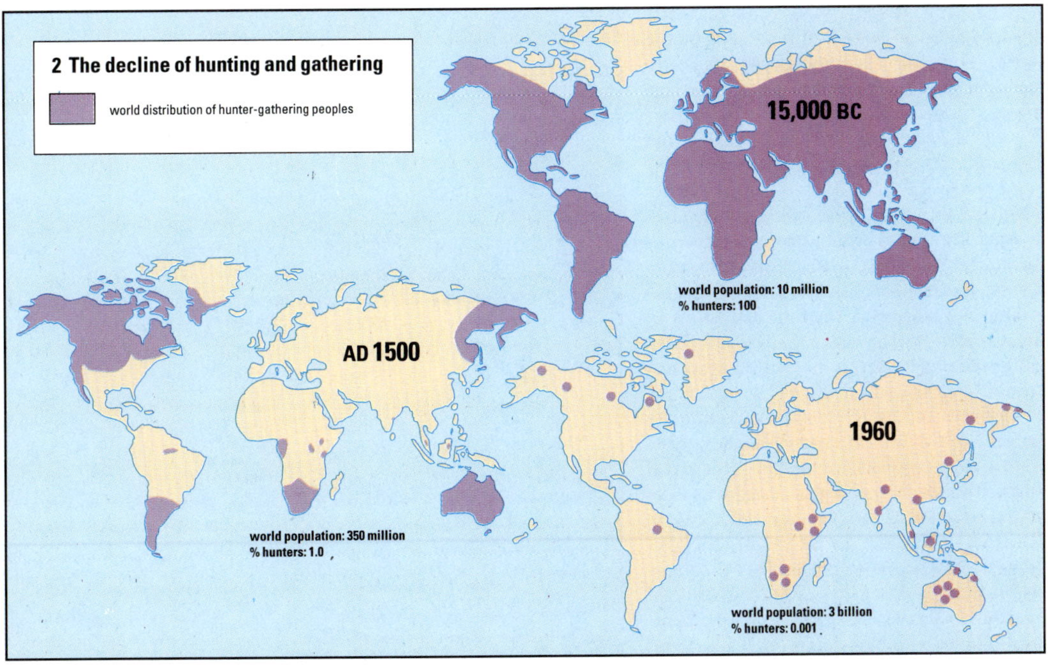

## 2 The decline of hunting and gathering

world distribution of hunter-gathering peoples

**15,000 BC**
world population: 10 million
% hunters: 100

**AD 1500**
world population: 350 million
% hunters: 1.0

**1960**
world population: 3 billion
% hunters: 0.001

15

# The first farmers of Asia

The first economies to be based on the husbandry of animal and plant staples came into being in the Near East. In the upland areas around the Zagros and Taurus mountains, and in Palestine, moister conditions as the ice-sheets released water that had been frozen led to the spread of large-seeded grasses – the ancestors of modern wheat and barley – which early hunters quickly appreciated for their nutrition and ease of storage. By 10,000 BC small villages of circular stone-walled huts developed, whose inhabitants lived from both the hunting and herding of gazelle and the harvesting of wild wheat. About 9000 BC, in northern Syria, some communities began to cultivate cereals outside their natural habitat while sheep were domesticated in Mesopotamia. By 7000 BC wheat and barley cultivation was established, as was the herding of goats, from Anatolia to the Zagros mountains, and this agricultural revolution spread shortly afterwards to Greece. Much of the Near Eastern lowland area, however, was too dry for cultivation. Only the development of irrigation – by spreading water from the rivers that drained from the mountains – allowed settlements to extend to the Mesopotamian plain in the sixth and fifth millennia.

Plants and animals were independently domesticated in many other parts of the world. Sedentary farming began in South Asia on the Kachi Plain of north-west India around 7000 BC. The early settlers cultivated barley and wheat, domesticated sheep, cattle and goats, and buried their dead with elaborate grave goods. From 6000 BC onwards, mud-brick storehouses divided into small compartments served as the focal point for food, tools and trade goods. By 5000 BC rice farmers had also established villages in the hills just south of the Ganges valley (map 3). In northern China the cultivation of millet, another cereal, began on the great loess plain around the Yellow River and its tributaries around 6000 BC. It remained the staple crop of the region for many centuries. Further south the principal cereal was rice, first cultivated in the Yangtze delta before 4000 BC (map 2). In addition, the ox-drawn plow began to be adapted throughout much of Eurasia, enlisting animal traction to increase the efficiency of farming. Villages acquired defensive walls, from

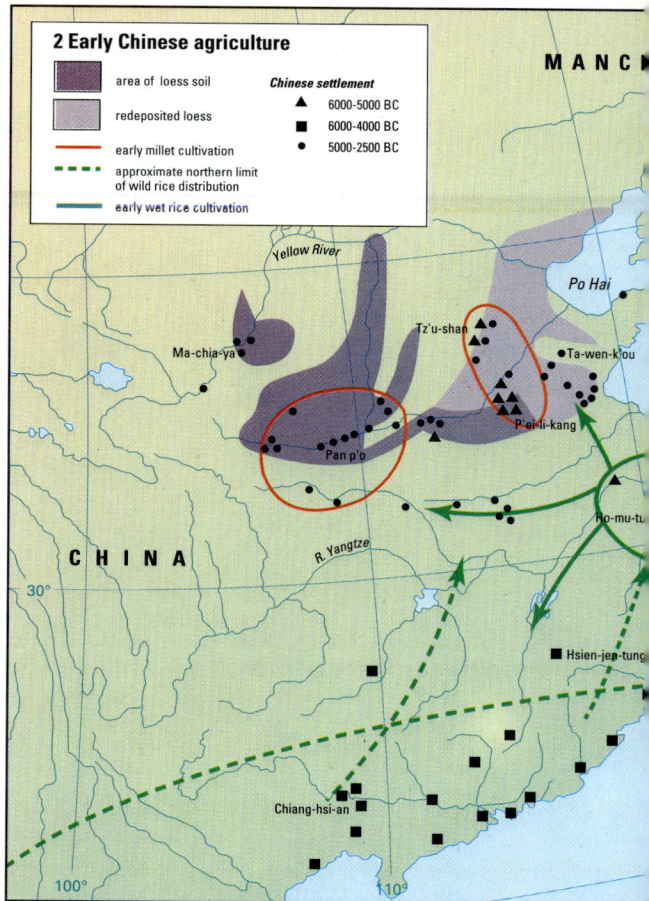

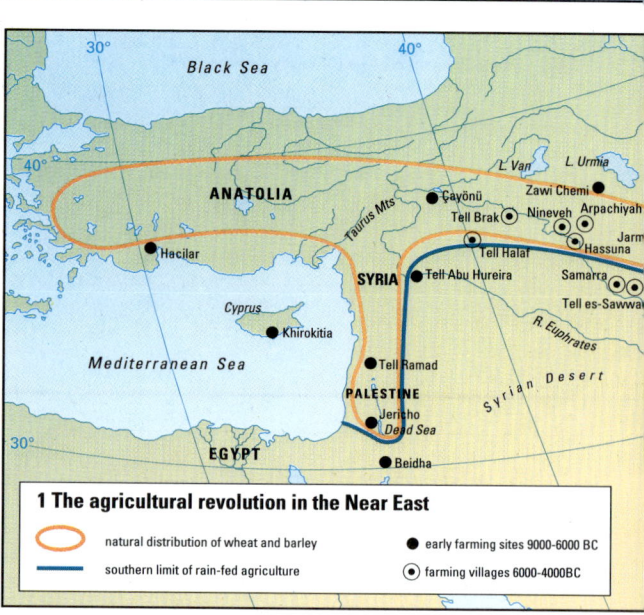

8,000 BC in the Near East (the first fortified community being Jericho) and from around 3,500 BC in China.

The greater size and permanence of farming settlements stemmed from three major factors: firstly, the exceptional productivity of the principal cultivated species, which could feed large concentrations of people all year round – something hunting and gathering can never do; secondly, the ability of plant foods to survive storage over many months, allowing the community to stay in one place and live off the previous harvest while a new crop grows and ripens. Finally, farmers need to live near their fields, both to protect them against human and animal predators and to minimize the travel and transport involved in preparing the ground, in weeding, and in harvesting.

Once the new settlement pattern had developed, it permitted a far richer lifestyle. A general increase occurred in the amount and variety of material goods and equipment. Hunters keep their possessions to a minimum, since everything must be carried around; but sedentary communities can produce and accumulate a wide range of items, both utilitarian and for ritual and pleasure – pottery and tools, ornaments and display items. The pace of change accelerated, and around 3000 BC a new threshold was reached, a critical stage in humankind's progress towards the modern world: the emergence of the first cities, and of the first ordered civilizations.

17

# The rise of civilization

The first civilizations arose in the alluvial basins of four major rivers which drain from the mountain fringes where agriculture began: the Tigris and Euphrates in Mesopotamia, the Nile in Egypt, the Indus in India, and the Yellow River in China. Each proved capable of supplying the high, regular yields needed to support large urban populations. Cities of thousands, and then tens of thousands, evolved. In Mesopotamia, a number already existed by 3500 BC. Egypt adopted urban civilization in about 3200 BC and the Harappan civilization arose in the Indus plain from about 2500 BC. Civilization in north China appears to have developed, again wholly or largely independently, around 1800 BC.

These societies shared many common features: the development of cities; writing; large public buildings; and the political apparatus of a state. The large agricultural surpluses produced by irrigation – some Mesopotamian communities harvested 60, 70 or even 80 grains for each grain sown – made it possible to employ a large segment of society in activities other than farming, such as manufacture and trade. This in turn led to the emergence of a ruling class which accumulated wealth through the exploitation of labour and the imposition of taxes. In Mesopotamia the ruler was also the chief priest and the temple centre provided a vital element of the political system, its monumental structure forming a visual reminder to all

citizens of the power that governed their daily life. The centralized control found in these societies fostered a special legal system, a standing army, a permanent bureaucracy, and the division of society into distinct classes. The state also supported scribes, who were usually trained and employed within the temples. The earliest writing was used as a means of keeping track of commodities, wages and taxes; but it soon served other purposes: to preserve religious traditions, which thereby became sacred books; to register social customs, which thereby became codes of law; and to record myths, which thereby developed into history and literature.

Since, apart from agricultural produce, the alluvial plains lacked most other natural resources, an extensive trading activity exchanged luxury goods and raw materials from other areas with the textiles and other manufactured goods of the cities and thus helped to develop other trading centres in a great arc from the eastern Mediterranean to the Indus valley and in China. The cities therefore exercised an influence out of all proportion to their comparatively small geographical extent. True, not all areas were affected: Australia, Africa, Europe and large parts of Asia had no cities; the first civilizations of the Americas did not emerge until about 1500 BC (and, when they did, owed nothing to ideas introduced from outside). Nevertheless the growth of the first urban centres, with their technology, literacy, and class divisions began a new phase in the development of human society.

# The Near East 3600-605 BC

The earliest of all known civilizations, Sumer, rested upon some 12 city-states in southern Mesopotamia. At first, pre-eminence passed from one to another, but the growing concentrations of people on the fertile plain eventually called for greater management than a single city could provide. In 2371 BC, a centralized authority spanning the whole valley grew up under the first of a series of legendary conquerors: Sargon of Agade (c.2334-2279 BC). Before long, his power extended far beyond Mesopotamia to Elam and the Zagros mountains in the southeast, and all the way to Syria and the Mediterranean coast in the north-west, while his grandson Naram-Sin extended the empire eastwards to the Iranian plateau. But Sargon's empire proved to be short-lived and its collapse, due both to external invasions and to internal strains, gave way to a new empire with Ur as its centre, its hegemony stretching from the Persian Gulf to Nineveh. But Ur also fell after little more than a century, and a kaleidoscope of shifting alliances brought new cities to prominence, most notably Mari and Babylon on the Euphrates. Under its powerful king Hammurabi, Babylon created another empire that covered the whole of southern Mesopotamia; but, once more, it did not long survive the death of its founder (map 1).

Even before Sargon unified Mesopotamia, Egypt was under the sway of a single ruler. Around 3100 BC an Upper Egyptian ruler, his power based on the exploitation of goldfields near the Red Sea, conquered the Nile delta and established a new capital at Memphis, which for almost 2000 years served as the administrative centre for a densely populated region of some 15,000 square miles running from the first cataract at Aswan to the Mediterranean coast (map 2). At about the same time, writing in hieroglyphic script commenced. During the 'Old Kingdom' period (2685-2180 BC) the rulers of Egypt built a series of massive pyramid-tombs along the desert edge opposite Memphis which emphasised their power and prestige. Then, after a century of invasion and anarchy, the Egyptian state entered a second period of cultural achievement under the able rulers of the Middle Kingdom (2040-1783 BC); and another era of expansion under the XVIIIth and XIXth dynasties (1570-1200 BC). At home they undertook vast building projects, like the rock-cut temple at Abu Simbel created by Ramesses II (1290-1224 BC); abroad they advanced through Palestine into Syria and created an empire that extended almost to the Euphrates.

The continuity of Ancient Egyptian history, although not unbroken, stood in marked contrast to developments in Mesopotamia. The two civilizations also differed in other respects. First, because of the annual Nile flood, Egypt did not depend to the same extent on irrigation canals and dams; second, although it possessed some cities, they lacked the geographical concentration found in southern Mesopotamia, so that its rulers tended to arise from rural rather than urban power bases. Third, and most important, Egypt rarely suffered foreign invasion. Admittedly the Hyksos, an Asiatic people, overran most of the country in the 18th century BC, but a new native dynasty expelled them c. 1570 BC and then pursued the invaders northwards to the upper Euphrates. Egypt's Asiatic empire lasted until about 1200 BC when the 'Sea Peoples', marauders from the Aegean and Asia Minor, attacked all the major civilizations of the Near East and initiated a 'Dark Age', concerning which very few historical sources survive, until about 900 BC and the emergence of Assyria.

The power of Assyria was based on the prosperous farming communities of the northern Mesopotamian plain. As early as the 11th century BC, Assyrian kings were campaigning as far to the west as the Mediterranean, but the greatest expansion of Assyrian power began in the 9th century BC, during the reign of Ashurnasirpal II (883-859 BC). Under Shalmaneser III (858-824 BC) Assyrian armies reached the Mediterranean, Lake Van and the Persian Gulf, and incorporated the Aramaean and other states east of the Euphrates into the Assyrian empire, although the heart of the state remained the upper Tigris and Euphrates.

Shalmanaser's reign ended in civil war, and a temporary set-back followed in Assyria's fortunes, but under Sargon II (721-705 BC) the empire expanded dramatically once more and, from his capital at Nineveh on the Tigris, Ashurbanipal (668-627 BC) ruled the whole of Mesopotamia,

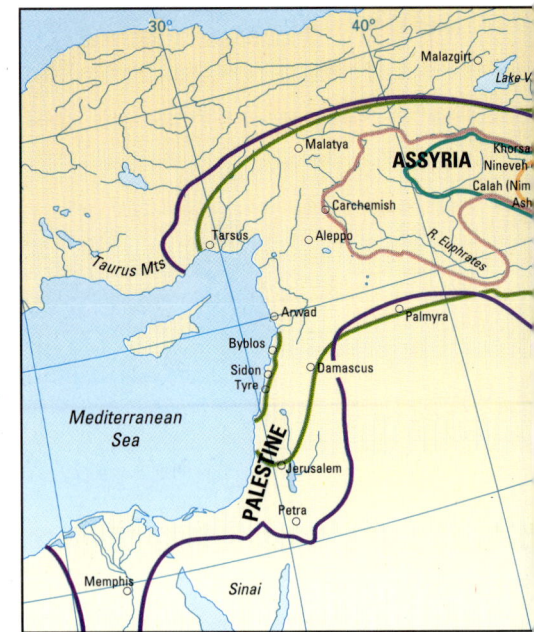

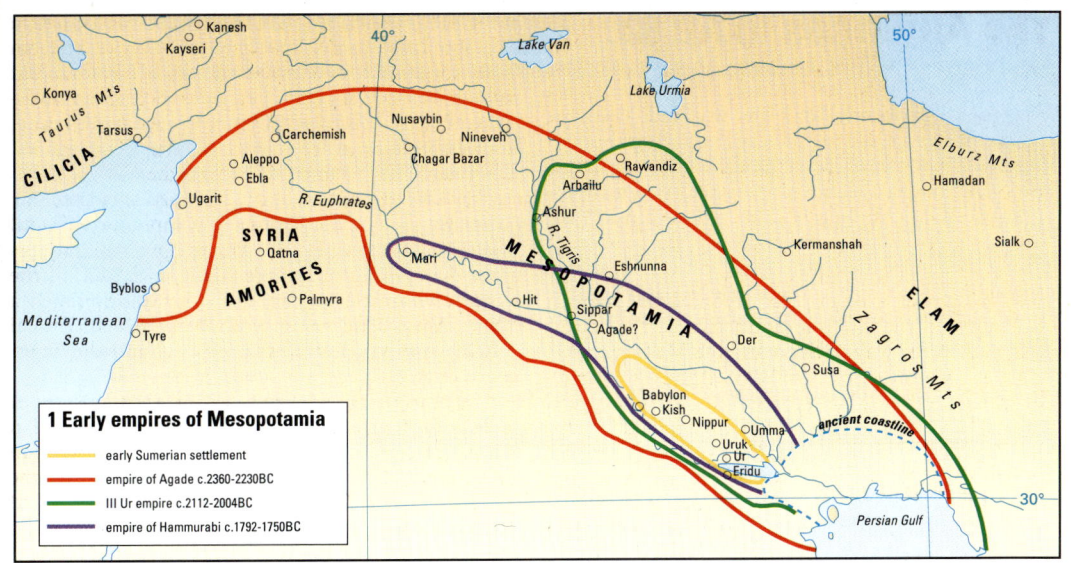

Syria and Palestine, and even (for a short time) the Nile delta (map 3). The Assyrians possessed a well-disciplined army and an efficient bureaucracy; to the Old Testament prophets, at least, they appeared invincible. Yet civil war, succession disputes and rebellions, particularly by the Babylonians, dogged the last century of Assyrian rule. In 612 BC Assyria fell before a coalition of her enemies: the Babylonians and Medes, aided by Scythian horsemen from the steppe. Nineveh was sacked and abandoned for ever.

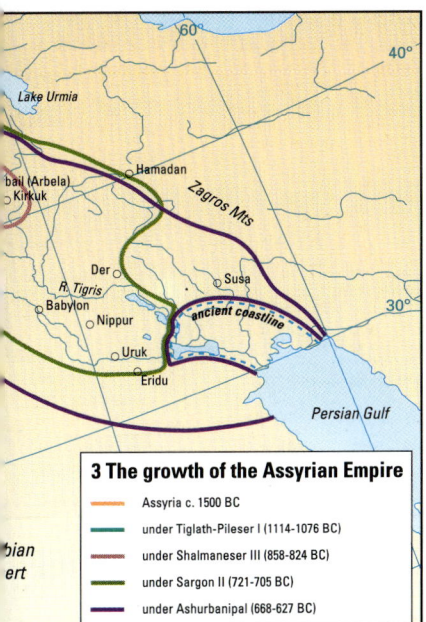

# The Americas to AD 800

The Americas, like Australia (page 24) were colonized from Asia during the last Ice Age, when lowered sea levels turned the Bering Strait into dry land. Then, the melting of the ice cut off the continent from Eurasia (page 12). It is one of the remarkable facts of human history that despite their geographical separation, development in Old and New Worlds followed much the same path: the adoption of agriculture; the creation of cities and empires; the invention of writing. These two geographical zones continued on parallel paths until the New World was invaded by Europeans after 1492 (page 68). The New World civilizations were highly inventive in their own right and in some ways in advance of their western counterparts. They produced – quite independent of the Old World – magnificent art, remarkable mathematical and astronomical skills, and monumental architecture.

The inhabitants of Mesoamerica and the central Andes began to experiment with plant cultivation around 7000 BC and by 1500 BC farming had allowed a rapid increase in population. By 800 BC the Olmecs on the Gulf of Mexico, the Zapotecs at Monte Albán, and the people of Chavín in Peru had developed complex societies with populations that numbered tens of thousands, with a hierarchy of social classes, an efficient civil service, a professional priesthood, and specialists in all kinds of tasks, from manufacturing to commerce and government.

Around and between these civilizations, other communities remained at the chiefdom level. Maize, beans and squash cultivation spread from Mexico to north America, and their arrival initiated a period of rapid development. In Ohio and Illinois, between 300 BC and AD 550, Hopewell chiefs built elaborate burial mounds and maintained trade contacts from Florida to the Rockies. Most American chiefdoms were agricultural, based on plant cultivation, but along the north-west coast rich fishing grounds and an abundance of whales and seals supported large villages and a complex ceremonial life by hunting and gathering alone. Towards the extremities of the continent, however, harsh conditions precluded farming, settlement remained sparse, and nomadic lifestyles persisted (map 1).

In Mesoamerica, new influences, especially among the Maya of Yucatán, complemented the early Olmec and Zapotec civilizations from the 4th century BC. Around AD 250 the Maya began to develop their own hieroglyphic writing and to erect carved stones bearing calendrical or historical inscriptions. They became preoccupied with the passage of time and their astronomers calculated the exact length of the solar year, the lunar month, and the revolution of the planet Venus, and predicted eclipses. To assist their calculations, they invented the idea of place value and the concept of zero.

Mayan civilization did not remain isolated. Important regional cultures developed elsewhere in Mexico: along the Gulf Coast (especially at El Tajín), in the valley of Oaxaca (where Monte Albán became a great city), and at Teotihuacán in the valley of Mexico. In its prime, around AD 600, the city of Teotihuacán, laid out in a precise grid plan, covered 8 square miles (20 km$^2$) and housed 125,000 people. Its wealth came from agriculture, crafts and trade, and it maintained diplomatic and commercial exchanges with the other civilizations of Mexico and with the Maya. But this prosperity did not last. Teotihuacán was destroyed and abandoned around AD 730; Monte Albán fell into disrepair during the 10th century; and Classic Mayan civilization collapsed, for reasons still not fully understood, between AD 800 and 900 (map 2).

A separate group of interrelated civilizations grew up in the central Andes, supported by spectacular irrigation systems in the lowlands and by ingenious raised fields in the highlands. The Andean peoples discovered sophisticated skills in working gold, silver and copper, and used these metals for tools as well as for jewellery. Although its vast distances and harsh topography made this region difficult to unify, the centuries between AD 600 and 1000 saw the rise of a truly imperial power based on Huari in the Peruvian Andes. Many elements of Huari religion and art originated at Tiahuanaco, further south, but were quickly adopted by Huari and then spread by force to many parts of the coast and highlands. For a short time Huari was the capital of a state embracing most of Peru, but around AD 800 the city was sacked and abandoned for ever. The fragile unity soon collapsed and not until the Inca conquests of the 15th and 16th centuries would the central Andes be reunified under a single government.

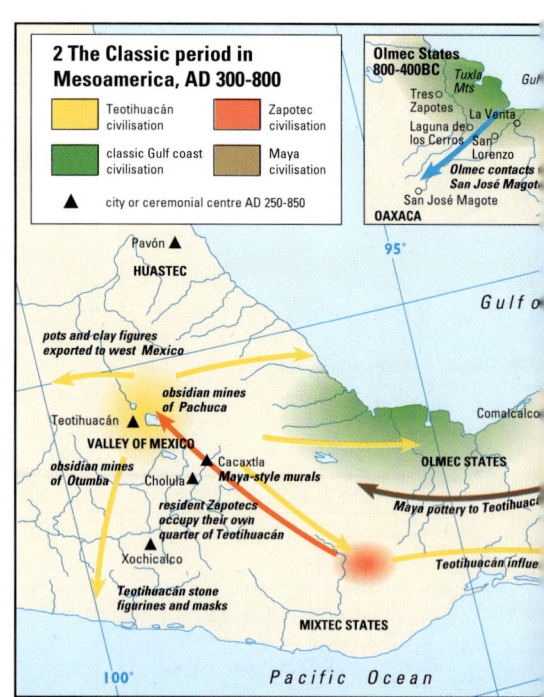

# Prehistoric Africa and Australasia

Both Australia and Africa were isolated from the rest of the Old World for most of prehistory, the former by sea, the latter by desert. Although the inhabitants of North Africa began the transition from hunting and gathering to farming around 8000 BC, the desiccation of the Sahara after about 4000 BC cut off Africa south of the Equator for centuries. In Australia, the aborigines mostly remained hunters and gatherers adapted to living in a large range of environments from tropical forest to harsh desert. They enjoyed a rich symbolic life, as evidenced by the decoration of their rock shelters with prolific designs. The colonization of the islands of Melanesia occurred considerably later, when settlers from New Guinea, associated with the distinctive Lapita pottery, reached Fiji around 1300 BC and then made their way into Polynesia via Tonga and Samoa, reaching the Marquesas islands in about AD 300 (map 2). From there they spread north to Hawaii (c. AD 800) and south-west via the Cook islands to New Zealand between 850 and 1100. But populations remained small: about 300,000 in Australia and 100,000 in New Zealand when the Europeans arrived there in the 18th century.

The geographical isolation of southern Africa was never complete. In the east settlers spread down the Rift Valley from Ethiopia during the first millennium BC, while trans-Saharan trade increased in importance after the introduction of the camel from Asia, around 100 BC, which facilitated the spread of iron tools and weapons, introduced earlier in the north by the Greeks and Carthaginians, but also arriving from the south via Nigeria. Aided by the new technology, Bantu-speaking farmers and cattle-herders began to colonize southern Africa in the early centuries AD. By the 13th century powerful Bantu chiefdoms had emerged, such as that centred on Great Zimbabwe, and on cattle-raising communities engaged in long-distance trade, long before the Portuguese arrived off both the south-east and south-west coasts of the continent at the close of the 15th century.

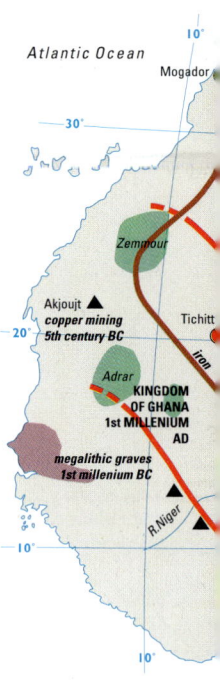

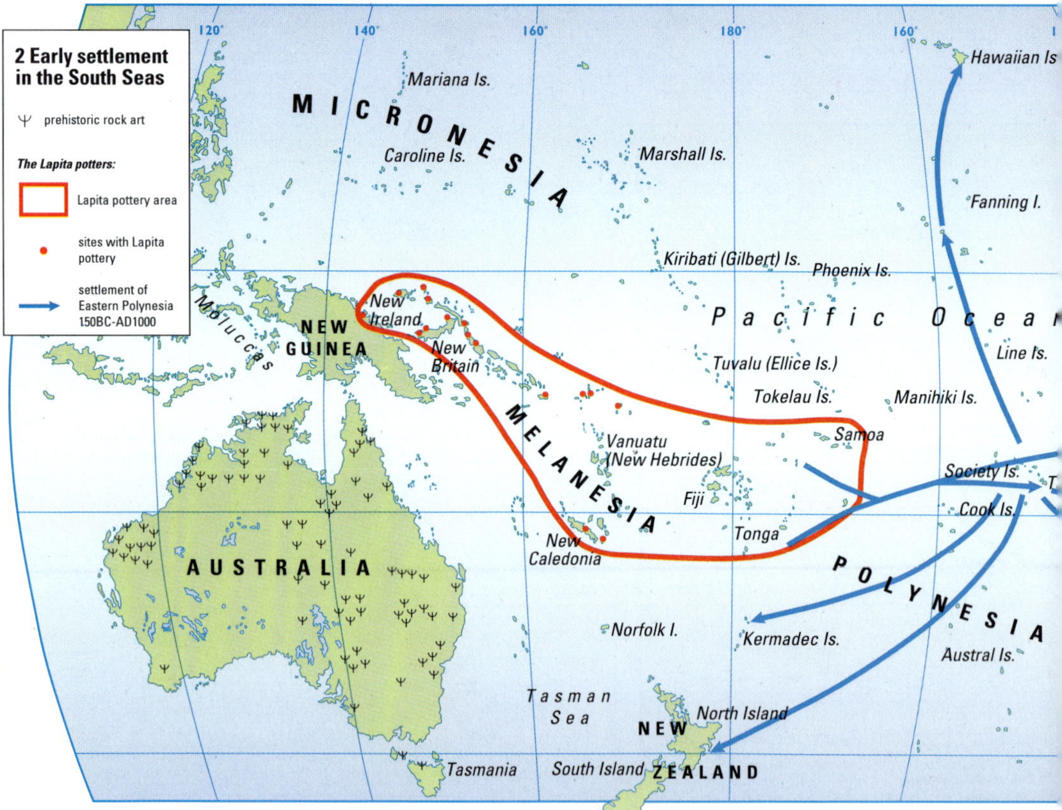

**2 Early settlement in the South Seas**

- Ψ prehistoric rock art

*The Lapita potters:*
- ▭ Lapita pottery area
- • sites with Lapita pottery
- → settlement of Eastern Polynesia 150BC–AD1000

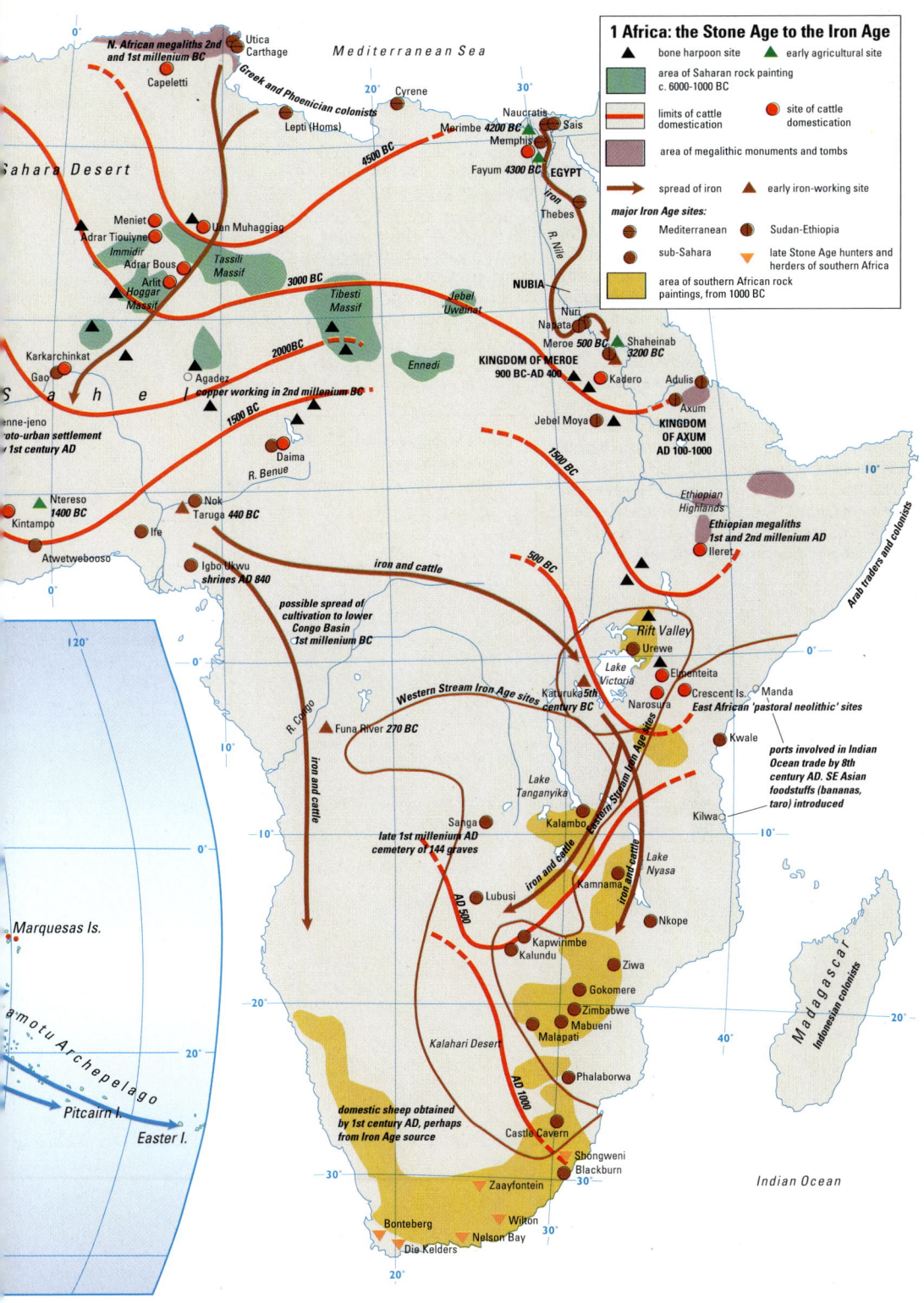

# South and South-East Asia to AD 500

The first civilizations of the Indus valley (page 12) collapsed around 1500 BC. When the picture becomes clear once again the population of northern India had been transformed, with a Hindu religion, a Sanskrit literature, a caste system and (by about 800 BC) iron working, which enabled the spread of farming communities eastward into the rich plain of the Ganges. By 600 BC at least 16 political units had grown up along the Ganges, the subcontinent's new centre of gravity. By 400 BC war had reduced the states to four, and no doubt the resulting social tensions helped to spread new ethical and religious systems, for in the 6th century Gautama (Buddha), founder of Asia's most pervasive religion, was born in one of these states, while in another Mahavira formulated the teaching of Jainism (see page 32).

A further turning point came in 320 BC when Chandragupta Maurya seized the state of Magadha on the lower Ganges, and occupied large parts of central India, and in 305 BC annexed the province of Trans-Indus from the successors of Alexander the Great (see page 30). Chandragupta's grandson Asoka (273-232 BC) expanded this Mauryan empire southwards, bringing the greater part of the sub-continent under his rule and inscribing edicts on pillars and rock-faces all over India as a permanent reminder of his power (map 1). The death of Asoka introduced a troubled period, punctuated by invasions of both Greeks and nomads who founded states in the north-west, such as the Kushan empire, where Hellenistic and Indian influences

**1 India's first empires, 297 BC–AD 150**
(approximate limits shown)

- Chandragupta Maurya's empire 297 BC
- Bindusara's empire 272 BC
- Asoka's empire 232 BC
- ▲ rock and pillar edicts
- Western satraps AD 150
- Kushan empire AD 150 (eastern limit)
- Satavahana kingdom AD 150

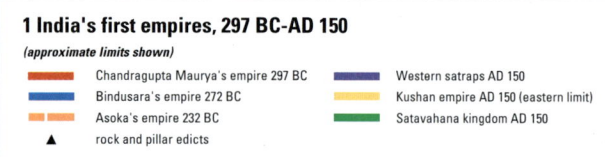

**2 Prehistoric sites in South-East Asia**
- Neolithic/Bronze Age settlements
- Dong Son drums
- Early Iron Age and urn burial sites

mingled. Further south, the Satavahanas of the Deccan ruled a state that straddled the peninsula by AD 150. Then, in the 4th century, the Gupta dynasty, again based on Magadha, created an empire which by AD 400 almost extended from the Indus to the bay of Bengal, and projected north Indian values and religions far beyond (map 3).

The barbarian invasions of the 5th century (see page 38) caused the collapse of Gupta power, but it was precisely during this period that Hindu and Buddhist influences began to spread to South-East Asia. The cultivation of rice in this area, beginning as early as 3000 BC, allowed the development of prosperous farming villages. Bronze came into use after about 1000 BC, reflected in distinctive bronze Dong Son drums, and iron followed after about 500 BC (map 2). By AD 300 trading links with India had burgeoned, and Buddhist images appeared by AD 500, notably in Burma, Cambodia, and Java. By AD 700 the construction of Hindu temples in the same three areas had begun.

27

# Early Europe 6000-1000 BC

Farming spread from the Near East to Europe about 6500 BC, beginning with Greece and Bulgaria. Agriculture in these regions involved wheat and barley, sheep and goats, just as in western Asia; but as farming spread north and west into more temperate zones, major adjustments became necessary. New, more robust types of cereal developed, and cattle and pigs became the dominant livestock. By about 5500 BC agricultural communities had developed along the Danube valley, and their descendants spread north-west from there until they reached the Paris basin around 4750 BC – an advance in the farming frontier of over one mile each year. After a brief pause, the final phase saw the spread of farming to the northern fringes of Europe, including Scandinavia and the British Isles, where it was adopted by existing hunter-gatherer communities by about 4000 BC (map 1).

Eventually these European farmers, like their Near Eastern counterparts before them, began to experience the difficulties caused by a shortage of suitable agricultural land to feed their growing population. The solution they adopted was not irrigation – temperate Europe, unlike the Middle East, never lacked rainfall – but the introduction, around 4000 BC, of the plough. This device required the maintenance of draught oxen which, although costly, provided a much more efficient way of breaking the ground than hoes and spades and allowed new areas to be farmed that would otherwise not have proved economic.

Meanwhile, in the Balkans, copper-working also began around 4500 BC and by 2500 BC it had become common to alloy the copper with tin to produce bronze.

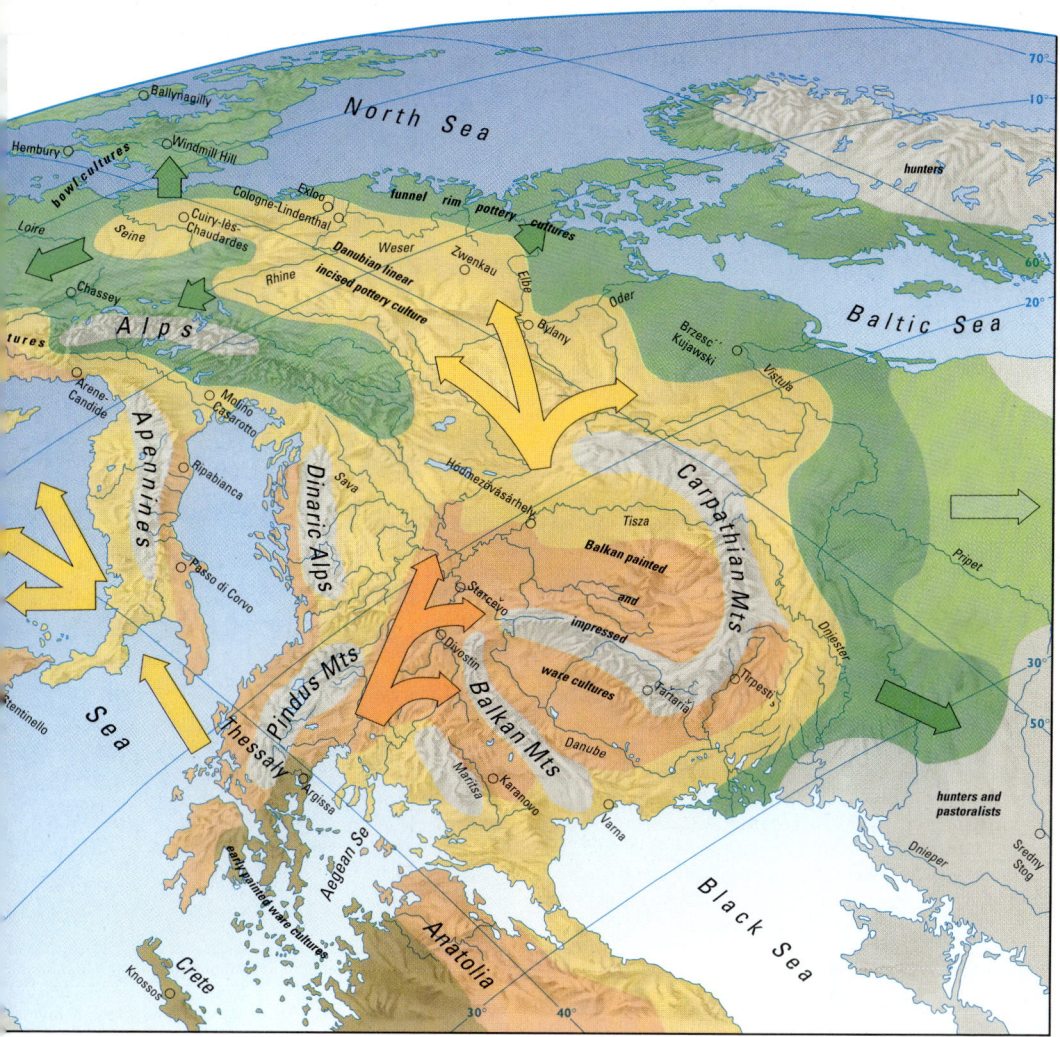

The need to acquire these two raw materials led to the development of extensive trade networks, which also conveyed other materials, such as amber from the Baltic, which is found as far afield as Mycenae, in southern Greece, where graves filled with sumptuous funerary offerings of gold and jewellery appeared from 1600 BC.

Mycenae was not the earliest European civilization: that honour belongs to the island of Crete where from about 2000 BC 'Minoan' culture, based on palaces decorated with colourful frescoes and equipped with advanced sanitary and drainage systems, developed. Bureaucracy and trade flourished, and an alphabetic script known as Linear A developed around 1600 BC. Two centuries later, however, the Mycenaeans, who take their name from the fortress of Mycenae in the eastern Peloponnese, conquered Crete and became the principal military and economic power in the Aegean (see map 2). They adapted the Minoan culture, including its script which they modified (to a form known as Linear B, clearly an early version of Greek) and used to administer their own empire. Mycenaean Greece was divided among a number of independent leaders, each of whom ruled a small kingdom, in much the same way as Greece in the classical period was divided into city-states (see page 30). The legend of the Trojan War, recorded centuries later in Homer's Iliad, is thought to recall a Mycenaean campaign of c. 1250 BC against the city of Troy, strategically situated at the entrance to the Dardanelles, and controlling access to the trade of the Black Sea. But this success, if indeed it occurred, must have been the final fling of the Mycenean warlords because by 1200 BC most of their palaces were in ruins, overthrown perhaps by rebellion or by outside attack, and a 'Dark Age' which left very few records ensued all over Greece for the next four centuries.

# The Greek world 750-300 BC

After the fall of Mycenae, Greece dissolved into a mosaic of small farming communities and chiefdoms dominated by local Greek-speaking tribes. By the 8th century BC, however, a new order had evolved, centred on about 150 city-states, each one a limited, independent self-governing community. Their emergence depended upon geography: 80 per cent of Greece is rock and mountain, but the coasts are studded with comparatively small plains. By 800 BC the main city-states had been founded, and new colonies of Greeks had been established on the Aegean islands and on the Anatolian coast at Ephesus and Miletus (map 1). Writing was reintroduced, coinage invented around 650 BC, the first temples founded, and new styles of sculpture, architecture and vase-painting developed.

There was an amazing explosion of Greek influence during the 8th and 7th centuries BC, with the foundation of far-flung colonies around the coast of the Mediterranean and the Black Sea. These included many cities which have remained famous to the present, such as Marseilles and Naples. In the central Mediterranean the Greeks came into conflict with the Carthaginians, who for many centuries disputed control of Sicily with them. In Asia Minor, however, the Greeks came up against the Persian empire, which first sought to annex the city-states of Anatolia and in 490 and 480-479 BC invaded the peninsula itself. The Persians met with defeat and the next 50 years marked the great age of Greek culture: the tragic drama of Aeschylus, Sophocles and Euripedes; the comedy of Aristophanes; the histories of Herodotus and Thucydides; the splendour of the Parthenon; the sculptures of Phidias. 50 years after the defeat of the Persians, however, Greece found itself embroiled in a desperate struggle between the city-states. The principal protagonists were Sparta, the militarized power in the Peloponnese, and Athens, which had built up a formidable fleet and used it to create an Aegean empire. The Peloponnesian war lasted over 25 years, from 431 to 404 BC. Despite victories on both sides, Athens fatally overstrained her resources with a disastrous expedition against Syracuse in Sicily (415-13) and in 404 BC succumbed (map 2).

The 4th century saw more jockeying for power, while Persia sought to intervene in Greek affairs, until the well-trained Macedonian army of King Philip II (359-336 BC) subdued the city-states and imposed the ambitious aim of invading Persia upon them. Philip's remarkable son Alexander (336-323 BC) invaded Asia Minor with an army of 35,000 men, both Greeks and Macedonians, in 334; moved on to annex Egypt (332) and the Persian empire (331); and campaigned successfully in India and Central Asia (map 3). Alexander's death in 323 and the ensuing struggles between his leading generals created three major powers: Macedon, Egypt, and the Seleucid kingdom (comprising the bulk of the Persian empire).

Although politically the empire of Alexander the Great proved ephemeral, in other respects its consequences endured. Alexander himself founded some 70 cities, not merely as military strongholds but as cultural centres and thus carried Greek civilization far to the east. Greek culture infused and Hellenized the whole *oikumene* (civilized world) as far as India and China.

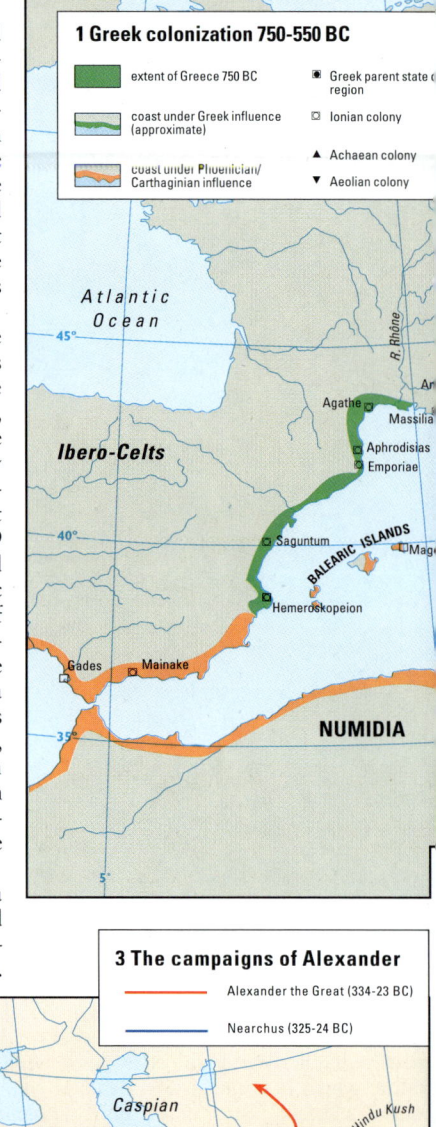

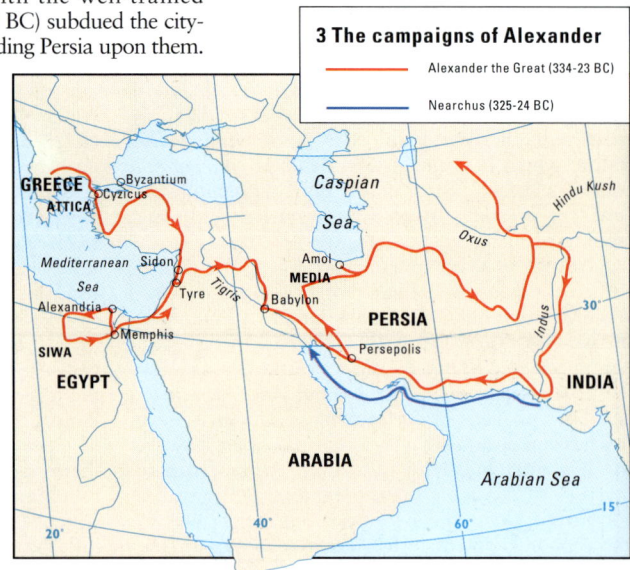

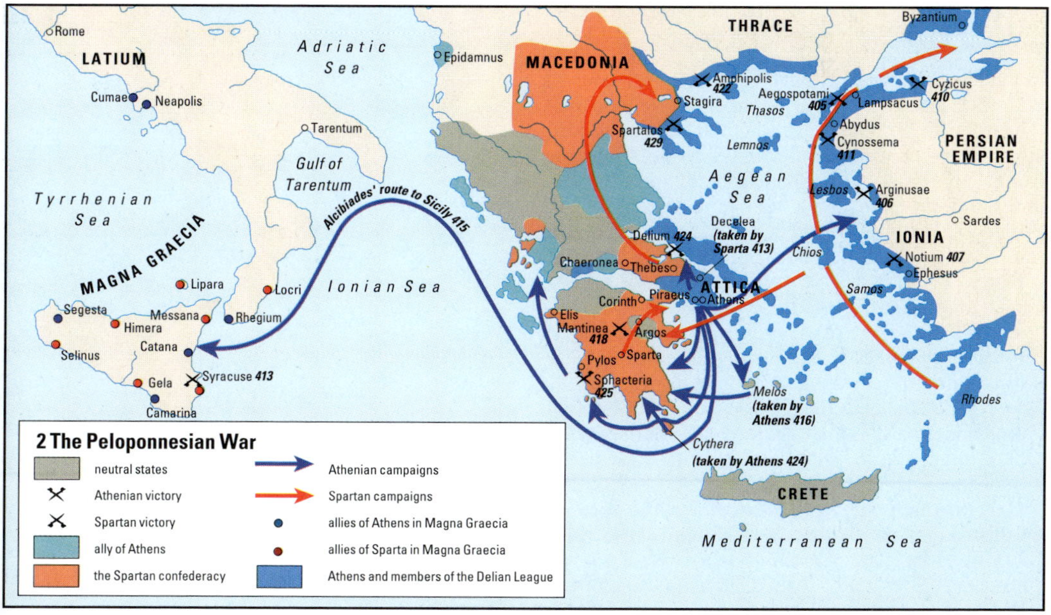

- Dorian colony founded by Corinth
- Dorian colony founded by Thera and Rhodes
- Dorian colony founded by Megara or Sparta
- Punic or Phoenician city
- other Greek colonies
- Philistine city
- Etruscan city

## 2 The Peloponnesian War

- neutral states
- ✕ Athenian victory
- ✕ Spartan victory
- ally of Athens
- the Spartan confederacy
- → Athenian campaigns
- → Spartan campaigns
- • allies of Athens in Magna Graecia
- • allies of Sparta in Magna Graecia
- Athens and members of the Delian League

31

# World religions

All the great world religions originated in Asia, and three of them – Judaism, Christianity and Islam – developed in the same small region. Moreover, several were either established or radically reformulated at much the same time: the outstanding prophets and reformers of Hinduism, Buddhism, Judaism, Confucianism and Taoism all lived in the 6th century BC. Their appearance perhaps reflected a need in the rising empires of the Old World for more universal creeds than local tribal deities could provide, and their diffusion – particularly the spread of the great missionary religions, Buddhism and Christianity – played an important role both in linking the different areas of civilization and in spreading the values of those advanced cultures to people living beyond the frontiers.

All the world religions shared, to some degree, a belief in a single spiritual reality. Hinduism, the oldest of them, although it reveres numerous gods emphasises the 'right way to live'; Buddhism, although it does not centre upon a god, instead stresses deliverance from suffering through the annihilation of desire. Originally a reformist movement within Hinduism, in its conservative, or Theravada, form, Buddhism soon spread throughout India and on to Sri Lanka, Burma, Thailand and South-East Asia. It later became perhaps the greatest of all missionary religions when it assumed the universalist, or Mahayana, form some 500 years after the death of its founder, Gautama (c. 565-483 BC). The first great landmark in Buddhist history was the reign of the Indian emperor Asoka (see page 26) in whose reign Buddhism spread to Sri Lanka. It had also reached China by the 1st or 2nd century AD, Korea in the 4th century, and Japan in the 6th century.

Judaism spread mainly as a result of the persecution of the Jews by more formidable neighbours, beginning with their forcible removal to Babylon (586-538 BC), which led to a change in the emphasis of the faith from observance and ritual to morality and righteous living. Oppressed by the Roman occupation (64 BC) and the destruction of the temple in Jerusalem (AD 70), Jewish groups spread far and wide until Judaism, too, became a worldwide religion. It also gave birth, directly or indirectly, to two other major creeds: Christianity (page 40) and Islam (page 46).

In the Far East the 6th century saw the rise of both the ethical system of Kung Fu-tzu or Confucius (551-479 BC) and the mystical religion of the Tao, or 'the Way', associated with the shadowy figure of Lao-tzu. Zoroastrianism, the other great religion of the period, which originated in Persia and saw life as a battleground between the forces of good and evil, spread widely through the Roman world in the form of Mithraism, with shrines as far afield as northern Britain. However, the decision of the Emperor Theodosius (379-95) to make Christianity the official

religion of the Roman empire doomed Mithraism. 'Heathen' temples were uprooted; rival creeds were condemned.

Most of the world religions spread along the trade routes, diffused by soldiers, administrators, merchants and ordinary travellers as well as by missionaries; and most tended to prosper under strong governments

that brought peace. Of course, innumerable other creeds survived without making the transition to world religions. The Greek pantheon, adopted and adapted by the Romans, honoured a sky-god Zeus (Jupiter) and numerous other deities, each with a special function. The Scandinavians (whose gods Wotan, Thor and others provided names for the days of the week), and countless others, long retained their own eschatology. But the world religions provided the bonds that eventually linked areas of the world previously separate.

# Rome 264 BC to AD 565

Rome's rise to power proved rapid and seemingly inexorable. In the 6th century BC the city was just a small fortress-town in central Italy commanding both the lowest crossing point on the river Tiber and a salt route between the mountains and the sea. By exploiting quarrels with its neighbours, the Roman Republic emerged as the dominant power first in central Italy and then in the whole peninsula. By 270 BC the entire area south of the river Arno lay under Roman control, and in 264 BC its army crossed into Sicily. This marked the beginning of Roman imperialism, for Sicily formed part of the Carthaginian empire, at the time the greatest sea-power of the Mediterranean. After three savage wars Rome acquired Sicily (241 BC), Spain (206 BC) and North Africa (146 BC). At the same time, conflict with the Hellenistic kingdoms further east resulted in the conquest of Macedon, Greece and Western Anatolia. In this way, almost by accident, Rome became an imperial power with far-flung possessions.

Administration of these provinces overstrained the Roman constitution, which had not been designed to manage an overseas empire, and the Republic finally collapsed in a series of civil wars. The last of these brought to power Octavian, who established himself as *Princeps* ('first citizen'), accepted the title Augustus (in 27 BC), and accumulated sufficient offices to allow him to reshape the constitution and extend the frontiers to a point where he hoped they would remain unchanged for ever. In fact, under his successors, Roman rule expanded further still until it stretched from Scotland to Egypt and from Spain to Assyria (map 1).

While maintaining undivided power in his own hands, Augustus allowed the Senate – the traditional government of Rome – to take a share in running the empire, with responsibility for several provinces. Thus, in theory, the Republican forms endured, and administration remained in civilian not military hands. Throughout the vast Roman world peace prevailed for over two centuries and population expanded, trade flourished and cities grew until, in the mid-3rd century AD, Germanic invasions in the west and Persian victories in the east brought the empire temporarily to its knees. A series of strong emperors between 268 and 284 restored a semblance of orderly government to the empire, but Diocletian (AD 284-305) realized that a single ruler could no longer hold the whole edifice together. He divided power between himself and a joint Augustus, with two deputies (Caesars), and split the empire into four prefectures and twelve dioceses (map 2). By now the military had triumphed over the civilian, and a new basis had to be found for imperial authority. Under the influence of eastern ideas, the Princeps became *Dominus* (lord), an absolute ruler, at the head of a vast bureaucracy. Gradually the centre of Roman power shifted towards the eastern part of the empire: Diocletian's successor Constantine (305-37) established a new capital at Byzantium (330), which he renamed Constantinople.

Although theoretically governed by joint rulers, the empire gradually broke into eastern and western halves, and when

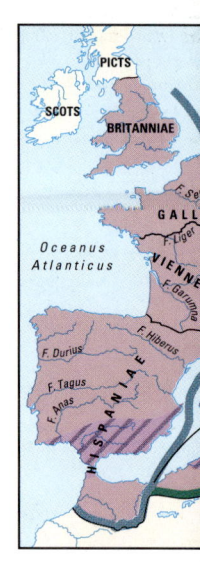

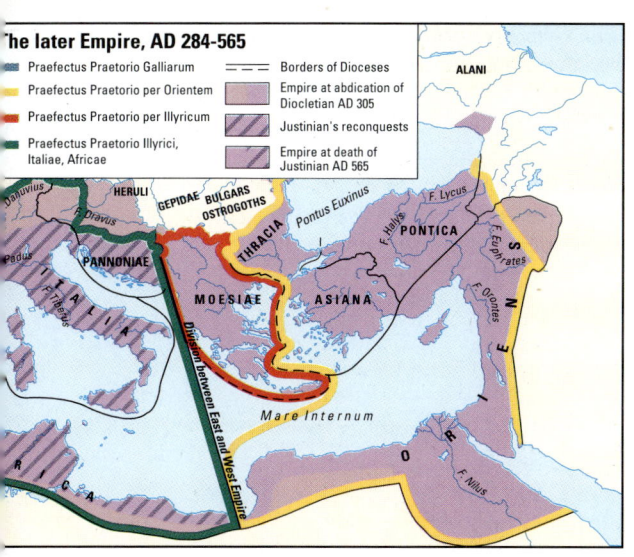

the western defences crumbled before a new wave of Germanic invaders in the early 5th century, little help arrived from the east. Rome itself was sacked in 410 and 455, and the Ostrogoths created their own kingdom in Italy in 493. Justinian (AD 527-565) did briefly recover some of the western provinces but failed to reunite the empire.

Nevertheless, the Byzantine state survived for another millennium, and many Roman traditions continued in the West. The Latin tongue, although developing into the derivative 'Romance' languages, long remained the language of churchmen and scientists; Roman Law forms the basis of most modern Western legal systems; many feats of Roman engineering genius survive to this day; and the Roman church lives on as a direct link with the past.

# China: the first empires

From the 16th to the 11th century BC China's first historical dynasty, the Shang, presided over a confederation of clans in the Yellow River valley. Around 1027 BC the Chou replaced them and extended their authority over the Yangtze valley as well, investing their supporters with fiefs to create a feudal hierarchy sustained by the services, food and clothes produced by peasant communities. Then in 771 BC western invaders sacked the Chou capital, and the feudatories seized the opportunity to break away. Over 100 belligerent political units sprang up. In the 5th century BC, however, bronze technology gave way to iron, animal power and irrigation transformed agriculture, increasing both food production and population, while warfare reduced the number of states. By 300 BC seven states still competed for hegemony; by 221 BC only one of them remained – Ch'in.

The Ch'in organized their subjects into groups which bore collective responsibility to maintain public order, and to provide manpower both for construction works (above all roads, canals and fortifications) and for the army (which was composed primarily of infantry). The defeated nobles suffered demotion and, instead of performing labour services to their lord, the peasants now paid taxes to the conqueror. A savage penal code, administered by a professional bureaucracy, enforced the new system.

In 221 BC Prince Cheng of Ch'in, took the title Shih Huang-ti (meaning 'first emperor'); ordered the construction of a national network of roads and canals, centered on his new capital at Hsiengyang; rebuilt and strengthened the Great Wall; introduced a uniform coinage whose distinctive shape (circular with a square hole in the centre) remained standard until 1911; and took steps to standardize the written language throughout the empire. Small wonder that his dynasty gave 'China' its name.

The burdens imposed by the autocratic first emperor provoked civil war shortly after his death in 206 BC; but before long a new dynasty, the Han, reunited China. At first they worked through feudal principalities allocated to their family and supporters, but by 100 BC the fiefs had again come under strong central control. The Han also extended the Great Wall far to the north-west, undertook several military expeditions against the nomad Hsiung-nu in the north, invaded northern Vietnam and Korea, and for a brief period after 59 BC controlled the Tarim basin. They also consolidated control over the Canton region, eliminating the Min-Yueh kingdoms of the south-east coast. A lively export trade, mainly in silk, began to Parthia and to the Roman empire (see map 1).

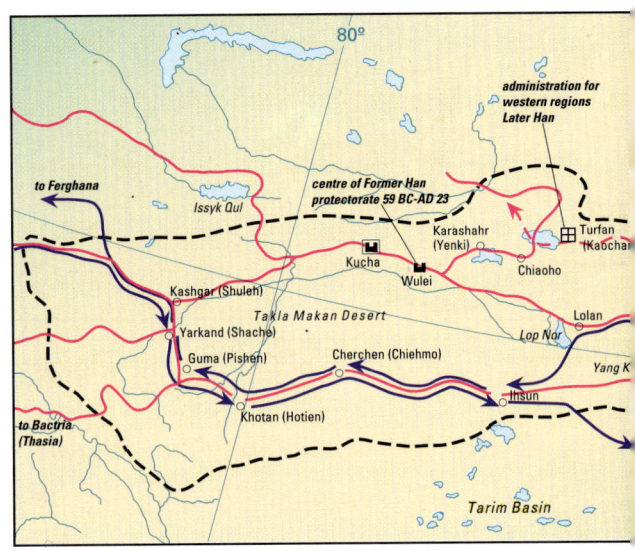

2 Han China in AD 2
- imperial capital
- enfiefed principalities
- commanderies
- highways
- canals

A census in AD 2 revealed some 57 million people in the empire. Great cities abounded, the largest – Changan, the capital – housing 250,000 people. The heart of the empire remained the Yellow River plain, where population densities in some areas approached 150 per square mile, and numerous fiefs survived (see map 2). Shortly afterwards, however, court families and great feudatories increased their influence, while agrarian unrest mounted. Real power lay in the hands of the regional commanders and warlords and the last Han emperor abdicated in 220. The Han empire fragmented into three regional states and a century later the Hsiung-nu burst through the Great Wall and overran northern China (see page 38). China was to remain politically fragmented until 589.

# The collapse of the ancient world

By the 3rd century AD, a continuous web of complex, advanced societies stretched across the southern half of the continents of Europe and Asia. In the West, Rome ruled the whole Mediterranean world and much of Europe; in China, the Han ruled a state that equalled the Roman empire in population and extended from the Pacific to the Takla Makan desert in central Asia; in between lay the Persian empire. The co-existence of these great states brought to vast areas of the Old World internal peace and efficient government, conditions that made possible commercial and cultural interchange on an unprecedented scale.

But most of this 'civilized world' formed only a narrow corridor, flanked to the north by the domain of nomadic tribes, expert horse archers who lived off their herds of sheep and cattle and possessed in war a speed and striking power that their sedentary neighbours could rarely match. In the 4th and 5th centuries AD, for reasons that remain mysterious, numerous nomad groups – although lacking central direction – launched devastating attacks against all the major civilizations. A confederation known as the Hsiung-nu from Mongolia broke through the Great Wall of China in 304 and within a decade reached the Yellow River, sacking the ancient Han capital Ch'ang-an (316). A succession of invaders from the steppes dominated northern China for the next three centuries.

At the same time another branch of the Hsiung-nu, the Huns, swept south-westwards through Asia, causing a chain reaction among the Germanic peoples along the Black Sea and the Danube. To escape them the Visigoths, perhaps 80,000 strong, forced their way into the Balkans and in 378 defeated a large Roman army outside Adrianople. Next, they moved into Italy and in 410 captured and sacked Rome itself. Meanwhile other Germanic tribes crossed the Rhine. The Vandals, the Alans and the Suevi invaded Gaul in 406 and plundered it for three years before passing on to Spain and north Africa. In their wake, the Franks, the Burgundians and the Alemanni also invaded Gaul, while the Picts from Scotland and marauders from the continent ravaged Britain. The empire's only success came in 451 when, with the aid of the Franks and Visigoths, a Roman army defeated and drove back a further onslaught by the Huns, led by Attila.

In 480 another branch of the Huns invaded India and destroyed the Gupta empire (page 27) before attacking the Persian empire, where they defeated and killed the ruler in 484. Finally, around 550, another group of warlike nomads from central Asia – the Juan-juan or Avars – moved west and within a generation ravaged Gaul and the Balkans, followed by the Slavs and Bulgars, who also invaded the Balkans, and the Lombards, who occupied northern Italy.

By AD 600 the great cities of Eurasia – Rome, Changan, and countless others – were in serious decline and the empires that built them had perished. Persia and southern China weathered the storm relatively intact, while in India and northern China, the invaders adopted native methods of government and co-operated with local elites, taking on their customs and culture as they did so. In all these areas, classical

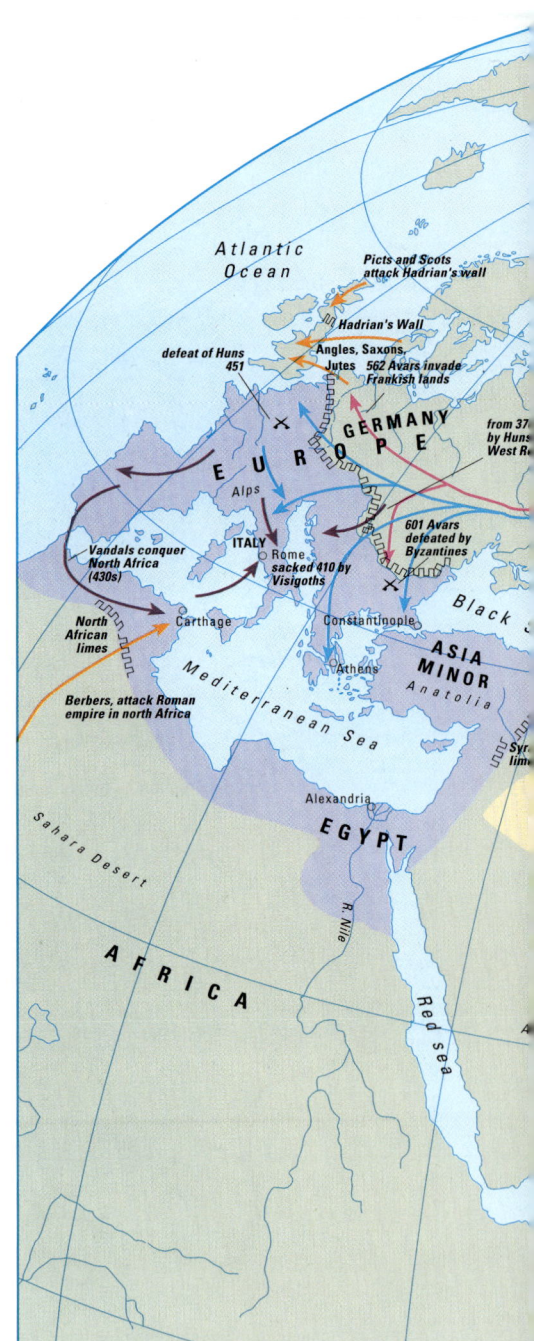

civilization emerged impaired but not extinguished. In Europe, too, the Roman tradition was modified rather than supplanted by the imposition of rulers of Germanic origin: the Franks in France; the Visigoths in Spain; the Ostrogoths in Italy. The deposition of the last Roman emperor in the west in 476 marked a further stage in the transformation of the west from classical to medieval. The Latin tongue survived, too, while knowledge of classical culture was transmitted through a handful of monasteries.

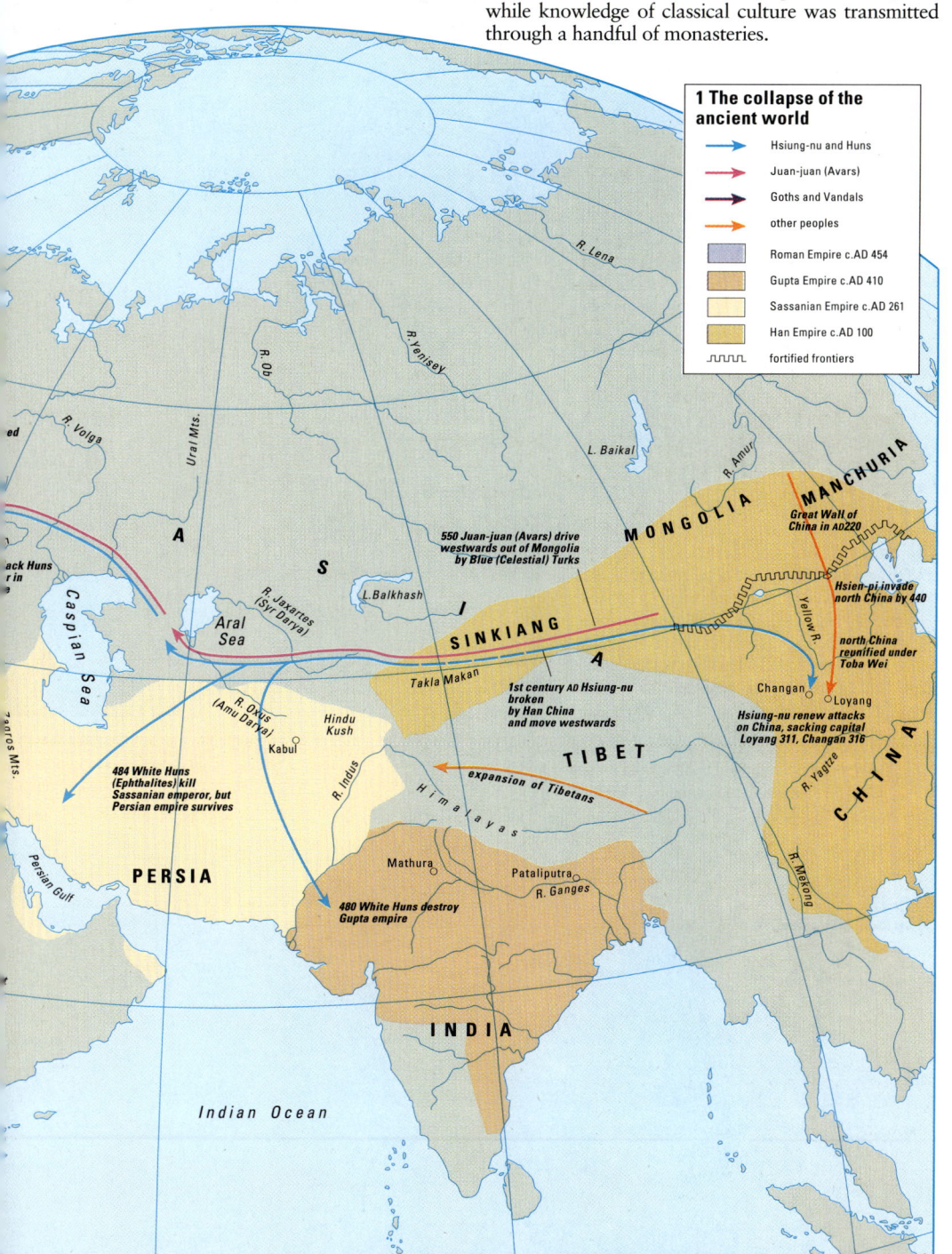

# The spread of Christianity to 1500

Christianity began as a Jewish splinter movement in Roman Palestine. Its founder, Jesus of Nazareth, claimed to be the Messiah, or Saviour, sent to prepare the Jews for 'the kingdom of God' but, after an initial, short-lived success, he was executed as a revolutionary (AD 29). Jewish orthodoxy rejected his message, but his followers turned instead to the conversion of non-Jews and by AD 200, despite repression and persecution, communities of Christians (as the followers of Jesus came to be called) flourished in several cities of the Roman empire (especially Antioch and Edessa). In 313 the Emperor Constantine granted the new faith toleration and in 325 at Nicaea presided over the first ecumenical council, representing the whole church, which defined beliefs for all Christians. A full ecclesiastical organization developed, with a hierarchy of bishops and a framework of patriarchates, provinces and dioceses throughout the empire (map 2).

The council of Chalcedon (451) attempted to enforce orthodoxy on the Christian world, but instead alienated the Monophysite (or Coptic) Christians of Egypt, Syria and Armenia, and the Nestorians who, expelled from Edessa, took refuge in Persia. Meanwhile the disintegration of the Roman empire in the West (page 34) undermined the position of the church. But salvation came from the periphery. The Coptic church of Egypt, with a strong monastic tradition, sent missionaries down the Nile from the 4th century, converting the peoples of Nubia and Ethiopia; while from the 7th century, the Nestorians of Persia expanded south into Arabia and east to China. In the west, the impetus for revival came from the monastic missionary church of Ireland, which evangelized first its Celtic neighbours in Britain and Brittany, and then in the 7th and 8th centuries the pagan tribes of continental Europe (map 1).

As the Muslim onslaught devastated the Christian Mediterranean (page 46), both Rome and Constantinople launched missions northwards among the Slavs. Russia opted for Orthodox Christianity, and in 988 the Russian prince Vladimir was baptized, while Poland (966) and Hungary (1001) chose Catholic Christianity. Although rivalry between the two patriarchates resulted after 1054

**1 Christianity in Europe**
- Monophysite Christians
- Orthodox Christians
- Catholic Christians
- original Catholic core
- Celtic churches
- Islam
- heathen peoples
- metropolitan see
- bishopric
- monastery/hermitage
- other churches
- routes of missionaries

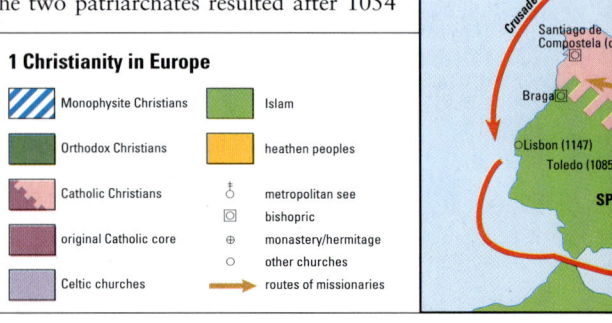

2 The spread of Christianity

- areas strongly Christian by 325
- areas largely Christian by 625
- ☦ patriarchate
- ☦ archbishopric
- ⊕ ecumenical council (with date)
- ◉ council
- ● the Seven Churches of Asia

in schism, the popes increased their authority by sponsoring Christian counter-offensives, in Iberia, the Baltic and the Near East: the crusades (page 44). The attempt to restore Christianity to Palestine proved a costly failure, but the militant crusading spirit remained alive. Meanwhile, within Europe, monks and (from the 13th century) friars joined the expanding network of parish clergy in Christianizing the countryside and combating heresy. In 1387 Lithuania, the last remaining heathen state in Europe, converted to Catholicism, just as persecution by Timur and other rulers (page 58) extinguished the faith in Asia, the continent of its birth.

# China 581-1279

After the barbarian invasions of the 4th and 5th centuries (page 38) the Sui dynasty (581-617) reunified China. They consolidated their empire through standardized institutions, a state-supported broad-based Buddhism, and the construction of a canal system linking the Yangtze with the Yellow River and the Loyang region. The T'ang dynasty (618-907) continued the process, creating a uniform administrative organization of prefectures, in which officials recruited through an examination system replaced the traditional aristocracy. The T'ang also extended their control to the Tarim basin and northern Korea: in the 660s, the Chinese empire reached its greatest extent and 88 Asiatic peoples recognised Chinese overlordship, adopting its culture, its written language and its political institutions (map 1).

In 751, however, at the Talas River, an Arab army defeated the Chinese, while a major rebellion rocked T'ang power in 755-62, causing many of the new conquests to be abandoned. Within the empire, power began to pass to the provinces until in 907, following a wave of peasant uprisings, China split into ten separate regional states. Although the Sung dynasty reunified the country between 960 and 979, they failed to regain the new territories. Nevertheless, Chinese economic growth continued. A massive movement of population into the fertile Yangtze valley and southern China produced large agricultural surpluses which stimulated trade and economic development. Between 750 and 1100, the population of the empire doubled; trade reached new heights; and a great concentration of industries arose around the capital, K'ai-feng, centre of the canal system and of the eastern road network.

In 1126-7 the Chin, a powerful nomadic state north-east of the Great Wall, invaded and conquered all of northern China, with terrible devastation. The Sung now controlled only the centre and the south, but stood constantly on the defensive, maintaining huge armies and paying vast subsidies to their aggressive neighbours (map 2). Even after the Chin invasion,

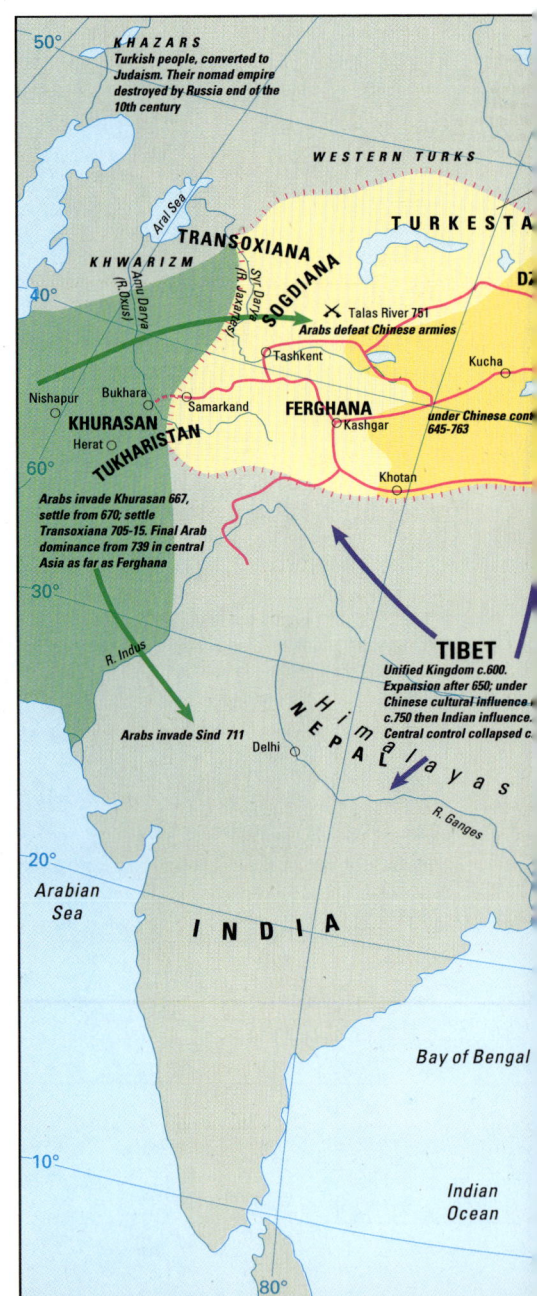

however, the Sung state remained immensely prosperous, since its southern territories proved far more productive than the old northern heartland of China. Population continued to increase rapidly; trade and industry boomed; and the new capital, Hangchou, became the world's largest city. This was also a period of great cultural achievement. The visual arts, literature, philosophy, science and technology all reached new heights; education became more widespread, aided by the dissemination of printing, which had been invented in T'ang times and now became commonplace. Merchants formed guilds and partnerships, setting up a complex commercial organization with banks, credit systems and paper money. The government was run by a mandarinate of career bureaucrats.

But their days were numbered. Between 1211 and 1234 the Mongols (page 56) had overrun the Chin empire, causing widespread devastation, and in the 1270s the forces of Kublai Khan – 'the most powerful man since Adam' according to a European visitor – annexed the entire Sung empire. For the first time, all of China lay under foreign rule.

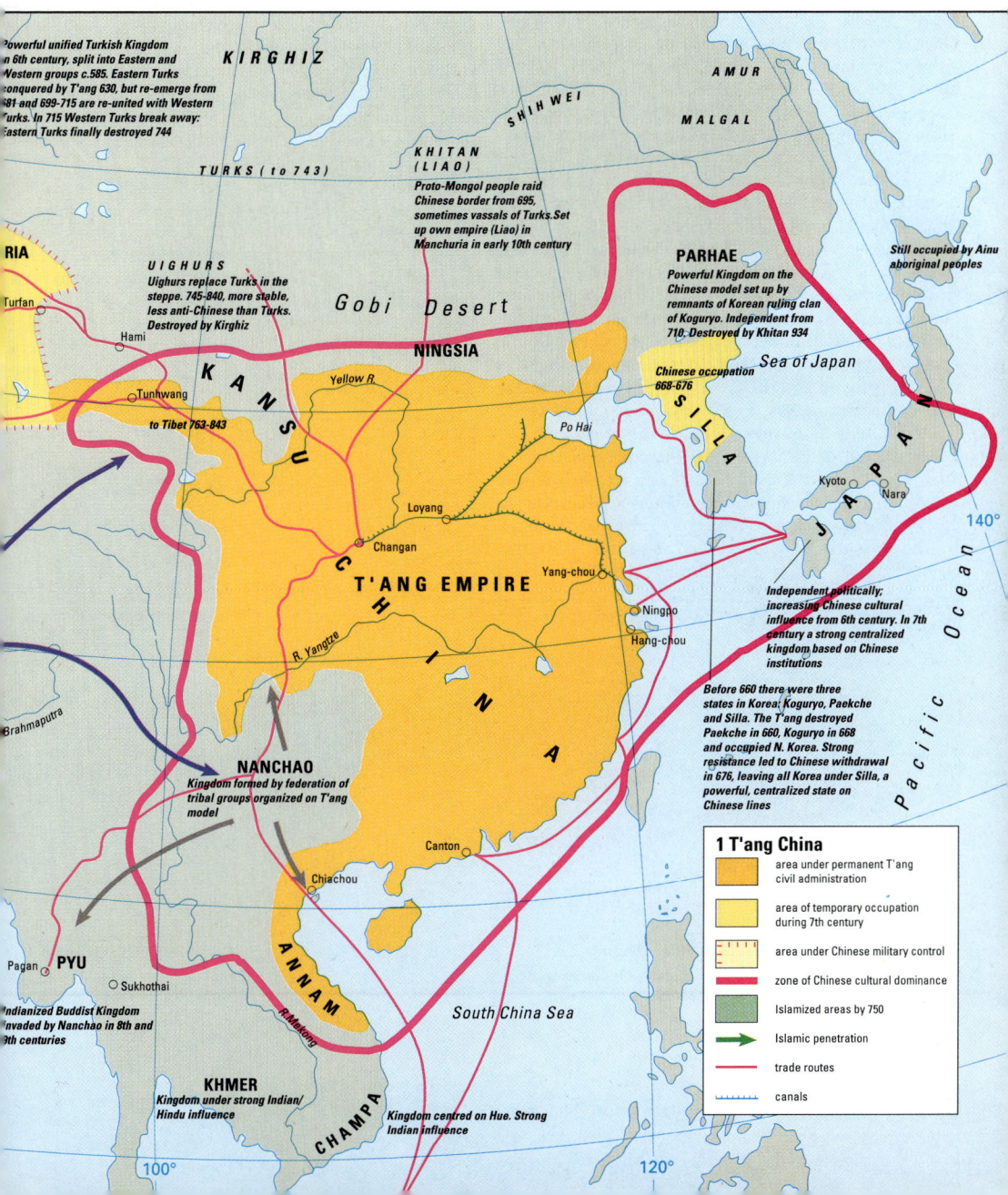

# The Byzantine world
## 610-1453

Almost from its inception, the Roman empire's centre of gravity moved to the east, first pulled by the lure of economic wealth in Egypt and western Asia; then pushed by the loss of the western provinces to Germanic invaders (page 34) and by the pressure of Sassanid Persia on its eastern frontier. Except during the reign of Justinian (page 35), the west was neglected and the Roman empire became an eastern, Greek-speaking state – normally known, from the reign of Heraclius (610-641), as Byzantium.

Heraclius ended the long contest with Persia victoriously, capturing Nineveh in 628, but almost at once Byzantium faced two even more redoubtable foes: Islam (page 46) and the Slavs. However, after the failure of two long Arab sieges of Byzantium (673-8 and 717-18), the empire launched a succession of vigorous counter-offensives. Basil II (976-1025) even managed to advance the imperial frontiers close to their earlier limits: the Arabs retreated into Palestine; the Russians met defeat at Silistra on the Danube; the Bulgars, who had advanced to within 60 miles of Constantinople, became imperial subjects; plans were laid to recover the former Byzantine territories in Italy. However, the constant campaigns imposed heavy financial strains, as well as profound and debilitating social change, and in spite of further phases of recovery, the frontiers steadily shrank (map 1).

The crucial development was the emergence, in the 11th century, of the Seljuk Turks (page 46), whose crushing victory over Byzantine forces at Manzikert in 1071 induced Emperor Alexius I (1081-1118) to call on the west for help, thus initiating the sequence of events that led to the First Crusade (1096-9). It proved a disastrous move since the Franks were less concerned to aid Byzantium than to set up their own principalities in Palestine and Asia Minor; the Normans, already in control of Sicily and Byzantine Italy, coveted lands in Greece; and the Italian cities, led by Venice, strove to increase their share of Mediterranean trade. After a century of mounting tension, the soldiers of the Fourth Crusade in 1204 conquered and pillaged Constantinople, partitioned the Byzantine empire, and established Latin states all over the Balkans (map 2).

The Latin Empire proved short-lived – its Greek-speaking subjects resented it and a new dynasty, the Palaelogogi, restored the Greek empire in 1261 – but the new Byzantine state was only a shadow of its former self and when, shortly afterwards, the Ottoman Turks established themselves first in Asia Minor and then advanced into Byzantium's European territories, its fate was sealed. The capital of the east Roman empire fell in 1453 (page 66).

Nevertheless, the history of Byzantium includes both greatness and lasting achievements. For centuries it transmitted Roman culture back to areas from which the barbarian invasions had effaced it. It also passed on its culture and its religion to the Balkan peoples and to Russia. 'Two Romes have fallen', a Russian monk wrote shortly after 1453, 'but the third is still standing and a fourth shall never be.' He referred to Moscow (page 52), now emerged as the heir to the Byzantine inheritance.

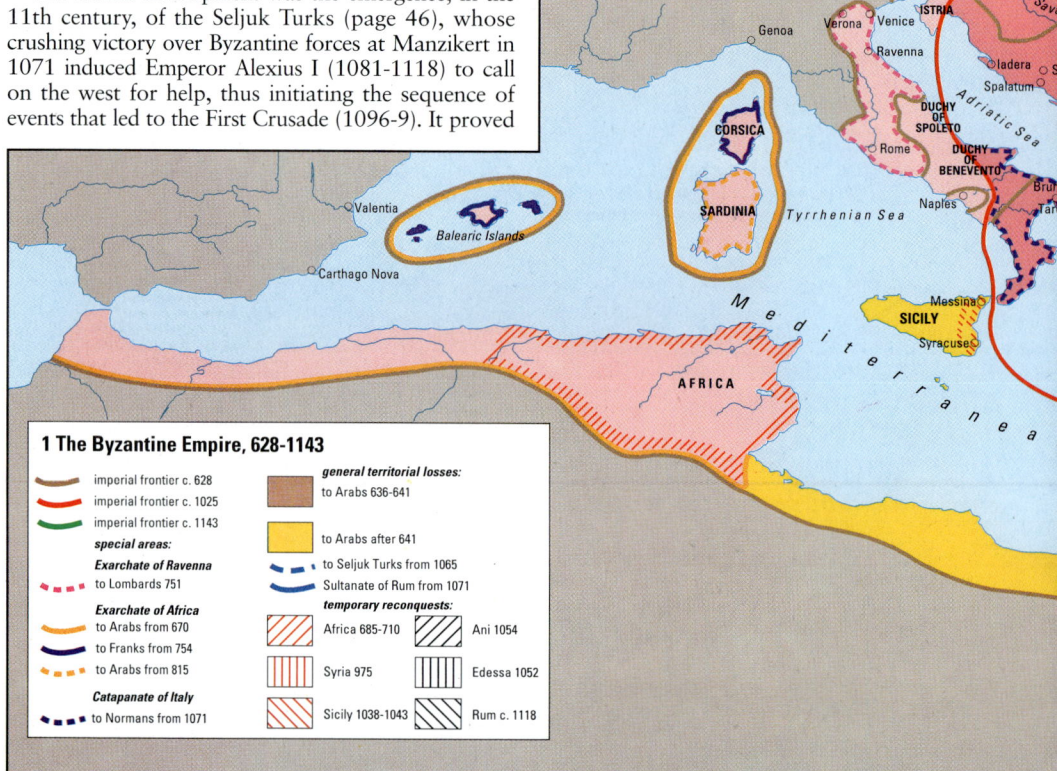

**1 The Byzantine Empire, 628-1143**

- imperial frontier c. 628
- imperial frontier c. 1025
- imperial frontier c. 1143

*special areas:*
- Exarchate of Ravenna
- to Lombards 751
- Exarchate of Africa
- to Arabs from 670
- to Franks from 754
- to Arabs from 815
- Catapanate of Italy
- to Normans from 1071

*general territorial losses:*
- to Arabs 636-641
- to Arabs after 641
- to Seljuk Turks from 1065
- Sultanate of Rum from 1071

*temporary reconquests:*
- Africa 685-710
- Syria 975
- Sicily 1038-1043
- Ani 1054
- Edessa 1052
- Rum c. 1118

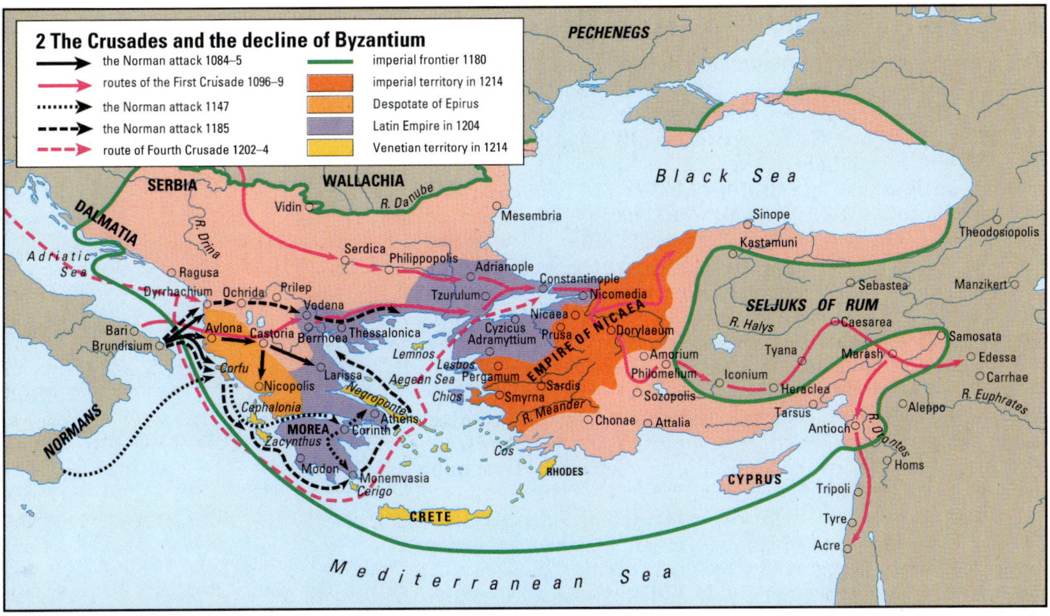
2 The Crusades and the decline of Byzantium
the Norman attack 1084–5
routes of the First Crusade 1096–9
the Norman attack 1147
the Norman attack 1185
route of Fourth Crusade 1202–4
imperial frontier 1180
imperial territory in 1214
Despotate of Epirus
Latin Empire in 1204
Venetian territory in 1214
PECHENEGS
Black Sea
SERBIA
WALLACHIA
R. Danube
Vidin
Mesembria
Sinope
Kastamuni
Theodosiopolis
DALMATIA
R. Drina
Adriatic Sea
Ragusa
Serdica
Philippopolis
Adrianople
Constantinople
Sebastea
Manzikert
Dyrrhachium
Ochrida
Prilep
Vodena
Tzurulum
Nicomedia
SELJUKS OF RUM
Bari
Brundisium
Avlona
Castoria
Berrhoea
Thessalonica
Nicaea
Cyzicus
Adramyttium
Prusa
EMPIRE OF NICAEA
Dorylaeum
R. Halys
Caesarea
Tyana
Samosata
Edessa
Carrhae
Corfu
Nicopolis
Larissa
Lemnos
Lesbos
Aegean Sea
Chios
Pergamum
Smyrna
Sardis
Amorium
Philomelium
Iconium
Heraclea
Marash
Sozopolis
R. Euphrates
NORMANS
Cephalonia
Negroponte
Athens
Corinth
MOREA
Zacynthus
R. Meander
Chonae
Attalia
Tarsus
Antioch
Aleppo
R. Orontes
Homs
Modon
Monemvasia
Cerigo
Cos
RHODES
CYPRUS
Tripoli
Tyre
Acre
CRETE
Mediterranean Sea

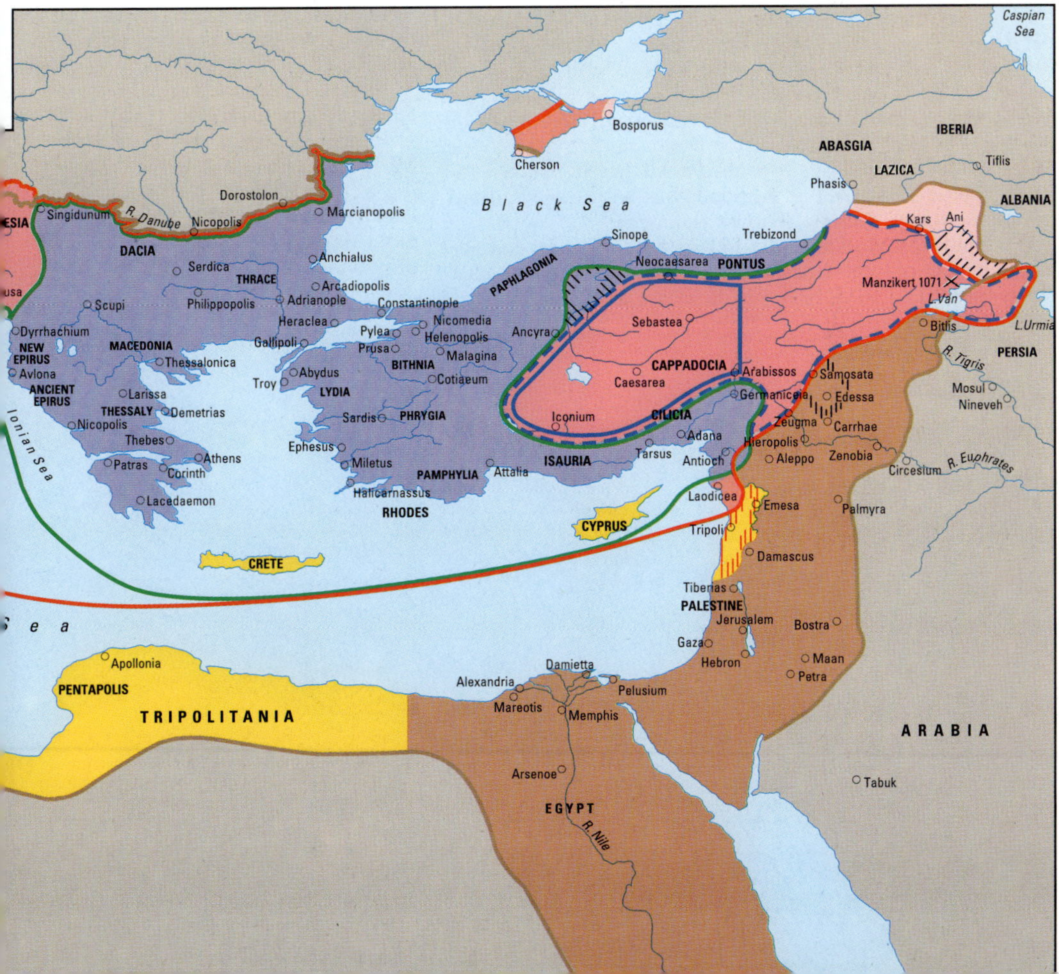
Caspian Sea
Bosporus
Cherson
IBERIA
ABASGIA
LAZICA
Tiflis
Phasis
ALBANIA
Black Sea
Dorostolon
Singidunum
R. Danube
Nicopolis
Marcianopolis
Sinope
Trebizond
Kars
Ani
DACIA
Anchialus
Neocaesarea
PONTUS
Serdica
THRACE
Arcadiopolis
PAPHLAGONIA
Manzikert 1071
L. Van
Scupi
Philippopolis
Adrianople
Constantinople
Nicomedia
Helenopolis
Heraclea
Pylea
Ancyra
Sebastea
Bitlis
L. Urmia
Dyrrhachium
NEW EPIRUS
MACEDONIA
Gallipoli
Prusa
Malagina
Thessalonica
BITHNIA
CAPPADOCIA
Arabissos
Samosata
PERSIA
Avlona
ANCIENT EPIRUS
Abydus
Cotiaeum
R. Tigris
Troy
LYDIA
Caesarea
Germanicea
Edessa
Mosul
Nineveh
Larissa
THESSALY
Demetrias
Ionian Sea
Nicopolis
Sardis
PHRYGIA
Iconium
CILICIA
Zeugma
Carrhae
Thebes
Ephesus
Adana
Hieropolis
Zenobia
Tarsus
Antioch
Aleppo
Athens
Patras
Corinth
Miletus
PAMPHYLIA
Attalia
ISAURIA
Circesium
R. Euphrates
Halicarnassus
Lacedaemon
RHODES
Laodicea
Emesa
Palmyra
CYPRUS
Tripoli
Damascus
CRETE
Tiberias
PALESTINE
Sea
Jerusalem
Bostra
Gaza
Hebron
Maan
Petra
Apollonia
Damietta
Alexandria
Pelusium
PENTAPOLIS
TRIPOLITANIA
Mareotis
Memphis
ARABIA
Arsenoe
Tabuk
EGYPT
R. Nile

# The Islamic world 632-1517

The rise and expansion of Islam ranks as perhaps the most significant development in world history between the fall of Rome and the European invasion of the Americas. Within a remarkably short time, a new world religion created a dynamic civilization which now embraces one-seventh of the global population: 600 million Muslims, spread from Morocco to Indonesia, and from Siberia to Zanzibar. 'Islam', which means 'submission to the will of God', was conveyed to humankind through the Koran, a volume of prescriptions on behaviour as well as belief, revealed by God to Mohammed his prophet, who was born in the religious and commercial centre of Mecca about 570. As Mohammed's followers grew in number, they aroused the hostility of the merchants of Mecca and in 622 the group withdrew to the neighbouring town of Medina (the *hijra*). But Mohammed returned to Mecca in triumph in 630, transforming it into the focal point for the new faith of Islam, and when he died in 632 his authority extended over much the Hejaz and much of central and southern Arabia.

For the next century Islam expanded rapidly: Arab armies defeated Latin Christian, Byzantine, Persian, Indian and Chinese armies to spread the new faith from the Himalayas in the east to the Atlantic in the west (map 1). In 711 they crossed over the Straits of Gibraltar and conquered Spain. Until 656 political control over the empire remained with Mohammed's relatives, but then a split occurred, with some Muslims following Ali, the Prophet's cousin and son-in-law (the Shi'ites), and others – the majority – accepting the rule of the Umayyad dynasty from Mecca who claimed to represent the Sunna or traditions of the Prophet. The Umayyads ruled from Damascus in Syria between 661 and 750, followed by the rival Abbasid dynasty, who created a new capital at Baghdad in Mesopotamia and opened government to non-Arab Muslims (known as *mawali*).

Gradually, the Muslim world lost its political unity and split into a number of local dynastic entities, some Sunnite and others Shi'ite (map 2). In 1055, however, the centre of the Islamic world was strengthened when the Seljuk Turks established themselves in Baghdad and shortly thereafter drove the Christians from most of Anatolia (page 44). Despite invasions from the west in the 12th century (the Crusades: page 45) and from the east in the 13th (the Mongols: page 56), Islam retained its hold over the Near East, while missionaries and merchants carried the faith eastwards to Malaysia, Indonesia and the Philippines, and southwards both to the sub-Saharan states and the cities of the Swahili coast of Africa (page 54). For a millennium after the birth of Mohammed, Islam remained the western hemisphere's leading and most extensive civilization.

**1 The expansion of Islam**
- empire under Mohammed
- growth under Abu Bakr (632-634)
- growth under Omar (634-644)
- growth under Othman (644-656) and Ali (656-661)
- expansion of Umayyad Caliphate (661-750)
- expansion 750-850
- routes of advance
- × battles

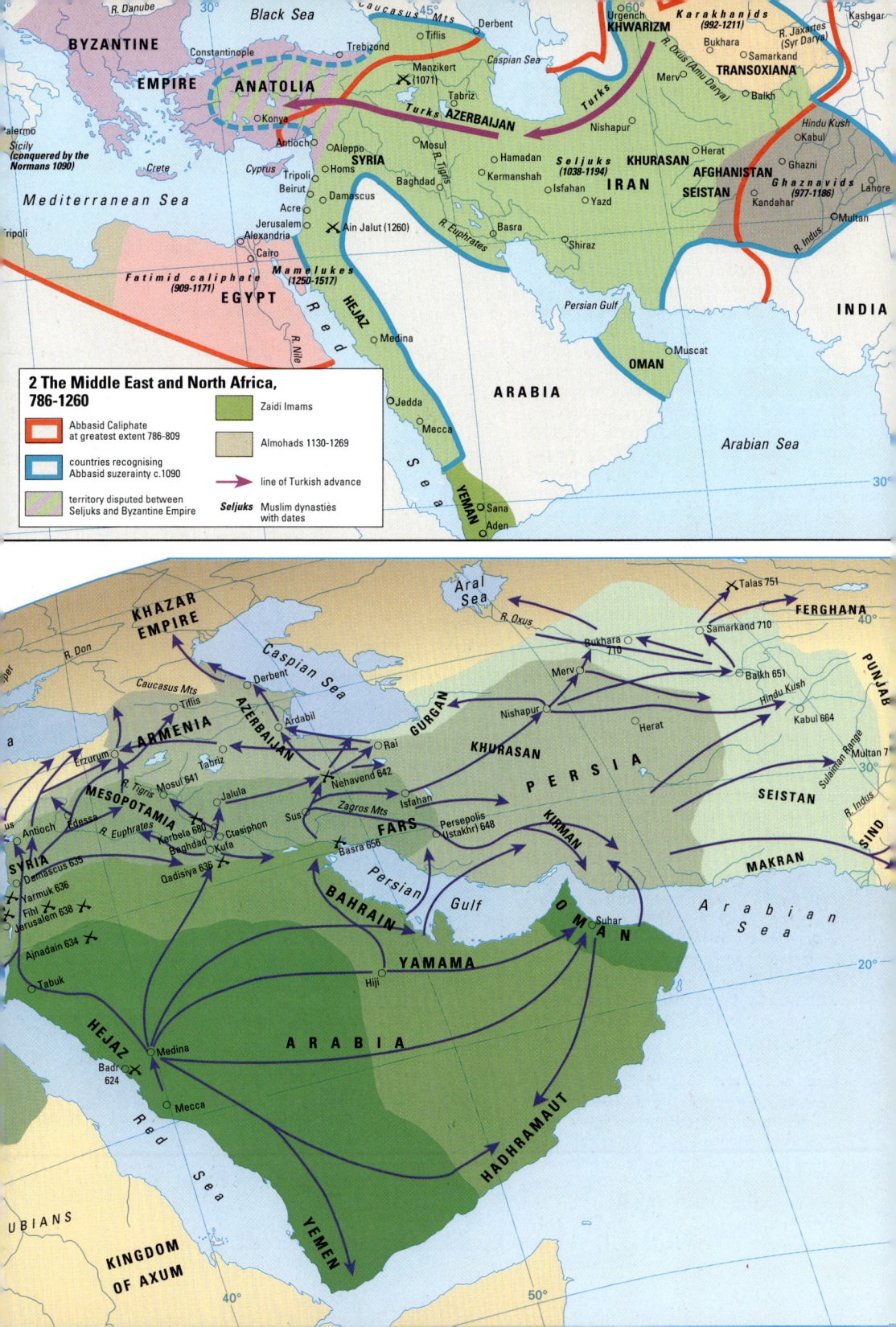

# Franks and Anglo-Saxons 714-814

Within a century of the Germanic invasions (page 38), settled kingdoms had grown up in western Europe, but not in Britain, where invaders from the continent met with resistance. During the 7th century, however, seven separate important kingdoms – which are traditionally known as the Heptarchy – emerged in England. Geographical obstacles seem to have prevented the states in the south-east (Sussex, Kent, Essex, East Anglia) from expanding, and leadership at first passed to Northumbria, whose progress benefitted from its early conversion to Christianity. Mercia led the opposition, sometimes in alliance with the 'Britons' on the periphery, and by the time of Offa (757-96) its pre-eminence was unquestionable: it controlled the four southeastern kingdoms, and even Wessex recognized Mercian overlordship (map 1).

On the continent, the Franks (whose original power base lay in what is now northern France, the Low Countries and the Rhineland) converted to Christianity under Clovis (486-511) and began to expand south and east. From their new capital at Paris, Clovis and his sons and grandsons defeated the Visigoths, conquered Burgundy and Provence, and extended their overlordship in Germany as far as the middle Danube.

Most of the new lands served to maintain the loyalty of the Frankish warriors, however, and when the conquests ceased in the mid-7th century the kings had to reward their followers and endow the Church by granting away their own estates and revenues. In doing so they diminished their resources and, in time, power passed to the families which had benefitted from royal favour. Eventually Pepin of Herstal, the leader of a prominent family from Austrasia achieved prominence, and at Tertry (687) defeated his chief rivals.

Pepin and his son Charles Martel (from whom the dynasty took the name 'Carolingian') restored Frankish fortunes and inaugurated a second surge of territorial expansion (map 2). Charles Martel (714-41) defeated the Arabs at Poitiers in 732, halting their rapid incursion into western Europe (page 46), while his son Pepin the Short (d. 768) expelled them from southern France. In 751, with the

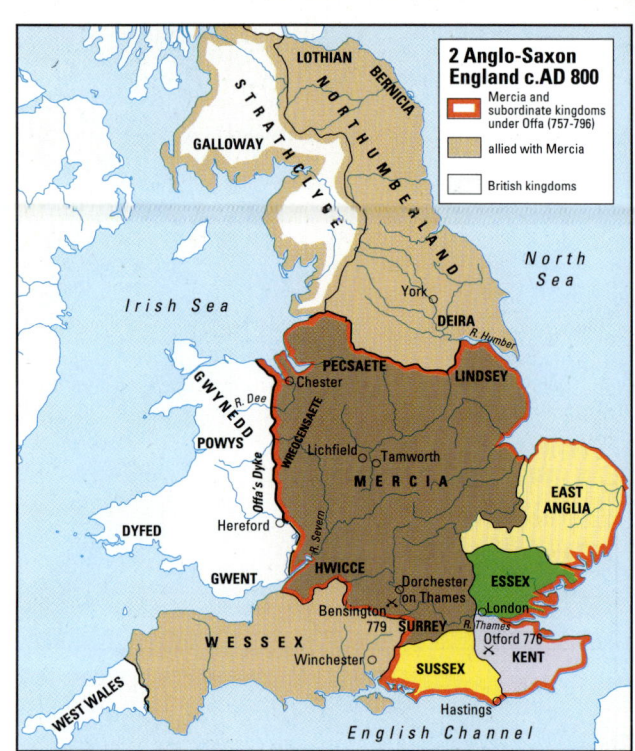

sanction and support of the pope, Pepin made himself king of the Franks. His son Charles the Great or Charlemagne (768-814) conquered Lombardy (774) and established Frankish rule in much of Italy. He won great victories over the Frisians (784-5), Bavarians (788), Avars (796) and Saxons (who were finally subdued in 804); and created a march, or boundary province, across the Pyrenees between 795 and 812. In 800 the pope in Rome crowned him emperor of the west.

However, Frankish custom called for the royal domain to be partitioned. Charlemagne's father had divided it between his two sons – Charlemagne only inherited the whole when his brother died in 771 – and the new emperor likewise planned in 806 to partition his possessions among his three sons, a scheme frustrated only by the early death of two of them, making it possible for the survivor, Louis the Pious (814-40), to inherit the whole empire. After his death, however, the treaty of Verdun (843) created three kingdoms: one in the east, one in the west, and a 'middle kingdom' which ran from the Low Countries to Italy. .

The Carolingians ruled through direct agents, rather than through Gallo-Roman bishops and counts as their predecessors had done; and throughout the 8th century these men generally remained loyal. After Charlemagne's death, however, their descendants tended to identify with the particular interests of their own localities, at the expense of the whole. Frankish hegemony in western Europe was thus disrupted by fragmentation just as it came under attack from merciless invaders, including the Vikings and Magyars (page 50).

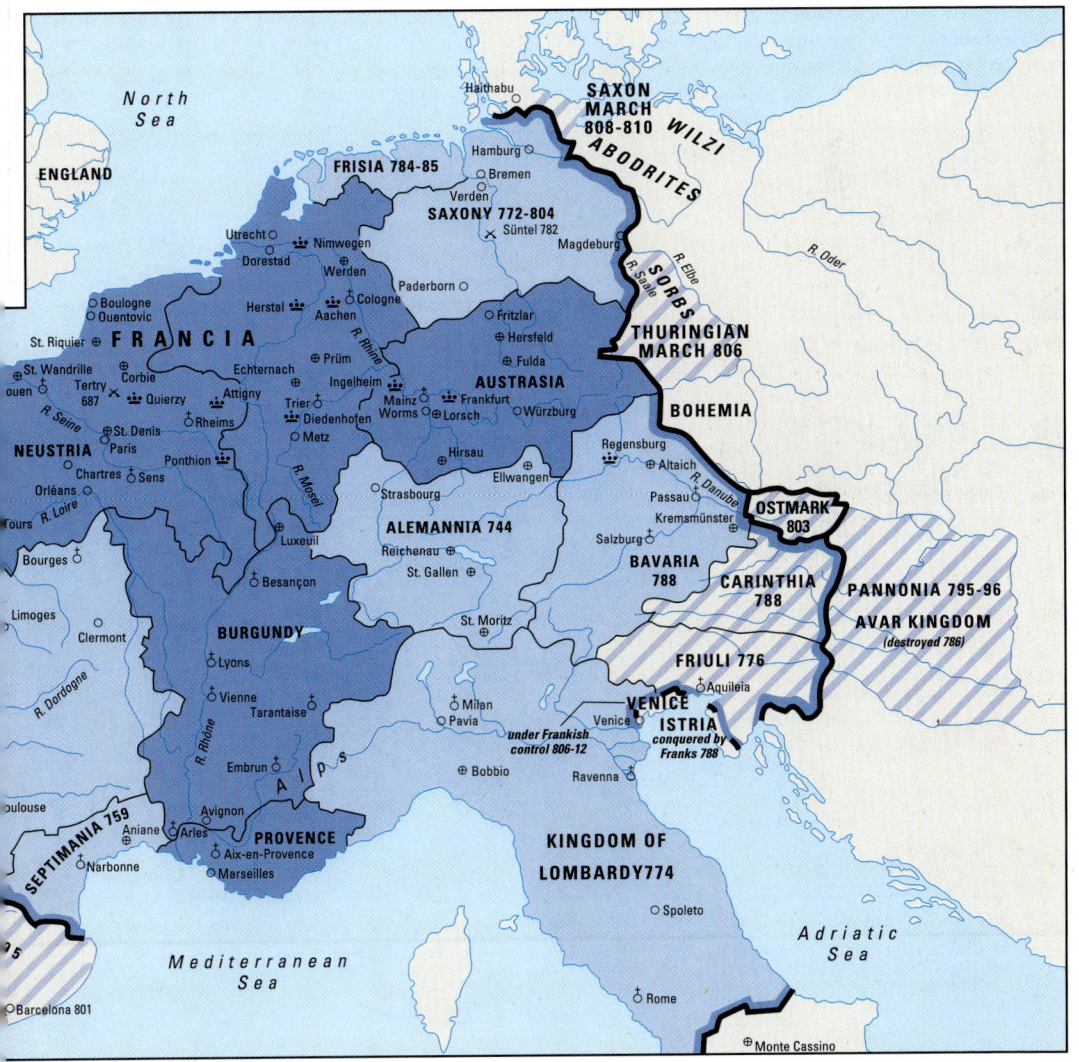

# Europe 814-1250

The activities of three separate groups of invaders in the 9th century shattered the relative stability achieved by Charlemagne in western Europe and by Offa of Mercia in England (page 48). The Saracens occupied the islands of the western Mediterranean and raided Italy and France; the Magyars of Hungary devastated northern Italy and Germany; the Vikings from Scandinavia not only plundered settlements around the European coast as far as the Mediterranean, but also created trade routes through Russia to Byzantium (page 44) and settled substantial parts of Britain, Ireland, northern France, Iceland and even Greenland.

The invasions disrupted royal authority and caused political fragmentation. In the Carolingian empire, the Frankish kings virtually capitulated to the Vikings, leaving defence to the local magnates who swiftly created their own power bases. In England, although determined resistance by Alfred the Great of Wessex (871-99) held the Danes at bay, a second wave of Scandinavian invasions a century later proved irresistible. However in the eastern half of the Frankish empire, Otto I's defeat of the Magyars at the Lechfeld (955) proved a turning point, and Germany became the first country in Europe to recover from the invasions. This achievement assured its predominance in Europe for almost three centuries.

German rulers rarely sought to assert control over the west Frankish lands but, as heirs to the Carolingians, they claimed the imperial title and the right to rule over Italy and the lands of the former "middle kingdom" (page 49). In 962 Otto I's coronation as emperor sealed the connection between Germany and Italy, and in 1034 his successors annexed Burgundy. However the emperors became increasingly dependent upon the wealth of Italy, and this embroiled Frederick I of Hohenstaufen (1152-90) with both the papacy and the populous fortified cities of the Lombard plain, all of whom saw Imperial power in Italy as a threat to their independence. The conquest of Sicily by Frederick's son Henry VI in 1194 made the Hohenstaufen the richest rulers in Europe; but the prospect of total encirclement once more alarmed the papacy and the

Lombard towns, leading to a long and costly struggle with Frederick II (1212-50). After his death, the Imperial position in Italy steadily deteriorated, and the last Hohenstaufen prince met defeat and death at the battle of Tagliacozzo in 1268.

Meanwhile, in Germany, the princes took advantage of their rulers' preoccupation with Italy both to consolidate their power and, on the eastern frontier, to direct a major expansion. The Slavs were driven out or enslaved, in favour of German settlers who, by 1250, had increased the German kingdom by about one-third and shifted its centre of gravity from the Rhine to the Elbe. The empire might no longer be the strongest or richest polity in Europe, but it remained the largest.

**2 The Hohenstaufen Empire 1152-1250**

- eastward spread of German peasant settlement 12th century
- German settlement by 1200-1250
- city with over 10,000 inhabitants
- member of Lombard Leagues of 1167 and 1226
- member of 1167 League only
- member of 1226 League only
- German invasions 1190-94
- Henry VI's Genoese and Pisan fleet 1194
- main Hohenstaufen palaces and castles
- mountain pass

# Early Russia 862-1242

Three factors shaped the early history of Russia: the eastward movement of Slav settlers; the impact of the Vikings (who were known to the Slavs as Varyagi or Varangians) from the north; and, most important of all, the division of the region into forests (in the north and centre) and treeless steppe (in the south). Before the arrival of the Vikings in the 9th century, the Slavs had begun to settle the central river basins, clearing the forests and living by agriculture, hunting, trapping and the fur trade, while nomadic tribes from Asia, such as the Pechenegs, occupied the grasslands of the south.

At first the Slavs resisted the Varangians, but in 862 they called in 'Rurik the Viking' to protect them from Pecheneg raiders. Since most of the rivers of Russia follow a north-south axis, great potential existed for trade between the Baltic and the Black Sea, and the Vikings sought to dominate and exploit these waterways and the territories adjoining them (map 1). Rurik therefore occupied Novgorod, and his followers soon pushed south to Smolensk and then down the Dnieper to Kiev (882). The principal trade route established by the Vikings ran from the Gulf of Finland up the river Neva, through Lake Ladoga to the river Volkhov, thence by portages to the Dnieper and on across the Black Sea to Byzantium.

Grand Prince Svyatoslav (962-72) campaigned to the south and east, greatly extending the frontiers of the Kievan state, which forged strong links with Byzantium, its chief trading partner; and from Byzantium it received the Christian faith during the reign of Vladimir Svyatoslav (980-1015). At the same time Kiev retained numerous connections with the West: one of Vladimir's granddaughters married the king of France, another the king of Hungary and a third the king of Norway. Half a century later, however, dynastic conflict and administrative inefficiency brought weakness and a new wave of Asiatic nomads, the Polovtsy, broke through the defences built by Svyatoslav and Vladimir. In 1093 they sacked Kiev itself.

A great northward exodus ensued to safer regions between the Oka and the Volga, where many new towns were founded (such as Vladimir, Suzdal, Rostov and Tver) and several new states developed – notably Vladimir-Suzdal, which included the fast growing commercial centre of Moscow (first mentioned in 1147), and Novgorod, which built up a fur-trading empire that reached to the Arctic and the Urals. Meanwhile, further south, Novgorod-Seversk, Vladimir-Volynsk and Galich broke away from Kievan rule (map 2).

Mongol invaders struck the final blow to the old order (page 56). In 1237-8, moving along the frozen rivers, they struck north and sacked the wealthy towns of Vladimir-Suzdal; in 1239-40 they advanced through southern Russia, systematically destroying settlements, including Kiev. Meanwhile Novgorod, although it escaped the Mongol onslaught as the onset of spring thawed the frozen rivers, faced repeated attacks by both Swedes and Germans in the Baltic region until Prince Alexander decisively defeated the former in 1240 on the river Neva (thus earning the title 'Nevsky') and the latter in 1242 on the ice of Lake Peipus. Despite these successes, however, even Novgorod had to recognize Mongol overlordship, exercised by the Golden Horde on the lower Volga, while the Lithuanian state expanded into the old Kievan heartland).

The Mongol invasion had other lasting economic, social and political effects. The destruction of so many towns decimated both trade and industry, while the elimination of the urban middle class smoothed the path of an autocracy which imitated its overlords in ruthless terror and extortion. The fall of Kiev destroyed the cultural centre of medieval Russia, with its rich Byzantine-based literature and art, while the Mongol forces, controlling the grasslands around the Caspian and the Black Sea, prevented almost all contact with Byzantium. Russia therefore inevitably developed a distinctive culture, society and political system of its own.

# African states and empires 900-1800

By the end of the first millennium AD great changes had taken place in Africa. The rise of a culture based on iron-working (page 24) led to the appearance of extensive states and empires based on trade. In the south, Zimbabwe, with its monumental stone buildings, exported gold and copper via the port of Sofala; in the west, the Kongo state carried on an important trade. Further north, Arab traders developed the trans-Saharan trade routes and so assisted the growth of major sub-Saharan states. Although Ghana rose to prominence before the Islamic era, its successors, Mali and Songhay, owed much of their wealth and culture – described in glowing terms by Arab travellers – to the impact of Islam. So did the Kanem-Borno empire around Lake Chad and the Hausa city-states. In the east Arab merchant colonies also spread down the Swahili coast as far as Kilwa and Sofala, bringing this part of Africa into an Indian Ocean trading complex. The staple exports in all cases were gold, ivory and slaves (map 1).

The arrival of the Portuguese in the 15th century at first had little impact on Africa. Their immediate object was to share directly in the gold trade, previously dominated by Muslim middlemen; the slave trade remained a secondary interest. However, with the development of labour-intensive sugar-plantations in the Americas (page 80), the slave trade attracted others. By the 18th century, nine European states maintained almost 50 fortified trading posts on the west coast, from Arguim to Whydah, to handle this burgeoning commerce, while the Portuguese continued to export slaves further south from Angola and Mozambique. Of some 15 million Africans shipped abroad by Europeans between 1450 and 1870, almost 90 per cent went to South America and the Caribbean, most of them during the 18th century. Muslim traders exported perhaps as many more again northward across the Sahara and from the Swahili coast. The effects on Africa of this appalling trade in human beings are hard to quantify, since the loss of population was not evenly divided. Some states, such as Kongo and Lunda, suffered disproportionately, while others seem to have profited. Thus, after the destruction of the powerful Songhay empire by Moroccan troops in 1591, the forest states of Asante, Dahomey and Benin, having direct access to the Atlantic and thus to European slave-traders, increased in importance and political power (map 2).

Apart from the Portuguese in Angola and Mozambique, and the fortified posts along the west coast, only the Dutch attempted to create a European colony in Africa before 1800: in the far south, around Cape Town. In the north-east, Islam continued to spread, but the Christian kingdom of Ethiopia still held its own. In the north, the Ottoman empire (page 66) maintained only nominal suzerainty over the states from Morocco to Egypt. In 1800, almost all of Africa thus remained independent of foreign control: a world unto itself, the 'dark continent'. However, precisely because of its autonomy, it would lack the ability to compete with the technological dynamism of the West in the 19th century (page 104).

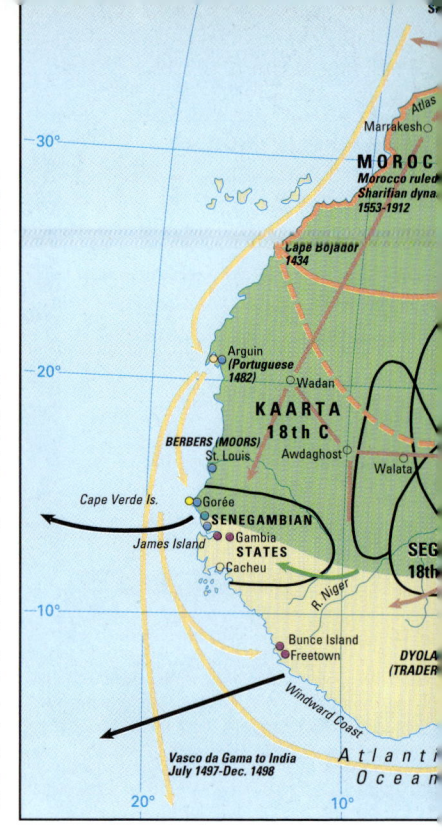

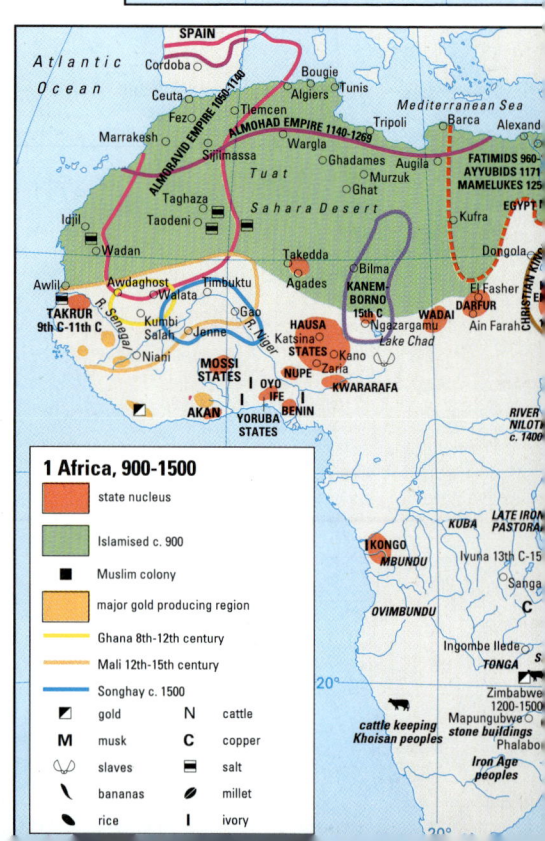

# The Mongol Empire
## 1206-1696

The Mongols, a nomadic people from the grasslands of Central Asia, staged a sudden and devastating irruption into world history in the first half of the 13th century (map 1). Theirs was not the first empire of the steppe, however. In the 7th century AD, in the wake of the upheavals that destroyed the ancient world (page 38), a confederation of Turkish tribes had managed to dominate the plains of Asia from the Great Wall of China to the Black Sea; but by 750 their rule had collapsed and the area disintegrated into feud and faction. Thus it remained for four centuries, when a charismatic leader, Temujin (1167-1227), gained recognition as supreme ruler and in 1206 took the title Genghis Khan, 'prince of all that lies between the Oceans'. Under his leadership the Mongols first invaded the Chin empire in north China and then turned

against the Islamic states to the west. By the time of Genghis's death, his empire stretched from the Pacific Ocean to the Caspian Sea. His successors continued the tide of destructive conquests: Kievan Russia (1237-40); the Abbasid Caliphate (1256-60); Sung China (1271-9). Europe and Japan were also threatened: one Mongol army reached the gates of Vienna while another defeated a German-Polish army at Liegnitz in 1241; two amphibious expeditions unsuccessfully attacked Kyushu in 1274 and 1281.

However the vast empire lacked coherence and stability, and the Mongols failed to develop appropriate institutions. On hearing of the death of Genghis's successor Ogedei in 1241, the victorious commander of the Mongol forces in Europe withdrew eastwards with his army, in order to take part in choosing a successor. They never returned. Likewise in 1260, on hearing of the death of Ogedei's successor, the victorious commander of the Mongol forces in the Near East decided to return to the Mongol heartland,

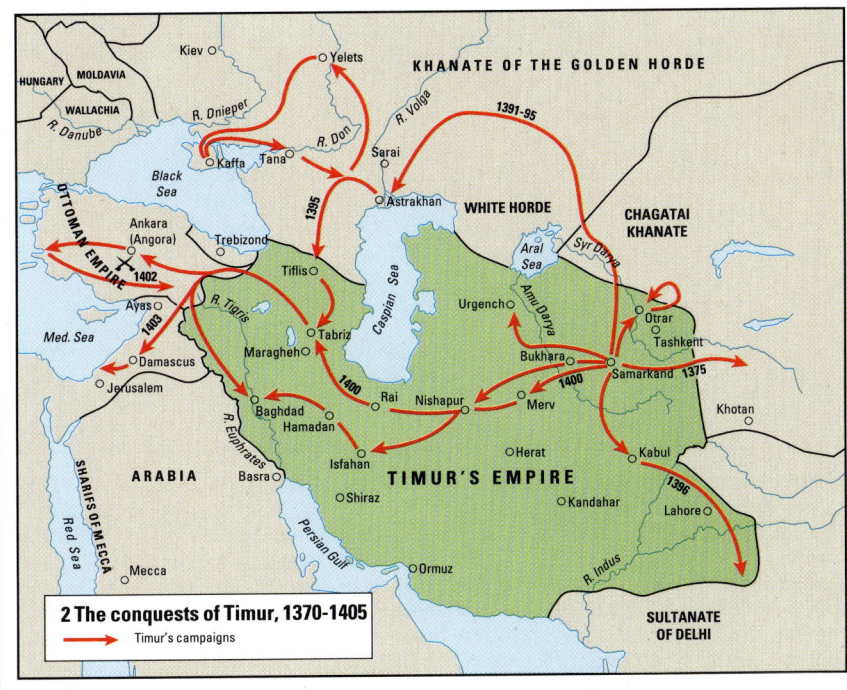

**2 The conquests of Timur, 1370-1405**
→ Timur's campaigns

leaving only a skeleton force behind him. This soon became known in Cairo, and the Sultan of Egypt marched to the defence of Islam, still reeling from the sack of Baghdad, the capital of the Caliphs, two years before. At Ain Jalut on 3 September 1260 the Mongols suffered a decisive defeat and withdrew to Persia.

The Mongol empire now fragmented. The title of Great Khan went to Kublai who, although never forgetting that he was the grandson of Genghis, spent most of his long reign (1260-94) seeking to reunify China and conquer Japan. The other Mongol states – the Golden Horde in the west; the Il-Khans in Persia; the Chagatai empire in the traditional Mongol heartland – went their own way.

Despite the widespread destruction of the Mongol onslaught, their temporary unification of Eurasia permitted the exchange of goods and ideas between the far east and the far west on an unprecedented scale. For over a century the 'Silk Road' of ancient times revived: silver and gold from Europe and the Near East reached China while Chinese silks and porcelain circulated in Europe. But the Black Death (see page 62) and the rise of Timur, or Tamerlane (1336-1405) changed all that, for he destroyed the Chagatai khanate, dislocated the Golden Horde, defeated the Ottoman empire at the battle of Ankara in 1402 (page 66), and initiated a policy of religious intolerance. However Timur died in 1405 before he had created the institutions and traditions required to ensure the survival of his vast empire (map 2). Instead, Mongol power in the west steadily lost ground to Russia (see page 78), and crumbled in China with the rise of the Ming dynasty (see page 88). Mongolia itself came under Chinese dominion in 1696.

57

# The Muslim Empires of India and Persia 1206-1707

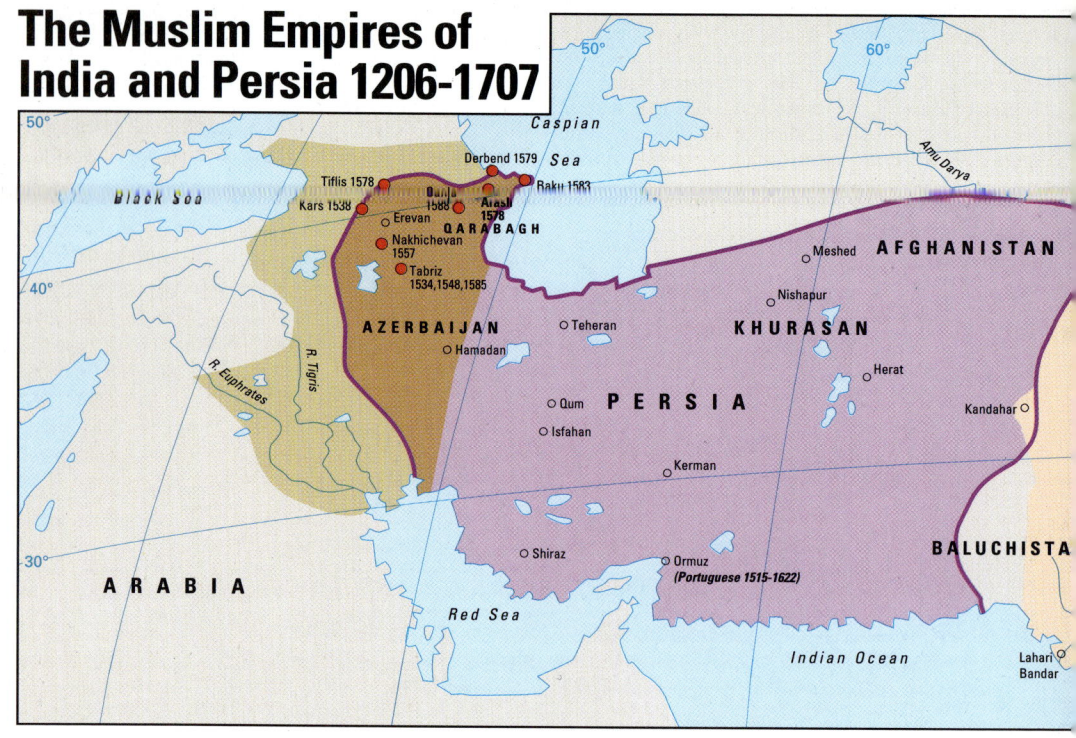

Delhi, founded in the 8th century by a Rajput chief, remained the focus of north Indian politics and also the centre of Muslim culture from the 13th to the 19th century. It served as the capital of the six Muslim dynasties, all of Turkish or Afghan extraction, who sought (unsuccessfully) to extend their rule into the Deccan between 1206 and 1526; and, after the defeat of the last of the Sultans of Delhi at Panipat (1526) by Babur – a descendant of Timur (page 56) – it became the headquarters of his descendants, the Mughals.

Babur's grandson, Akbar (1556-1605), extended the frontiers of the empire to Bengal in the east, to Gujerat and the river Godavari in the south, and to Kashmir in the north. New territories were added under Akbar's grandson, Shahjahan (1627-56) and his son Aurangzeb (1656-1707), who annexed Bijapur and Golconda in the south, and Orissa in the east. However, these achievements depended absolutely upon the acquiescence of the 150 million or so Hindu peasant farmers and petty landlords who paid the taxes that supported the Mughals' 4 million warriors, and the court grandees who commanded them. It was a delicate balance, for if the peasants and landlords were overtaxed, they would revolt; and if the grandees were not rewarded with office and wealth they would desert the court. Around 1700 the Hindu Marathas began to ravage southern regions, while some Rajput states and the Sikhs rebelled. All this reduced tax yields, and after the death of Aurangzeb several frontier provinces split off from the empire (page 90).

Meanwhile, to the West, after 1500 the leader of a fanatical sect of Shi'a Muslims, Ismail Safavi, re-unified Persia – which had been in a state of chaos since Timur's invasions – and proclaimed himself Shah. However the Sunnite Ottomans under Selim I (page 56) invaded in 1514, defeated Ismael at the battle of Chaldiran and captured Tabriz, thus initiating a duel between the two powers that lasted for over a century. The conflict centred around the key cities of Mesopotamia, and Baghdad, Tiflis, Derbend and Basra changed hands repeatedly; but its intensity stemmed from the religious division within Islam between Sunnite and Shi'ite (page 46), which excited the same passions as the split between Protestant and Catholic Christians at the same time. Eventually Shah Abbas (1587-1629) with assistance from both Russia and the Christian West, managed to regain most of the lost territories; but the Turks recaptured much of Mesopotamia in the 1630s.

Both empires boasted a rich civilization. Akbar and Abbas each built luxurious new capital cities – at Fatehpur Sikri and Isfahan respectively – and attracted to their courts local and foreign writers, artists and craftsmen. Shahjahan built the magnificent Taj Mahal outside Delhi. Nevertheless, two developments threatened these achievements. On the one hand, as in all autocracies, government authority could suddenly collapse under a weak ruler. Thus

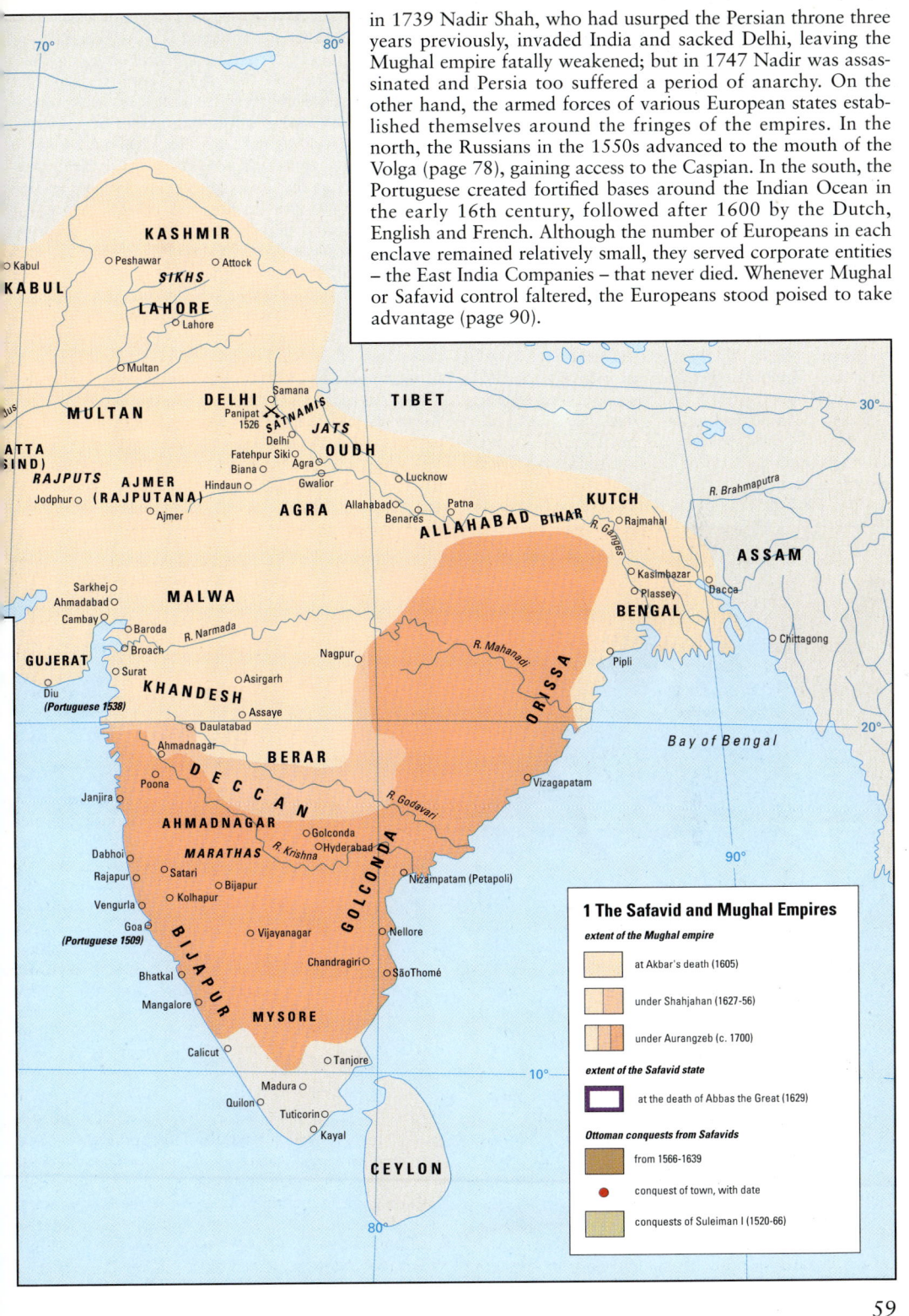

in 1739 Nadir Shah, who had usurped the Persian throne three years previously, invaded India and sacked Delhi, leaving the Mughal empire fatally weakened; but in 1747 Nadir was assassinated and Persia too suffered a period of anarchy. On the other hand, the armed forces of various European states established themselves around the fringes of the empires. In the north, the Russians in the 1550s advanced to the mouth of the Volga (page 78), gaining access to the Caspian. In the south, the Portuguese created fortified bases around the Indian Ocean in the early 16th century, followed after 1600 by the Dutch, English and French. Although the number of Europeans in each enclave remained relatively small, they served corporate entities – the East India Companies – that never died. Whenever Mughal or Safavid control faltered, the Europeans stood poised to take advantage (page 90).

# South-East Asia to 1511

Situated at one of the world's main cross-roads, civilization developed early in South-East Asia: traces of 'Java man' date from the middle Pleistocene and remains of *homo sapiens* from c. 40,000 BC; rice cultivation in Thailand began about 6000 BC and bronze working in Thailand and Vietnam in 1000 BC or earlier (pages 10 and 16). Early trade routes linked India with ports along the coasts of Burma, Thailand, Cambodia and Vietnam; Hindu-Buddhist influences from India reached the area around the 2nd or 3rd century AD; and by the 5th century Buddhist images and votive tablets appeared, along with Sanskrit inscriptions. These influences never obliterated the unique character of South-East Asian civilization; instead, the next thousand years saw their assimilation to produce distinctive societies in the area. The culture of Java and southern Sumatra likewise became Indianized, but these areas also developed commercial and political links with China, which welcomed tribute missions from a growing number of states. From the 8th century temple complexes, each combining Hindu and Buddhist influences, evolved in four main areas: central Java (notably at Borobudur and Prambanan, from the 8th to 10th centuries), Cambodia (especially at Angkor, from the 9th to 13th centuries), Burma (Pagan, from the 11th to 13th centuries) and, associated with the Hindu-Buddhist kingdom of Champa, along the coast of central Vietnam. Meanwhile Palembang (a centre of Sanskrit culture from perhaps as early as the 7th century) emerged as the capital of the maritime empire of Srivijaya, which for centuries controlled international trade passing through the straits of Malacca and Sunda, and across the Isthmus of Kra (map 1).

The great temple-states fell into decline after the 12th century. In Java, the area of Prambanan was superseded in importance by eastern Java, where three states developed in succession: Kediri (12th century), Singhasari (13th century) and finally Majapahit (late 13th-early 16th century). On the mainland, first Mongols and then Shans sacked Pagan in the 13th century, while Angkor fell to Thai attacks after 1369. Sukothai, the first of the lowland Thai cities, was itself in decline by the late 14th century. New political centres replaced the old temple cities: in Burma,

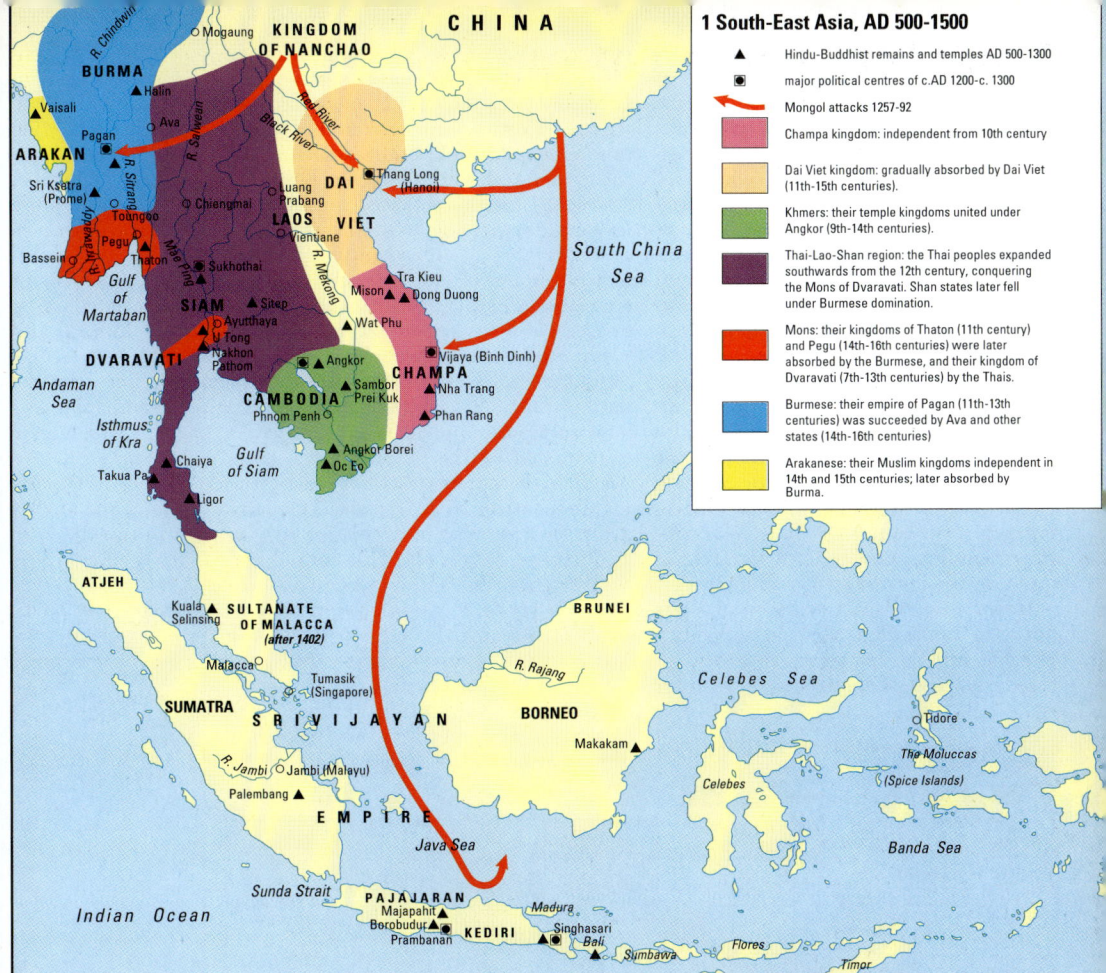

Toungoo (1347), Ava (1364), and Pegu (1369), capital of a new Mon kingdom in the south; in Thailand, Chiengmai (1296) and Ayutthaya (1350); in Cambodia, Phnom Penh and other cities along the Mekong; in Laos, Luang Prabang (1353). All were Theravada Buddhist in the Singhalese tradition, with stupas rather than temples. Meanwhile, in Vietnam, after the failure of Chinese attempts at reconquest (despite invasions in 1075-7 and 1285-8) a new kingdom, called Dai Viet, emerged and gradually absorbed Champa (annexing its capital, Vijaya, in 1471). Further south, Srivijaya declined and a powerful new Muslim state developed after 1400 at Malacca, commanding the narrow straits through which most east-west trade passed. By that time the east Javanese empire of Majapahit was in decline, and the west Javanese kingdom of Pajaran also collapsed before Muslim pressure from the northern coastal ports in the early 16th century.

Islam had began to influence northern Sumatra just before 1300; now it spread further, often under Malaccan influence, to the north Javanese trading ports, the Spice Islands, Borneo and, in the 16th century, the Philippines (map 2). When the Spaniards arrived, Mindanao had already been converted and the spread of Islam in Luzon was only halted by the Spaniards' capture of the Moorish fort at Manila in 1571 and their determined promotion of Christianity (page 74).

Meanwhile, in Vietnam, Confucian scholarship strengthened, despite the failure of another attempt at reconquest under the Ming; and all over southeast Asia the series of voyages made by the Muslim admiral Cheng Ho in the early 15th century revived and reinforced China's system of tributary relationships (page 70). From the 1430s, however, China abandoned its interest in the wider world and southeast Asia began to assume its modern pattern of cultures and polities which even the arrival of the Europeans, starting with the Portuguese capture of Malacca in 1511 (page 74) influenced little until the 19th century.

# Europe 1250-1500

The 14th century brought to an end the rise and consolidation of national monarchies in western Europe (page 50). Though growth in population and productivity was steady until the later 13th century, both began to decline thereafter. Part of the problem lay in a sudden climatic deterioration which terminated the agricultural boom that had prevailed since 1150: crop yields fell, marginal areas brought into cultivation were abandoned. In 1315-17 Europe experienced the first of many famines; and the weakening of human powers of resistance through inadequate nourishment may have accelerated the spread of the 'Black Death', or bubonic plague, which killed perhaps 20 million Europeans between 1346 and 1353, wiping out in some areas as much as a third of the population within two years (map 1).

However, the impact of the plague was not even. Some areas escaped altogether, and Eastern Europe seems to have suffered relatively little: Bohemia under Charles IV (1333-78), Poland under Casimir III (1339-70) and Hungary under Louis the Great (1342-82) all made rapid strides – aided in part by skillful exploitation of their natural resources, such as the silver mines of Kutna Hora in Bohemia. Above all, in the wake of the Mongol invasions (page 56) Lithuania expanded into the former heartland of Kievan Russia and united in 1386 with Poland to form the largest state in Eastern Europe (map 2).

But elsewhere the setback proved more serious. All the western states had overextended themselves financially, and the new economic and demographic crisis exacerbated by the Black Death – combined with the tensions caused by the fragmentation of Italy and Germany after the end of Hohenstaufen rule in 1250 (page 51) or the Hundred Years' War between England and France – produced a series of popular uprisings in both cities and the countryside: the Jacquerie (1358) in France; the Peasants' Revolt (1381) in England; urban insurrections in Spain, Italy and the Low Countries. Few rebellions achieved their aims, but they all weakened state power even further.

# China and Japan 1279-1644

The Mongol invasion of China caused immense destruction. During the conquest of the north (1211-34: page 56) much of the land went out of cultivation, many cities and industries perished, and countless people died or became slaves. The conquest of the south (1270-9) brought similar hardships, and Mongol rule proved harsh. Popular resentment erupted in a wave of popular uprisings after 1335, exacerbated by disastrous floods in coastal regions in the 1350s. One of the rebel leaders, Chu Yüan-chang, gradually overcame his rivals and in 1368 established a new dynasty, the Ming.

The Ming rebuilt irrigation and drainage works in great numbers, reforested on a grand scale, and moved vast numbers of people to repopulate the devastated north. New crops were introduced and the canal system extended to transport produce: by 1421 the 'Grand Canal' stretched from Hang-chou to just south of Peking and carried some 200,000 tons of grain northwards every year. Thanks to these measures, the Chinese population rose from some 60 million in 1393 (40 per cent fewer than a century before) to about 130 million by 1580. The great cities of the Yangtze delta became major industrial centres, particularly for textiles, while the southern ports fitted out the enormous fleets sent by Chu's son, the Yung-lo emperor (1402-24), to the South China Sea and the Indian Ocean.

The Ming entrusted control over the vast population to a gentry class of degree-holders, who had passed through the examination system and shared the value of the bureaucracy without actually holding office. But the system discouraged innovation and was over-centralized, with all major decisions dependent upon the emperor; and few of Yung-lo's successors possessed the dedication necessary for such heavy responsibilities. Nevertheless, the early Ming engaged in an aggressive foreign policy. They restored Korea to vassal status in 1392, occupied Annam from 1407 to 1427, and invaded Mongolia (map 1). However, after a northern campaign in 1449 resulted in the capture of the emperor, the Ming reverted to a defensive strategy, strengthening the Great Wall until it ran for almost 2,500 miles, and increasing the garrisons in the north and north-west. China remained relatively stable for another century, but in the 1430s the government banned all overseas trade by sea, except under close supervision. Not surprisingly, by 1500 smuggling had become commonplace in the south-eastern provinces and by 1550 heavily-armed bands of smugglers and pirates infested the seas around China and terrorized the coastal regions from their bases in Japan.

Central authority in Japan had collapsed in the 1330s and the country became plagued by local and provincial wars – almost continuously in the century after 1467. By about 1560, some nine leading families had formed alliances that covered most of the country, and competed openly for supreme power (map 2). In 1568 Nobunaga, leader of the Oda clan, captured Kyoto, the imperial capital, and by the time he was assassinated in 1582 by a jealous rival he had forced almost all the other lords to accept his orders. Within a decade, his ablest general Toyotomi Hideyoshi had completely reunified Japan, reorganizing the tax system and redistributing land to provide sufficient funds for his ambitious policies – including the invasion of Korea in the 1590s. After his death in 1598 another of Nobunaga's generals, Tokugawa Ieyasu, assumed power and in 1603 established the dynasty of shoguns who ruled Japan until the 19th century (page 82).

The Tokugawa put an end to the pirate problem, thus easing the pressure on the Chinese coast; but at just this time a new threat arose in the north-east, where the Manchu gradually expanded their power into the areas immediately to the north of the Great Wall and (in 1637) into Korea. Ming authority now collapsed. After 1627 a wave of rebellions broke out in the wake of repeated crop failures in the north-west, and much of central and northern China soon came under rebel sway. In 1644, one of the rebel leaders captured Peking and the last Ming emperor committed suicide. Almost immediately the Manchus intervened, seized Peking, and began the conquest of China (page 88).

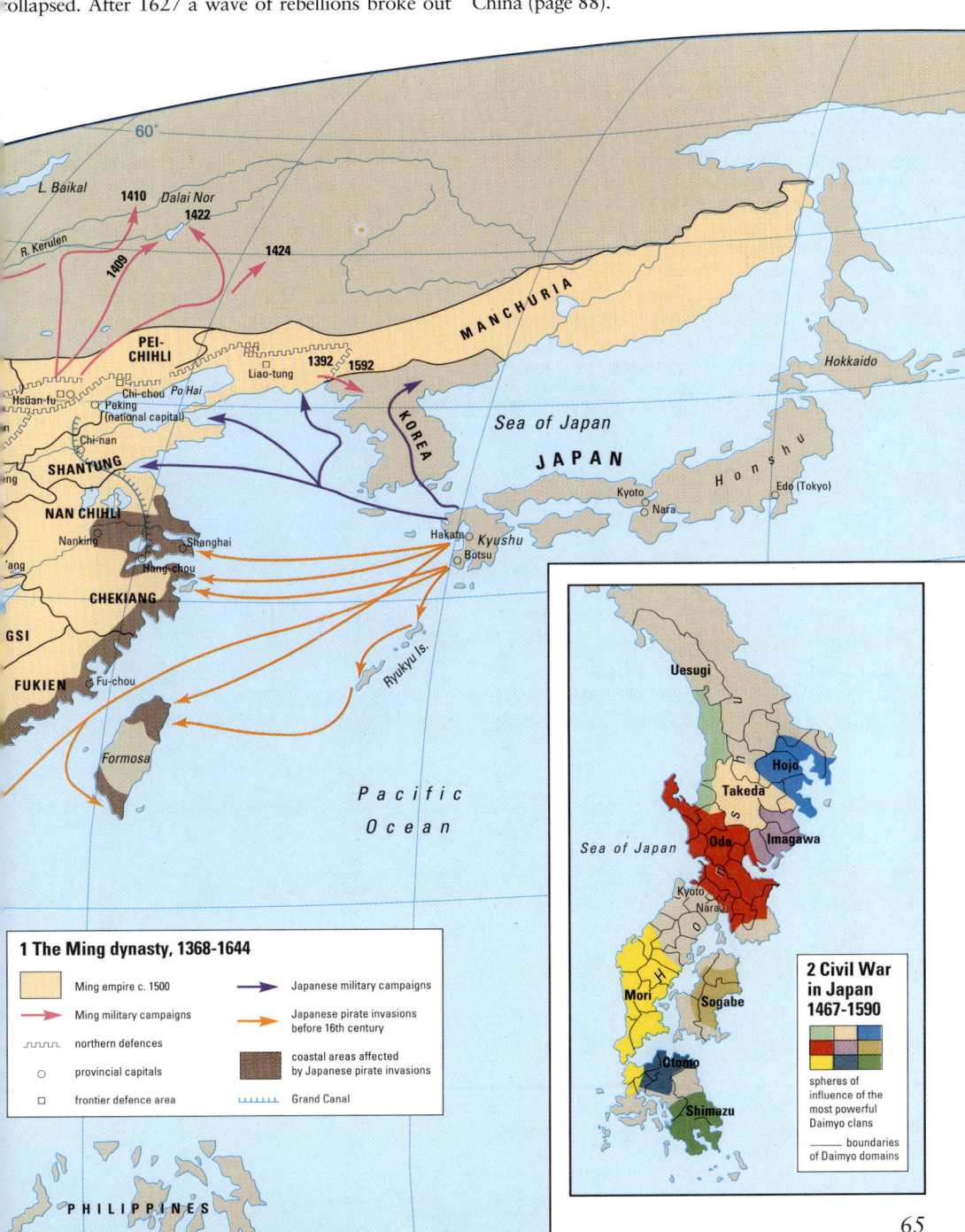

# The Ottoman Empire
## 1300-1699

The overthrow of the Abbasid Caliphate by the Mongols in 1256-60 (page 56) left the Muslim world in disarray for half a century. One of the centres of recovery lay in north-west Anatolia where, around 1300, a Turkish leader named Osman founded a state which became the core of the future Ottoman empire (map 1). The damage to the structure of the Byzantine empire caused by the Fourth Crusade in 1204 (page 44) facilitated the Ottomans' rapid advance in the 14th century. By 1354 the Turks had crossed the Dardanelles to Gallipoli, and their victories at Kosovo (1389) and Nicopolis (1396) left them masters of the Balkans. The invasion of Timur (page 57) and his destruction of the Turkish army at Ankara (1402) gave the hard-pressed Byzantine empire some respite, but the renewal of expansion under Murad II (1413-51) and Mohammed II (1451-81) sealed its fate. In (1574), although his fleet of galleys met with defeat at the hands of a Christian coalition at Lepanto (1571). However the wars of his successors against Persia (1578-90 and 1602-39) and against the Austrian Habsburgs (1593-1606) resulted in the loss of the Caucasus to the former and of annual tribute for Hungary from the latter.

The end of expansion, coupled with rapid price inflation (from 1584), a rising population and a static economy provoked a spate of popular and military uprisings between 1596 and 1610 in the Anatolian heartland of the empire (map 2). Nevertheless, Mesopotamia was regained from Persia in the 1630s and Crete conquered from the Venetians in the 1660s; and in 1683 a great army laid siege once more to Vienna. But it failed, and a Christian counter-attack drove the Turks out of Hungary by 1699 – although the Turks still remained a formidable power, controlling the entire Arab world east of Libya and most of the Balkans until the 19th century.

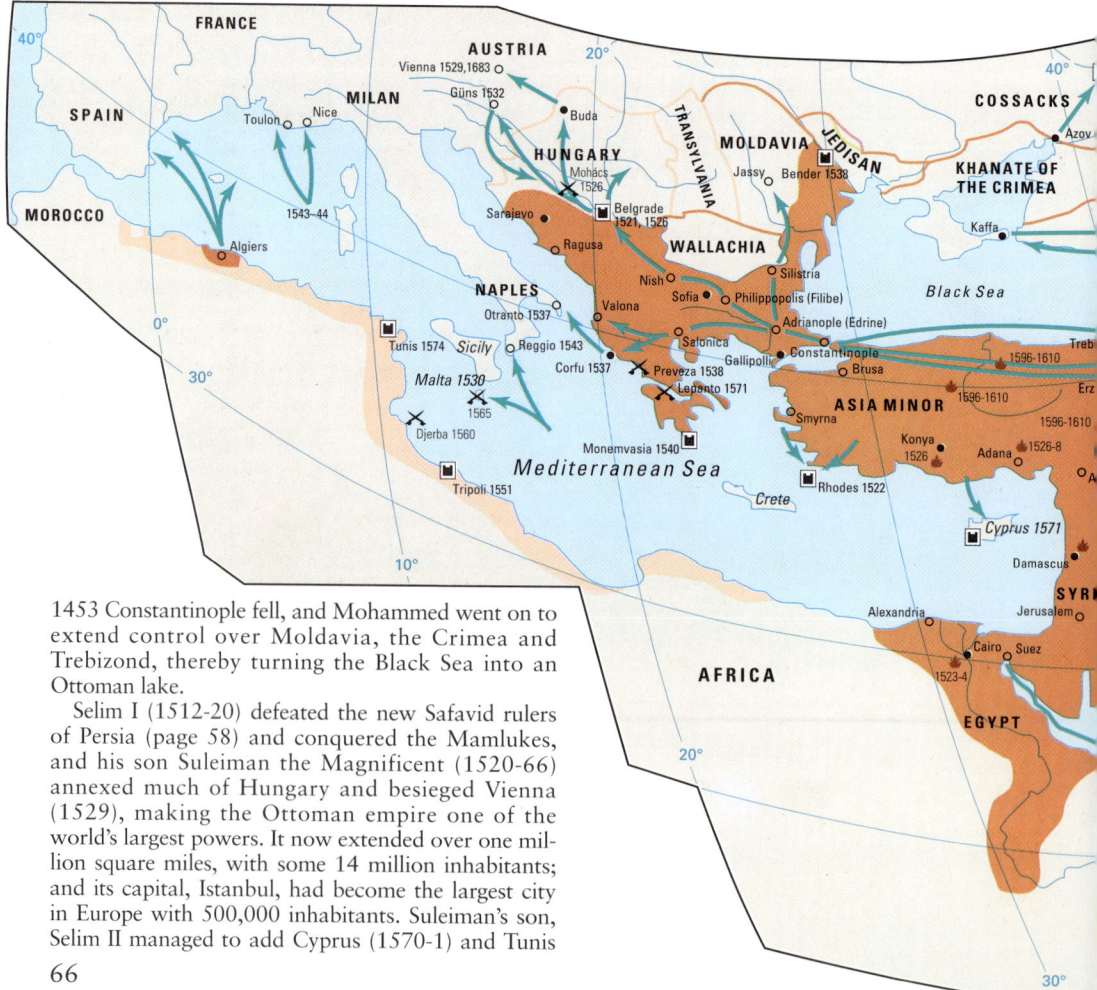

1453 Constantinople fell, and Mohammed went on to extend control over Moldavia, the Crimea and Trebizond, thereby turning the Black Sea into an Ottoman lake.

Selim I (1512-20) defeated the new Safavid rulers of Persia (page 58) and conquered the Mamlukes, and his son Suleiman the Magnificent (1520-66) annexed much of Hungary and besieged Vienna (1529), making the Ottoman empire one of the world's largest powers. It now extended over one million square miles, with some 14 million inhabitants; and its capital, Istanbul, had become the largest city in Europe with 500,000 inhabitants. Suleiman's son, Selim II managed to add Cyprus (1570-1) and Tunis

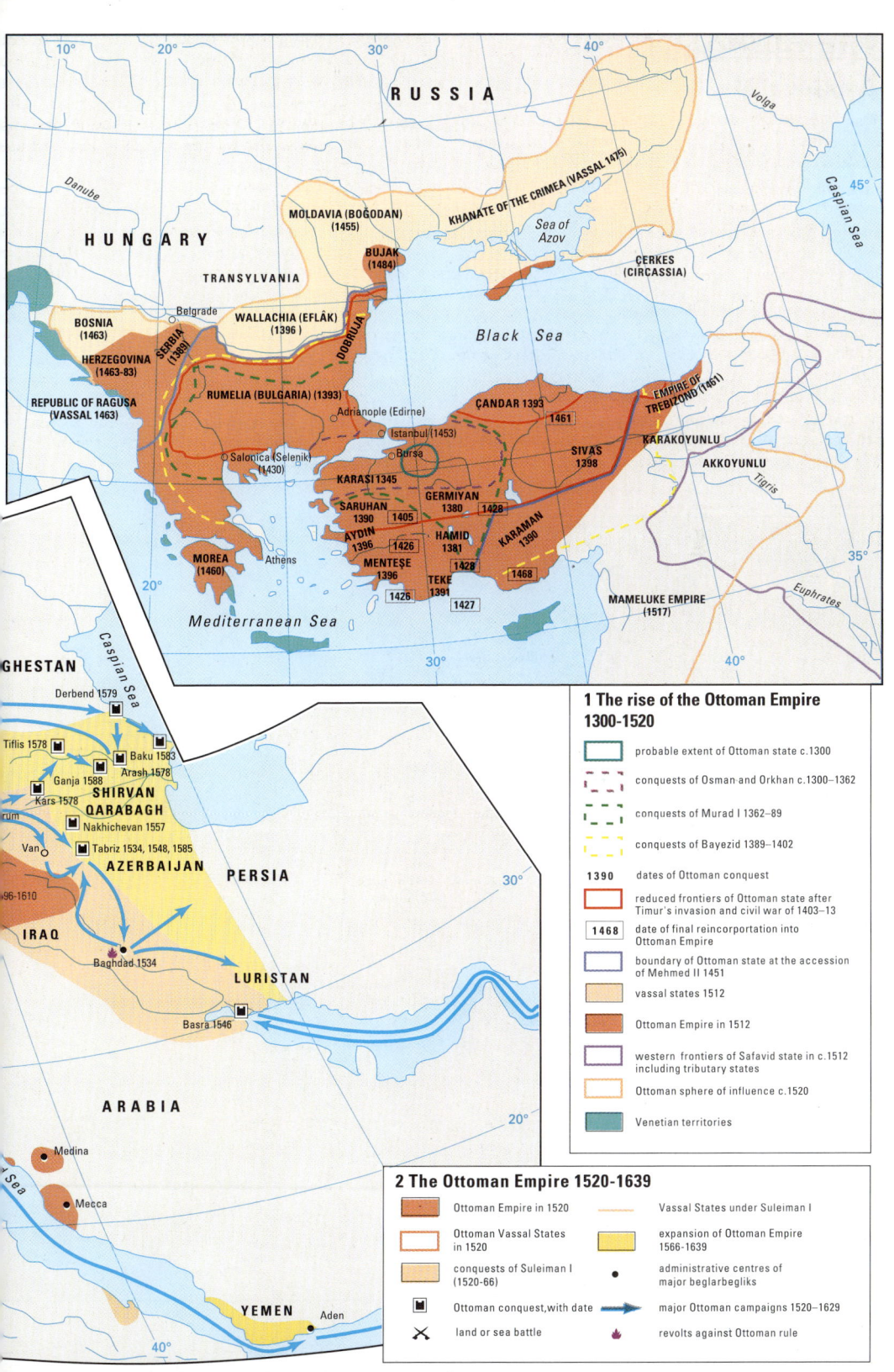

# Precolumbian America

Two major civilizations confronted the Spaniards when they arrived on the American mainland in the early 16th century: the Aztec Empire in Mexico, with a subject population of perhaps 12 million, and the Inca empire in Peru, ruling some 6 million. The rest of the continent remained sparsely inhabited – perhaps 1 million people lived north of the Rio Grande with another million in the rest of South America – divided among more than a thousand small tribal societies with distinct languages. Few regions, particularly in the north, had reached the stage of settled agriculture, despite some contacts in the north-east with Europeans around the year 1000 (map 1).

The Aztec and Inca Empires differed markedly in character, and no evidence exists of any contact between them. Like the Toltecs, who between 968 and about 1170 controlled much of the valley of Mexico from their capital at Tula, the Aztecs came from the north. In 1325 they arrived in the valley and settled on a group of islands in the swampy margins of Lake Texcoco, where they built their capital, Tenochtitlán (site of Mexico City). Serving at first as mercenary warriors for neighbouring towns, by 1428 they had overthrown them all and, led by a priest-king and an hereditary warrior aristocracy, embarked upon an ambitious programme of conquest. When the Spaniards arrived in 1519, the Aztecs controlled the greater part of Mexico and had entered Maya territory in Yucatán (map 2).

The Inca formed one of the numerous tribes of Quechua stock inhabiting the central Andes, but until the accession of Pachacuti Inca in 1438 they played only a

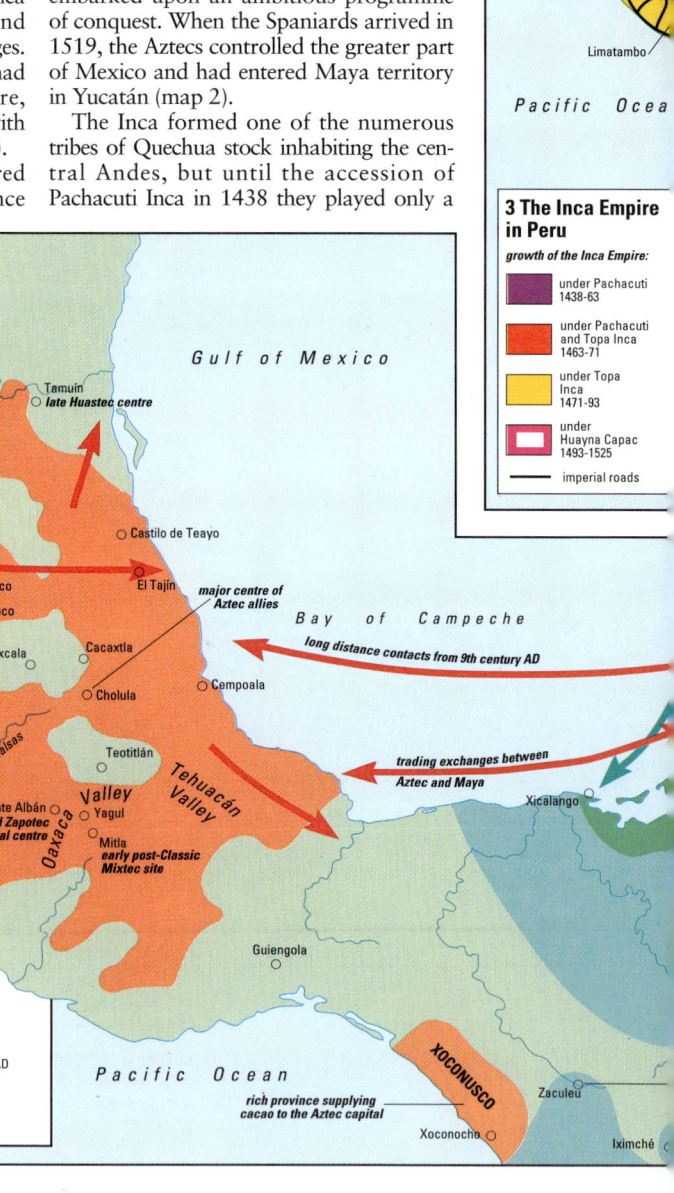

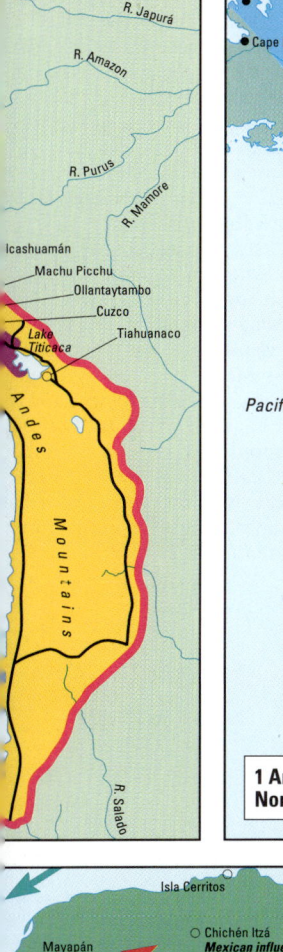

**1 Archaeological sites in North America, from AD 1000**

minor role. Within 45 years, however, Pachacuti's conquests extended Inca control from Lake Titicaca to Huánaco in the north, while his son Topa pushed north into Ecuador and south to Chile, and from the Pacific coast to the Upper Amazon. This created an empire 200 miles wide and 2500 miles long, held together by an impressive system of highways, post-stations and relay runners (map 3).

The Incas created a genuine imperial system, with an hereditary dynasty of absolute, 'divine' Incas, a Quechua aristocracy, and a highly trained bureaucracy. All land was state-owned, with a complex system of irrigation. The ordinary Inca subject spent 9 months working for the state, but in return received protection from famine (through state-owned food stores) and support during sickness and old age. The Aztec Empire, on the other hand, exercised harsh military dominion over vassal peoples who enjoyed political autonomy provided they paid heavy tribute to Tenochtitlán in food, textiles and other goods – increasingly in humans for ritual sacrifice to the Aztec gods (up to 50,000 a year by 1510). These demands help to explain why so many people in the valley of Mexico welcomed the Spaniards, just as a recent succession dispute provided allies for the European invaders in Peru. Although both the Aztec and Inca polities expanded faster than any 15th-century state in Latin Christendom, neither empire proved as stable as it seemed. Mexico fell to a force spearheaded by under 2,000 Europeans in 1519-22, Peru to a band of less than 200 in 1531-3 (see page 80).

69

# The world c. 1492

The central feature of world history since the 1490s has been the expansion of Europe and the spread of European civilization throughout the globe. Until then, the world had, on the whole, pressed in on Europe; thereafter the roles became reversed. In the 16th century, however, Europe continued to stand on the periphery of the civilized world, eclipsed by Ming China (the most powerful and advanced state of the period, with over 100 million inhabitants – equal to the whole of Europe) and by the rising Ottoman, Safavid and Mughal empires of the Middle East. Meanwhile Islam won converts in central and Southeast Asia, and among the peoples of sub-Saharan Africa.

The total area occupied by the major civilizations, roughly co-terminous with the area of plough cultivation, nevertheless remained relatively small. Almost 80 per cent of the world's surface was inhabited either by food gatherers or herdsmen (as in Australia and most of Siberia, North America and much of Africa) or by hand cultivators (especially in South-East Asia, West Africa and Central and South America). But plough cultivators proved far more productive, and the relatively small area that had been brought under the plough probably housed between two-thirds and three-quarters of the global population (map 1).

Until the 1490s, worldwide racial segregation prevailed. Although Christians and Muslims from all over Eurasia made pilgrimages to their Holy Places in the Middle East, they seldom settled; and although merchants travelled widely across and around Asia, their numbers remained few. In the early 15th century a succession of Chinese voyages, commanded by the Muslim admiral Cheng Ho, secured tribute and extended recognition of the new Ming dynasty; but they led to no lasting interchange of population.

Until the 1490s, therefore, the Negroids remained concentrated in sub-Saharan Africa and a few Pacific islands; the Mongoloids in Asia and the Americas; the Caucasoids in Europe, North Africa, the Middle East and India; and the Australoids in Australia and South India (map 2a). By 1800, however, the pattern had fundamentally altered as the

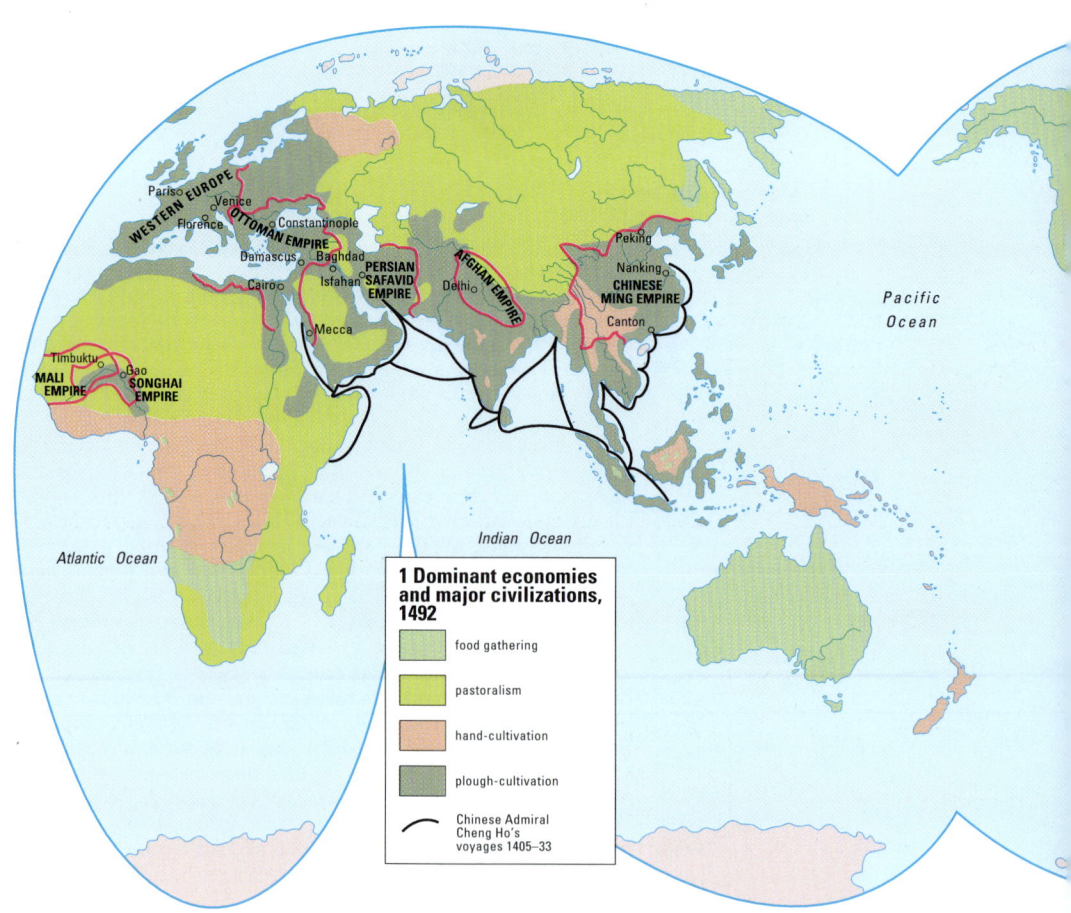

result of six inter-continental migrations: from Europe and Africa to the Americas; from northern Europe to Africa and (later) Australasia; from Russia into Siberia; from China to South-East Asia; and from India to Africa, South-East Asia and the Caribbean. By far the greatest change occurred in the Americas, where the native population declined dramatically in the century following the first contact with the Europeans – in some cases by 90 per cent – to be replaced by Europeans, Africans, and in some parts of Latin America by a mixed race of mestizos (map 2b).

Nevertheless, the tempo of change must not be exaggerated. Although in America the Aztec and Inca empires collapsed suddenly in 1521 and 1533 respectively (page 68), elsewhere the political impact of Europe remained limited until the 18th century. China and Japan survived intact, and India kept the Europeans at arm's length for 250 years following the arrival of Vasco da Gama in 1498. There, as in Africa and South-east Asia, the European presence long remained confined largely to trading stations and fortresses along the coast. The cultural influence of Europe was even more negligible: Christianity made little headway, except when imposed by the conquerors (as in the Americas and the Philippines), until it received the backing of western technology in the 19th century.

The comparative fragility of the Aztec and Inca civilizations in the Americas, and of the African kingdoms immediately south of the Sahara, despite their outstanding achievements, may be partially explained, first, by their geographical isolation and relative lack of external stimulus and, second, by their dependence on hand cultivation. After 1492, when all the continents came into direct contact with each other for the first time, many of these non-Eurasian civilizations proved unable to offer more than a feeble resistance to outside aggression. To be sure not until the 19th century, with the opening of the Suez Canal and the construction of the transcontinental railways in North America, Siberia and Africa, did areas that had previously been separate finally blend into a single world economy; but the first stages of global integration were completed in the three centuries following 1492.

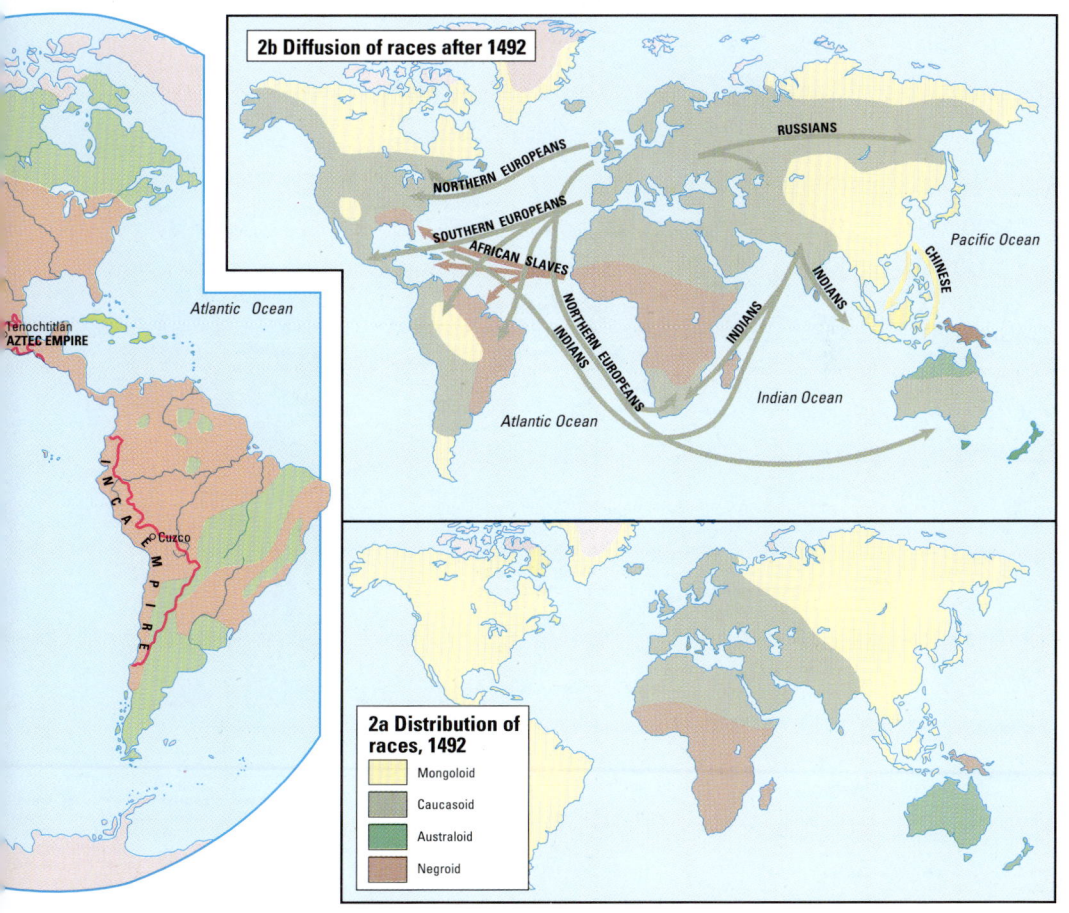

# The great discoveries 1480-1616

In 1480 European shipping remained largely confined to the North Atlantic, the Baltic and the Mediterranean, while the West African coast had been explored cursorily, and only very recently by Europeans; Indian, Persian, and Arab vessels plied the northern Indian Ocean; Chinese and Indonesian junks sailed in the western Pacific, but rarely went beyond Japan, the Philippines and the Indonesian archipelago; and local craft navigated the Caribbean and the coasts of Peru and Ecuador. No shipping used the southern Indian Ocean, the South Atlantic, or the main basin of the Pacific. In the course of the next 150 years, however, European navigators opened all the seas, except in the regions of circumpolar ice and the South Pacific, to European ships. Initially, in the 15th century, two series of voyages sought a sea passage to southern Asia in the hope of initiating direct trade in spices. One series, mounted from Portugal, sailing by a south-eastern route and employing local navigators in the East, eventually reached their declared destinations: the entrance to the Indian Ocean (1488), Malabar (1498), Malacca (1509), and the Moluccas (1512-13). The other series, based on Spain and sailing west or south-west, proved less successful in its immediate purpose but

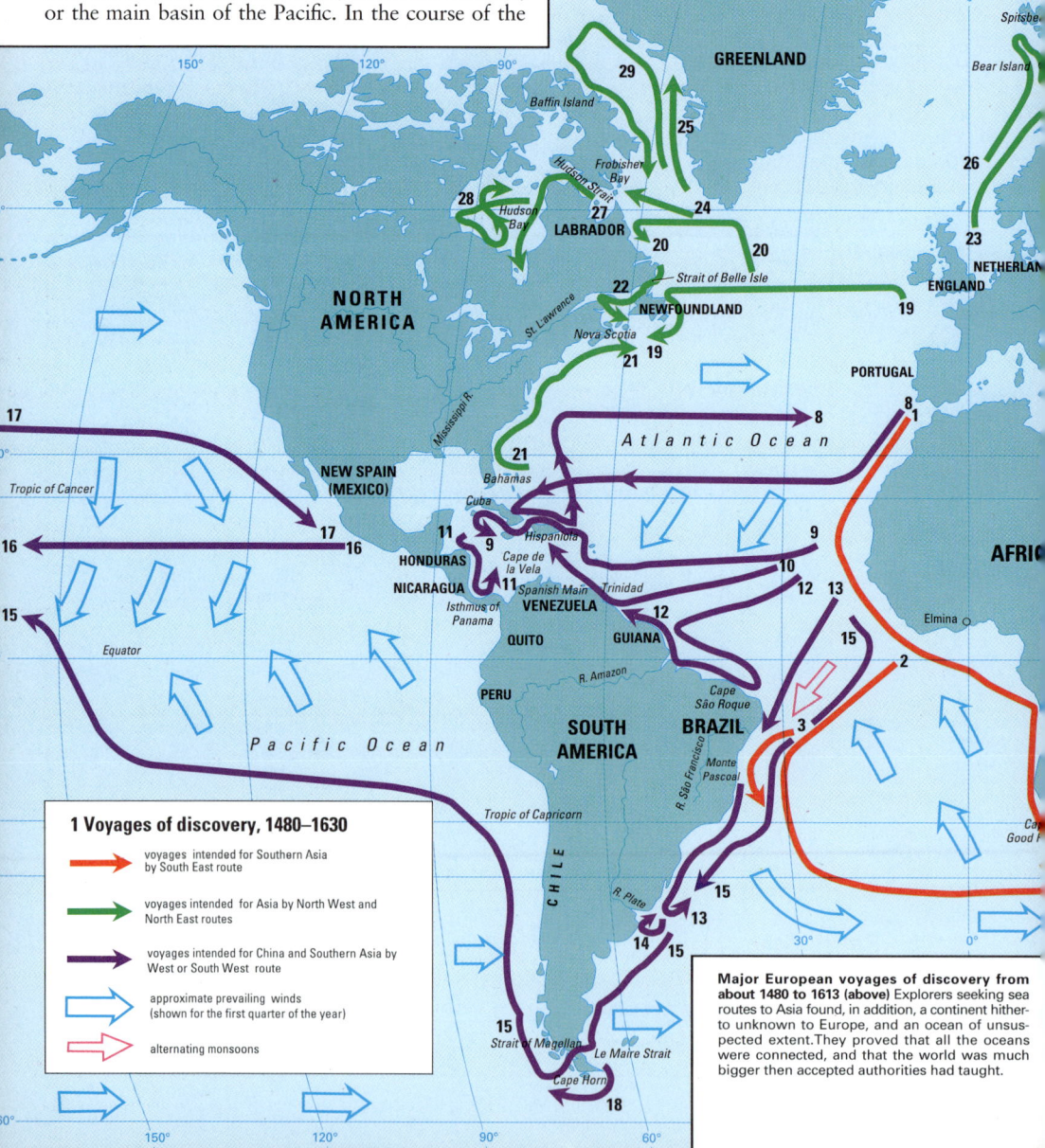

**1 Voyages of discovery, 1480–1630**
- voyages intended for Southern Asia by South East route
- voyages intended for Asia by North West and North East routes
- voyages intended for China and Southern Asia by West or South West route
- approximate prevailing winds (shown for the first quarter of the year)
- alternating monsoons

Major European voyages of discovery from about 1480 to 1613 (above) Explorers seeking sea routes to Asia found, in addition, a continent hitherto unknown to Europe, and an ocean of unsuspected extent. They proved that all the oceans were connected, and that the world was much bigger then accepted authorities had taught.

more fruitful in incidental discovery: the Spaniards hit upon the West Indies (1492) and the Spanish Main (1498). Eventually they too reached South-east Asia (1521), but by a route too long and arduous for commercial use – for to reach the Pacific they had to circumnavigate an immense land-mass which, although it was initially thought to be a peninsula of Asia, by the 1520s had been recognized as a new world. They immediately began to settle the area (page 69). Taken together, the Spanish and Portuguese discoveries proved that all the oceans of the world, at least in the southern hemisphere, were connected.

For most of the 16th century, by the use and threat of force, the Iberian powers managed to prevent other Europeans from using the connecting passages, except for occasional raids. The third great series of voyages, therefore, mostly by English, French and Dutch navigators, searched for alternative routes to Asia in the northern hemisphere, in the west, north-west, and northeast. Although unsuccessful in their primary purpose, they revealed another continental land-mass with a continuous coast extending from the Caribbean to the Arctic, and opened the way for the European exploration and settlement of eastern North America (page 80).

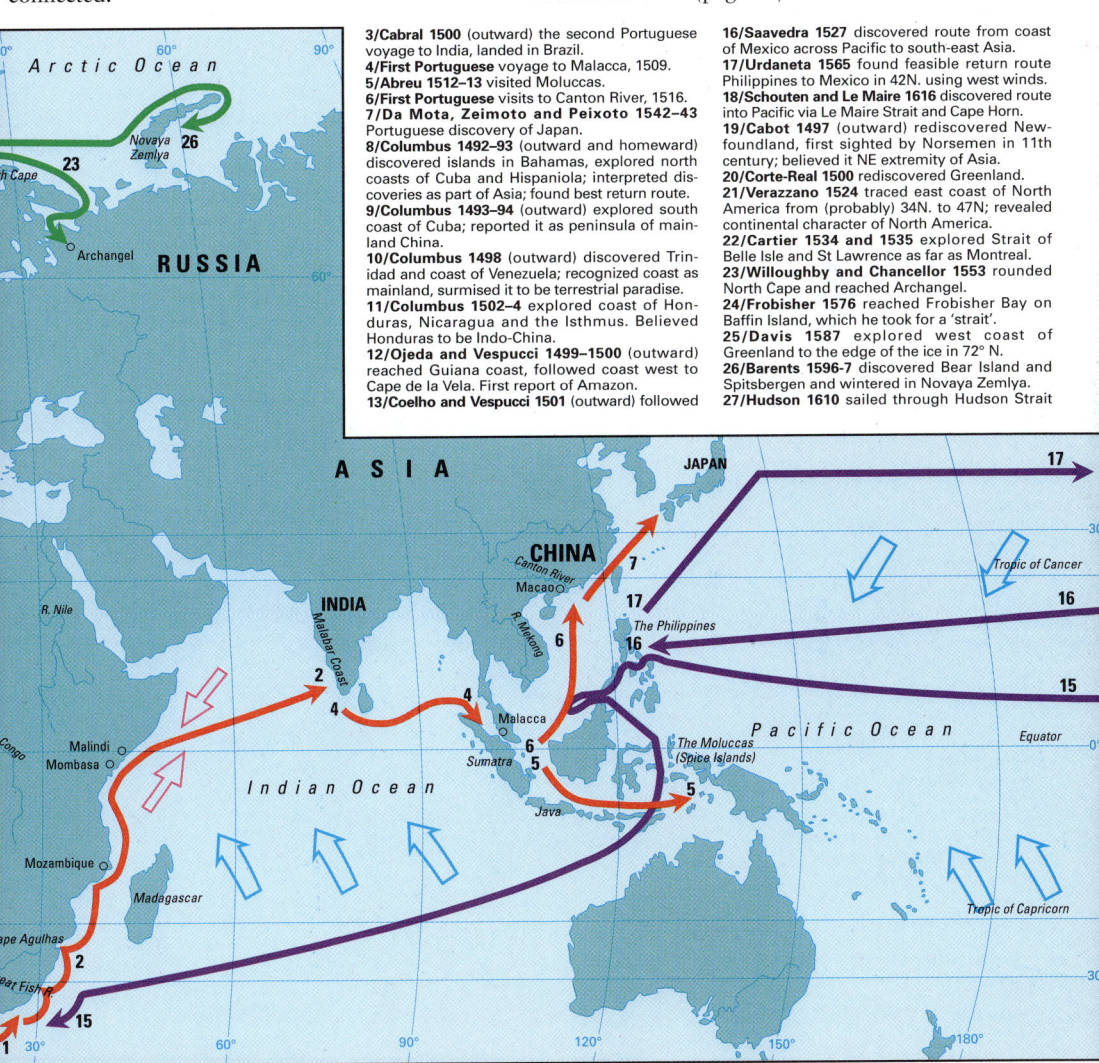

**3/Cabral 1500** (outward) the second Portuguese voyage to India, landed in Brazil.
**4/First Portuguese** voyage to Malacca, 1509.
**5/Abreu 1512–13** visited Moluccas.
**6/First Portuguese** visits to Canton River, 1516.
**7/Da Mota, Zeimoto and Peixoto 1542–43** Portuguese discovery of Japan.
**8/Columbus 1492–93** (outward and homeward) discovered islands in Bahamas, explored north coasts of Cuba and Hispaniola; interpreted discoveries as part of Asia; found best return route.
**9/Columbus 1493–94** (outward) explored south coast of Cuba; reported it as peninsula of mainland China.
**10/Columbus 1498** (outward) discovered Trinidad and coast of Venezuela; recognized coast as mainland, surmised it to be terrestrial paradise.
**11/Columbus 1502–4** explored coast of Honduras, Nicaragua and the Isthmus. Believed Honduras to be Indo-China.
**12/Ojeda and Vespucci 1499–1500** (outward) reached Guiana coast, followed coast west to Cape de la Vela. First report of Amazon.
**13/Coelho and Vespucci 1501** (outward) followed

**16/Saavedra 1527** discovered route from coast of Mexico across Pacific to south-east Asia.
**17/Urdaneta 1565** found feasible return route Philippines to Mexico in 42N. using west winds.
**18/Schouten and Le Maire 1616** discovered route into Pacific via Le Maire Strait and Cape Horn.
**19/Cabot 1497** (outward) rediscovered Newfoundland, first sighted by Norsemen in 11th century; believed it NE extremity of Asia.
**20/Corte-Real 1500** rediscovered Greenland.
**21/Verazzano 1524** traced east coast of North America from (probably) 34N. to 47N; revealed continental character of North America.
**22/Cartier 1534 and 1535** explored Strait of Belle Isle and St Lawrence as far as Montreal.
**23/Willoughby and Chancellor 1553** rounded North Cape and reached Archangel.
**24/Frobisher 1576** reached Frobisher Bay on Baffin Island, which he took for a 'strait'.
**25/Davis 1587** explored west coast of Greenland to the edge of the ice in 72° N.
**26/Barents 1596-7** discovered Bear Island and Spitsbergen and wintered in Novaya Zemlya.
**27/Hudson 1610** sailed through Hudson Strait

**1/Dias 1487–88** (outward) discovered open water south of Cape Agulhas; entered Indian Ocean; reached Great Fish River.
**2/Vasco da Gama 1497–98** (outward) made best use of Atlantic winds on the way to Cape of Good Hope; reached India, guided by local pilot.

coast south from Cape São Agostinho to (possibly) 35S.
**14/Solis 1515** entered River Plate estuary and investigated north bank.
**15/Magellan and Elcano 1519–22** discovered Strait of Magellan, crossed Pacific, reached Moluccas via Philippines. First circumnavigation.

to the southern extremity of the of Hudson Bay, which he and others took to be the Pacific.
**28/Button 1612** explored the west coast of Hudson Bay, concluded Bay landlocked by the west.
**29/Baffin and Bylot 1616** explored whole coastline of Baffin Bay and came to the conclusion that no navigable NW passage existed in that area.

73

# European overseas expansion 1492-1713

By 1492, Portugal already possessed several archipelagos in the Atlantic and the Gulf of Guinea, some fortresses in Morocco, and a few trading stations in West Africa (above all the castle at Elmina). In the next half century she established some 50 forts and trading posts around the shores of the Indian Ocean, as well as coastal enclaves in Angola and Brazil. Strategically, the most important bases were Mozambique (1507), a port of call for fleets sailing to India; Goa (1510), headquarters of Portuguese Asia; Malacca (1511), a major market on the strait connecting the Indian Ocean with the South China Sea; and Ormuz (1515), a key entrepot of the international spice trade. East of Malacca the position of the Portuguese was far more precarious and their activities remained purely commercial. A few bases, some fortified, grew up in the Moluccas; a clandestine settlement developed at Macao on the Chinese mainland after 1557; and from 1580 Jesuit missionaries held a lease on the Japanese port-city of Nagasaki (map 1).

In Africa and Asia the Portuguese generally sought to control trade rather than production; and though they could not eliminate the commerce of others in the Indian Ocean, they forced many ships to use harbours under their control, and extorted tolls or duties from the rest. The Spaniards in the Americas, by contrast, embarked on a deliberate policy of conquest and colonization: from the 1490s in the Caribbean islands; from the 1520s in Mexico; from the 1530s in Peru; and from the 1570s in the Philippines.

Few dared to challenge the Iberian monopoly – apparently enhanced by the union of Portugal and Spain in 1580 – before the 17th century. However, the foundation of East India Companies by the Dutch, the English and (later) the French brought the Portuguese under increasing attack. Dutch forces first established independent bases in the East (above all at Batavia, the heavily fortified headquarters of the Dutch East India Company) and then between 1640 and 1660 wrested Malacca, Ceylon, most South Indian ports and the lucrative Japan trade from the Portuguese. In 1652 they also created a useful south African base on the route to the East at Cape Town. The English and French also established modest settlements in India, and developed a promising trade with China. Even the Spaniards undermined the Portuguese, exporting Chinese goods after 1572 through their colony in the Philippines (map 2). Elsewhere in Asia, however, Europeans during this period traded in competition with local merchants on terms laid down by local rulers, and their efforts constituted but a fraction of Asia's total commerce.

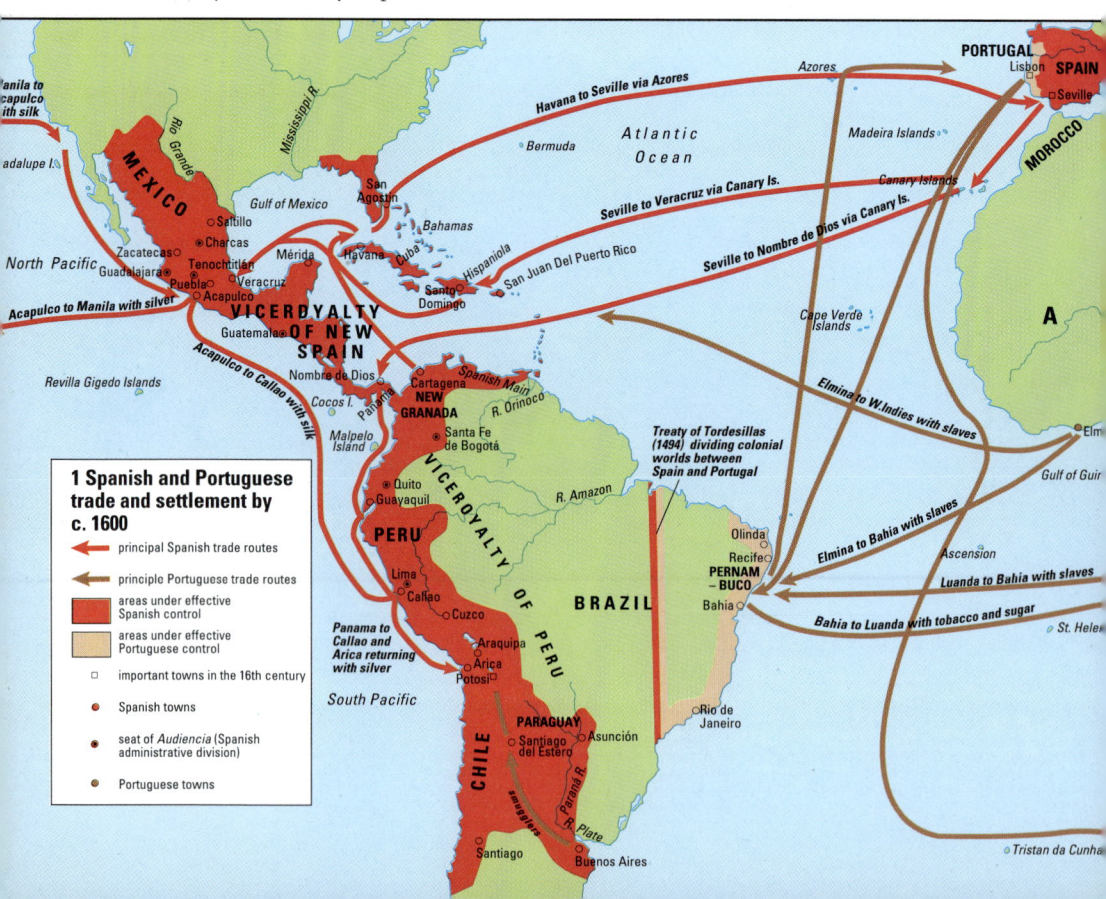

1 Spanish and Portuguese trade and settlement by c. 1600

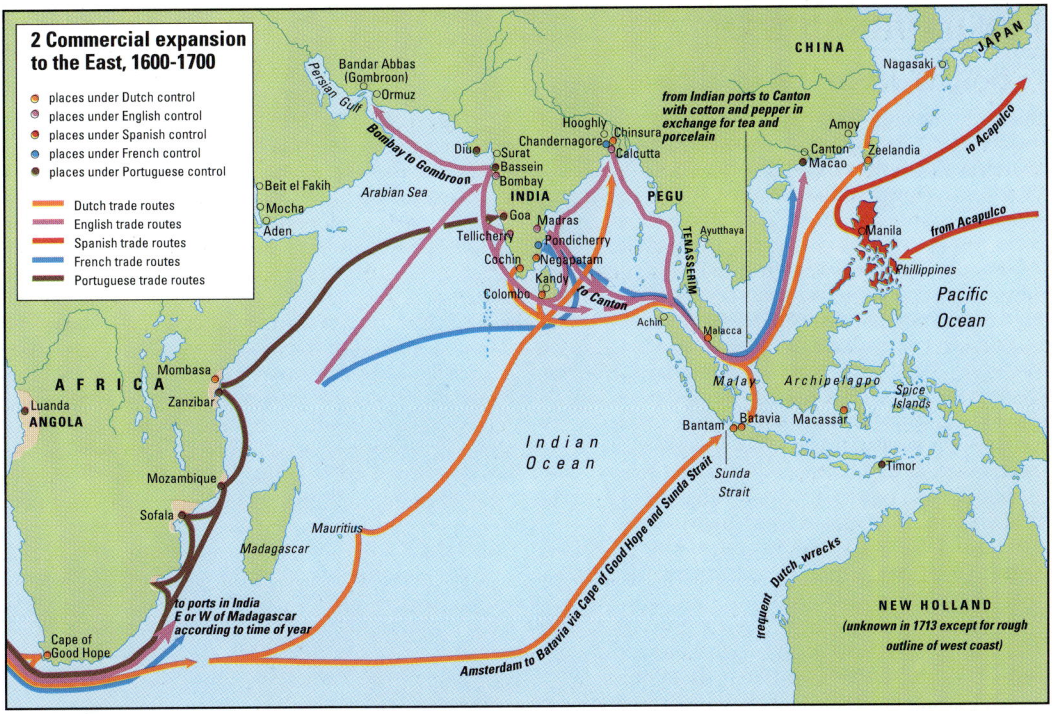

2 Commercial expansion to the East, 1600-1700
places under Dutch control
places under English control
places under Spanish control
places under French control
places under Portuguese control
Dutch trade routes
English trade routes
Spanish trade routes
French trade routes
Portuguese trade routes
CHINA
JAPAN
Nagasaki
Persian Gulf
Bandar Abbas (Gombroon)
Ormuz
from Indian ports to Canton with cotton and pepper in exchange for tea and porcelain
Hooghly
Chinsura
Chandernagore
Calcutta
Amoy
Canton
Macao
Zeelandia
to Acapulco
Diu
Surat
Bassein
Bombay
Bombay to Gombroon
Beit el Fakih
Mocha
Aden
Arabian Sea
INDIA
PEGU
Goa
Madras
Tellicherry
Pondicherry
Cochin
Negapatam
Kandy
Colombo
to Canton
TENASSERIM
Ayutthaya
Manila
from Acapulco
Phillippines
Pacific Ocean
Achin
Malacca
AFRICA
Mombasa
Zanzibar
Luanda
ANGOLA
Malay Archipelago
Spice Islands
Bantam
Batavia
Macassar
Indian Ocean
Timor
Sunda Strait
Mozambique
Sofala
Mauritius
Madagascar
Amsterdam to Batavia via Cape of Good Hope and Sunda Strait
frequent Dutch wrecks
NEW HOLLAND
(unknown in 1713 except for rough outline of west coast)
to ports in India E or W of Madagascar according to time of year
Cape of Good Hope


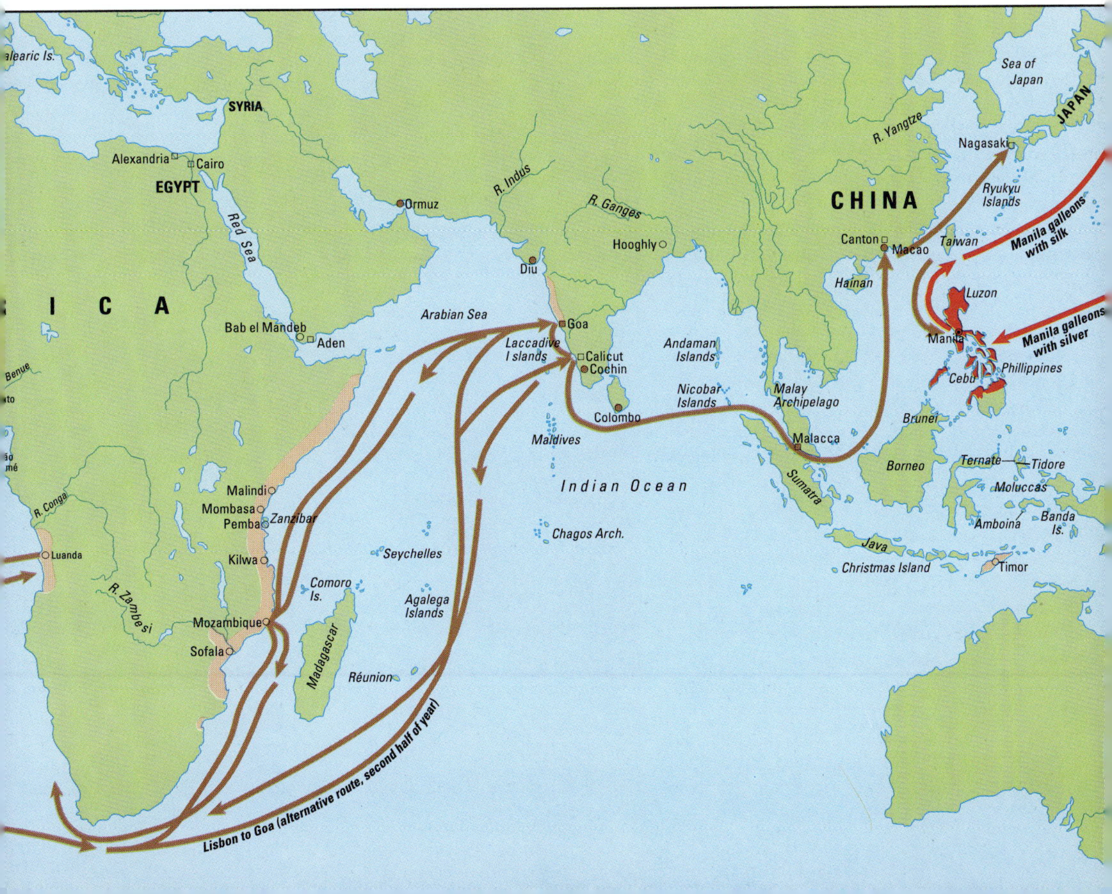

Balearic Is.
SYRIA
Alexandria
Cairo
EGYPT
Red Sea
Ormuz
R. Indus
R. Ganges
Hooghly
Diu
R. Yangtze
CHINA
Sea of Japan
JAPAN
Nagasaki
Ryukyu Islands
Canton
Macao
Taiwan
Manila galleons with silk
Hainan
Luzon
Manila
Manila galleons with silver
Phillippines
Cebu
AFRICA
Bab el Mandeb
Aden
Arabian Sea
Goa
Laccadive Islands
Calicut
Cochin
Andaman Islands
Nicobar Islands
Malay Archipelago
Colombo
Maldives
Malacca
Brunei
Borneo
Ternate
Tidore
Moluccas
Indian Ocean
Sumatra
Amboina
Banda Is.
Benue
R. Congo
Malindi
Mombasa
Zanzibar
Pemba
Luanda
Kilwa
Chagos Arch.
Seychelles
Java
Christmas Island
Timor
R. Zambesi
Comoro Is.
Agalega Islands
Mozambique
Sofala
Madagascar
Réunion
Lisbon to Goa (alternative route, second half of year)

# The expansion of France 1440-1789

In 1415 English troops invaded France and by 1429 had established suzerainty over almost half the kingdom (map 1). In the 1440s, however, with the aid of a powerful artillery train, Charles VII (1422-61) began a rapid reconquest which by 1453 had expelled the English from all but the port-city of Calais, and doubled the size of the royal domain. His successors annexed Burgundy (1477), Brittany (1491) and Bourbon (1527) by force, and inherited Anjou and Provence (1481). Several other semi-independent fiefs came to the crown at the accession of Louis XII (1498), Francis I (1515) and Henry IV (1589).

After Henry's death in 1610, continuing religious division, costly foreign wars and aristocratic faction, culminating in the Fronde revolt (1648-53), brought France to the brink of dissolution again. However Henry's grandson Louis XIV (1643-1715) restored order and made France the dominant state of Europe. During the relatively peaceful years between 1659 and 1672 the king and his ministers struggled to develop the French economy (agriculture, manufacture and trade), to extend overseas possessions, and to expand the army and navy. They also developed commercial harbours and sponsored public works, such as the Languedoc Canal connecting the Atlantic and the Mediterranean. The richness of resources available to the French, including a population of perhaps 20 million (the largest of any 17th-century European state), undoubtedly played a part in these achievements; but so did the ceaseless efforts, directives, and resources emanating from the Court (map 2).

Despite France's gains at the peaces of Westphalia (1648) and the Pyrenees (1659), Louis still feared Habsburg encirclement (page 86). He sought both to secure territories that might plug the gaps in his frontier (in wars fought in 1667-8 and 1672-8 which brought the acquisition of territory from the Spanish Netherlands and of Franche-Comté), and to create an 'iron frontier' of state-of-the-art fortresses, thickest on the ground in the north and east, to create a defence in depth that would prevent any enemy forces from penetrating to the heart of the realm as the English and the Habsburgs had done in the past. Perhaps his success in this endeavour

made him too bold, for in 1700 he accepted the will of the childless Spanish Habsburg Carlos II which bequeathed to Louis's grandson Philip the entire Spanish empire – Spain, Spanish America, the South Netherlands and half of Italy – even though he knew this sudden concentration of territory in the hands of the Bourbon dynasty would provoke a general European war. After some French initial victories (1702-3), followed by a string of searing defeats (1704-9), the 'iron frontier' showed its worth and forced France's exhausted enemies to conclude the compromise peaces of Utrecht (1713) and Rastatt (1714), by which Philip retained Spain and Spanish America, while Savoy, Britain and the Austrian Habsburgs partitioned the rest (map 3).

Louis had thus secured the integrity of France's frontiers, and ended for ever the threat of Habsburg encirclement; but the ruinous cost of his wars created a legacy of financial disorder and internal discontent which served to hamstring his successors. Although Louis XV (1715-74) managed to incorporate Lorraine in 1766, and his successor Louis XVI (1774-93) assisted the successful rebellion of the American colonies against Great Britain (page 98), both monarchs sacrificed (as Louis XIV had done) France's overseas possessions and accumulated such monstrous public debts that, in 1789, the government summoned a representative assembly, the States-General, to solve the financial crisis. In doing so, it unleashed revolution (page 93).

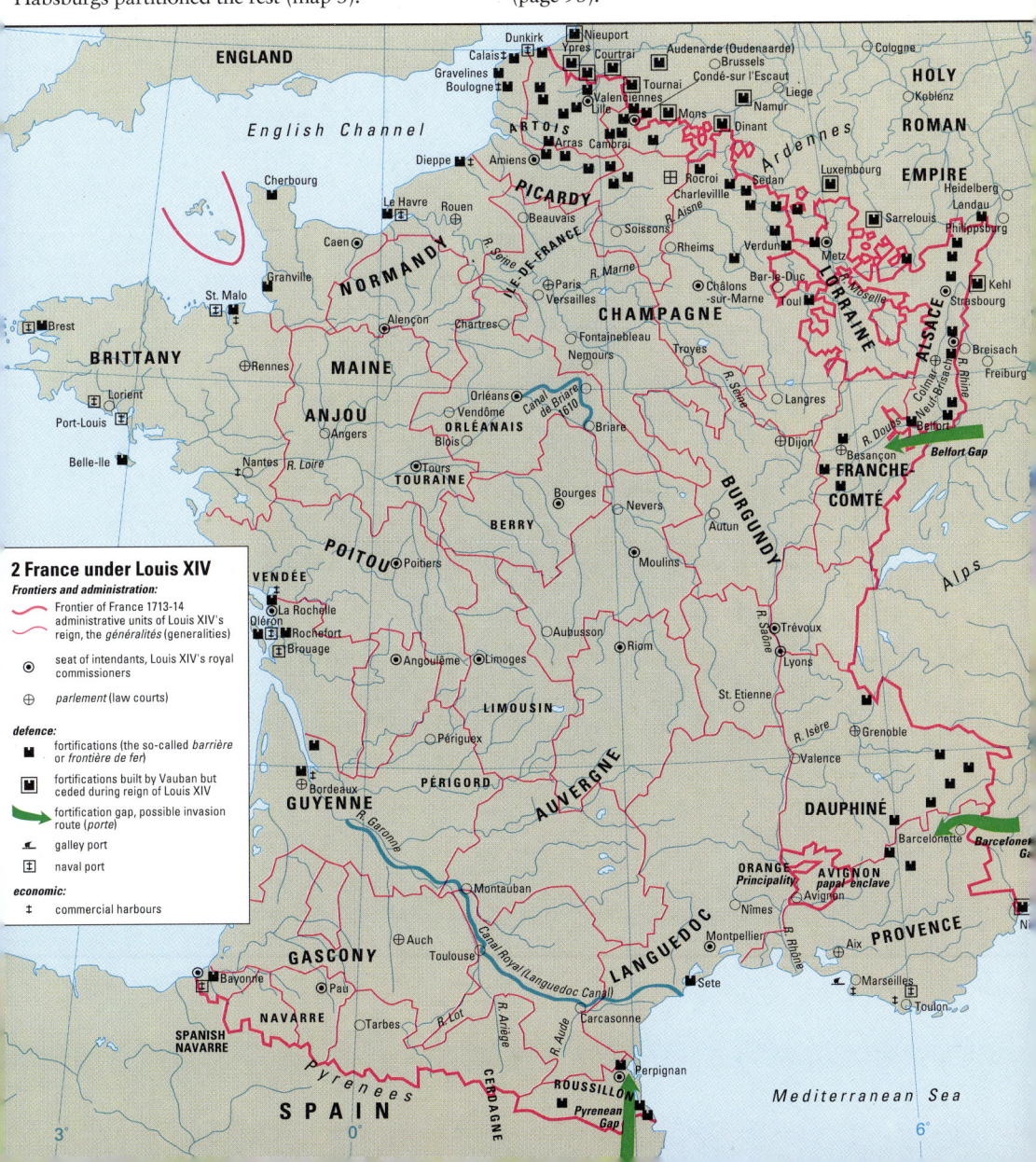

# The expansion of Russia 1462-1815

After the Mongol invasion of the 13th century (page 56), the lands which had formed part of Kievan Russia fragmented. Lithuania expanded in the west, while the east and south became subject to Mongol overlords, in whose service the principality of Muscovy rose to prominence. Ivan III (1462-1505) opened another phase of expansion: in 1478 he annexed the city republic of Novgorod and in 1480 proclaimed independence from the Mongols. In 1510 his son Vassily (1505-33) overran the republic of Pskov, bringing Muscovite control close to the Baltic; and his grandson Ivan IV (1533-84) conquered the Tatar states of Kazan (1552) and Astrakhan (1556), gaining control of the Volga down to the Caspian Sea. In addition, from the 1580s, the lucrative fur trade lured enterprising Russians deep into Siberia. Crossing the Urals, they followed the River Ob until they came within portage of the Yenisey, where they built and fortified Turukhansk (1607); thence they reached the Lena river system, where they built Yakutsk (1632), and finally the Pacific, where they built Othotsk (1649) – some 6,000 miles (9,700km) east of Moscow (map 2).

However Ivan IV failed to realise his principal territorial ambition, the acquisition of Livonia and direct access to the Baltic, while his attempt to break the power of the traditional nobility by creating a 'private domain' (the *oprichnina*) around Moscow resulted in massive depopulation. Muscovy was also still not entirely safe from the Crimean Tartars, who sacked Moscow in 1571. Then succession disputes following the extinction of the old Muscovite ruling house (the 'Time of Troubles', 1598-1613) caused the loss of much territory to Poland and Sweden.

Recovery came only in the mid-17th century, when successful wars with Poland (1632-4 and 1654-67) brought substantial gains, including Kiev and the Ukraine. Meanwhile the settlement of Siberia continued: 23,000 Russians lived there by 1622, 105,000 by 1662 and 230,000 by 1709. However the Amur Basin, acquired in the 1650s, had to be ceded to China in 1689 (albeit in return for useful trading concessions: map 2) and attempts to force access to the Black Sea failed. Instead, Peter I ('the Great', 1682-1725) concentrated on achieving a 'window on the west', wresting Estonia and Livonia from Sweden in 1721, acquiring the ancient port of Riga and founding the new one of St Petersburg (1703). Peter's successors reverted to his policy of expansion on the Black Sea. Catherine II ('the Great', 1762-96) annexed the Tatar khanate of the Crimea and also acquired large parts of Poland – although the cost of her campaigns, on top of the oppressive social system which required serfs to spend almost all their time labouring on the lords' lands, provoked a major peasant uprising under Emelyan Pugachev (1773-5). The period 1772 to 1815 saw the Russian land frontier expand 600 miles (970 km) at the expense of Poland. Finally, despite a French invasion which reached Moscow in 1812, the Congress of Vienna in 1815 confirmed Russia's acquisition of Finland, Poland, Bessarabia and Transcaucasia (page 110).

The population ruled from Moscow had grown, both by territorial acquisition and by natural increase, from some 10 million in 1600, to over 15 million in 1725 and to almost 43 million in 1812, and the empire – the largest in the world – now stretched over 11 of the world's 24 time-zones.

# Colonial America 1519-1783

The daring conquest of Mexico by Hernán Cortés in 1519-20 and of Peru by Francisco Pizarro in 1531-3 (page 69) laid the foundations of a huge Spanish colonial empire in the Americas. By 1535, when the crown established viceregal government in Mexico and Lima became the capital of Peru, all the major centres of indigenous population in the former Aztec and Inca empires lay in Spanish hands: an area four times the size, and containing eight times the population, of the country from which the conquerors had come. Although the frontiers of colonial settlement continued to advance – with new viceroyalties in New Granada (1739) and Rio de la Plata (1776) and new military governments in Texas (1718) and California (1767) – none of these later, sparsely inhabited conquests compared with Mexico and Peru in wealth and importance. Potosí in Peru and Zacatecas in Mexico became the largest producers of silver in the world, and by 1560 silver formed America's principal export to Europe.

Elsewhere on the continent colonization proved slower. The Portuguese only settled the Atlantic coast of South America after 1549 for fear that the French might do so. By 1600, although coastal Brazil had become studded with profitable sugar plantations and mills, worked by slaves from Africa, the Brazilian interior remained the domain of native Indian tribes until the 1690s, when the discovery of enormous gold deposits in the interior provoked a new wave of colonization. In the northwest, Russian explorers and traders pressed on; but by 1819 only 19 settlements existed between the Aleutian islands and California (map 1).

The Atlantic seaboard of North America, with its harsher climate and poor soil, also at first attracted few Europeans (who came mostly for fish and furs). Settlement only began with the foundation of Acadia (Nova Scotia) by the French in 1604, of Virginia (1607) and Massachusetts Bay (1620) by the English, and of New Amsterdam (later New York) by the Dutch (1624). Gradually, however, the Europeans pressed inland: the French advanced down the St Lawrence and (after 1682) the Mississippi, creating a chain of fortified posts all the way to the Gulf of Mexico and founding New Orleans in 1718; the English spread out around the rich fur-hunting grounds of Hudson Bay. Wars between the European states now regularly involved the Americas, with England gaining first the Dutch colonies along the Hudson (1664) and then French Canada (1763). By 1700, perhaps 250,000 Europeans lived in North America, but by 1820 that number had soared to 9 million (compared with just over 3 million in Spanish America).

The Spaniards in America relied from the first on Indian labour, both in ranching and mining, and readily intermarried; hence an extensive mestizo population developed, especially in Mexico and Peru. The British, however, who wanted land for farms and plantations, expelled or exterminated the native population: by 1820, only 600,000 lived in the English speaking areas (compared with 7.5 million in Spanish America). Instead, in Virginia, and then later in the Carolinas, where tobacco was introduced as a cash-crop, African slaves were imported to work on the plantations (like those of the sugar producers of Brazil and the Caribbean islands). By 1820, almost 2 million Africans lived in North America (compared with 800,000 in Spanish America).

Throughout the period, each mother country maintained a tight grip on its colonies. The colonists tolerated this as long as they felt insecure – whether from the threat of native uprisings or through the series of wars between the mother countries. Britain's resounding victory over France in 1763, however, brought total security to her American colonies, whose elites soon came to resent the continuing tax demands of the government in London. In 1776 they demanded their independence (page 98) and the colonies of Latin America followed suit in 1808. (page 106).

# South-East Asia and Japan 1511-1830

In 1603 the Japanese emperor conferred the title of Shogun (military leader) on Tokugawa Ieyasu, who had established control over the state re-unified in the 1590s (page 64). The Tokugawa dynasty exercised power until 1868, giving Japan a much-needed period of political stability. A complex system of government emerged in which the shoguns in Edo (modern Tokyo) dominated or regulated the 250 or so fiefs of the feudal lords, organized society in a hierarchy of classes, and enacted a comprehensive legal code. From 1612 they banned the Christian missionaries (active in many areas since the mid-16th century) and persecuted their adherents. They also forbade all Japanese to travel abroad; limited foreign contacts to the Dutch (who maintained a trading post at Nagasaki), the Chinese and the Koreans; and until 1853 successfully repulsed various attempts by the Russians, British, French and Americans to open trade (map 1). Yet despite this isolation, Tokugawa Japan prospered: trade and cities grew rapidly; the population rose from 20 to 30 million; high literacy rates prevailed; industry and credit spread widely. By the mid-19th century, Japan was far better prepared than any other part of Asia to meet the challenge of Western expansion (page 116).

Initially, however, Western traders showed far more interest in the spices of South-East Asia. The disintegration of the empires of Srivijaya and Majapahit (page 60) left behind scores of petty states, with little cohesion, opening the way to Portuguese acquisition of Malacca (1511) and footholds in the Moluccas (page 74). Their presence at first changed little: in Asia they came to dominate the spice trade through a chain of fortified stations, linked by naval power, not to acquire territory. The arrival of the Dutch and then the English after 1595 (page 74) did not initially change this, for they too sought primarily to monopolize the spice trade, and even after the establishment of a fortress at Batavia (1619) the Dutch directed most of their territorial ambitions towards acquiring Portuguese and English bases, rather than to conquering native states. The only substantial European colony in the area remained the Philippines, where the Spanish authorities began to foster the cultivation of tobacco, sugar, hemp and other commercial products from the later 18th century (map 2).

The mainland monarchies of South-East Asia – Arakan, Burma, Siam, Cambodia, Luang Prabang and Annam – had little direct involvement in European trade, and concentrated instead on extending their power at the expense of their neighbours. Over the period as a whole, Annam (Vietnam) and Siam expanded at the expense of Luang Prabang (Laos) and Cambodia. Burma almost disintegrated after the Mons rebelled in 1740, set up a king of their own at Pegu, and in 1752 captured the Burmese capital

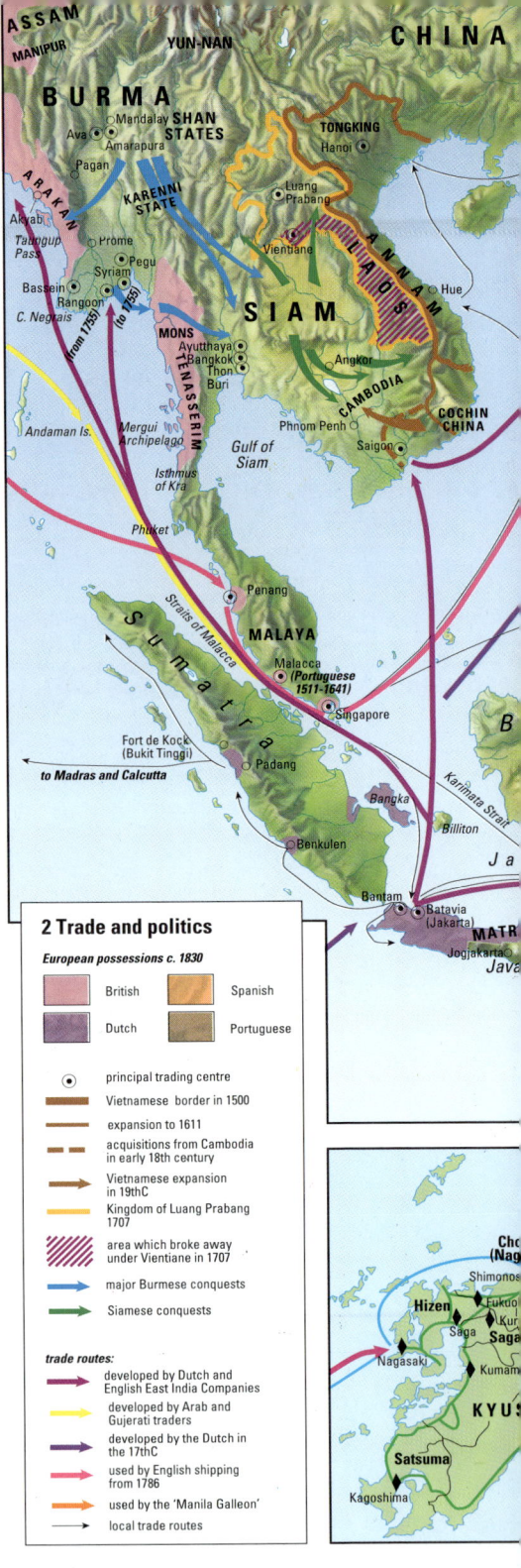

of Ava. However a charismatic leader, Alaungpaya (1735-60), defeated the Mons and established Rangoon as the southern port of a reunited Burma (1755), while his successors invaded Siam (1767) and conquered Arakan (1785).

Two factors complicated state-building in the area: the constant pressure of the hill peoples of the interior (like the Mons), always eager to assert their independence, and the steadily increasing interference of the Europeans. A group of Iberian adventurers temporarily seized power in Cambodia in the 1590s; the French briefly garrisoned some Siamese strongholds in the 1680s; both the French and English East India Companies intervened in Burma in the 1750s. Meanwhile, the Dutch began to extend their control over Java and the Spice Islands, and at the same time the British established their base at Penang (1786) and a free trade port at Singapore (1819) on the Malayan peninsula.

These acquisitions led to tension between the two colonial powers, which only abated after a treaty in 1824 obliged the British to withdraw from Sumatra and the Dutch from Malacca. Secure in the east, the British now turned on Burma and, after a short war (1824-6), annexed Arakan, Assam and Tenasserim. The future Dutch and British colonial empires in South-East Asia were taking shape, but their control remained loose and indirect. Only after the industrial revolution, and the expanding demand for raw materials and markets, did the Europeans seriously impinge upon the lives and fortunes of the peoples of the region.

# The Reformation 1517-1660

The decades around 1500 saw a great revival of popular religion in Latin Christendom, which the established church could not control. The fall of Constantinople (page 44) allowed the Roman church to ignore the Orthodox areas; and, except in Bohemia and Moravia, heresy scarcely existed in the West. Complacent, the Papacy failed to deploy its immense wealth adequately, producing widespread pluralism and absenteeism; this, coupled with the materialism of the hierarchy, discredited the Western church in the eyes of many Christians. Some, like Erasmus of Rotterdam (1466-1536) and Thomas More (1478-1535), hoped for spiritual renewal within the church; but in Saxony Martin Luther (1483-1546) criticized clerical abuse and in 1520 called upon the German nobility to reform the church. Meanwhile, inspired by Huldreych Zwingli (1484-1531), the magistrates of the Swiss canton of Zürich renounced allegiance to Rome.

These successful protests sparked others. By 1560, seven out of every ten inhabitants of the Holy Roman Empire no longer accepted papal authority, and Protestantism (as the dissident creeds became known) also prevailed in Scandinavia, the Baltic lands, and England. Further defections from Rome came through the teaching of John Calvin (1509-64) in Geneva. Calvinism made rapid progress in France, Poland, Hungary and Scotland (where it became the official creed after 1560).

In addition, a number of more radical sects sprang up, called 'Anabaptists' by their enemies because of their belief that only adult baptism was valid. They rejected ritual, spiritual and temporal authority, and many social conventions in favour of Biblical simplicity. Many combined evangelism with social protest, and participated both in the major rising of the German peasantry in 1524-5 and in the radical government of the city of Münster in 1534-5. Both movements were brutally repressed and Anabaptism, where it survived, became a secret, separate creed.

Eventually the Catholic church reformed itself. The Council of Trent (three sessions 1545-63) condemned abuses, defined doctrine, and created a more effective and educated clergy; at the same time new religious orders (most notably the Jesuits, incorporated in 1540) targeted key areas for reconversion. By 1650 the Protestants had been expelled from Bavaria (1579), Austria (1597) and France (1685), and the number of Protestant churches in Poland had declined from 560 in 1572 to 240 in 1650. Spain eradicated its small Protestant minorities, and in 1609 expelled its substantial Moorish population. In the Holy Roman Empire, however, the Protestants fought back, provoking the savage religious conflict known as the Thirty Years' War (page 86).

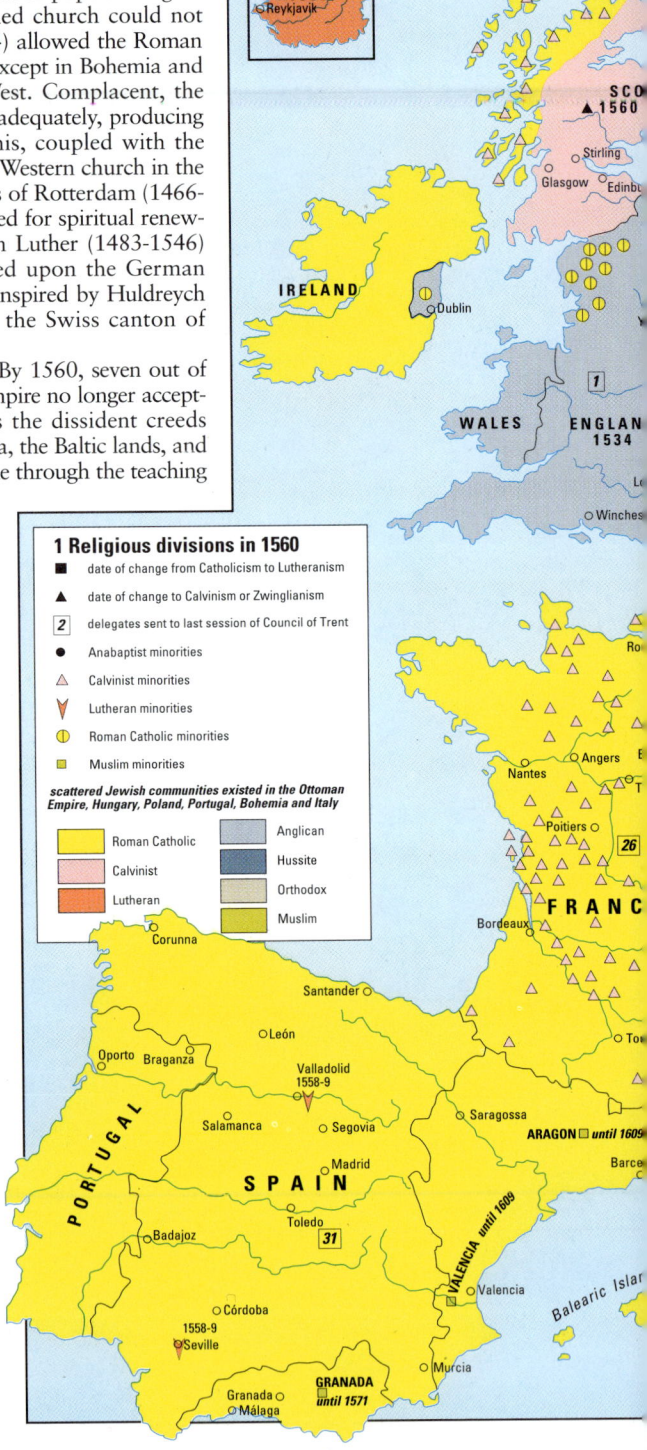

# The Habsburg ascendancy in Europe 1519-1659

Charles V's election as Holy Roman Emperor in 1519 created a Habsburg hegemony in Europe. He already ruled lands in Austria, South Germany and the Netherlands, and the realms bequeathed by his maternal grandparents in Spain, Italy and North Africa. Each of these inheritances soon increased. In 1526 his brother Ferdinand succeeded to the crowns of Bohemia (which included Moravia, Silesia and Lusatia) and Hungary. In 1535 Charles himself acquired both Lombardy and Tunisia, and throughout his reign he added to his holdings in the Netherlands (map 1). Moreover, in America, his Castilian subjects toppled first the Aztec and then the Inca states (see page 80). Although at Charles V's death in 1558 the central European lands (and the Imperial title) passed to Ferdinand and his successors, Charles's son Philip II also ruled a formidable inheritance. He, too, managed to extend it – adding the Philippines by conquest after 1571, and Portugal with her overseas possessions by inheritance after 1580.

Such centralization did not prove popular, however. Apart from provoking the enmity of France, which felt encircled, Charles V faced rebellions from his subjects in Spain (1520-2) and Germany (1552-5), the former provoked by taxation, the latter arising from religious dissent provoked by the Reformation (page 84). Philip II (1556-98) contended, in the Netherlands, with the longest-lasting revolt in modern European history (map 2). The various provinces inherited or acquired by Charles V became part of a single state only in 1548. Local customs, often guaranteed by charter against central government interference, nevertheless survived and Philip II's attempts to override them – both to raise taxes and to persecute heretics – provoked insurrection. A timely display of force stifled an uprising in 1566; but in 1572 the provinces of Holland and Zealand sustained rebellion, helped by the threat of a French invasion which made difficult a concentration of Spanish forces, until the cost of opposing them compelled Philip to withdraw his troops in 1576-7. Although forces loyal to (and maintained by) Spain reconquered many areas in the 1580s, fighting went on with the northern rebels for more than 20 years. Only in 1609 did Spain finally conclude a 12-year truce with the largely Calvinist Dutch Republic.

The Netherlands' struggle resumed during Emperor Ferdinand II's war against his rebellious subjects in Bohemia and Austria (map 3). The

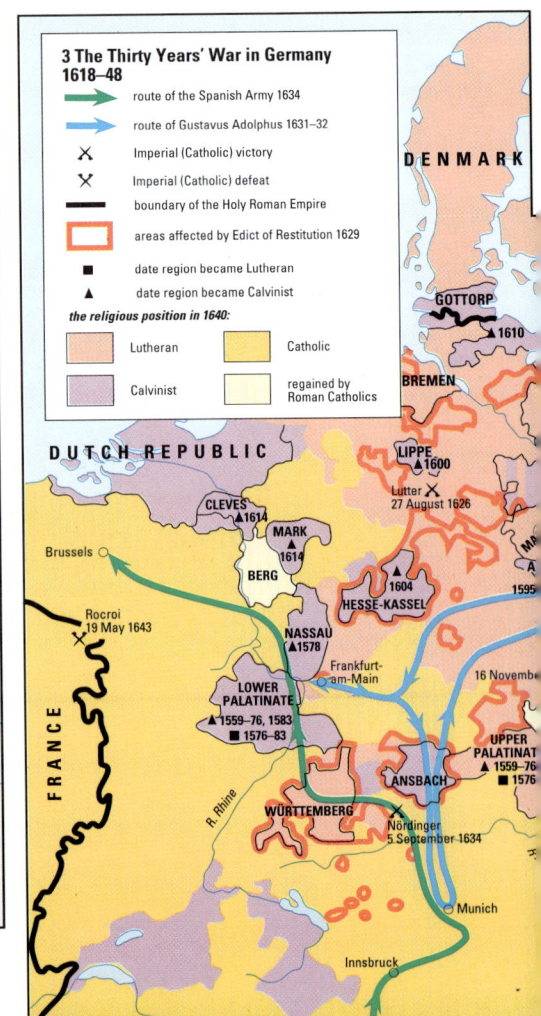

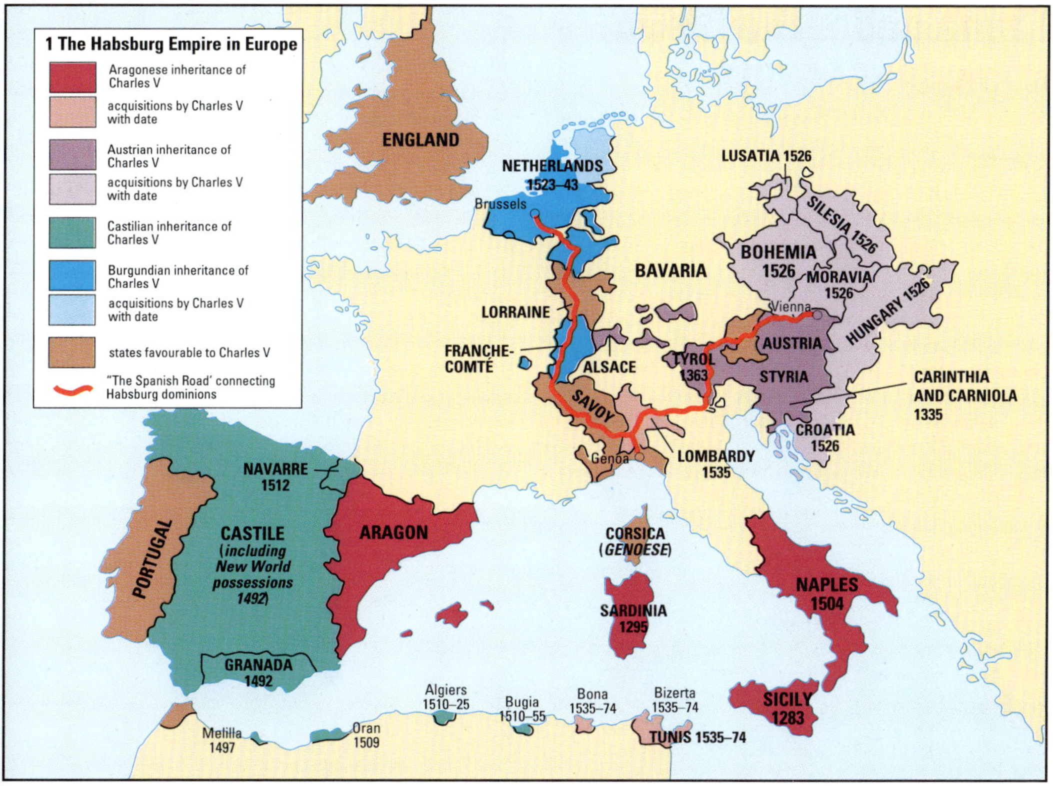

### 1 The Habsburg Empire in Europe

- Aragonese inheritance of Charles V
- acquisitions by Charles V with date
- Austrian inheritance of Charles V
- acquisitions by Charles V with date
- Castilian inheritance of Charles V
- Burgundian inheritance of Charles V
- acquisitions by Charles V with date
- states favourable to Charles V
- "The Spanish Road" connecting Habsburg dominions

Protestants were expelled from Austria (1597) and from Styria (1600). Encouraged by his success, with Spanish and Papal support Ferdinand turned in 1621 against the German Protestant states, especially the Calvinists. Despite aid from Britain, Denmark and the Dutch, they lost and in 1629 Ferdinand issued an 'Edict of Restitution' by which he reclaimed Church lands acquired by Protestant rulers. Swedish military aid turned the tables against the emperor, and saved the German Protestants from collapse: an army led by King Gustavus Adolphus routed the Imperialists at Breitenfeld (1631) and drove them from much of Germany. A Spanish army intervened to restore Habsburg fortunes but, although victorious at Nördlingen (1634), their aid to the emperor also provoked France to declare war first on Spain (1635) and then on the emperor (1636). The war turned into a free-for-all with fighting spreading to almost the whole continent.

After many more years of largely unsuccessful campaigning, at the peace of Westphalia (1648) the emperor was forced to abandon virtually all his powers in Germany, to agree to toleration for Protestants and Catholics, and to promise not to assist his Spanish cousins in their war against the Dutch rebels; by the peace of Münster (1648) Spain formally recognized the independence of the Dutch Republic (and their possession of all territories conquered since 1621); and by the peace of the Pyrenees (1659), Spain ceded all areas gained by France on the frontiers of both Spain and the Netherlands. The religious and political frontiers of central Europe which were agreed by these treaties lasted unchanged for 100 years. The Habsburg bid for European hegemony had failed.

# China under the Ch'ing dynasty 1644-1911

A new era in Chinese history opened in 1644 when the Ming dynasty, beset for a century by Japanese raids, civil wars, and northern invaders (see page 64), fell to the forces of a Manchurian dynasty which ruled the country until 1911. The Manchu, or Ch'ing, rulers met with resistance in southern China for half a century, but quickly established a working relationship with the gentry who staffed the Chinese bureaucracy and, with its support, began a successful policy of territorial expansion which continued until the mid-18th century (map 1).

At the same time population trebled from about 100 million in 1650 to 300 million in 1800 and reached 420 million by 1850, while vast quantities of tea, silk, cotton, lacquer and porcelain were exported (mostly to Europe). But the financial strain of the wars of expansion and the pressure of the growing population on land and food caused hardships that led to recurrent unrest and revolt, not only among the ethnic minorities who were harshly exploited by Chinese and Manchus alike, but also in the heartland itself, beginning with the 'White Lotus' rebellion, 1795-1804. China remained the world's largest and most populous state, but its economic difficulties and inadequate bureaucracy prevented effective resistance to the pressures of the Western powers who sought to open the Chinese market for the goods produced by their empires.

China's defeat in the Opium War (1839-42) resulted in the cession of Hong Kong to Britain and the opening of the first five Treaty Ports (their number steadily increased) in which foreigners enjoyed extra-territorial rights. More seriously, it served to weaken imperial authority and encouraged the Taiping rebellion

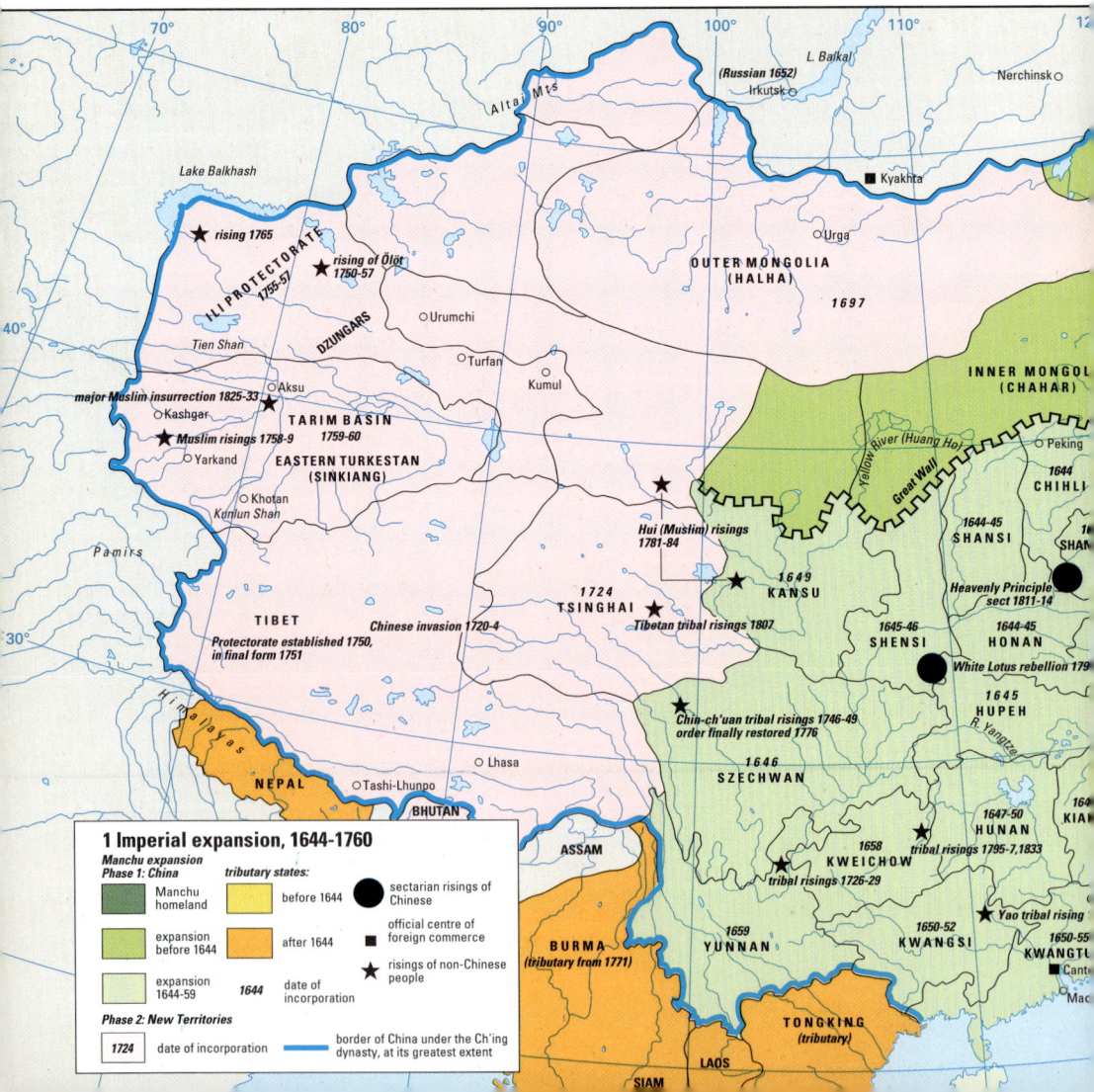

2 The dismemberment of the Chinese Empire, 1842-1911

(1850-64), the most serious of the many revolts that shook Manchu power. The Taiping and Nien uprisings alone left 25 million dead. These grave disorders also convinced the Western powers that Ch'ing China stood on the verge of collapse and encouraged them to secure a share: Russia gained the Amur basin, the Maritime Province (1858-60) and, temporarily, the Ili valley in Turkestan (1871-81); France occupied Indo-China (1884-5); Britain took Burma (1886); Japan annexed Taiwan (1895) and Korea (1910) (map 2). These losses convinced many Chinese that radical changes were inevitable, and when in 1911 a small mutiny broke out among the Manchu army, disaffection spread rapidly throughout the whole country and the imperial government collapsed (page 122).

# India 1707-1947

Shortly after Aurangzeb's death in 1707 (page 58), Mughal power declined. In the north, Oudh and Bengal became effectively independently, owing only nominal allegiance to Delhi; in the centre, the power of the Maratha confederacy increased; in the south the Muslim state of Mysore expanded rapidly. Meanwhile European influence in India continued to increase, with both the French and English East India Companies acquiring new territory in the southeast. Robert Clive's victory at Plassey in 1757 gave the English control over the lands and resources of Bengal, Orissa and Bihar, allowing the Company to maintain an army of over 100,000 men – most of them Indian soldiers (sepoys) trained to fight in European fashion – with which they not only destroyed France's Indian ambitions but also extended their control over the entire eastern coast of the subcontinent (map 1). Mysore went down to defeat in 1799, the Marathas in 1805, both delivering extensive new territories to British control, and most other major Indian rulers soon recognized British suzerainty.

Over the next half-century the conquest of Sind (1843) and the Punjab (1849), brought the dominions of the Company up to the country's natural frontier in the northwest, while a war with Nepal (1814-16) extended them to the Himalayas. To the east the British clashed with the Burmese empire and in 1824-6 annexed Assam and Arakan (page 83). Within India, the 'Doctrine of Lapse' introduced by Governor-General Dalhousie (1847-56) resulted in the absorption of autonomous but dependent states, such as Oudh and several Maratha kingdoms, into the directly administered territories (map 2). Not surprisingly, this policy provoked disaffection which found violent outlet in 1857. Beginning as a mutiny of the Company's native soldiers, the revolt soon involved princes, landlords and peasants throughout northern India; but the loyalty of the Sikhs and the passivity of southern India enabled the British to restore control after 14 months of bitter fighting.

The mutiny proved a watershed in the history of British India. It thoroughly discredited the Company and in 1858 the London government assumed direct control. The subcontinent now acquired a pivotal position in Britain's Imperial system, leading to intervention in Afghanistan

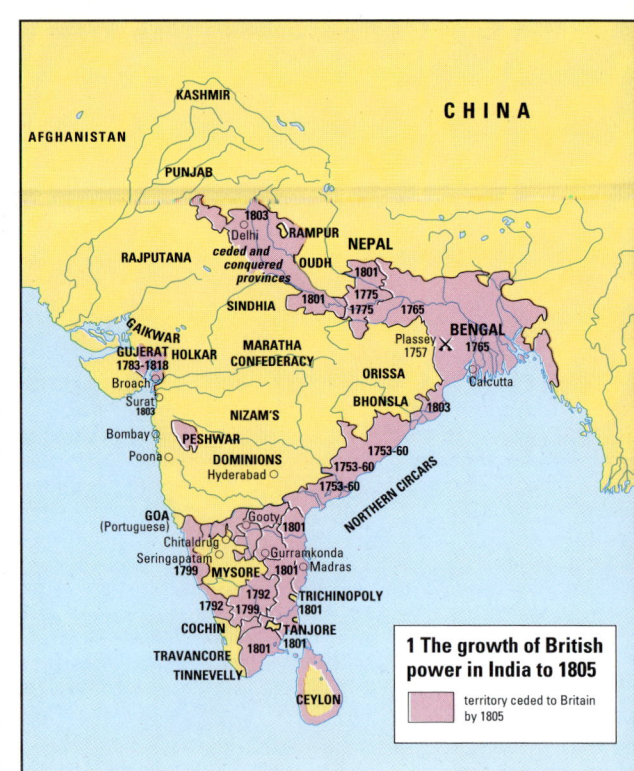

**1 The growth of British power in India to 1805**
- territory ceded to Britain by 1805

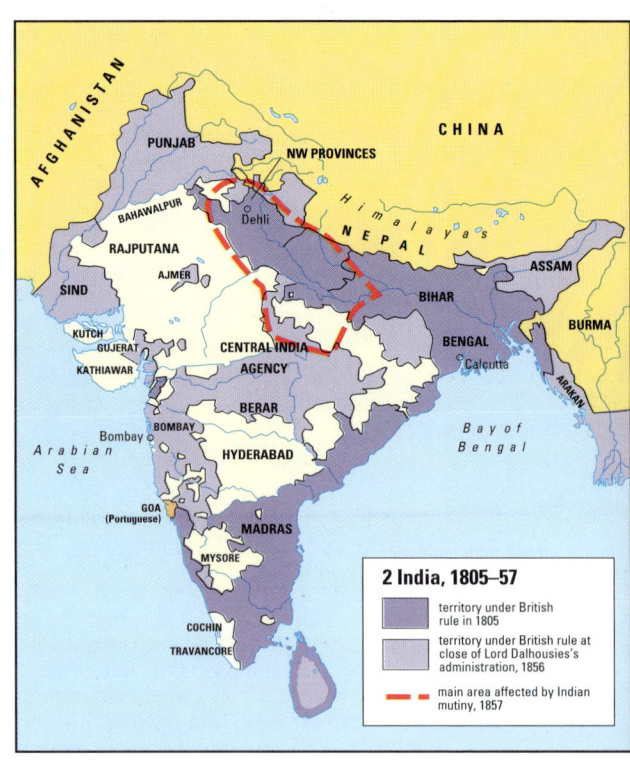

**2 India, 1805–57**
- territory under British rule in 1805
- territory under British rule at close of Lord Dalhousie's administration, 1856
- main area affected by Indian mutiny, 1857

to block Russian expansion into central Asia (page 108), and in Burma to counter French influence in Southeast Asia. From East Africa to China, the Indian army regularly acted to advance British interests. Within India, the autonomy of the princes was henceforth respected and active steps were taken to develop the economy: the construction of first-class roads and a major rail network, together with the opening of the Suez Canal in 1869, made possible the exploitation of raw materials and the introduction of export crops, such as tea. Between 1869 and 1929 India's foreign trade increased sevenfold. However, although some modern industries developed under Indian entrepreneurs, most of the trade involved importing British manufactures and exporting raw materials; and in most areas neither the character of the economy nor traditional agriculture experienced any basic change (map 3). The gross national product increased only slowly, while from 1921 (thanks to sustained population growth) per capita income declined.

The rise of a new middle class, partly through industry but more through the recruitment of educated Indians into the colonial administration, coupled with overt British racism, awakened a new political consciousness. The Indian National Congress (established with official blessing in 1885) at first accepted British rule, but soon developed an extremist wing which questioned the foreigners' right to rule India. The decision to partition the province of Bengal in 1905 provoked mass agitation and terrorist attacks; and from 1919, under the leadership of Mohendas K. Gandhi (1869-1948), Congress fought actively for home rule and, after 1929, for independence. Profiting from the unrest caused by unemployment and the world economic depression, Gandhi launched a civil disobedience campaign (1930-4) that galvanized the Indian masses, and forced Britain to pass the Government of India Act (1935) which provided a framework for participation in central and provincial government.

By 1937 Congress controlled 11 of the 14 provincial administrations, but failed to represent adequately the interests of the large Muslim minority whose leaders in 1940 passed a resolution calling for an autonomous Islamic state in the subcontinent: Pakistan. In 1942 Gandhi launched a 'Quit India' campaign and in 1946-7, faced by massive disaffection, a naval mutiny, and strong pressure from the United States, the British drew up hasty plans for partition along sectarian lines. India and Pakistan became independent in 1947, Burma and Ceylon in 1948 (page 152).

# The age of revolution
## 1755-1815

The later 18th century saw unprecedented uprisings throughout the western hemisphere (map 1). Many reflected a long-standing desire for independence, as in Corsica (1755, 1793), Haiti (1791), Sardinia (1793), Ireland (1798), Serbia (1804) and Spain (1808). Most, however, owed something to the Enlightenment, a European intellectual movement which emphasized certain fundamental rights of human beings and rejected traditional authority. Paradoxically, this could lead to rebellions by conservative elements against reforming rulers – such as the Austrian Netherlands (1787)

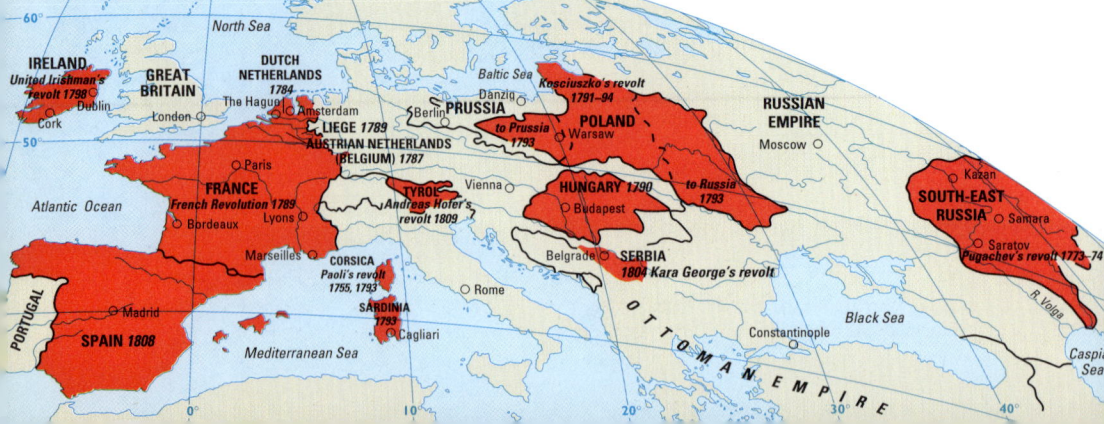

1 Revolts and revolutions in Europe and America
— borders in 1789
▮ areas affected by revolution 1773-1814

and Hungary (1790) against the 'Enlightened' policies of Emperor Joseph II – or the resistance of colonial societies to the centralizing policies of the home government – as in North America after 1775 (page 98) and in South America after 1808 (page 106). More commonly, however, opposition came from the middle classes: against a closed patriarchate in the Dutch Republic (1785-7); against the absolute monarchy and its aristocratic supporters in France.

In France, between 1789 and 1791 a representative assembly, summoned to solve a financial crisis, abolished feudalism, and created a constitutional monarchy and equality before the law. The king, however, refused to cooperate and was deposed in 1792, provoking Austrian, Prussian and (from 1793) British attempts to overthrow the Republic by force. They failed: instead, the revolutionary government in Paris purged its opponents at home and, by mobilizing unprecedented numbers of its citizens, conquered the Low Countries, Switzerland and Italy, imposing satellite republics.

In 1799 a successful general, Napoleon Bonaparte, took power as military dictator. He secured peace abroad (1802), and reorganized French local government, laws and education. But Britain declared war again in 1803 and, although her command of the seas (confirmed at Trafalgar, 1805) provided immunity from invasion, Napoleon defeated her continental allies – Austria, Prussia and Russia – in a brilliant series of battles (1805-7). Next, in order to create a continental blockade against British trade, Napoleon overran Spain (1808) and extended France's frontiers to Catalonia, the Baltic and Rome (1809-10). However Britain supported his opponents in the Iberian peninsula, expelling French forces by 1814. Meanwhile Russia's refusal to cooperate in the continental blockade led to a French invasion in 1812 which, although it reached Moscow, exhausted Napoleon's resources and led to his defeat and abdication in 1813-14 and again in 1815 (the 'Hundred Days').

Nevertheless, despite his failure, Napoleon's success inspired even his enemies: throughout the 19th century, Spanish, German and Italian reformers envisaged the state in essentially Napoleonic mode (page 110), while his administrative, legal and educational reforms in France survived the restoration of royal power.

# The Industrial Revolution in Europe c.1750-1914

The Industrial Revolution, which began in England in the later 18th century, became the catalyst of the modern world. Nevertheless the speed of change can be exaggerated. Even in continental Europe its impact remained limited before 1850 to a few enclaves; and not until the last quarter of the century did the great surge forward occur. Outside Europe, except for the United States, industrialization took place even later (page 120). In 1895, even in Germany, one-third of the population still worked on the land, and most of eastern and southern Europe remained virtually untouched by industry.

Until 1900, when its lead began to be challenged by Germany and the United States, Great Britain remained the workshop of the world and its industrial strength, which enabled it to dominate world markets, explains its pre-eminence in the age of imperialism (page 112). Britain's precedence rested upon many factors. On the one hand, unlike much of the rest of Europe, it possessed abundant coal, iron and other basic materials, and it enjoyed an advantageous position in the Atlantic trade which generated much capital. On the other hand, it possessed several unique advantages. First, it escaped direct damage from the various wars that ravaged Europe between 1688 and 1815; second, unlike most continental states which bristled with customs barriers and internal frontiers, after the union of England and Scotland in 1707 Great Britain formed a single economic unit; third, again in contrast to continental Europe, the early disappearance of serfdom in England meant that the surplus labour released by rising agricultural productivity could move, without legal obstacles, to the growing industrial centres. Finally, England possessed a unique network of navigable rivers and canals (map 1), which proved of immense importance before the railway age for moving both raw materials and finished goods.

In its earliest phase, English manufacturers had also relied on water as a source of energy; but in the century to 1870 industrial power depended on steam, generated by the combustion of coal. At first, except in Britain and (from 1820) Belgium, steam

power came only slowly, held back by political fragmentation, lack of capital and, above all, poor communications which severely limited markets. The steel firm of Krupps, founded in 1810 and later to be a giant of German industry, still employed only 7 men in 1826 and 122 in 1846. The pace of industrialization only accelerated with railway development. Between 1830 and 1870 the rail networks of Britain, Belgium and Germany became virtually complete, and construction began elsewhere. At much the same time, barriers to trade came down: France demolished her internal tariffs in 1790, Prussia followed suit in 1818 and in 1834 joined the German Customs Union, which included 17 states and some 26 million people.

A new period, sometimes called the Second Industrial Revolution, opened in the 1870s (see map 2). The new German empire (page 111) led the way, increasing its coal output from 38 million tons in 1871 to 279 million tons in 1913, and its iron output from 1.5 million tons to 15 million tons. But it also led in new areas of industrial enterprise, especially chemicals, electricity and steel. By 1910, Krupps employed 70,000 men. At a time of growing international tension (page 118), such rapid economic growth was bound to produce a reaction among Germany's neighbours and Russia began a campaign of rapid industrialization in 1890 (page 108), France in 1895 and Italy in 1905. In all these states, much heavy industry was keyed to armaments. Although the bulk of the population of Europe remained largely untouched, industrialization had both changed the face of the continent and rendered its future uncertain.

# The emerging global economy *c.* 1775

In 1775, the areas of Spanish conquest and settlement in central and south America still ranked as the most valuable European overseas possession, thanks to the silver production of Mexico and Peru and the gold exports of Brazil, most of which went to Europe in return for manufactured goods. Along the Atlantic coast from Brazil to the Chesapeake, but above all in the Caribbean islands, plantation societies had developed to meet the rising demand both in Europe and in British North America (where over 2 million whites now dwelt) for tropical agricultural produce: cacao, tobacco, cotton and (especially) sugar. Since most plantations depended on the labour of African slaves, increased consumption in Europe meant increased shipments of slaves from Africa.

A closely integrated Atlantic economy had thus emerged. By 1775 the mainland colonies throughout the Americas were generally self-sufficient in food and some supported limited manufacturing. But their white populations consumed prodigious quantities of imported European manufactured goods, and prosperity almost everywhere depended on the ability to export to Europe. Transatlantic commerce, in turn, contributed substantially to the economic development of Spain, France and Britain (almost 40 per cent of whose total exports in 1775 went to America).

In Asia, although the volume of European trade also greatly increased in the 18th century, it remained largely confined to ports or small coastal enclaves to which Asian merchants delivered goods. The Dutch and English East India Companies, founded in 1600-2 (page 74), still dominated trade with maritime Asia, but the shipment of spices to Europe had by the 18th century been overtaken by a boom in textiles (above all silks and cottons) and new drinks (tea and coffee). Since, however, in contrast to the Americas, few European manufactures proved competitive in Asia (except in the Mediterranean ports of the Ottoman empire), increased imports of Asian goods generally depended on shipments of American silver, either re-exported from Europe or carried across the Pacific to the Philippines and thence to China.

**1 The Atlantic economy**

exports of goods in £ millions (x25 for approximate modern equivalent)
movement of migrants and slaves
*sugar* New World export commodities
GUIANA areas linked economically with Europe

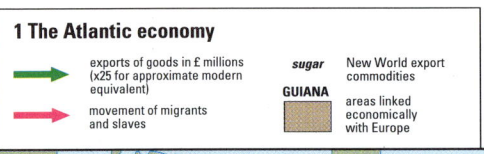

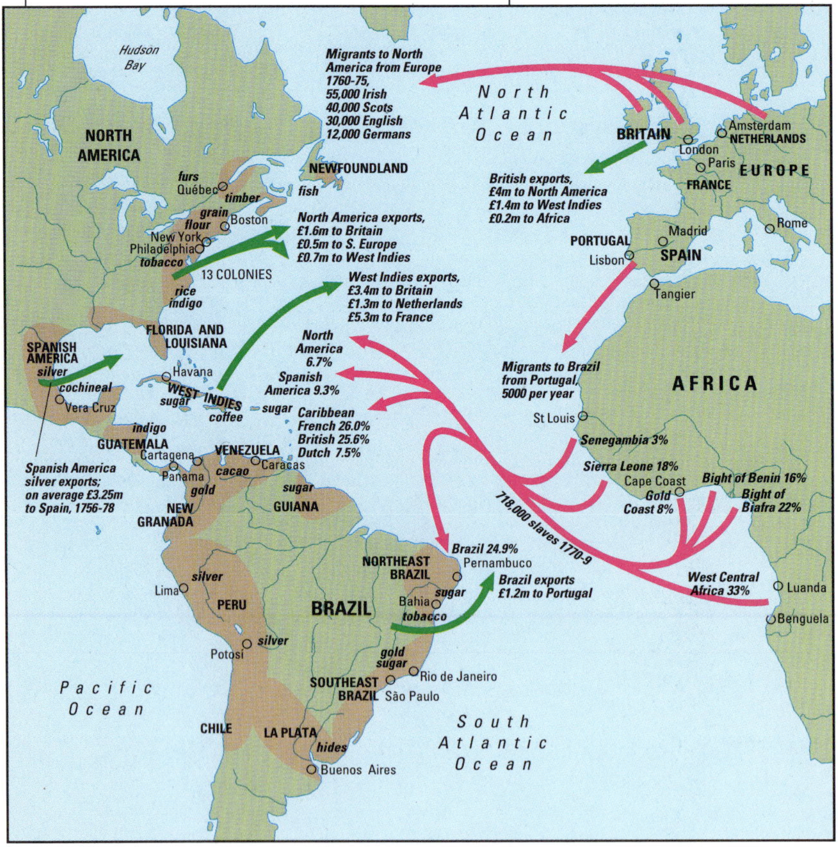

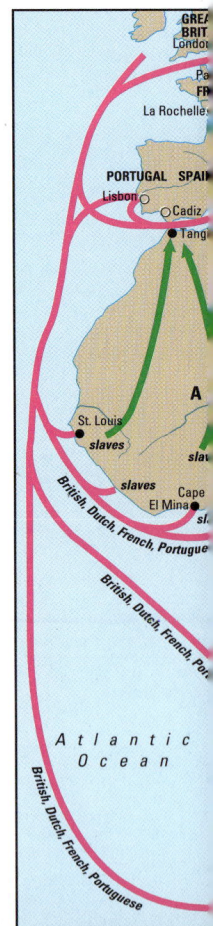

European trade also stimulated the demand for export commodities from, and injected large quantities of silver into, India and China; but most of Asia's economic life remained relatively unaffected by contact with the West, and much of its long-distance trade continued to be conducted by Asian merchants using their own caravans of pack-animals or ships. However, conditions were changing rapidly in two areas of great economic importance: the British had gained control of Bengal, a major centre of textile manufacture, in the 1760s and now used its huge tax revenues to maintain a substantial army ready to annexe other areas of the subcontinent; and the Dutch in Java could impose commercial controls and receive commodities (above all coffee) as tribute.

Only Africa remained almost totally resistant to European penetration. Although the slave trade reached its apogee in the 18th century, with some 2.3 million slaves shipped out between 1770 and 1800, the prices paid by the Europeans for each slave steadily rose – suggesting that the African rulers who dealt in slaves more than held their own, despite the disruption arising from wars and slave-raiding, and the sustained loss of population.

In short, Europe's rapid commercial expansion overseas (for better or worse) hastened the economic integration of the world. The Americas outside the plantations enjoyed a degree of self-sufficiency, but Europe still determined the economic development of much of the continent. Although, except in Bengal, Java and the Philippines, the West could not yet shape the economies of Asia and Africa, with Britain now poised to conquer India (page 90) and with the Industrial Revolution underway in Europe (page 94), the stage was set for the creation of an integrated global economy.

## 2 Trade in Africa and Asia

| | routes of European trade |
|---|---|
| | routes of trade primarily of African and Asian merchants |
| coffee | African and Asian export commodities |
| • | centres of European trade in Africa and Asia |

**East India Company trade:** value of imports to Europe

| | British | Dutch |
|---|---|---|
| Bengal | £800,000 | £200,000 |
| China | £300,000 | £250,000 |
| Madras | £200,000 | - |
| Bombay | £100,000 | - |
| Batavia | - | £200,000 |
| Ceylon and Coromandel | - | £150,000 |
| **Total** | **£1,400,000** | **£800,000** |

**Levant trade:** value of imports to Europe

| French | £2,200,000 | Dutch | £1,100,000 |
|---|---|---|---|
| British | £600,000 | Venetian | £600,000 |

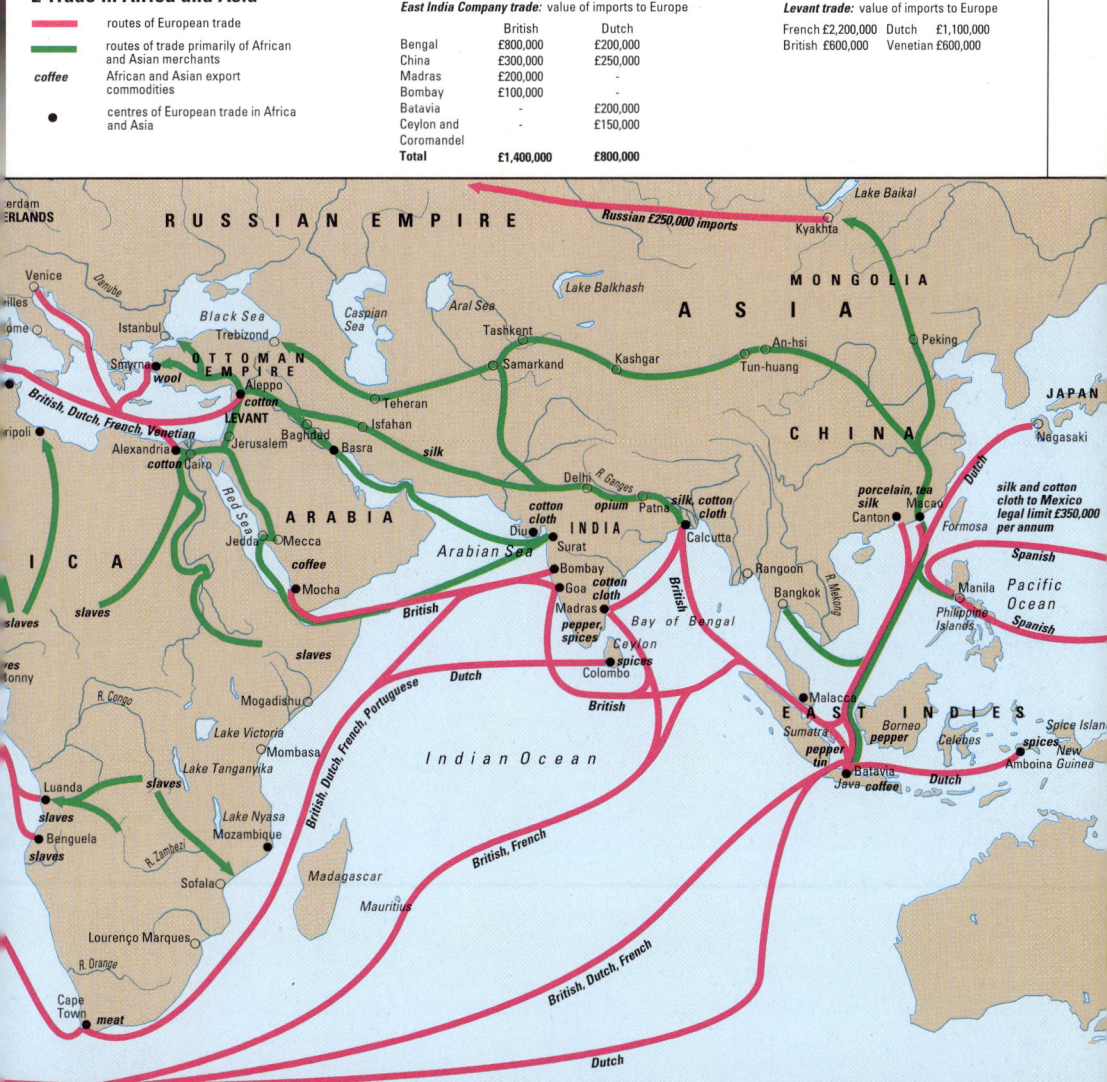

# The United States 1775-1865

The disputes and difficulties leading to the American War of Independence and the foundation of the United States began almost immediately after the English victory over France. In the Seven Years' War (page 80) Britain began to reorganize her vastly expanded North American possessions, establishing a huge Indian reserve west of the Alleghenies (1763) and extending the boundaries of Quebec (formerly French Canada) to the Mississippi and Ohio rivers (1774). The 'thirteen colonies' bitterly resented both this check to their westward expansion and the simultaneous insistence by Britain that its colonies should henceforth bear a greater share of the costs of their defence. Armed opposition began at Lexington and Concord in Massachusetts in 1775 (map 1). The colonies' representatives declared Independence in 1776, compelled the main British field army to surrender at Yorktown (1781), and fought on until the Treaty of Versailles (1783) recognized their sovereignty and extended the frontiers of the 'United States of America' to the Great Lakes and the Mississippi.

Expansion now proceeded rapidly. In 1783 the new republic comprised some 800,000 square miles (2,072,000 km²) of territory, but the purchase of Louisiana from France (1803) more than doubled its size. West Florida was taken by force in 1812 and East Florida (60,000 square miles, 155,400 km²) during the presidency of James Monroe. Thereafter extensive territories in the south and west were added, largely at the expense of Mexico (map 2), and in 1846 a compromise with Britain was reached over Oregon, increasing the number of states from 13 to 34. The population expanded from 3 million in 1783 to 31 million in 1860, fuelled by the arrival of a new wave of European immigrants, predominantly German and Irish.

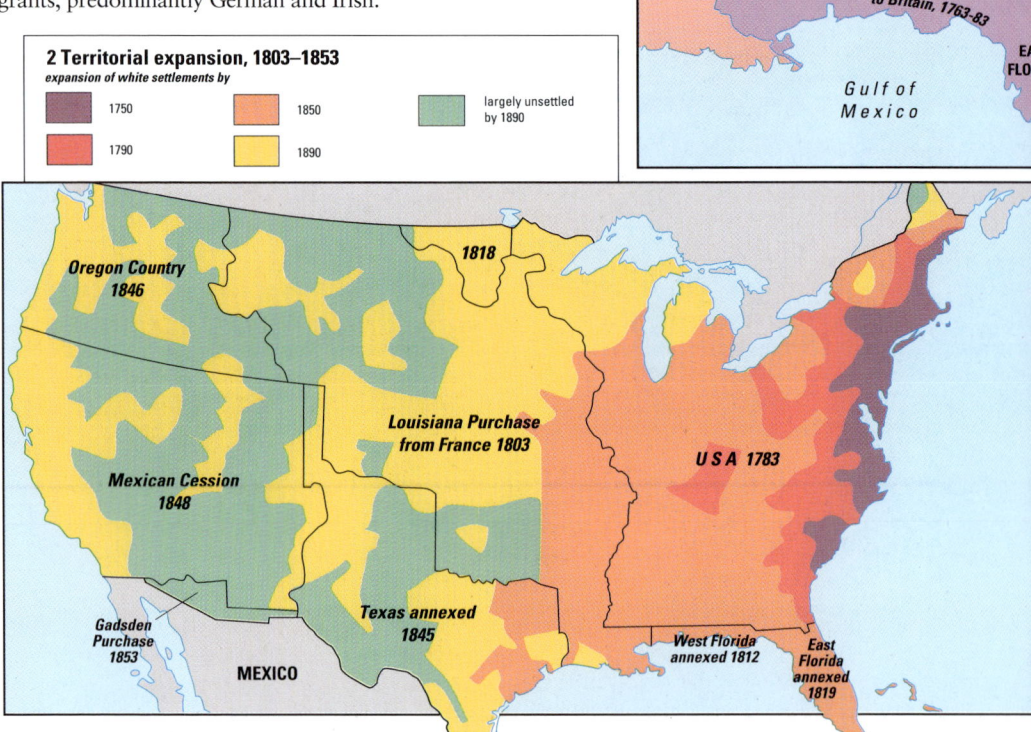

2 Territorial expansion, 1803–1853

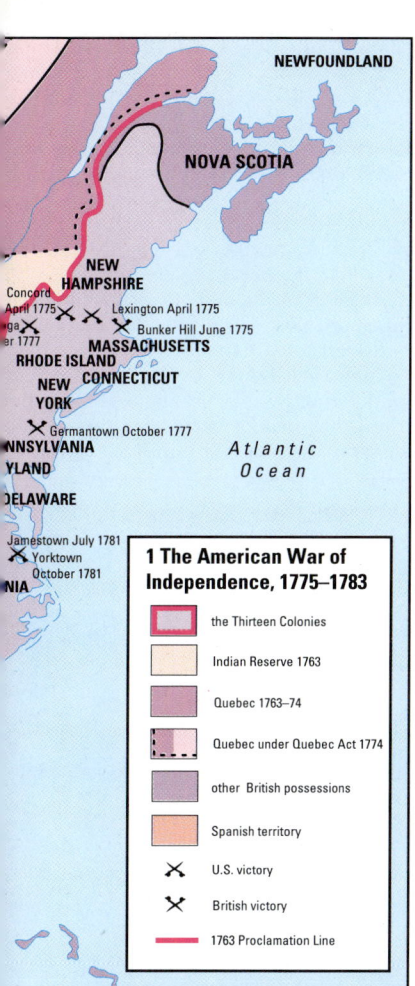

**1 The American War of Independence, 1775–1783**

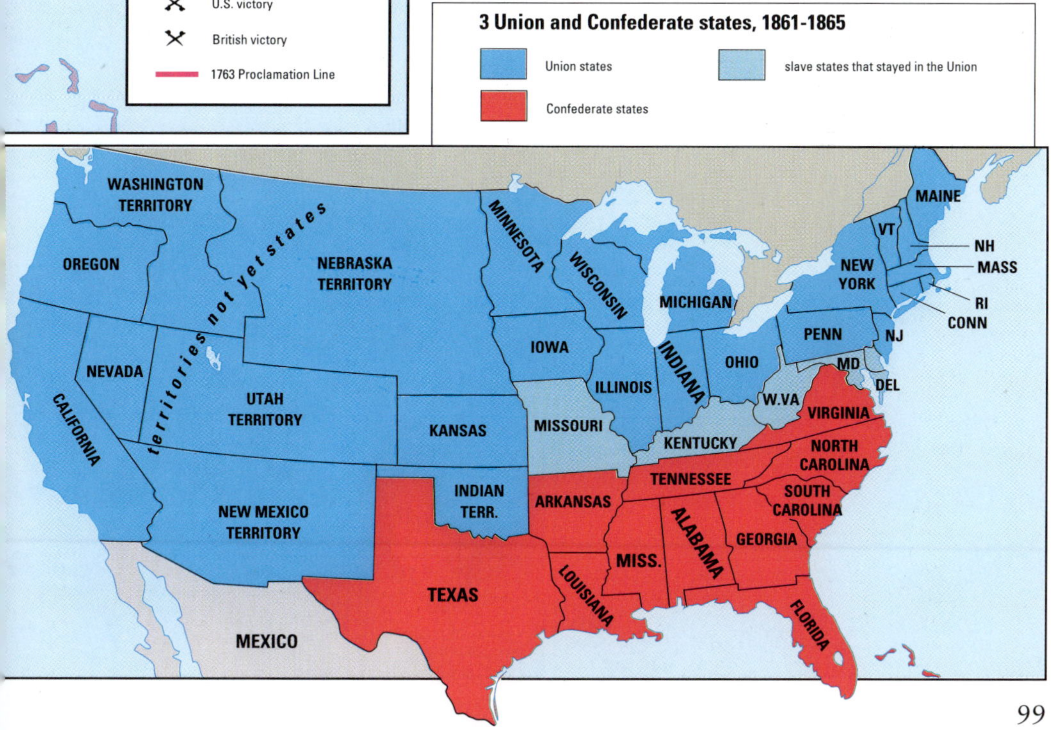

- the Thirteen Colonies
- Indian Reserve 1763
- Quebec 1763–74
- Quebec under Quebec Act 1774
- other British possessions
- Spanish territory
- ✕ U.S. victory
- ✕ British victory
- 1763 Proclamation Line

These developments had important political consequences. The ruling elites of the southern states, with their plantation economy and large black slave population, felt increasingly threatened by the industrializing north and the growing Midwest. This, rather than the issue of slavery, underlay the American Civil War (1861-5); but the issues in fact proved inseparable because, with over 90 percent of the black population living in the South, the moral question was also a regional question. Abraham Lincoln, elected President in 1860 by the votes of the Northern states, was right to claim that the nation could not permanently remain 'half slave and half free'.

Soon after Lincoln's election, South Carolina seceded from the Union and was quickly joined by ten other states which came together as the Confederate States of America with their capital at Richmond, Virginia (map 3). For Lincoln the fundamental issue was whether a constitutional republic could preserve its territorial integrity; he recognized no constitutional right of secession. By 1863, however, pressure from radical Republicans added the aim of freeing the slaves in the rebel states to the commitment to restore the Union. Thanks to the superior military skill of their commanders, and to their shorter lines of communications, the confederacy fought on for four years (1861-5). The Northern strategy was to deny the South vital resources by a naval blockade, to gain control of key river routes and forts in the west and to capture Richmond. Eventually the superior demographic and economic resources of the North prevailed – albeit at the cost of 635,000 Union and 383,000 Confederate military casualties – and created the 'second American Revolution' which, by crippling the southern ruling class and liberating its labour force, determined that the thrusting, urban, industrialized North, with its creed of competitive capitalism, would stamp its pattern (for good or ill) on the entire United States.

**3 Union and Confederate states, 1861-1865**

- Union states
- Confederate states
- slave states that stayed in the Union

# Australia and New Zealand from 1788

Although Australia and New Zealand were reconnoitred by the Dutch explorer Abel Tasman in 1642, colonization only began in 1770 when James Cook raised the British flag at Botany Bay. New South Wales served as a penal colony from 1788 to 1839, as did van Diemen's land (later Tasmania) from 1804 to 1853, but in 1829 the British government, in order to forestall the French, claimed the whole Australian continent. Fear of France also led to the annexation of New Zealand in 1840. However, the geographical obstacles, the lack of exportable goods (at first chiefly seal products and sandalwood), and (especially in the case of New Zealand) the opposition of the indigenous population complicated the colonization process in both territories. In 1850, the total white population of Australia still numbered only 350,000, and that of New Zealand was less than 100,000.

The discovery of gold in New South Wales and Victoria in 1851 initiated a new phase, and encouraged the growth of the inland population. Even more important was the rapid growth of sheep-farming: in 1850 Australia sent 17,000 tons of wool to Great Britain, but 134,000 tons in 1879. Nevertheless, as centralizing systems of communications and transportation developed, the dominance of the coastal cities – especially Sydney and Melbourne – increased. By the 1890s, two-thirds of Australia's population lived in urban areas along the coast (a pattern that steadily intensified throughout the 20th century.) In New Zealand, where wool

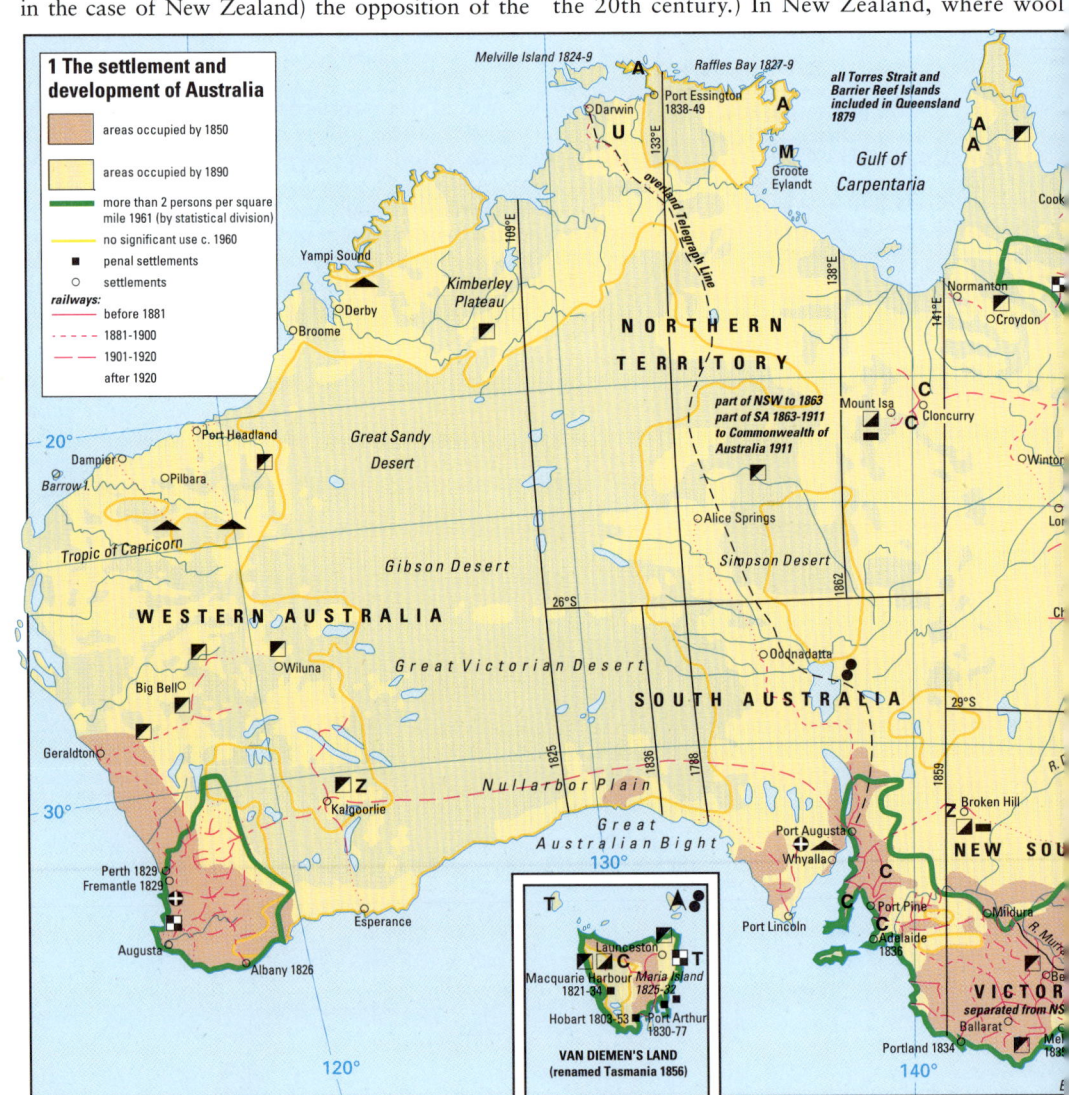

remained largely a South Island product, exports rose in value from £67,000 in 1853 to £2.7 million twenty years later. The development of the North Island, which was held back by the bitter Maori Wars (1860-71), only came after the introduction of refrigeration, which made possible the export of frozen lamb, butter and cheese. Dairy farming developed rapidly, and the North Island now drew ahead of the South in population.

Political development kept pace with economic growth. In 1855 New South Wales, Victoria, South Australia and Tasmania became self-governing colonies, followed by Queensland in 1859; in 1901 they joined together to form the Commonwealth of Australia. New Zealand, which had been divided in 1852 into six provinces, each with an elected council, became a united Dominion (after measures had been taken to safeguard the rights of the Maori population) in 1876. Both countries achieved sovereign status under the Statute of Westminster in 1931. The economy of both dominions remained heavily dependent on primary exports – wool, meat, grain and dairy products – which enjoyed preferential treatment in the British market. Even the spectacular discoveries of minerals, coal, oil and gas in and about Australia after 1950 went largely into exports. However Britain's decision to join the European Economic Community and dismantle 'imperial preference' in 1973 (page 156), coupled with the conviction that the countries of the Pacific Rim will become the economic hub of the world in the 21st century, drove both Australia and New Zealand to develop new economic activities and to foster trade with countries outside the British Commonwealth.

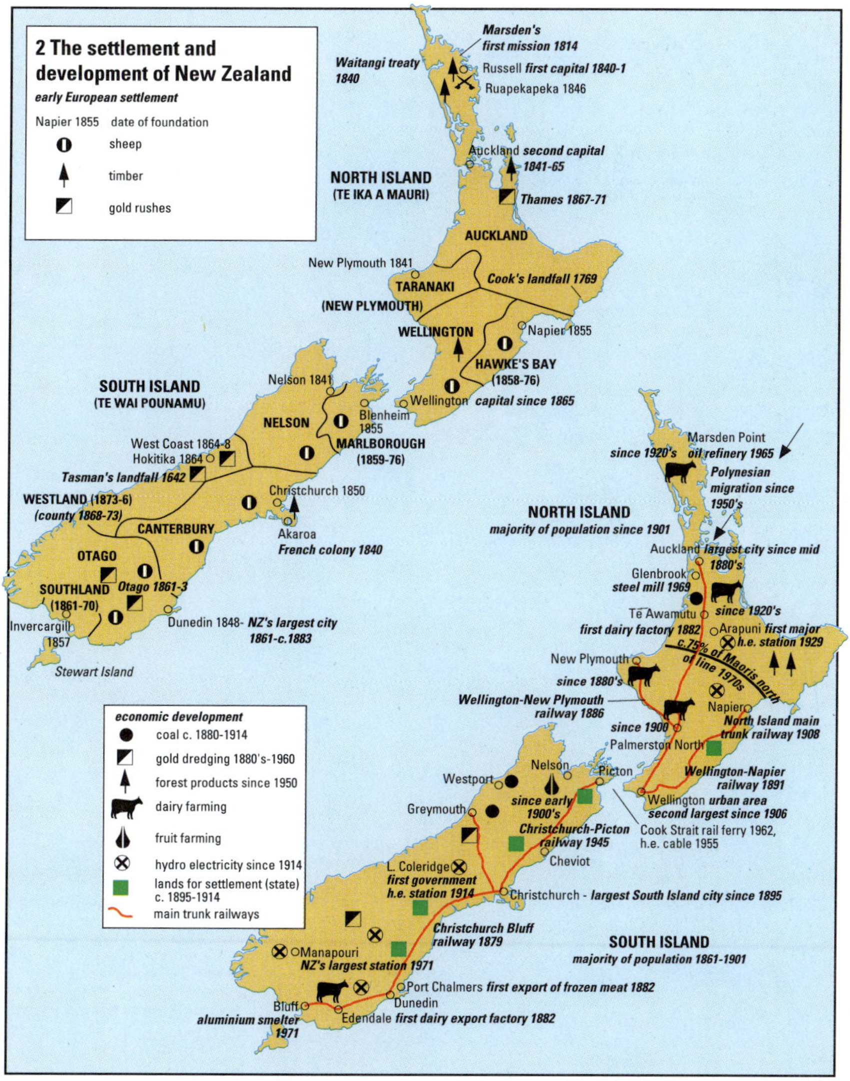

## 2 The settlement and development of New Zealand

# The decline of the Ottoman Empire 1798-1923

The period between 1798 and 1923 saw the disintegration and final collapse of the Ottoman Empire, the major power in the Near East since the 16th century (see page 66). Plagued by foreign invasions, wars, and the revolts of subject peoples demanding national independence, the empire steadily lost territory.

In 1798 a French army led by Napoleon Bonaparte invaded Egypt and Syria, only to be defeated by the British. Peace was arranged in 1802 and three years later the sultan appointed Mohammed Ali governor of Egypt. Under his rule, however, the province gained *de facto* independence and in 1841 Mohammed was recognized as hereditary viceroy. Meanwhile, between 1830 and 1847 the French conquered Algeria, and in 1881 they annexed Tunis; the following year the British occupied Egypt. There were also wars with Russia, rebellions in the Arab provinces and almost constant revolts in the Balkans – starting with the Greek War of Independence in 1821, which resulted (following the pressure of foreign powers) in the recognition of a sovereign Greek state in 1830. Foreign intervention also precipitated the Crimean War (1853-6) and the Lebanese crisis of 1860-1, while Russian and Austrian demands helped secure the independence of Bulgaria, Montenegro, Serbia and Romania by 1878. By 1882, the Ottomans had lost 40 per cent of their empire.

Their finances also deteriorated rapidly until in 1875 the state became virtually bankrupt and Sultan Abdul-Aziz suspended payment of the interest due on the Ottoman debt. In 1881, he agreed to supervision of his treasury by European bankers: the empire's survival became dependent on foreign governments who preferred the preservation of a weakened Ottoman state to the

dangerous power vacuum that would follow Turkish collapse. Nevertheless, further territorial losses followed: Italy annexed Libya in 1911 and, at the end of the Balkan wars in 1913 (page 118), the Ottomans surrendered Crete, most of the Aegean islands, Thrace, Macedonia and Albania. In all, between 1908 and 1911, the Turks lost 30 per cent of their remaining possessions.

Throughout the 19th century the sultans made various attempts to modernize their empire, but not always successfully: Selim III, who aimed to create a modern army, was deposed in 1807 when his troops mutinied against the proposed reforms. The Janissaries rebelled in 1826 against reforms decreed by Mahmud II, but this provoked their abolition. After a decade of agitation, in 1876 Sultan Abdul Hamid II introduced a constitution, and a Parliament met the following year; but it was dissolved almost immediately and only pressure by the Ottoman Society for Union and Progress (the 'Young Turks') forced its restoration in 1908. The following year Abdul Hamid abdicated, and the Young Turks came to dominate the administration. However, their nationalist policies and opposition to any further surrender of territory contributed substantially to the Arabs' willingness to seek accommodation with the Turks' enemies, once the Ottoman empire entered World War I on the side of Germany and Austro-Hungary (page 124).

Despite tenacious resistance, the Turks were eventually defeated and the Middle East (despite earlier promises to the Arabs) came under the control of the victorious French and British governments. The Sultan collaborated with Great Britain after his defeat, and in 1920 agreed to the treaty of Sèvres which envisaged the dismemberment of the empire. However, the arrival of Greek troops at Izmir provoked a nationalist uprising which crystallized around the Turks' only undefeated general, Mustafa Kemal. The sultanate was abolished and, after some reverses, Turkish forces drove the Greeks back and secured recognition of the sovereignty of the Turkish Republic at the treaty of Lausanne in 1923.

# Africa in the 19th century

By 1870 the Western powers had finally ended the slave trade, responsible for the forced migration of at least 10 million Africans to the Americas since 1500. Otherwise, however, Europe's impact on the African interior remained limited to two areas: Algeria, conquered by France between 1830 and 1847, and Cape Colony, where Dutch settlers (subjected to British rule after 1806) moved north-east in the Great Trek (1835) in search of land and freedom, and founded settlements which eventually became the Orange Free State and Transvaal. In West Africa, the followers of a Muslim religious leader from Hausaland, Uthman dan Fodio, conquered much of Upper Nigeria after 1804, and Uthman's son became sultan of Sokoto. Somewhat later, two other charismatic Islamic leaders also carved out new states: al-Hajj Umar north of the Niger in the 1850s, and Samory south of it in the 1870s and '80s. In the north-east, Mohammed Ali of Egypt conquered northern Sudan in 1820, and his grandson Ismail consolidated Egyptian control over much of the littoral of the Red Sea. Finally, in the south, the formation of the Zulu kingdom by Shaka in 1818 led to widespread disruption as neighbouring peoples moved away from the aggressive new state.

Meanwhile, the progress of industrialization in Europe (page 94) created a demand for new sources of raw materials and new markets, while the mass-production of quinine (which offered protection against the malaria endemic in Africa) and machine-guns gave the Europeans the ability to satisfy these demands by force. In the 1870s the French advanced inland from Senegal while the British began the conquest of Nigeria. In 1882 the British invaded and occupied Egypt, and the Belgians advanced up the Congo river. Next, Germany laid claim to Togoland, the Cameroons, South-west Africa and East Africa, each move provoking parallel actions by other powers. Portugal revived her effort to colonize the interior of Angola and Mozambique, while Britain claimed parts of East Africa (later Kenya and Uganda) and, on the initiative of the Cape politician and industrialist Cecil Rhodes, central Africa (later Zimbabwe, Zambia and Malawi).

Even larger gains accrued to the French, who swept into sub-Saharan Africa from three directions and gained control over almost one-third of the continent (map 1). With the conquest of Libya and Cyrenaica by Italy in 1911 and the partition of Morocco between France and Spain in 1912, of the 40 political units into which Africa had been arbitrarily divided, only two could claim any real independence: Ethiopia, which had defeated an Italian attempt at annexation in 1896, and Liberia, which enjoyed financial support from the United States. In little more than a generation, the Europeans had gained control over an additional 12 million square miles of territory.

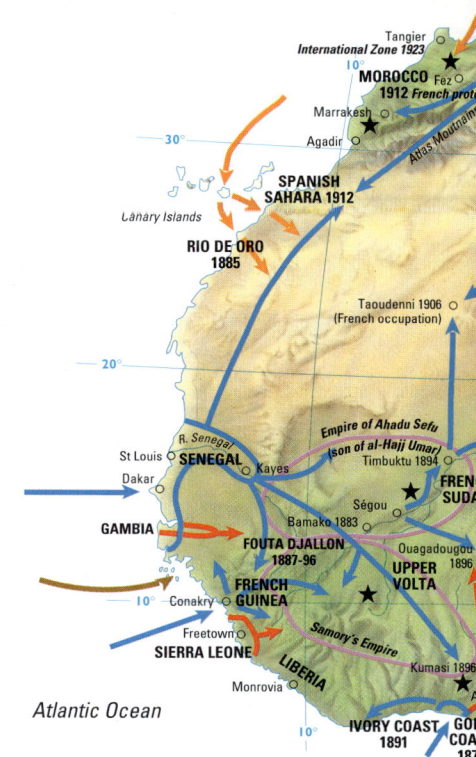

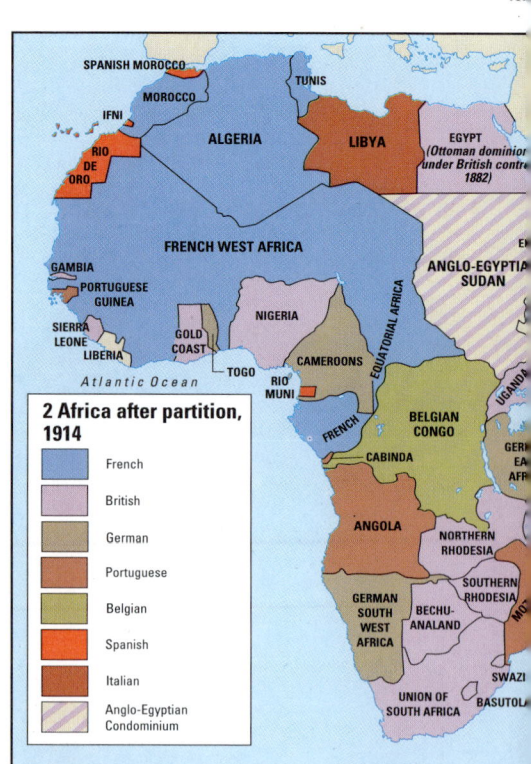

2 Africa after partition, 1914

# Latin America 1808-1929

Napoleon's invasion of Spain and Portugal in 1808 (page 93) enabled these countries' American colonies to gain independence. The revolt began in Argentina in 1810 and in Venezuela in 1811, helped by the decision of Great Britain and the United States to oppose intervention by the Iberian powers. The fall of Lima (1821) and Simón Bolívar's victory at Ayacucho (1824), deprived Spain of control over South America. In the North, early rebellions in Mexico were suppressed, but in 1823 a republic was proclaimed, and a last Spanish attempt at reconquest in 1829 met with defeat. Only Brazil made the transition to independence peacefully, as Portugal agreed to provide a constitution and in 1822 the Portuguese king's eldest son became Emperor Pedro I of Brazil. Only in 1889 when, following the abolition of slavery (1888), disgruntled plantation owners rose in revolt, did a federal republic replace the empire.

Independence remained in essence a political movement confined to the colonial aristocracy, who desired a transfer of authority without social change. The next half-century was dominated by military dictators who ruled in the interests of the privileged classes and squandered their assets on repeated territorial disputes. Mexico lost most, forfeiting vast territories to the United States (see page 98); but it was also the first state to introduce limited social reforms after the election of the Indian Benito Juarez as President in 1858.

A subsistence economy still prevailed in most areas. Although Brazil with its slave-operated coffee plantations offered an exception, elsewhere the great rural estates showed little interest in producing for the market. After 1880, overseas investment increased rapidly but selectively, concentrated mainly in Argentina, Brazil, Mexico and Chile. Moreover, even there, the foreign stimulus shifted those economies sharply towards the export of primary products: grain and meat from Argentina, nitrate from Chile, coffee and rubber from Brazil, oil from Mexico, and fruit from the so-called 'Banana Republics' of the central isthmus.

Most of these countries modernized and commercialized their production, and built docks and railways to expedite the export of food and raw materials. This attracted a new wave of immigrants and created a new urban and industrial proletariat as well as a middle class prospering from the export trade; but it left the majority of the rural population in abject poverty. Mexico under the repressive regime of Porfirio Díaz (1876-1911) exemplified these trends until in 1910 the country erupted in revolution: eventually, in 1917, a constitution incorporating major social and political reforms was adopted. Elsewhere, as long as prosperity continued – that is, until the Great Crash of 1929 (see page 130) – political and social pressures remained under control (albeit sometimes only thanks to armed intervention by the United States); but rapid and unbalanced economic expansion steadily undermined the regimes that promoted it.

# The expansion of the Russian Empire 1815-1917

For 40 years after the Congress of Vienna (1815) Russia remained the strongest military power in Europe, focusing her interests on the Balkans and on the straits leading from the Black Sea. Since most Balkan subjects of the Ottoman empire were Orthodox Slavs, Russia considered herself their natural protector; and because Turkey lay in the way of Russia's access to the Mediterranean, it desired Constantinople to remain amenable to Russian influence alone. However, France and Austria also had imperial ambitions in these areas, while Britain opposed any further Russian expansion. In 1854, therefore, following Russia's invasion of Turkey's Danubian provinces and destruction of the Ottoman fleet, France and Britain (supported by Austria) declared war and invaded the Crimea, eventually forcing Russia to evacuate the Balkans and to dismantle its Black Sea fleet. A further Russian attempt to liberate the Balkan Slavs from Turkish rule in 1877-8 also failed (page 102).

Russia proved far more successful in Asia (map 1). Her forces subdued the Kazakhs (1816-54), completed Russian control of the Caucasus (1857-64) and annexed the khanates of central Asia (1865-76). The imperial frontier now reached – and sometimes penetrated – the great mountain chains that separated it from Persia, Afghanistan, India and China. The colonization of North America also continued into the early 19th century, and forts were built as far south as California; but most were soon abandoned and Alaska was sold to the United States in 1867. On the other hand, China ceded to the Tsar the Amur basin and parts of the Pacific coast (where Vladivostok was founded in 1860), and leased Port Arthur (1898). This warm-water harbour, unimpeded by winter ice, was soon linked to the main Trans-Siberian railway (completed in 1903). But Russian expansion conflicted with Japanese designs. The two powers had already clashed over their interests in Korea and south Manchuria, following Japan's victory over China in 1894-5 (page 116), and in 1904-5 Japan attacked Russia, forcing her to return most of her gains in the Far East.

This humiliating defeat fanned the flames of domestic unrest. Shaken by the backwardness exposed in the Crimean War, Tsar Alexander II (1855-81) had initiated a number of reforms in the 1860s: new local government organizations; educational improvements; and radical changes to the legal system. The emancipation of the serfs in 1861 was the cornerstone of the reforms. However, still confined to their villages, many peasants felt aggrieved that they often had to acquire by purchase less land than they had previously worked. At the same time, from 1890 the government embarked on an industrialization programme with railways at its centre. Many of the lines aimed to facilitate the movement of troops to frontier areas in case of war, but it allowed not only migration from overcrowded central Russia to western Siberia, but also the movement of peasants to urban areas to man a growing number of factories. Between 1863 and 1914 Russia's urban population increased from 6 to 18.6 million.

In 1905, in the wake of Japan's victory, revolutionary parties proved quick to exploit the low incomes and general hardships created by these rapid changes, while the new professional classes pressed for political

reform (map 2). Unrest in the towns spread to the countryside and even to the Black Sea fleet, led by the battleship Potemkin, forcing Tsar Nicholas II (1894-1917) to grant a constitution, including a *duma*, or parliament; but by 1907 the government had regained full control. Nevertheless the 1905 revolution irreparably weakened the old order, and after 1912 another wave of social unrest swept the empire. Internally, Russia was in no position to meet the challenge of the First World War in 1914.

# Nationalism in Europe 1815-1914

Nationalism flourished in Europe in the wake of the French Revolution (page 93), but it remained confined largely to the middle classes and proved relatively short-lived. The Great Powers at the Congress of Vienna in 1815 aimed to restore Europe (as far as possible) to its pre-war condition by combating both liberalism and nationalism and by creating a barrier around France. To that end Holland received the Austrian Netherlands (later Belgium); Prussia took over Westphalia and much of the Rhineland; Sardinia-Piedmont annexed Genoa; Russia retained Finland and most of Poland; and Austria gained Venetia and Lombardy.

By 1830, however, when a new wave of liberal and national agitation arose, the Great Powers no longer worked in unison, enabling Greece (page 102) and Belgium to obtain independence. In 1848-9, when an outburst of nationalism erupted into full-scale revolution, the solidarity of the conservative powers – coupled with divisions among the nationalists themselves – still sufficed to maintain

1 The unification of Italy, 1859-70
- Kingdom of Sardinia in 1815
- territory annexed 1859
- territory annexed May 1860
- territory annexed November 1860
- territory annexed 1866
- territory lost to France 1860
- French from 1768, formerly Genoese
- Italian border 1914

2 The unification of Germany, 1815-71

- Prussia in 1815
- acquired by Prussia 1815-66
- boundary of German Confederation of 1815
- boundary of North German Confederation 1866
- Imperial territory of Alsace-Lorraine 1871
- free city
- boundary of German Empire 1871
- Austro-Prussian forces attack Denmark 1864
- Prussian armies in the war with Austria 1866
- German armies in the Franco-Prussian war 1870-71

the status quo. Shortly afterwards, a new generation of statesmen began to use nationalism for their own ends. Cavour sought a unification of Italy along conservative lines, in the interests of Piedmont-Sardinia, and was hostile to the more revolutionary nationalism of Garibaldi and Mazzini. Bismarck in Prussia, too, wanted unification to achieve his aim of a conservative, Prussian-dominated German state. Both used diplomacy and war to achieve their objectives: Cavour allied with France before attacking Austria in 1859, securing the unification of Italy (except for Venetia and the Papal States) by 1861 (see map 1). Bismarck allied with Austria in order to defeat Denmark (1864), then in concert with Italy attacked Austria (1866), and finally defeated France (1870-1),

achieving in the process the unification of Germany (map 2).

Liberal nationalists later endorsed both achievements, but neither satisfied the nationalism they had aroused. Italy still laid claim to the Alto Adige and Istria; Bismarck's 'Small German' solution, which excluded Austria, disappointed those who hankered after a Greater Germany. Nevertheless, the four short wars fought between 1859 and 1871 solved the Italian and German questions, and re-drew the map of Central Europe. Moreover, the Great Powers now remained at peace for over four decades, and although nationalist grievances continued to fester, territorial disputes within Europe ceased to divide most governments.

# Imperialism 1830-1914

Until 1830, the search for oriental luxuries remained the driving force behind European imperialism, and (with the important exception of India: page 90) the European stake in Asia and Africa remained confined to trading stations and the strategic outposts necessary to protect trade. Thereafter two new factors transformed the situation. First came the enforced 'opening' of the key markets – Turkey and Egypt (1838), Persia (1841), China (1842), Japan (1858) – to European, particularly British, commerce. Then, from the 1870s, a new phase of the Industrial Revolution (page 94) provoked a search for raw materials to feed the new industries. In the scramble for these resources between 1880 and 1914, Europe added almost 9 million square miles (23.4 million km$^2$) – one-fifth of the land area of the globe – to its overseas colonial possessions.

France and Britain took the lead. The former conquered Algeria after 1830, annexed Tahiti and the Marquesas in the 1840s, expanded its colony in Senegal in the 1850s and began the conquest of Indo-China in 1859. Britain, both to forestall the French and to safeguard its position in India, claimed sovereignty over Australia and New Zealand (page 100), and acquired Singapore (1819), Malacca (1824), Hong Kong (1842), Burma (1852), and Lagos (1861) (map 1).

The same imperatives underlay British expansion after 1880, except that the number of competitors to forestall increased. Thus the French empire grew between 1871 and 1914 by nearly 4 million square miles (10.4 million km$^2$) and 47 million people (mainly in north and west Africa and Indo-China, where Laos and Tongking were added to Cambodia and Cochin-China, but she also secured Madagascar and some Pacific islands); Germany also acquired an empire of 1 million square miles (2.6 million km$^2$) and 14 million colonial subjects (in South-West Africa, Togoland, the Cameroons, Tanganyika and the Pacific islands); Italy obtained several outposts in Africa; the United States annexed the Philippines, Guam, Hawaii and some Caribbean islands; and Russia began to expand in central Asia. Britain too managed to acquire extensive new territories in Africa which almost linked Cape Town with Cairo, more Pacific islands (including Fiji), and parts of the Indonesian archipelago (map 2). She added 88 million subjects to her empire and, by 1914, exercized authority over a fifth of the world's landmass and a quarter of its peoples.

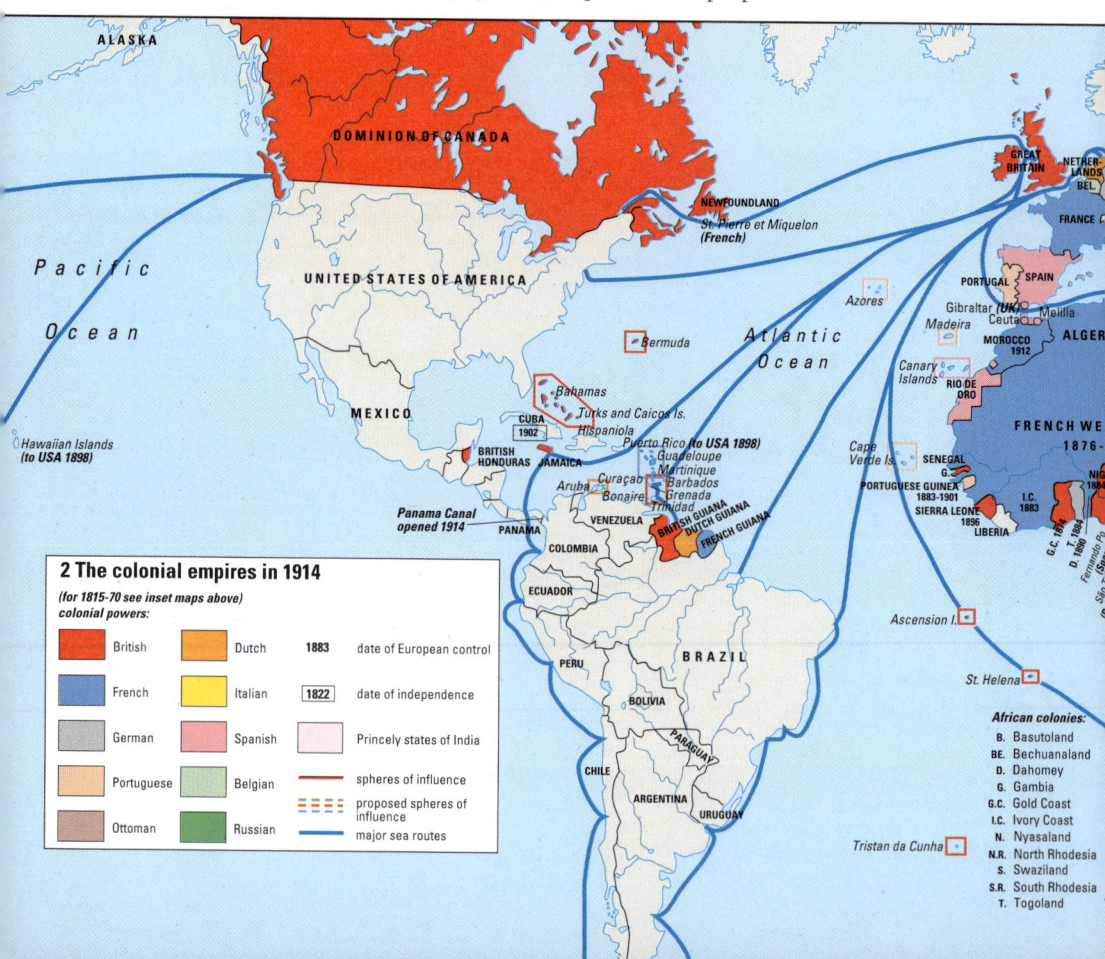

In retrospect, the fragility of these European empires, so hastily assembled, is obvious. None of the imperial powers possessed the resources to govern them effectively and European imperialism proved more ephemeral than anyone at the time imagined; yet it left an indelible mark on the peoples of Africa and Asia, propelling them willingly or unwillingly into the 20th century.

# North America 1865-1929

Although the United States made a remarkably rapid recovery after the Civil War (page 99), development remained very uneven. In the defeated South, the period of Reconstruction (1865-77) proved a bitter experience. South Carolina, which in 1860 had ranked third in the nation in per capita wealth, ranked 40th ten years later; and other once-prosperous states did scarcely better. The 4 million liberated black slaves fared worst, being left (as Frederick Douglass wrote) without money, property or friends. Although the population of the Union surged from 31 million in 1861 to 92 million in 1910, most of the increase by-passed the South and concentrated wealth and power in the north-east and the upper Mid-West. Only around 1920 did cheap labour attract textile industry to the South (map 1).

The settlement of the Great Plains, made possible by the railway boom after 1870, constituted perhaps the most striking achievement of the post-war period. The track in operation increased from 30,000 miles (48,000 km) in 1860 to 163,000 (262,000 km) in 1890 (at which point it exceeded the size of the entire European rail system); the number of farms rose from 2 million in 1860 to 6 million in 1910; and the population living west of the Mississippi grew from 6 million to 26 million. Yet the bulk of the population remained concentrated in the north-east (map 3), and most of the 25 million immigrants arriving between 1870 and 1914 stayed there, providing cheap labour for American industry.

Railways played an even more prominent role in the development of Canada. The United States made no secret of its hope to absorb the provinces and thus create a continent-wide empire. After the acquisition of Alaska by the United States, this pressure grew, but the Canadians frustrated their neighbours' intentions by forming the Canadian Federation in 1867, completed by the purchase of Rupert's Land from the Hudson's Bay Company (1869) and the adhesion of

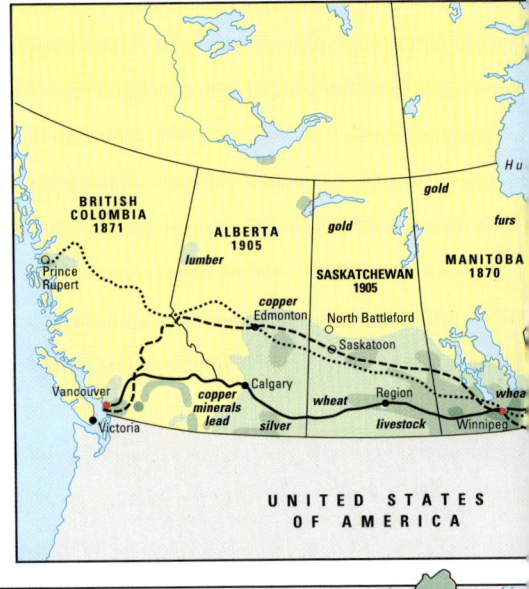

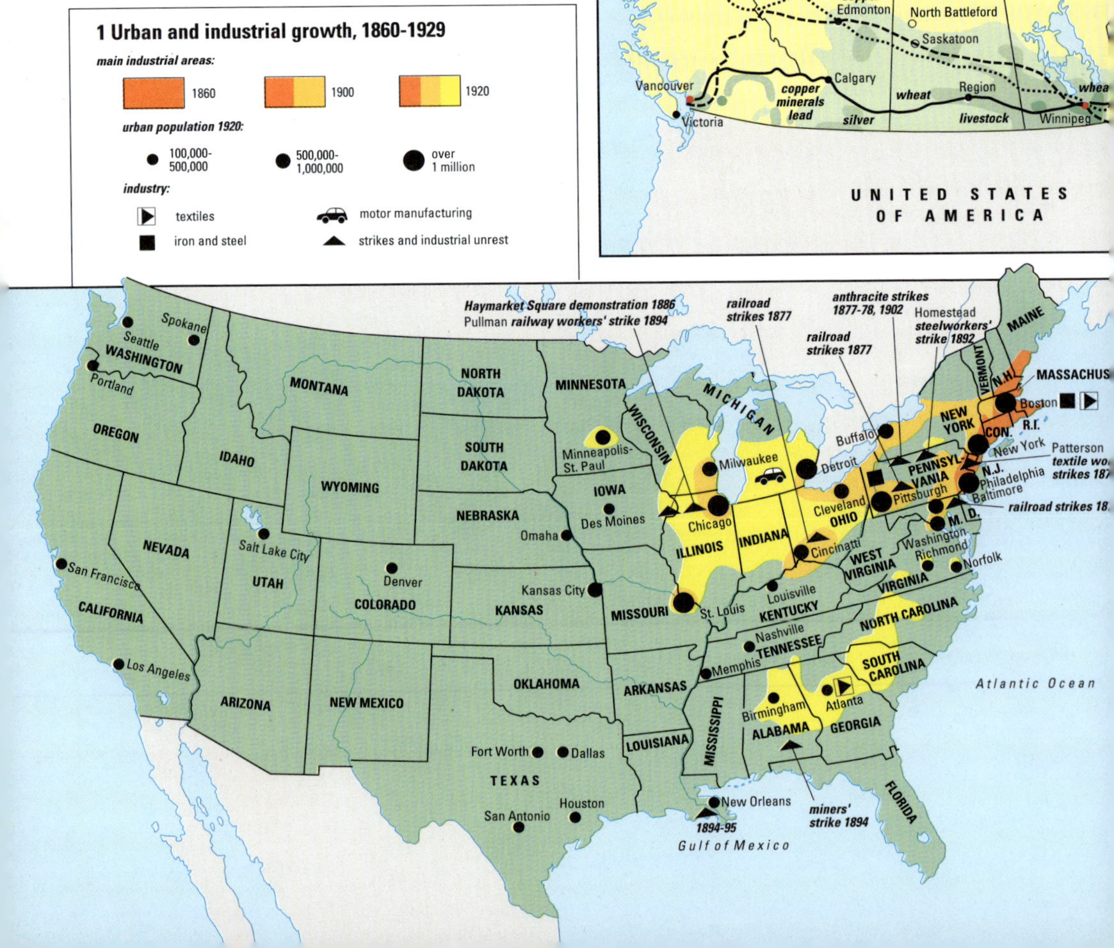

Manitoba (1870) and British Columbia (1871). The great transcontinental railways – the Canadian Pacific (completed 1885) followed by the Canadian Northern and the National Transcontinental – became the lifeblood of the new Dominion, opening Manitoba and Saskatchewan, and turning Canada into one of the world's leading wheat producers. It also facilitated the exploitation of rich wheat deposits, particularly copper and nickel (map 2). Overall, Canada's industrial output increased from $190 million in 1890 to over $500 million in 1914.

This achievement was dwarfed, however, by the economic and territorial growth of the United States. Output of iron and steel increased 20-fold between 1870 and 1913, by which time steel production exceeded that of Britain and Germany combined, and the United States remained the world's leading agricultural producer. Meanwhile, in 1867 Alaska was purchased from Russia; in 1898 (following a successful war with Spain) the Philippines, Guam, Puerto Rico and Hawaii were annexed, the latter after many years of American encroachment in the islands' affairs; and in 1903 Cuba and the Panama Canal Zone became protectorates. The United States now possessed the political and economic might to intervene almost anywhere on the world stage: in Mexico in 1914 and again in 1916, and – on a far greater scale – in Europe in 1917-18 (page 124).

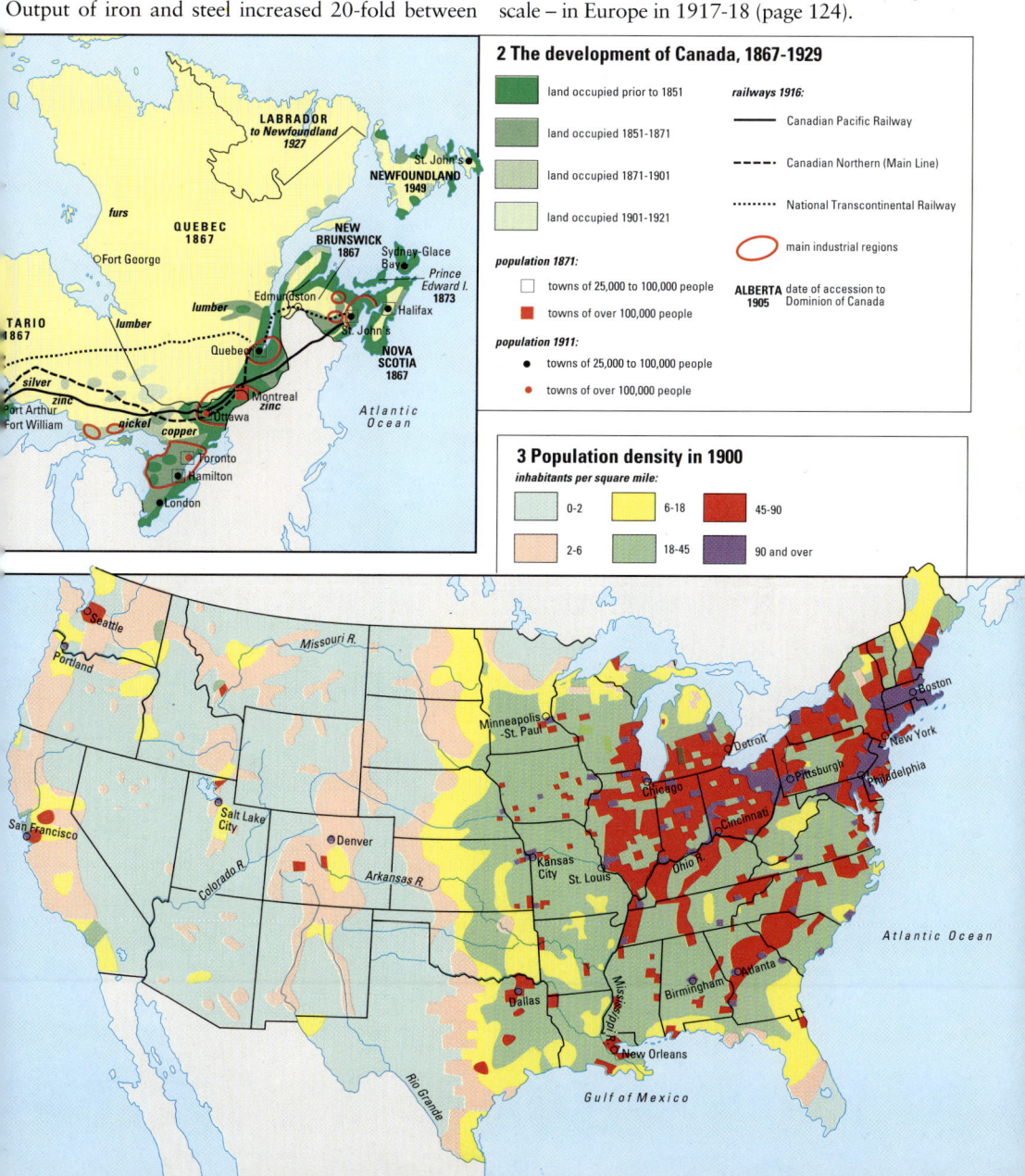

# Japan 1868-1941

The Tokugawa shoguns (page 82) gave Japan over two centuries of peace and prosperity. In 1868, however, internal tensions, combined with the pressure of Western powers to open Japan to foreign trade, resulted in a revolution (known as the Meiji Restoration) which replaced the shogun and the feudal structure with a modern system of government. The new Japanese leaders implemented widespread reforms in the belief that a modern economy and military would ensure Japan's international independence and equality. They instituted a national education system (which by 1900 provided teaching for 90 per cent of children), a conscript army, and a navy with modern ships. Legal codes, largely based on French and German models, were introduced from 1882. The economic reforms were wide-reaching; the first railway opened in 1872 and by 1906 the system linked most parts of the country; up to one-third of state expenditure went on developing commerce and industry (map 1); and a land tax reform in 1873 provided a secure source of revenue for the government. The shifting structure of Japanese foreign trade (see inset table) illustrates the dramatic impact of these changes. Whereas in 1878-82, manufactured goods represented half of all imports but only 7 per cent of exports, in 1918-22 the ratio had reversed: finished manufactures now accounted for over 40 per cent of sales and only 15 per cent of purchases. Moreover the total value of Japan's exports rose in this period from 30 million to 1.8 billion yen.

International recognition of Japan's new status was nevertheless slow in coming: consular jurisdiction survived until 1894, and the unequal treaties negotiated in the 1850s with the Western powers remained in force until 1911. As Japan's strength and confidence grew, however, so did nationalist and imperialist ambitions. In 1894-5 a victorious war against China, arising from disputes in Korea, ended in a treaty granting Taiwan to Japan. Russo-Japanese rivalry over Manchuria led to clashes in Manchuria and culminated in Japanese victory in the war of 1904-5. The Treaty of Portsmouth (1905) which ended that war gave Japan a lease of

territory in China and extensive rights in South Manchuria. In 1910 she acquired Korea. Japanese support for the victorious Western powers in World War I brought few further rewards, however, and the country's military leaders became frustrated. After 1931, under the impact of the Great Depression (page 130), Japan overran first Manchuria and then – despite strong opposition from the United States – northern China in an attempt to achieve economic self-sufficiency (map 2). Germany's victory over France and the Netherlands in 1940 offered an opportunity to expand southwards – thereby gaining control over valuable oil fields in Borneo and Burma – precipitating full-scale war with the Western powers (page 134). Paradoxically, Japan's total defeat and the ensuing American occupation propelled her even more decisively into the modern world than the Meiji restoration had done.

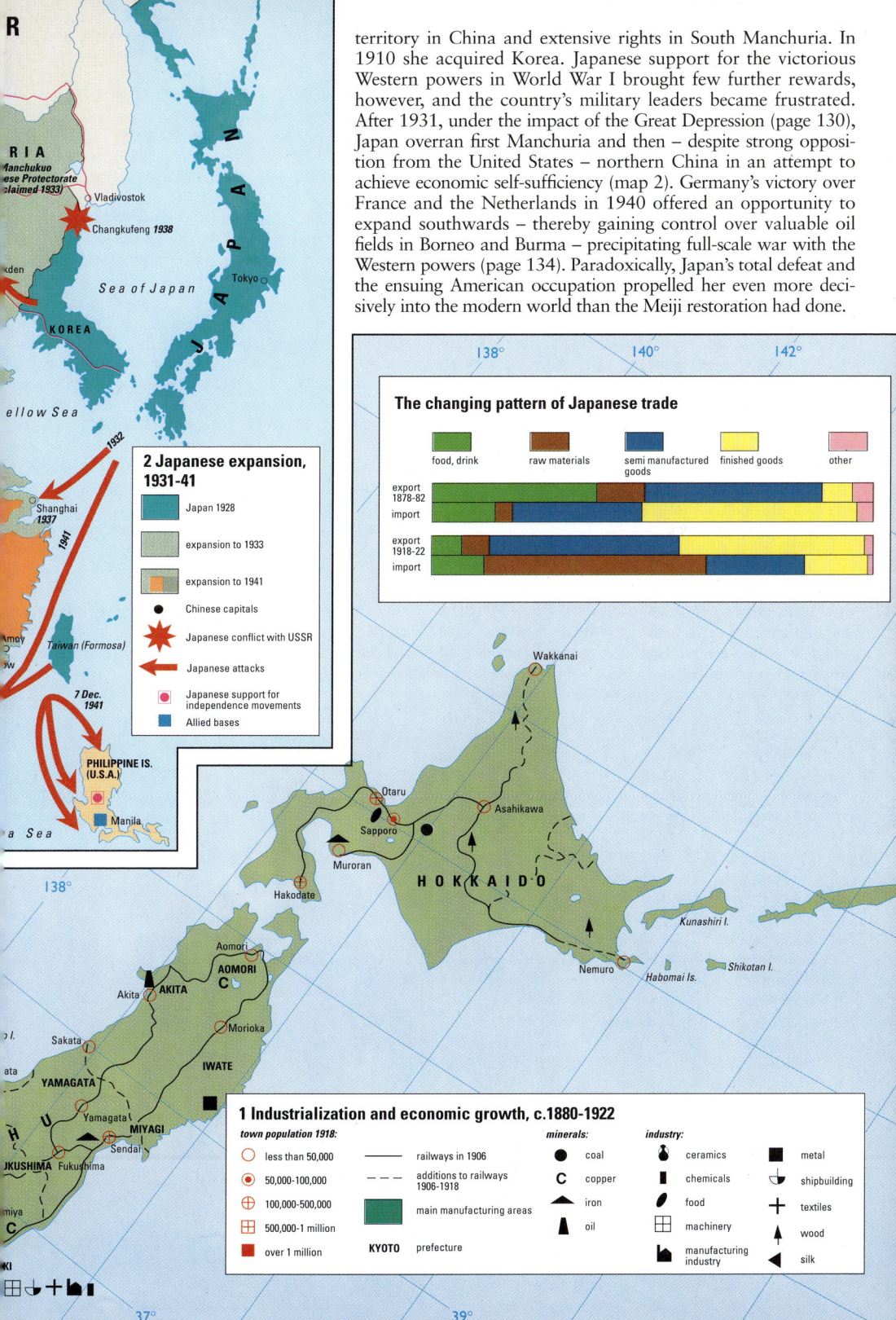

# The European powers 1878-1914

The unification of Germany and Italy (page 110) seemed for a time to have resolved the major questions which had disturbed the peace of Europe since 1848. Bismarck, the architect of German unification, concentrated after 1871 on building a system of alliances that would ensure the future of the new empire, mainly by isolating France, which proved unable to reconcile itself to the rise of the new German empire, and for almost 20 years he succeeded in convincing the rest of Europe of Germany's conservative and pacific intentions. In time, however, the alliances that had seemed defensive became aggressive and destabilizing. Meanwhile, although the achievements of Bismarck and Cavour reduced nationalist fervour in central Europe, they stirred up a hornet's nest in the Balkans, where the struggles of various national groups for independence from the Turks inevitably involved the neighbouring powers, Russia and Austria (which, after its exclusion from Germany in 1866 became far more interested in the Balkans: map 1).

Revolts in the Balkans between 1875 and 1878, culminating in Russian intervention and war with the Turks, resulted in the treaty of Berlin (brokered by Bismarck) which either confirmed or established the independence of Serbia, Montenegro, Romania and Bulgaria and granted Austria a mandate to govern Bosnia and Herzegovina. In 1879 Germany and Austria signed a defensive alliance, expanded to include Italy in 1882 (map 2a). Russia, satisfied that Slav interest had been met in the Balkans, turned increasingly to her interests in Central Asia and the Far East. The main European rivalries were now between Britain and Russia in Asia, and Britain and France in Africa. Britain remained isolated in Europe, while France and Russia signed an alliance in 1894 as a counterweight to the strength of the alliance bloc based around Germany.

The situation changed after 1897, however, when Germany began to seek a 'place in the sun'. This was not unreasonable; but by then most places in the sun had been occupied by others, and German policy – which involved building a High Seas Fleet to rival that of Britain – therefore seemed a constitute a threat to the established imperial powers. As a result, Britain resolved its differences with France in 1904, and with Russia in 1907, and France settled its long-standing dispute with Italy in 1902. Thereafter, the Triple Entente with France and Russia became the lynch-pin of British foreign policy, the only firm assurance against the German 'threat'. Germany, on the other became concerned with the danger of 'encirclement' by a hostile ring constructed by Great Britain (map 2b).

As a result, a dangerous simplification of alignments occurred into a bi-polar system: the Triple Alliance and the Triple Entente drew tighter, and Germany in particular grew closer to its only dependable ally, Austria. When Austria annexed Bosnia and Herzegovina in 1908, Germany gave her qualified support, though enough to rekindle Austro-Russian antagonism in the Balkans. During the Balkan wars (1912-13), in which a Russian-sponsored Balkan League consisting of Serbia, Greece and Bulgaria attempted to drive the Turks out of Europe, the two diplomatic systems still cooperated; but Austria stood aghast at the consequent enlargement of Serbia – which almost doubled its size – and feared Serb agitation for an independent south Slav state (map 2c).

The assassination of the heir to the Austrian throne in Sarajevo (Bosnia) in June 1914 provided what seemed to the Austrian government like its last chance to deal with Serbia before it grew too powerful, and Germany threw its entire weight behind its ally. Russia, however, could not afford to leave Serbia in the lurch and began to mobilize against Austria. Germany regarded this as a direct threat, and also began to mobilize. However, fearing attack from Russia's allies in the West, German Grand Strategy called for an immediate attack on France – in the hope that it could be knocked out of the war before Russia advanced in force. On 28 July, Austria declared war on Serbia; on 1 August 1914 Germany declared war on Russia, and two days later on France. The diplomatic system created by Bismarck, coupled with the volatile situation in the Balkans, had produced a world war (page 124).

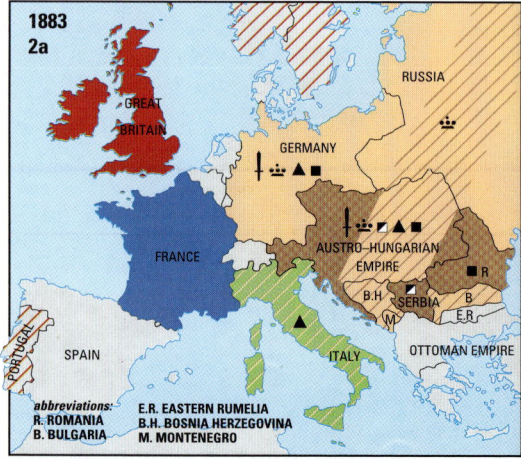

**2 European alliances**
- Austro-German alliance (the Dual Alliance) 1879-1918
- Three Emperors' Alliance 1881-87
- Austro-Serbian Alliance 1881-95
- Triple Alliance 1882-1915
- Austro-German-Romanian Alliance 1883-1916
- Franco-Russian Alliance 1894-1917
- Russo-Bulgarian military convention 1902-13

*stripes, similar and identical colours indicate an entente or community of interests*

abbreviations:
R: ROMANIA  E.R. EASTERN RUMELIA
B: BULGARIA  B.H. BOSNIA HERZEGOVINA
             M. MONTENEGRO

# The world economy on the eve of the Great War

The integration of the world's economy into a single interdependent whole formed one of the principal developments of the period 1870-1914. Europe (and to a lesser extent the United States) stood at the heart of this process, emitting the impulses that opened up the remaining areas of the globe to Western exploration and exploitation.

Three interrelated aspects deserve special attention. First came the development of better means of communication. In 1870, railways remained largely confined to Europe (60,400 miles, 97,250 km of track) and North America (56,300 miles, 90,600 km): the rest of the world could boast only 9100 miles (14,650 km). By 1911, however, the total network of tracks had increased to 657,000 miles (1.06 million km) – 175,000 miles (280,000 km) of them outside Europe and North America – and included some spectacular transcontinental links: across the United States (four between 1869 and 1893), Canada (1885), Russia (1904) and the Andes (1910). The expansion of world shipping was equally striking, with not only a spectacular rise in the total tonnage, but a shift from sail to steam which increased the speed and regularity of shipments. However, the main shipping traffic, both passenger and freight, took place among the advanced countries and the white dominions, or between them and the producers of the raw materials they required. Canal construction also continued apace – above all the Suez Canal, completed in 1869, which carried 437,000 tons in 1870 and over 20 million in 1913; and the Panama Canal, completed in 1914, which carried 5 million tons of cargo in its first year. These spectacular totals reflected the enormous savings in distance – 41 per cent for vessels sailing from Liverpool to Bombay, 60 per cent for vessels sailing from New York to San Francisco.

Finally, messages travelled around the world with increasing speed. Cables laid beneath the oceans linked the continents – between Britain and North America (1858); from Vancouver to Brisbane (1902) – followed by telephones (with international lines from 1887) and wireless stations (from 1897). These developments paralleled a boom in commerce.

Foreign trade tripled in volume between 1870 and 1914, although (again) most of the activity occurred among the industrialized countries, or between them and their suppliers of primary goods or their new markets. In 1913, only 11 per cent of the world's trade took place between the primary producers themselves. Britain ranked as the world's largest trading nation in 1860, but by 1913 it had lost ground to both the United States and Germany: British and German exports in that year each totalled $2.3 billion, and those of the United States exceeded $2.4 billion.

3 The share of world trade

Britain remained the world's financial capital, however, as well as its largest lender, with almost $20 billion in foreign investments by 1914 – slightly more than those of France, Germany, Holland and Belgium combined. The United States and Russia were in fact net borrowers of foreign capital. Investments within Europe and North America on the whole assisted and accelerated economic advancement, helping to create the costly infrastructure (such as railways and other public works) for developing nations that would in time repay these debts. By contrast, investments in non-industrial regions (such as the Russian and Ottoman empires) and overseas territories that lacked both the knowledge and the power to direct the capital flow, served to colonize rather than develop them, destroying native industries and creating dangerous political and economic pressures which would, in time, produce conflict between rich nations and poor nations and demands for a new economic order (page 160).

# The Chinese republic 1911-1949

By 1911 the imperial government of China was thoroughly discredited (page 89) and an army mutiny led to the emperor's abdication. But the Republic proclaimed in 1912, with Sun Yat-sen as its first president, was overwhelmed by its inherited problems, and Sun was soon deposed by Yuan Shih-k'ai, the most powerful general of the old regime. After Yuan's death in 1916 power passed to provincial warlords, whose armies caused untold damage and millions of casualties. Compounding this misery were the expansionist policies of Japan and the foreign powers, based in the Treaty Ports (page 88), who interfered in the Chinese economy and in Chinese politics.

In 1919, the refusal of the Paris Peace Conference to abrogate foreign privileges provoked spontaneous urban uprisings. These provided a new constituency for Sun Yat-sen, who in 1923 reorganized his Nationalist (Kuomintang; KMT) Party, allied with the Chinese Communist Party (founded 1921), and prepared to reunite the country. But Sun died in 1925 and it was Chiang Kai-shek, the Moscow-trained general of the KMT army, who in 1926 marched northwards to eliminate the warlords. Helped by peasant and workers' uprisings along his route, Chiang proved remarkably successful, but in 1927 he turned on his allies, massacring the Communists in Shanghai. However KMT direct rule remained limited to the lower Yangtze (map 1). Nevertheless, the Japanese, fearing the potential challenge from a reunited China, decided to reinforce their hold in the north and overran Manchuria (1931) and Jehol (1933).

Although KMT purges had virtually eliminated Communism from the cities, peasant disaffection – arising from the absence of land reform – offered an alternative constituency. From his base at Chingkang Shan, Mao Tse-Tung and others created a new centre of revitalized communism, developing a peasant-based party rather than an urban, proletarian party on the Russian model. In 1929 KMT pressure compelled Mao and his followers to move first to Kiangsi, and then in 1934 to the north-west (the 'Long March': map 2).

In 1937 Japanese forces invaded northern and central China and the KMT retreated to the interior, where they remained until the Japanese surrender in 1945. A race to occupy the liberated areas now ensued, with the Communists gaining much of the north and most of Manchuria, and the KMT re-occupying the south. In 1947 hostilities between the two sides erupted into a civil war from which the Communists emerged victorious. The People's Republic of China was proclaimed in October 1949, and soon afterwards the KMT fled to Taiwan. For the first time since 1911, a strong regime controlled all of mainland China – albeit most of the country had been devastated by the warlords, the Japanese occupation and the civil war.

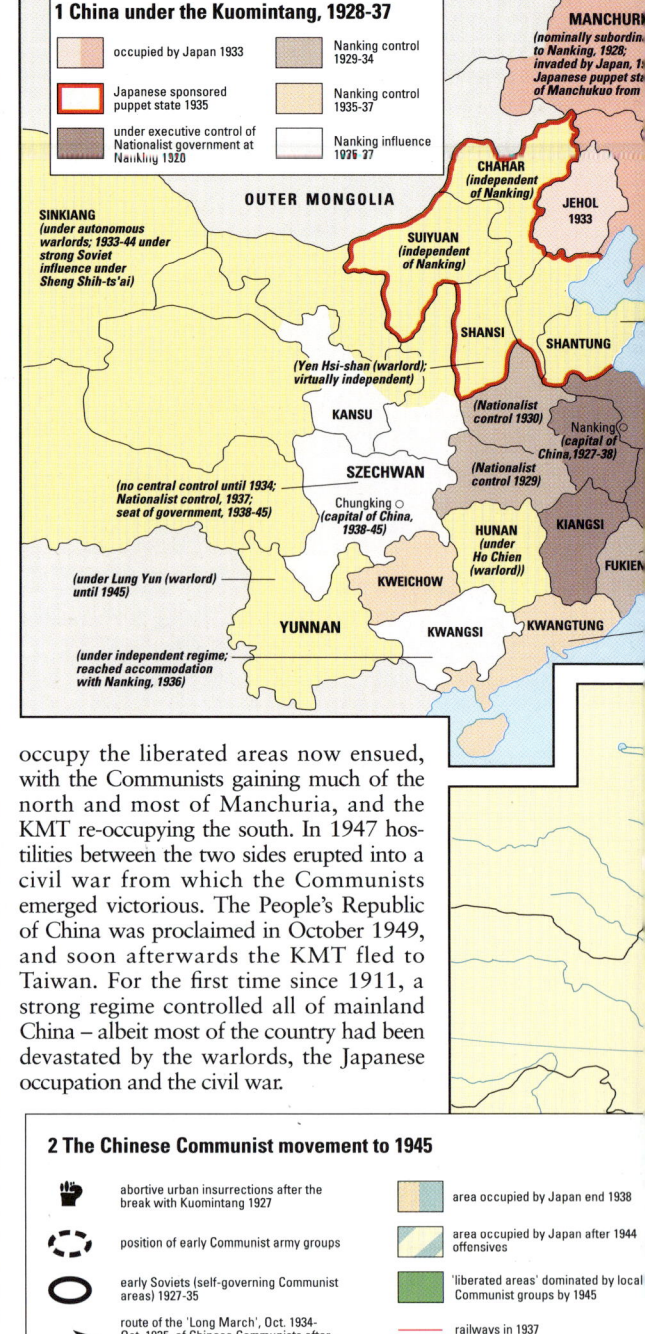

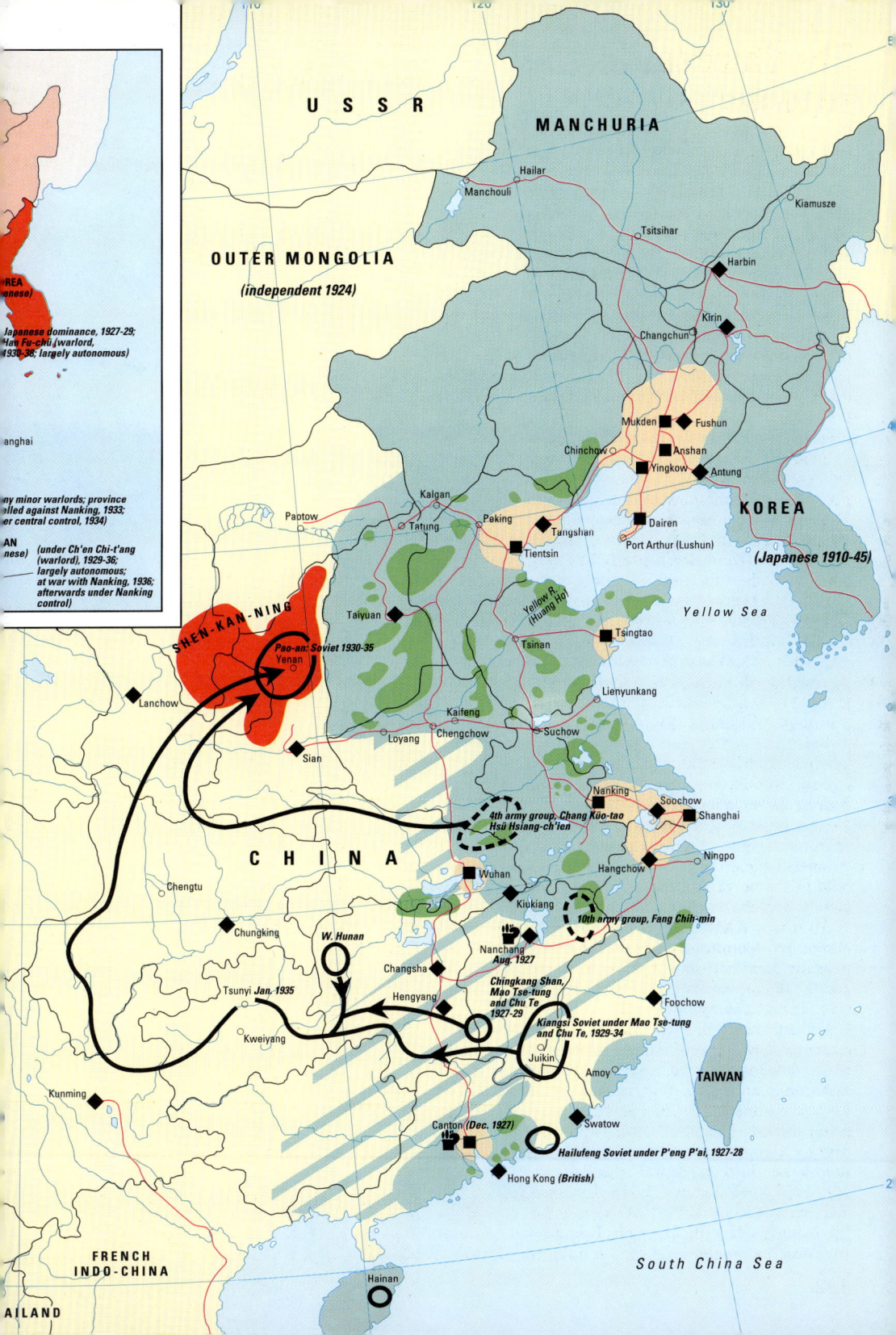

# The First World War
## 1914-1918

All the war-plans of the Great Powers in 1914 envisaged a short war. The German Schlieffen Plan called for an attack on northern France through Belgium, leading to the rapid collapse of the French government before Russia had time to mobilize (page 118). It almost succeeded: the Germans came within 40 miles of Paris, but not before Russian armies had invaded East Prussia. Although their advance was halted at Tannenberg (August), important German reserves were diverted from the Western front just as a spirited counter-attack by French and British troops began at the Marne (September). The two sides now spread their forces out and dug in, until their trenches stretched from the Channel coast to Switzerland.

The war in the west (map 2) turned into a war of attrition. Each side launched repeated offensives, with appalling casualties but little gain, for railways were able to bring up reinforcements before the slow-moving front-line troops could make good any advantage. In 1916 the British, under Field Marshal Douglas Haig, made a major frontal assault on German lines at the river Somme. On the first day of the battle there were 60,000 British casualties, mowed down as they advanced through the barbed wire. Haig threw his forces into an unwinnable conflict for another four months. Both sides experienced terrible losses and little was achieved. Neither side could break the trench stalemate by pursuing alternative strategies. The British and French attempted a series of attacks from the rear: in the Dardanelles and Mesopotamia against the Ottoman empire, which entered the war in November 1914 on the side of the Central Powers (Germany and Austria); on Austria's southern frontier after Italy declared war in May 1915; at Salonika in Greece in support of Serbia. All failed. The Germans countered by building a fleet of submarines with the express intention of bringing Britain to its knees by attacking vulnerable food imports on which Britain relied. In 1917 unrestricted submarine warfare failed to reduce Britain's food supply by more than a fraction, but provoked the United States into war with Germany.

On the eastern front, which stretched for twice the distance of that in the west, warfare remained more mobile and both Germany and Austria scored major successes. In 1915 the former overran a huge area of Poland, whose resources it ruthlessly exploited, while the latter occupied most of Serbia. In 1917 the combination of huge losses and economic chaos broke the fighting spirit of the Russian forces and provoked revolution and military collapse (page 126). At the peace of Brest-Litovsk in March 1918 Germany gained the Ukraine, Poland, Finland and the Baltic provinces.

Instead of moving its forces across to the West, however, Germany sent its troops to occupy these new territories – even Finland – and at the same time launched a final, all-out offensive in the West, in an attempt to break the deadlock. Once again it came close to success but the Allied line held and in July, aided by tanks and reinforced by American forces and money, a counter-attack began that not only pushed the German army back towards the German frontier, but that won the war. The German line began to fall back and morale collapsed: by October 1918, with Austria close to disintegration and with Germany facing a grave political crisis at home, the Berlin government sued for an armistice, granted on 11 November 1918.

At the peace conferences held in and around Paris in 1919, the victors imposed upon Germany, Austria, Hungary, and Bulgaria notable losses of territory, huge reparations and stringent reductions in their armed forces. The draconian nature of the settlement made it inevitable that, although over 8 million men had perished in the fighting, and the financial cost of the war totalled over $186 worldwide, it would not be (as so many had hoped) 'the war to end all wars'.

# The Russian Revolution 1917-1945

By 1917 the strain of war had fatally weakened the Tsarist government: liberals, businessmen, generals and aristocrats all plotted its overthrow. In the end sheer hunger turned a general strike and bread queues into a revolutionary movement which in February forced the Tsar to abdicate, and power passed to a provisional government of prominent *duma* (parliament) politicians. The revolutionary committees (soviets) did not disband, however, and gradually the 'peace, bread and land' programme of the Bolshevik group, led by V. I. Lenin, gained support. In October, the Bolsheviks seized control of strategic points in Petrograd (formerly St Petersburg), arrested the Provisional Government, and assumed power in the name of the soviets. The same soon happened in other cities (map 1).

No one thought they would retain power for long. The overriding need was for peace, and Lenin insisted, on accepting the onerous terms imposed by Germany in the treaty of Brest-Litovsk (March 1918: page 124); but almost immediately the Bolsheviks (who now took the name 'Communists') faced massive invasions by forces loyal to the Tsar and assisted by troops from Britain, France, Czechoslovakia, Poland and other 'Entente' (anti-Bolshevik) powers. Nevertheless, by 1920 the civil war had been won, albeit at the cost of 13 million lives and immense damage to property. Lenin now introduced his 'New Economic Policy', which by 1925 allowed the Russian economy to regain its pre-war industrial level. In 1928 Lenin's successor, Joseph Stalin, introduced a Five Year Plan of industrialization, and the following year embarked on the forced collectivization of agriculture, which transformed small, individual peasant holdings into huge state and collective farms. The results of the policy proved disastrous, however. It was implemented without adequate machinery, and poorly organized. Crop yields fell, and a great famine in 1932-3 claimed millions of victims. This rural catastrophe caused some 40 million people to move into the cities, where their fresh labour was used mainly for construction, making the industrial growth rates of the Soviet economy under the first and second Five Year Plans (1928-37) look both startling and unique.

But this industrialization took place against a background of state-directed terror as Stalin consolidated the Communist dictatorship. The security forces (the NKVD) executed perhaps 12 million people, while a further 10 million suffered imprisonment in forced labour camps (see map 2). Economic growth enabled Russia to survive the German invasion in 1941 (page 132) partly because over 1500 factories were moved to safety further east. Nevertheless the setback remained undeniable: a further 20 million Soviet citizens died in the conflict and, although the USSR mobilized more fully than any other state in World War II, its industrial output in 1946 stood at only 70 per cent of the 1940 level.

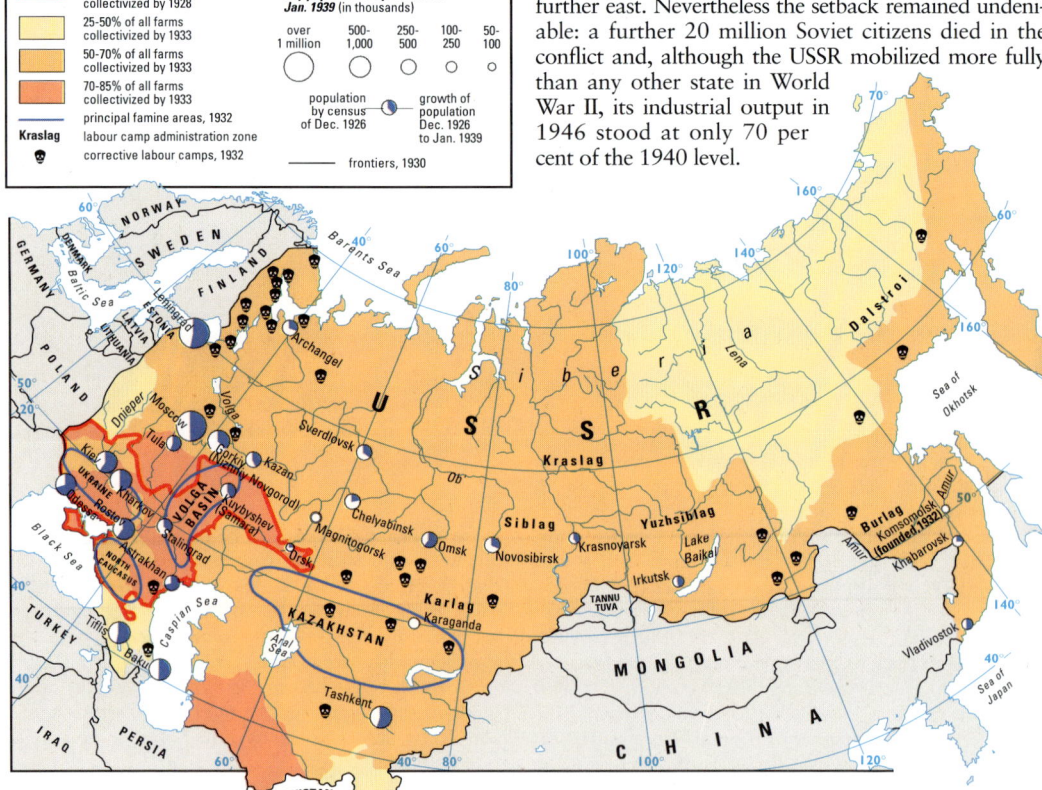

2 Collectivization and population movements, 1923-39

# European political problems 1919-1939

The collapse of the Central Powers in the autumn of 1918, and the subsequent peace treaties (page 124), brought about major frontier changes, the emergence of several new states, and the enlargement of others on the winning side (see map 1). The dismemberment of the Austro-Hungarian empire, the disarmament and the imposition of reparation payments on Germany and her allies, and the effects of the Russian Revolution and civil war (page 126) completely altered the balance of political power in Europe (map 1). In terms of population and industrial strength, however, Germany, although weakened, still had no rival in central Europe. The only hope of those who stood to lose by a revision of the peace treaties was the maintenance of overwhelming collective military strength against any revival of German strength. France tried to restrain Germany by signing alliances with the new states of Poland and Czechoslovakia, but Britain proved reluctant to enter into new continental commitments, and the United States withdrew into isolationism. However, Germany's formal recognition of the post-war frontier settlements with France and Belgium by the Locarno treaties (1925) inaugurated a new spirit of cooperation. Germany was welcomed back into the community of nations and after 1928 many nations signed the 'Kellogg-Briand Pact', which outlawed aggressive war.

But indications of stability proved illusory. Many states, especially in eastern Europe, displayed alarming political instability; and all European participants emerged economically weakened from the World War. Italy – which had run up huge debts and lost 600,000 men in the war, but gained only 9000 square miles (14,400 km²) of new territory at the peace – soon became ungovernable, with civil war between left- and right-wing extremists prevailing in many cities until in

1922 the Fascist party, led by Benito Mussolini, took power. In other parts of Europe, the cost of the war and the defects of the peace settlements, coupled with the strains of economic readjustment and disastrous inflation, strengthened anti-parliamentary and revolutionary movements of both left and right. And with the onset of the Great Depression in 1929 (page 130), financial and economic chaos returned to the entire continent. Unemployment rose drastically, especially in Germany where after 1930 the anti-parliamentary movements of both right and left, the Nazis (National Socialists) and the Communists, increased their strength enormously until in 1933 the Nazi leader, Adolf Hitler, became Chancellor and proceeded to absorb or abolish all the other parties.

Hitler's victory, combined with the economic weakness of Britain and the political instability of France, irretrievably damaged the precarious balance of peace in Europe. The League of Nations, created in 1920 to regulate international disputes and protect member states from aggression, remained only as strong as its members; and its failure to prevent Italy's annexation of Ethiopia in 1935-6, or Germany's remilitarization of the Rhineland in 1936 encouraged further aggression (map 2 and insert). Hitler, who rapidly increased and modernized Germany's armed forces, annexed Austria and parts of Czechoslovakia in 1938, then Bohemia and Memel in spring 1939, while Italy invaded and occupied Albania (1939). Whether an early alliance between the western democracies and the Soviet Union would have halted the aggressors is a matter of dispute. However, fearing that he might be next in line, and already engaged in hostilities with Hitler's ally, Japan, in August 1939 Stalin signed a non-aggression pact with Germany. The collapse of the unstable system created after World War I was now unavoidable.

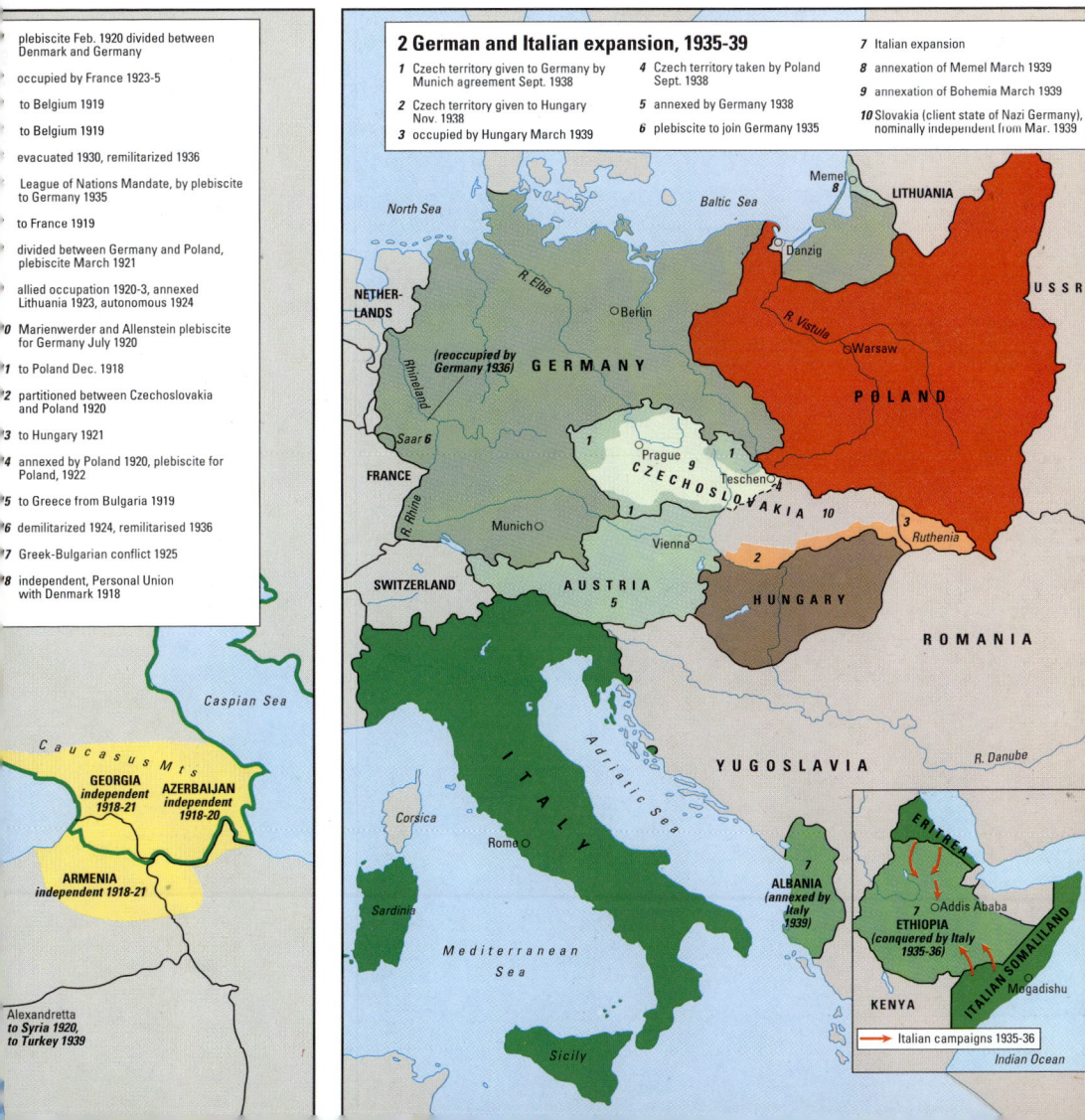

# The Great Depression 1929-39

The New York Stock Market crash in October 1929 reflected deep weaknesses in the world economy. Commodity prices world-wide had been falling since 1926, reducing the capacity of exporters such as Australia and Latin America to buy products from Europe and the United States. Within the latter, wages lagged behind profits, impairing the development of domestic markets and limiting the potential of new industries, such as automobiles, to replace old ones, such as textiles. International finance never recovered from the strains of World War I, which caused a dramatic increase in productive capacity, particularly outside Europe, without a corresponding increase in sustained demand. Fixed exchange rates and free convertibility gave way to a compromise – the Gold Exchange Standard – that lacked the stability necessary to rebuild world trade.

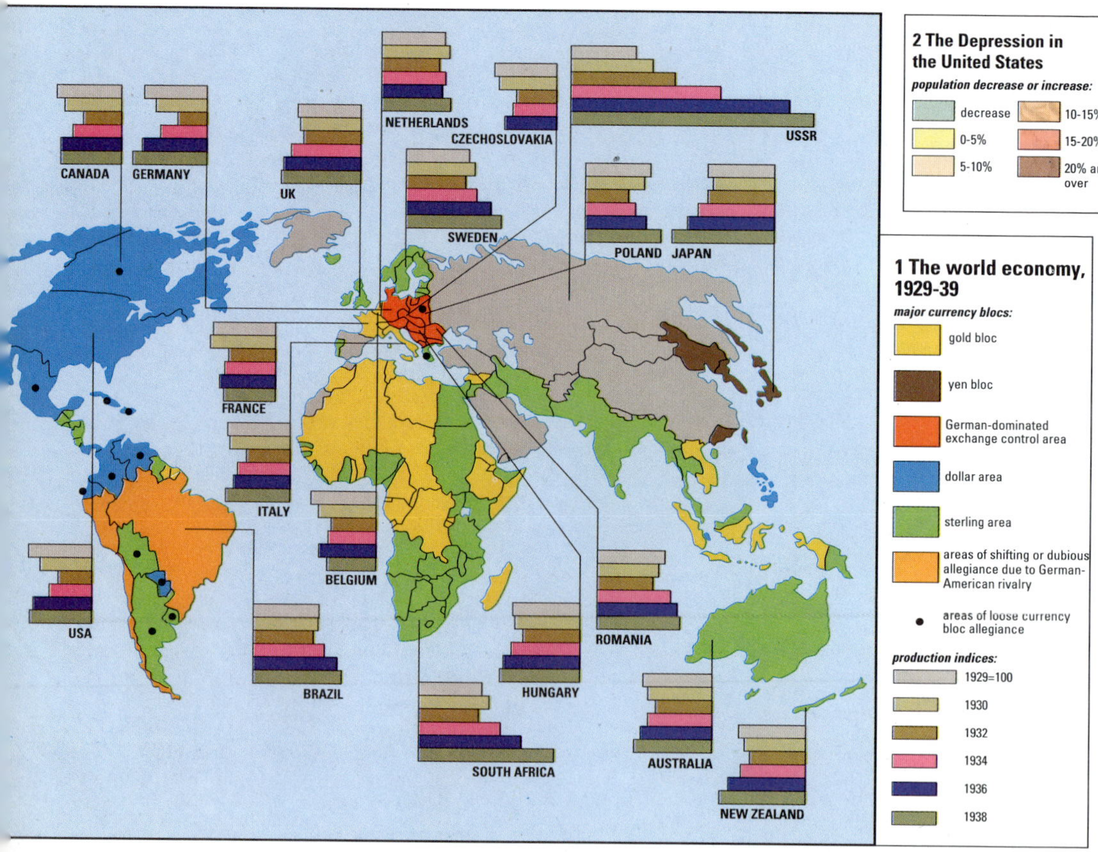

In the scramble for liquidity that followed the Great Crash, funds flowed back from Europe to America and Europe's fragile prosperity crumbled. In many industrial countries one-quarter of the labour force was thrown out of work. Prices and wages plummeted, industrial production fell to 53 per cent of its 1929 level in Germany and the United States, and world trade sank to 35 per cent of its 1929 value (see diagrams and map 1). Early attempts to solve the problem did more harm than good. In 1930 the United States imposed the highest tariff in its history; in 1932 Britain responded with the Ottawa agreements, a

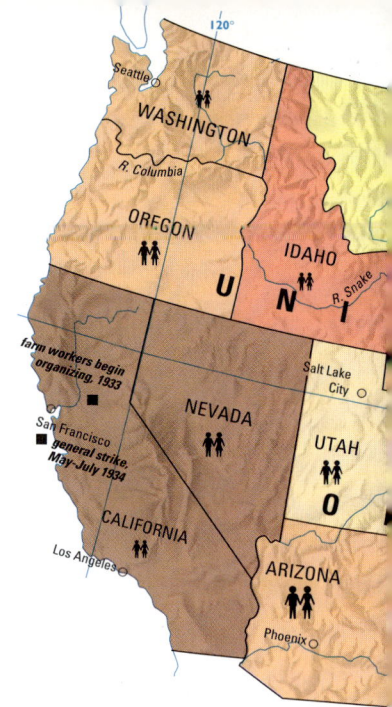

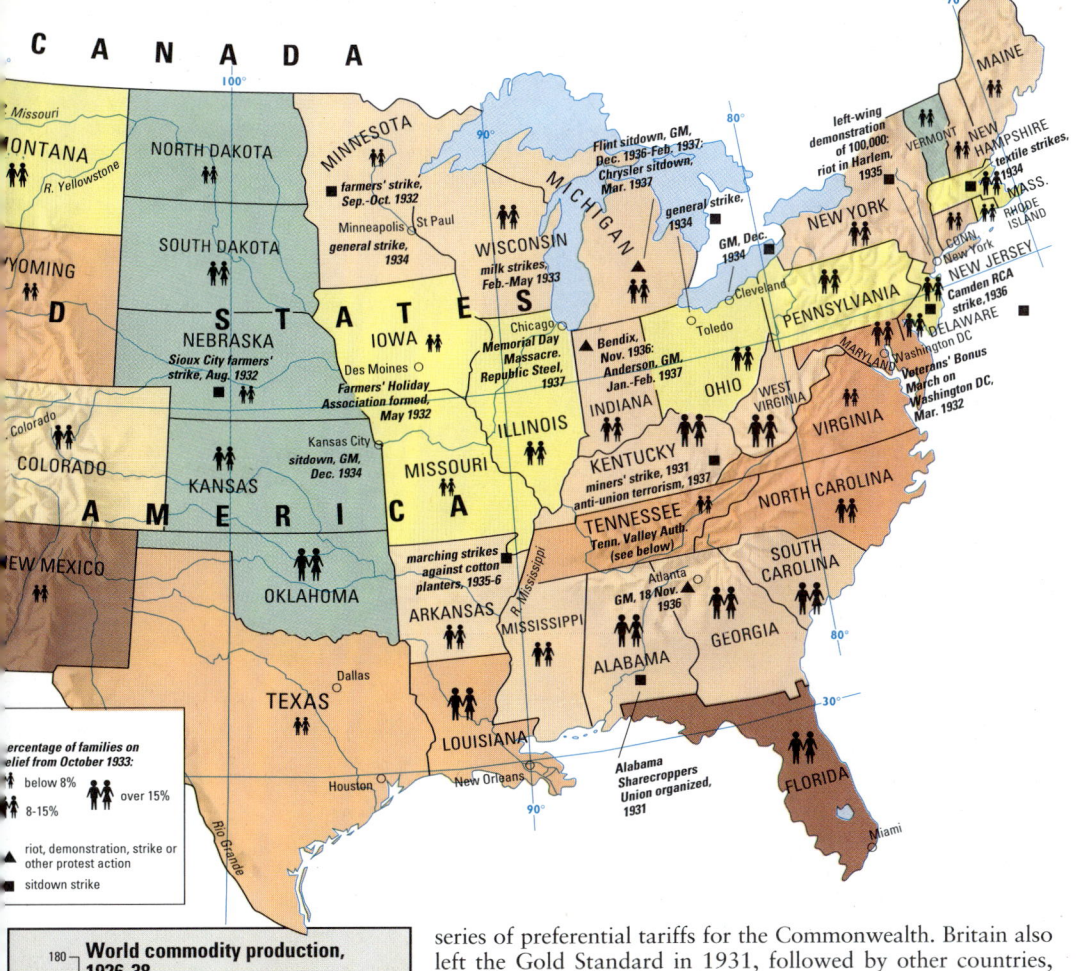

series of preferential tariffs for the Commonwealth. Britain also left the Gold Standard in 1931, followed by other countries, dividing virtually the entire world into closed currency blocs which inhibited trade still further. Only Soviet Russia, largely isolated from the world economy, continued to increase its industrial production (page 126).

Economic nationalism fostered political nationalism, just as mass unemployment and the erosion of middle-class living standards fostered political extremism. In Japan, the fall of the Hamaguchi government in 1931 marked the end of constitutional democracy and the beginning of aggression in Manchuria (page 117). In Europe, Hitler rose to power in 1933 partly in response to the deflationary policies of his predecessors that raised unemployment from 3 million in 1930 to 6 million in 1932 (page 129). Even in Britain and the United States, fascist movements exercised considerable pressure. In the former, a right-wing National Government, formed in 1931, preserved democratic rule; in the latter, President Franklin Roosevelt, elected in 1932, implemented a 'New Deal' that laid the foundations for recovery. Nevertheless in 1934 some 20 billion days were lost in the US through industrial action and in 1938 over 10 million Americans remained out of work (map 2). Only World War II, and the boost it gave to production, pulled the United States out of the Depression.

# The Second World War: the West 1939-45

Hitler's accession to power in 1933 added a new dimension to international politics. At first his expansionist designs had to await economic recovery, but his virtually unopposed annexation of Austria and Czechoslovakia (1938-9) and the Nazi-Soviet Pact of August 1939 (page 129) led him to expect similar acquiescence when, the following month, he invaded Poland. This time he miscalculated: the western democracies declared war (though this did nothing to aid the Poles).

Over the next two years, Germany rapidly secured first Denmark and Norway, then France and the Low Countries, and finally Yugoslavia and Greece, while Italy annexed Albania and invaded Egypt (map 1). Despite the Nazi-Soviet pact, however, Hitler's ultimate goal was the conquest of Russia: his operations in the West, like the Schlieffen Plan in 1914 (page 124), merely aimed to eliminate Germany's western enemies before the main struggle began in the east. In this Hitler failed because Britain – though defeated on the continent and subjected to sustained aerial bombing – refused to concede defeat. Nevertheless, in June 1941 Hitler launched his forces on Russia and, thanks to the combination of strategic surprise and tactical superiority, made rapid progress, taking over 3 million Russian prisoners-of-war. But the winter killed many Germans, who had far outrun their logistical support and lay stranded outside Moscow, Leningrad and Rostov. At precisely this point, on 7 December 1941, Japan attacked the United States (page 134), and Hitler – in an act of egregious folly – also declared war.

Although Germany launched another major thrust in Russia in 1942, reaching the Volga at Stalingrad, that too failed, with the loss of a major army, and her

troops fell back in the face of superior Soviet forces, supplied both by the industrial complex built up beyond the Urals (page 126) and by the United States. Meanwhile, Anglo-American troops cleared Axis forces first from Africa and then from Sicily in 1942-3, leading Italy to make peace (though German forces there fought on); partisans gradually took over Yugoslavia; and from June 1944 allied armies liberated France and Belgium before moving into Germany. They met the Soviets on the Elbe in May 1945.

The costs of the war were appalling: 15 million military personnel and 35 million civilians had perished, 20 million of them Soviet citizens. The Germans had murdered prisoners of war (Canadians, Americans and Britons in the West as well as Russians in the east); they had murdered all captured partisans and members of the communist party; and they murdered all Jews they could find, many in mass shootings and at least 6 million in special extermination camps. However, they also lost heavily: the Anglo-American strategic bombing offensive reduced most of their major cities to rubble, and the Soviet troops carried out a systematic campaign of destruction as they advanced in 1944-5. By war's end, almost all Europe lay in ruins, yet already the differences between the victors had appeared which would darken the post-war years (page 154).

**2 The defeat of Germany, 1942-45**

# The Second World War: Asia and the Pacific 1941-45

Japanese expansion in Asia after 1931 (page 117) stemmed from a desire for economic self-sufficiency, military security and a self-imposed leadership of East Asia. By 1940, however, with no end in sight to the Chinese war, Japan widened its ambitions to include the empires of the colonial powers – those of France and the Netherlands, recently defeated by her ally Germany, and those of Britain, at war with Germany (page 132) – as an alternative source of raw materials and markets that would free Japan from economic dependence on an increasingly unfriendly United States.

In September 1940 Japan occupied French Indo-China and the United States promptly placed an embargo on sending all iron and steel scrap to Japan. Next, following a sharp defeat at Nomonhan (Kalkhin Gol), Japan concluded a neutrality pact with Russia – which had been seen as the empire's principal potential enemy since the Russo-Japanese war (page 116) – and prepared to occupy the rest of the European colonies in South-East Asia. But first she felt it necessary to forestall a counterstrike by the United States: at dawn on 7 December 1941 her aircraft attacked and partially destroyed the US Pacific fleet at Pearl Harbor, Hawaii.

Japan hoped to fight the world's greatest industrialised power to a stalemate that would result in a negotiated peace recognizing Japanese hegemony in east Asia. Within six months, her forces had conquered

the American outposts of Guam and the Philippines, and occupied the British and Dutch colonies throughout South-East Asia. Their forces also overran the Bismarck archipelago and much of New Guinea, and captured most of the island redoubts necessary to create a defensive perimeter in the mid-Pacific (map 1). In June 1942, however, at Midway Island, aggressive tactics shaped by superb intelligence allowed the aircraft carriers of the US Pacific fleet (which had not been in Pearl the previous December) to destroy a major Japanese carrier force. The United States, although following a 'Europe first' policy in the world war, still possessed abundant resources to advance on two distinct axes against Japan: in the south Pacific, an island-hopping strategy (by-passing the major centres of Japanese resistance and executed by amphibious forces) aimed for the Philippines; in the central Pacific, carrier-borne forces advanced towards the Marianas, from whose airbases bombing raids could be launched on Japan itself. At the same time, Allied forces moved into Burma; and in August 1945 Russia finally broke her neutrality pact and invaded Manchuria (map 2).

But Japan, though utterly exhausted, succumbed to none of these conventional threats: rather two atomic bombs, dropped on Hiroshima and Nagasaki in August 1945, precipitated the unconditional surrender of the millions of her troops still in arms. The brief Japanese colonial adventure had caused almost as much destruction as Hitler's war in Europe; but it also unleashed forces of revolutionary nationalism that would shape events throughout Asia over the next five decades (page 142).

# The United States since 1945

The requirements of wartime production solved the unemployment problem (page 130) of the United States at last, and the gigantic output achieved to meet the needs of army, navy, air force and allies demonstrated the economic potential which, when realized, would create an era of unprecedented prosperity for the United States. Gross national product almost trebled in real terms between 1950 and 1990, while real income per head nearly doubled.

A number of factors brought about the economic surge: rapid population increase (from 132 million in 1940 to 250 million in 1990); technological advances coupled with the emergence of new consumer goods; the sudden spending of wartime savings between 1945 and 1948; and the rearmament programmes connected with the Cold War and the Korean War (page 154 and 142). Affluence came to seem entirely normal and business confidence was seldom less than buoyant: on this basis of wealth and hope most American people began to transform their entire way of life. The expansion of the suburbs constituted perhaps the most obvious change. Easy credit, cheap fuel (both for homes and cars), mass production of housing and automobiles, and giant road-building programmes (40,000 miles of interstate highways by 1980), all helped encourage Americans in their millions to move off the farms and out of the cities into endless miles of suburbs. So although the population of the central cities grew from 48 million to 79 million between 1950 and 1990, that of their urban fringes also rose from 21 million also to 79 million (map 1).

By 1990, less than one-third of the US population lived in non-metropolitan areas, but the flight from the farms did not reduce productivity: on the contrary, the number of people fed by one farm worker doubled from 15 in 1950 to 30 in 1970. Thanks to mechanization (by 1990 almost 100 per cent of the cotton crop was harvested by machine, as against only 10 per cent in 1949), improved seeds and fertilisers and government subsidies, the United States provided a significant proportion of the world's staple foods, such as wheat, maize and soya beans. The economy at large grew steadily, with the service sector (as in western Europe: page 156) expanding far more rapidly than manufacturing.

But beneath the prosperity lurked tensions. American capitalists tended to spend their profits rather than re-invest them, and industrial workers claimed higher wages and easier conditions of work without regard to the effect such claims (if successful) might have on prices and on the international competitiveness of American industry. The Vietnam War (1965-73: page 152) created high inflation and bitter internal divisions. Explicit discrimination against Blacks and Asians exploded in urban riots during the 1960s and gave rise to a widespread movement for civil rights led by Dr Martin Luther King (map 2). Then came the policies of Presidents Ronald Reagan (1981-9) and George Bush (1989-93), who cut taxes by a third (releasing a flood of spending power on the markets), slashed welfare programmes (turning the inner cities into ghettoes), vastly increased expenditure on armaments (so creating the biggest deficit in history), and failed to remedy the structural defects of American industry (so that the new purchasing power went overwhelmingly into imports, creating an equally unprecedented trade deficit).

On the other hand, winning World War II, engineering the reconstruction of western Europe through the Marshall Plan (page 138), the space exploration programme, major advances in the rights, education, income and social acceptance of minorities, and the successful resistance to Soviet expansionism without war were all achievements of which Americans could feel proud.

**1 Growth of metropolitan areas, 1940-75**

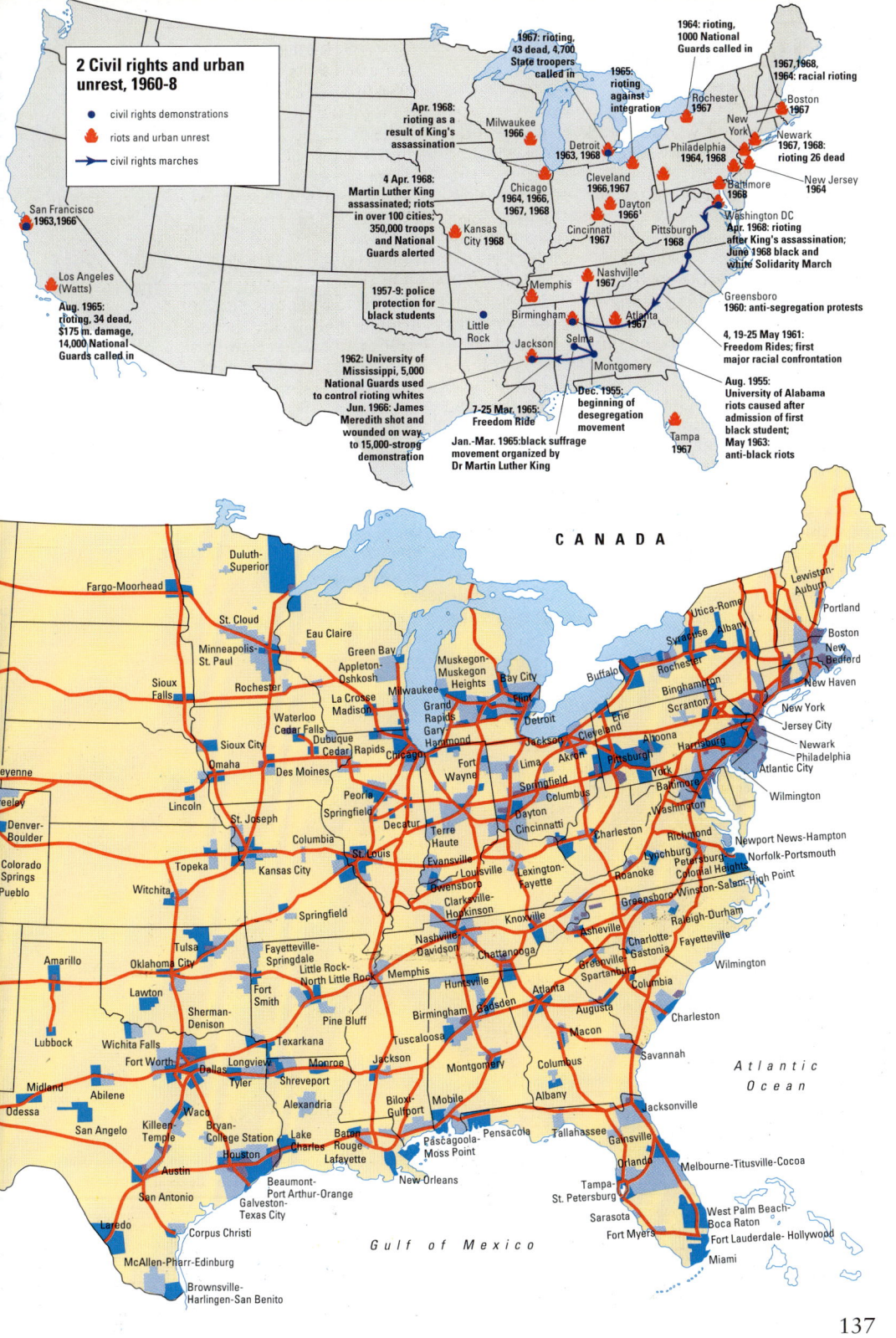

# Europe 1945-73

World War II left Europe politically disorganized and economically prostrate, a situation greatly exacerbated by large-scale population movements. The German collapse released millions of incarcerated prisoners-of-war and slave-workers, and a further 5 million Russian prisoners, refugees and servicemen were repatriated. Two more lasting shifts of population also occurred: some 12 million Germans abandoned (voluntarily or forcibly) their prewar homes in the east, especially in lands annexed by the Nazis after 1938; and over 2 million Russians moved into the territories annexed by the Soviet Union during its westward advance (map 1).

The political frontiers of the new Europe were established at conferences between the victors (USA, USSR, Britain and France) held at Yalta and Potsdam in February and July 1945: the union of Germany and Austria decreed by Hitler in 1938 was dissolved and Germany lost territory to Poland and the Soviet Union; both countries were divided into occupation zones under four power control. In Austria the system worked relatively smoothly, and in 1955 the country achieved independence, albeit as a permanently neutralized state; but co-operation between the USSR and her allies in Germany broke down in 1948. Britain and the United States had already amalgamated their zones in 1947 and, in conjunction with France, they now prepared for the formation of a West German government (the Federal Republic: BRD). After an attempt to prevent this by means of a blockade on Berlin, the Soviets prepared their zone for quasi-independence as the German Democratic Republic (DDR): the two states came into existence in 1949 (map 2).

2 Post-war Germany 1945-90

- border of Germany in 1937
- border of German Democratic Republic 1949-90
- border of German post-war administrative regions
- administrative capital

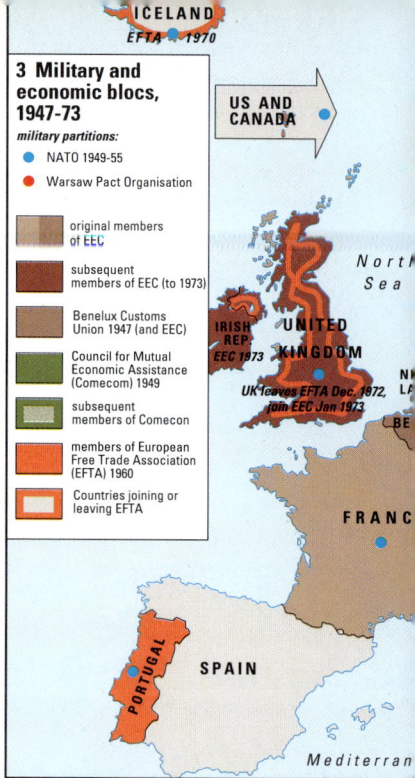

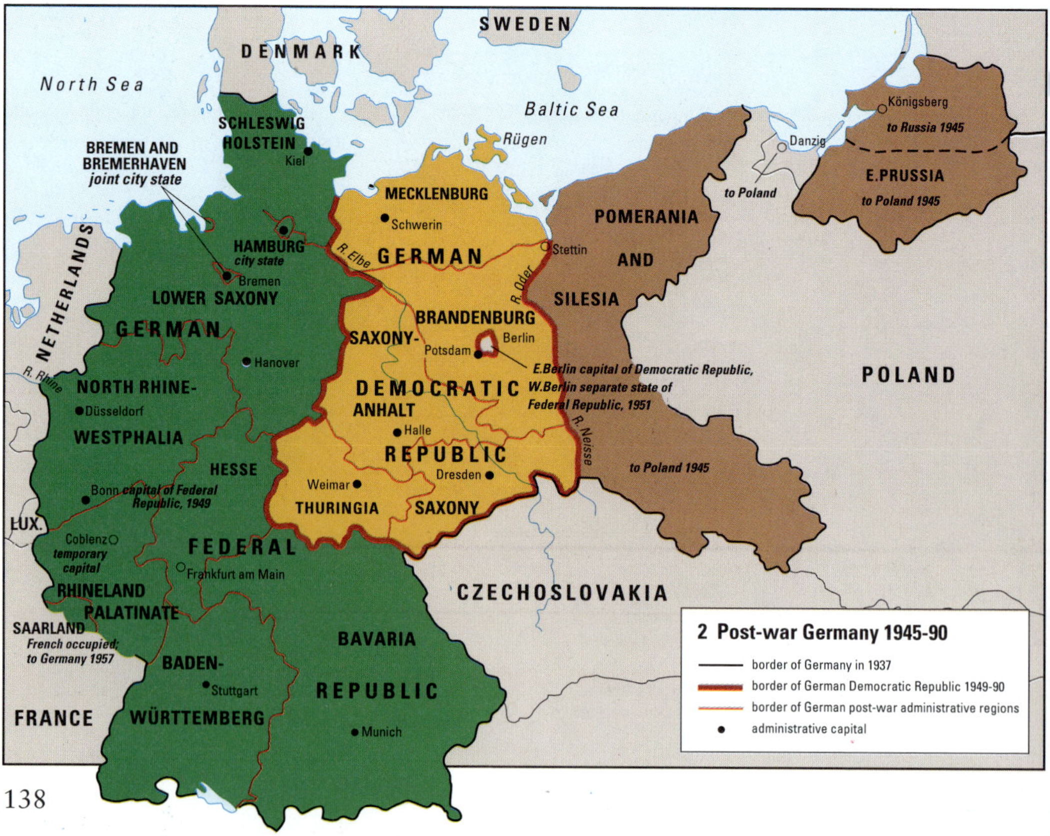

They immediately took their place in the two political blocs into which Europe had become divided. The eastern republics had all come under communist rule by 1948 and economic growth, though continuous, remained slow thanks to Stalinist methods of production. In the western democracies, thanks largely to lavish American aid (the Marshall Plan from 1947), an economic miracle took place, with smooth and rapid growth year after year. The two blocs had their own military groups – NATO in the west (1949) and the Warsaw Pact in the east (1955) – and their own economic organizations – in the east Comecon (1949) and in the west the European Community (six members 1957; 12 by 1986) and the less successful European Free Trade Association (map 3). However the growth surge suffered a serious check in 1973 when the Arab-led Organization of Petroleum Exporting Countries (OPEC) increased the price of oil by 250 per cent.

# The Soviet Union 1945 to 1991

Despite the extensive loss of life and property inflicted on Russia during World War II (page 133 above), remarkable economic recovery began after 1945. The output of heavy industry rose steadily and light industry, neglected under Stalin (who died in 1953), also progressed under his successors. The agricultural problems created by collectivization (page 126) remained – grain production only increased in the late 1950s, and even then the USSR continued to depend on imports – but vast reserves of oil, gas and mineral ores were discovered and exploited in Siberia. Russia's east European satellites were obliged to supply high-quality engineering products and expert personnel (as well as more basic items), which immensely assisted the USSR's economic progress. The development of the atom bomb (1949), of the first satellite (the sputnik: 1957), and of the first manned space flight (1961) all indicated the ability of Russian science to innovate.

After 1945 the Soviet military became a central feature of the state (map 2). One-fifth of the budget was devoted to military spending while between 1952 and 1976 101 military leaders became full members of the Central Committee of the Communist Party. The Soviet Union, along with the United States, had become a 'superpower', with a comparable degree of military strength. Although its gross national product fell well short of its rival's, the USSR overtook the USA in the production of iron ore, cement, steel and oil. Nevertheless the Soviet economy entered a period of crisis in the 1970s. Increasingly, the USSR found the arms-race more costly than did the USA (not least because the latter enjoyed far better credit and so could finance much of its expenditure through loans: page 136), and the position became critical when the USA threatened to extend its defence system into outer space (the 'Strategic Defense Initiative'). In 1985 a new Soviet leader, Mikhail Gorbachev, came to power with a programme of reform designed to achieve a 'revolution within the revolution'.

From 1985 to 1990 Gorbachev successfully improved relations with both China and the west in order to provide peaceful external conditions for reconstruction. He introduced *glasnost* (openness) in the media to encourage criticism of deficiencies in the economy and society; but he could not assure an adequate supply of food, and unrest in the cities grew. In desperation, in 1989 he withdrew Soviet forces from eastern Europe, hoping to reduce costs and thus improve the situation at home; but the resurgence of nationalism in many constituent republics began to threaten the entire union. The Soviet Union comprised many different ethnic, religious, linguistic and cultural groups (map 1). The majority of the

**1 The nationalities of the Soviet Union, 1989**

| | | |
|---|---|---|
| Russians 53.19% | Moldavians 1.23% | Kazakhs 2.98% |
| Latvians 0.54% | Ukrainians 16.18% | Kirghiz 0.93% |
| Lithuanians 1.10% | Mordvins 0.42% | Chuvash 0.31% |
| Estonians 0.38% | Turkmen 1.00% | Tatars 2.44% |
| Belorussians 3.78% | Uzbeks 6.12% | Bashkirs 0.53% |
| Poles 0.41% | Tajiks 1.55% | Georgians 1.46% |

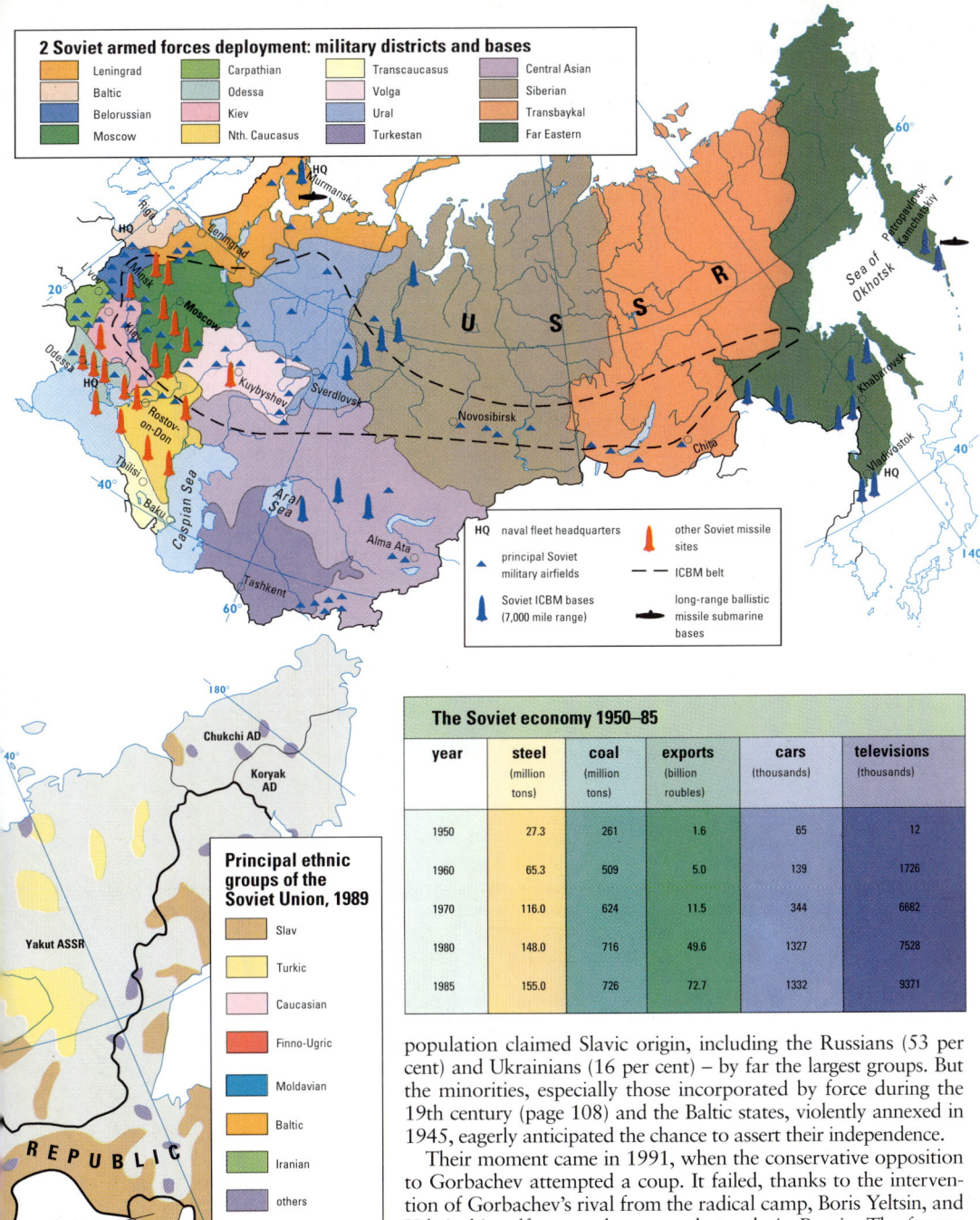

### The Soviet economy 1950–85

| year | steel (million tons) | coal (million tons) | exports (billion roubles) | cars (thousands) | televisions (thousands) |
|---|---|---|---|---|---|
| 1950 | 27.3 | 261 | 1.6 | 65 | 12 |
| 1960 | 65.3 | 509 | 5.0 | 139 | 1726 |
| 1970 | 116.0 | 624 | 11.5 | 344 | 6682 |
| 1980 | 148.0 | 716 | 49.6 | 1327 | 7528 |
| 1985 | 155.0 | 726 | 72.7 | 1332 | 9371 |

population claimed Slavic origin, including the Russians (53 per cent) and Ukrainians (16 per cent) – by far the largest groups. But the minorities, especially those incorporated by force during the 19th century (page 108) and the Baltic states, violently annexed in 1945, eagerly anticipated the chance to assert their independence.

Their moment came in 1991, when the conservative opposition to Gorbachev attempted a coup. It failed, thanks to the intervention of Gorbachev's rival from the radical camp, Boris Yeltsin, and Yeltsin himself assumed power – but only in Russia. The former republics now became 15 independent states. The break-up of the USSR did not bring peace, however: a bitter civil war raged in Georgia; Armenian forces occupied most of Nagorno-Karabakh, claiming it from neighbouring Azerbaijan; and separatist movements arose in parts of the Russian federation itself, jeopardizing the prospects for Yeltsin's programme of economic reform, and with it the very existence of democratic forms of government.

# East Asia since 1945

Japan, like Germany (page 138), was occupied by the victors following her surrender in 1945. The Far East Commission, which contained representatives of all the countries that had fought Japan but remained an American enterprise, sought to demilitarize Japan and create a peaceful, democratic state. It reformed the education system (removing from the syllabus all material which had encouraged military and authoritarian values), made the Diet (parliament) the highest political authority, established an independent judiciary, introduced a programme of land reform, and sought (with little success) to break up the great concentrations of corporate power. With the advance of communism in east Asia, however, the United States increasingly saw Japan as a potential ally, and worked to reconstruct the economic power destroyed by the war. The occupation formally ended in 1951.

Japan's defeat in 1945 also ended its harsh rule of Korea and led to its occupation by the victors: Japanese forces north of the 38th parallel surrendered to Soviet Russia, those in the south to the United States. The Soviets supported the establishment of a communist state in the north under Kim Il-sung, a guerrilla leader who had spent considerable time in the Soviet Union; and the Americans retaliated by sponsoring a representative regime under Syngman Rhee, a strong anti-communist. Both new governments entertained strong ambitions to unite the country under their own rule, and in June 1950 the North attacked, pushing the South Korean and remaining United States forces back toward Pusan (map 1). The US forces counterattacked in September with a daring amphibious landing at Inchon, leading to a further offensive that promised to unify Korea. In November, however, the Chinese committed substantial forces that regained most of the north. A stalemate ensued and an armistice was signed in 1953.

The establishment of the People's Republic of China in 1949 (page 122) marked a fundamental turning point in the modern history of China. After a century of severe internal conflict and disintegration, usually provoked or exacerbated by external aggressors, China was now reunified and strongly governed by leaders who had a decisive vision of the society they wished to create. Whatever the excesses and failures since 1949, that fundamental achievement must be recognized. For most of the 1950s, China closely followed the Soviet model of directed economic planning and achieved some modest progress in developing heavy industries. But in 1958 Mao Tse-Tung, the communist leader, became impatient and sought to mobilize the revolutionary energies of China's vast population, creating huge rural communes and urban associations for production in the 'Great Leap Forward'. It was abandoned in chaos three years later. In 1965 Mao once more became impatient and again tried to mobilize the energies of the masses in the 'Great Proletarian Cultural Revolution', intended to prevent the creation of vested interests and bureaucratic arrogance in the party and the state. Once again, however, ideology triumphed over expertise, producing chaos and misery. Nothing in China grew as fast as the population. After Mao's death in 1976, the new dominant figure Deng Xiao-ping authorized a major shift in economic policy. Material incentives were re-established and foreign trade and investment encouraged (map 2). Political dissent, however, remained prohibited, and pro-democracy protests in Peking in 1989 were brutally crushed.

With the end of occupation in 1951 Japan began a period of exceptionally high economic growth and within 20 years had become an economic super-power. The 1950s saw strong emphasis on the development of heavy industry: Japan soon became the world's principal ship-builder and third largest producer of iron and steel. But from the 1960s Japanese industry also produced high-technology consumer manufactures – cars, cameras and computers – largely directed towards export markets across the world. Many major Japanese companies established production or assembly plants overseas, notably in South-East Asia but also in Europe and North America. Hence Japan's foreign investment rose dramatically from the 1970s, much of it in other countries in East and South-East Asia (diagram 3), helping to make the Pacific Rim a lynchpin of the global economic system (page 160).

**1 The Korean War**

**3 Japanese industrial production and exports, 1945-90**

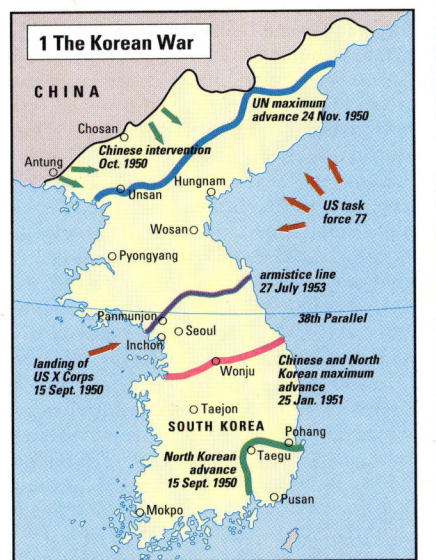

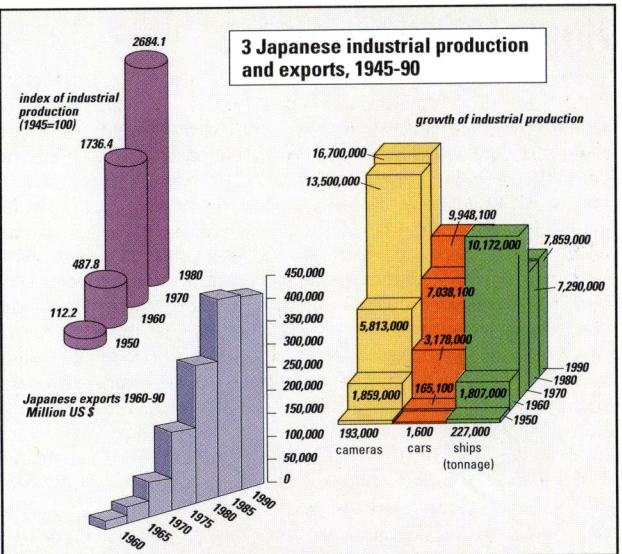

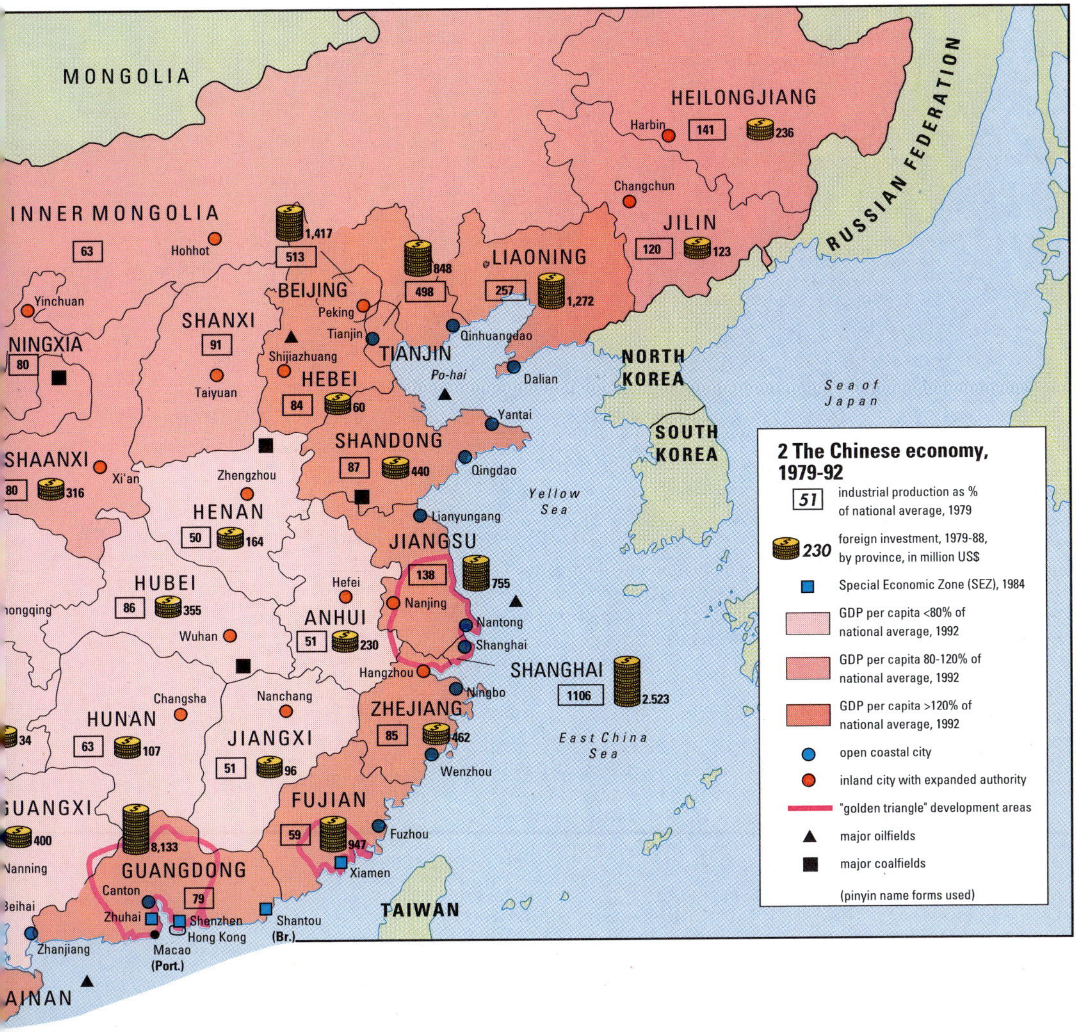

# Retreat from empire after 1947

The Western empires created in the 19th century (page 112) remained intact in 1939, though most German and Ottoman possessions had passed to Britain, France and Japan as League of Nations mandates. The United States planned to grant independence to the Philippines, acquired in 1898, and did so immediately after World War II; but none of the seven remaining European colonial powers – Britain, France, Spain, Portugal, Belgium, Italy and the Netherlands – surrendered their empires voluntarily. Only Britain even conceived of independence as the ultimate goal, albeit with continued membership of the Commonwealth, a goal already attained in 1939 by Canada, South Africa, Australia and New Zealand. The continental colonial powers thought more in terms of evolution towards a common citizenship, with their colonies as overseas parts of the metropolitan territory. Such plans were complicated, however, by the resistance of European settlers, with consequent inter-racial tensions, and by clashes between the European ideal of evolution along Western lines (in education and economic development) and the powerful Hindu, Muslim, Buddhist and Confucian cultures of the 'subject peoples'.

France fought stubbornly to maintain its control of Indochina (page 152), and the Netherlands struggled to contain the nationalists of Java, who had proclaimed the Indonesian Republic in 1945. Neither succeeded. Continual unrest forced Britain to grant independence to India and Pakistan (1947), followed in 1948 by Burma and Ceylon (page 152). Nevertheless Britain fought (and won) a long war against communist insurgents in Malaya, and resisted Indonesian attempts to annexe Sarawak and Brunei. Only after the evacuation of Aden in 1967 did Britain abandon its presence east

of Suez – save only for Hong Kong, to be retained until 1997, its economic success being of some benefit to Communist China.

In Africa resistance to independence was strongest in colonies with substantial white settler populations. In Algeria, with 1 million whites, a savage war of liberation occurred between 1954 and 1962; but conflict proved bitter, too, in Kenya and Rhodesia. However by 1974 all had achieved independence (page 150). By then, although Britain showed in the Falklands War (1982) her determination to fight on behalf of the few outposts still directly ruled from London, the formal structures of European imperialism had been dismantled and largely replaced by different forms of association such as the British Commonwealth or the French Community.

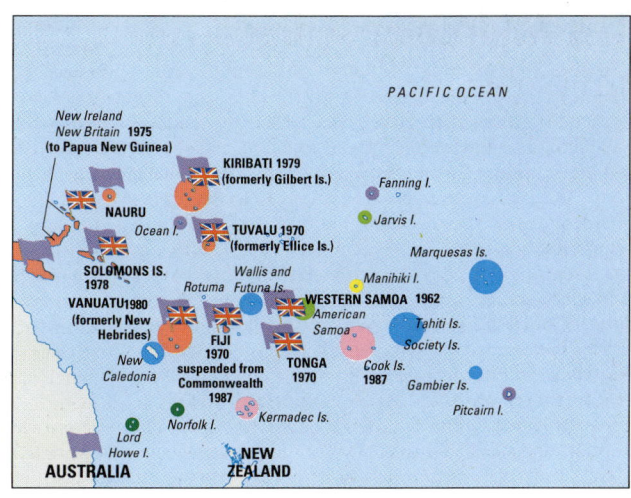

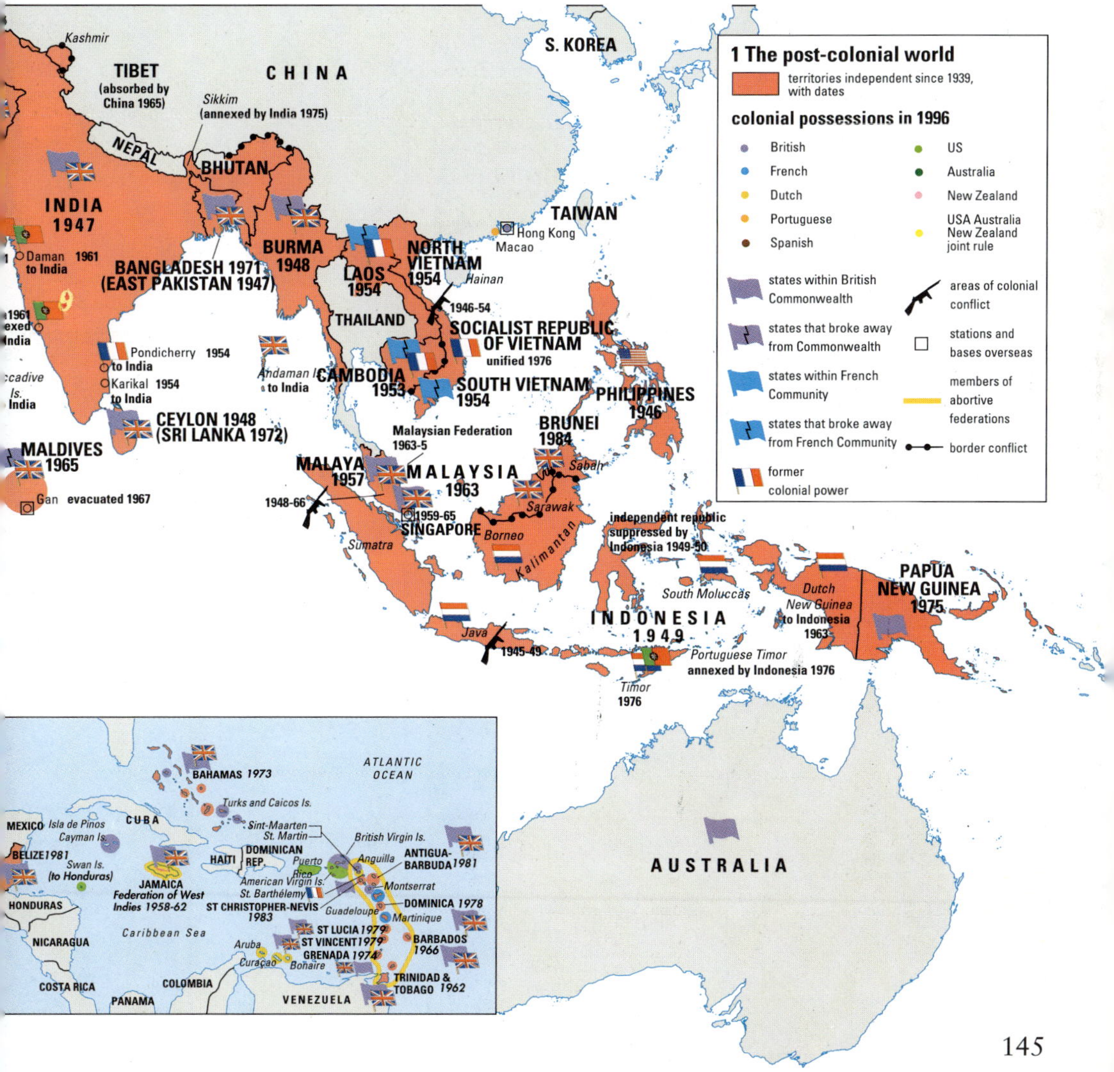

1 The post-colonial world

# The Middle East since 1917

The Middle East has occupied world attention more consistently than any other region since 1945: Israel and its neighbours have engaged in four full-scale wars; Israel has invaded Lebanon twice; two Gulf wars have been fought; military coups have reinforced a regional pattern of internal repression; waves of refugees, from Cyprus to Afghanistan, have been forced to flee.

American support for the state of Israel (founded in 1948), sponsorship of the Baghdad Pact (1955), and intervention in Lebanon (1958) seemed to threaten the Soviet southern frontier, and so assistance was offered to Syria, Egypt and (after the revolution of 1958) Iraq. The Soviets also championed the Arab states during the Arab-Israeli war of 1967, despite which Israel occupied the west bank of the Jordan, Sinai and the Golan heights, provoking further large-scale Arab emigration (map 2). In 1973 an Egyptian and Syrian attack on Israel met with limited military success, and opened a new phase of negotiation. Egypt and Israel concluded the Camp David Accords (1978) which resulted in the return of Sinai in 1982; but the Israelis showed no intention of returning the other territories occupied since 1967, instead installing large numbers of new Jewish settlements. Moreover in 1982, to counter Palestinian guerrilla activity, they invaded and held south Lebanon. Nevertheless, in the wake of a prolonged period of resistance to Israeli rule in the West Bank and Gaza, which excited much outside sympathy, in 1991 the US succeeded in bringing Israel and its Arab neighbours into extended peace talks, which resulted in limited Palestinian self-rule in 1994-5.

As open conflict between Israel and her neighbours abated, it began in the Gulf. The replacement of the Shah of Iran by Ayatollah Khomeini in 1979 seemed to President Saddam Hussein of Iraq to offer the chance of territorial gain. He attacked in 1980.

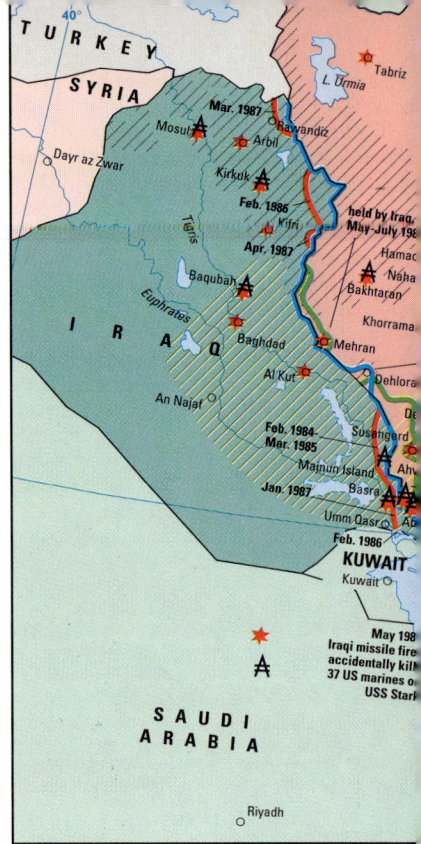

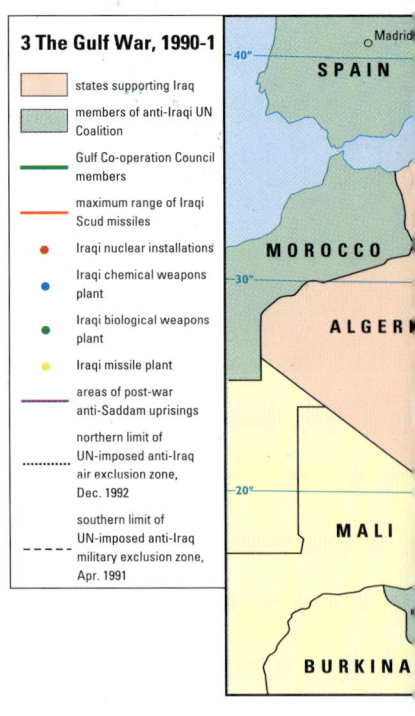

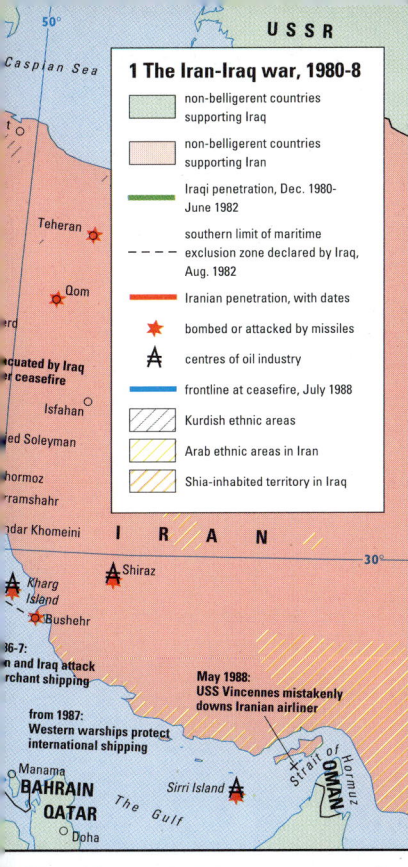

However, eight years of attritional warfare achieved virtually nothing and in 1990 (map 1), in an attempt to gain new resources with which to liquidate his war debts, Saddam invaded and annexed another neighbour, Kuwait. The United Nations, led by the US, put pressure on Saddam to withdraw and, when he refused, in 1991 used armed force to expel him (map 3). These events had a catastrophic effect on the oil production of the Persian Gulf, much of it located in the war zone. The area's share of global output fell from 41 per cent in 1979 to 26 per cent in 1991, with production in Iraq and Kuwait reduced almost to zero.

Nevertheless, oil remained the region's most valuable natural asset. Output and revenue both increased dramatically after the OPEC price-rise in 1973 (page 139), creating some of the highest per capita incomes in the world in the Arab Gulf states. Their prosperity also attracted massive immigration from Egypt, Jordan, Yemen and the Indian sub-continent, creating a potential problem. The rise of Islamic fundamentalism posed another. After 1979 it became a badge of hostility towards the West in Iran and towards Russia in Afghanistan, and elsewhere toward the regime in power – unless, as in Iran, that regime was an Islamic theocracy. In Algeria, the attraction proved so strong that the government in 1992 cancelled a second round of elections to prevent the fundamentalists gaining power.

Although the collapse of the Soviet Union (page 141) ended the superpower rivalry which once dominated the area, the Western powers continued to exert their influence, both to safeguard the oil supplies on which their economies still depended and to protect blatantly persecuted minorities like the Kurds of northern Iraq. Moreover, the enormous concentrations of conventional weapons – and the interest in developing chemical and biological weapons – in so many antagonistic states ensured that the Middle East continued to occupy world attention.

# Latin America since 1930

The Great Depression (page 130) struck Latin America a shattering blow, cutting off supplies of foreign capital and lowering the price of its primary products in the world markets. Chile's exports fell by over 80 per cent between 1929 and 1933; those of Bolivia and Peru by 75 per cent. Only oil-exporting Venezuela more or less weathered the storm. The economic collapse led to widespread disillusion with middle-class liberal or radical parties: in 1930 and 1931, 11 of the 20 republics south of the Rio Grande experienced revolutionary changes in government. Mexico, where Lázaro Cárdenas (1934-40) revived the land distribution policies of 1911 (page 106), experienced a shift to the left; but elsewhere the swing was mainly to the right. The new dictators tended to be populists, appealing directly to the masses and cooperating with organised labour and the trade unions. They also introduced programmes of industrialization – following Soviet or, more often, Fascist models – to reduce dependence on overseas markets and hasten economic development.

Manufacturing industry received a further boost during World War II, which cut off imported consumer goods and stimulated the industrial sector. But industrialization made Latin America dependent upon imported capital goods, raw materials, technology and finance – especially from the United States – creating enormous foreign debts (map 2). Multinational corporations exploited the cheap labour of Latin America without stimulating economic development. Social tensions arose from income concentration, unemployment, lack of opportunities, and from the intrusion of foreign interests. Social revolutions were attempted but frustrated in Guatemala, Bolivia and Chile (map 1), underlining the obstacles to change in economies too narrowly based to sustain welfare programmes, where local elites were prepared to collaborate with the United States.

Cuba after 1959 attempted to achieve social change, economic growth and freedom from the United States simultaneously; but although its revolution led to greater social equality and some improvement in the lot of rural workers, it also brought a repressive regime and dependence on the Soviet Union. Moreover its attempts to spread revolution in Central and South America all failed.

In the face of revolutionary change, with some support from the upper and middle classes, the military seized power in many areas and combined political repression with economic liberalization. But by the late 1980s their policies too had largely failed and, in the face of economic recession and popular protest, their power gradually weakened. Instead, democratic government resumed in several states of the subcontinent, and in 1992 Mexico signed a free trade agreement (NAFTA) with Canada and the United States, creating the largest integrated trading bloc in the world.

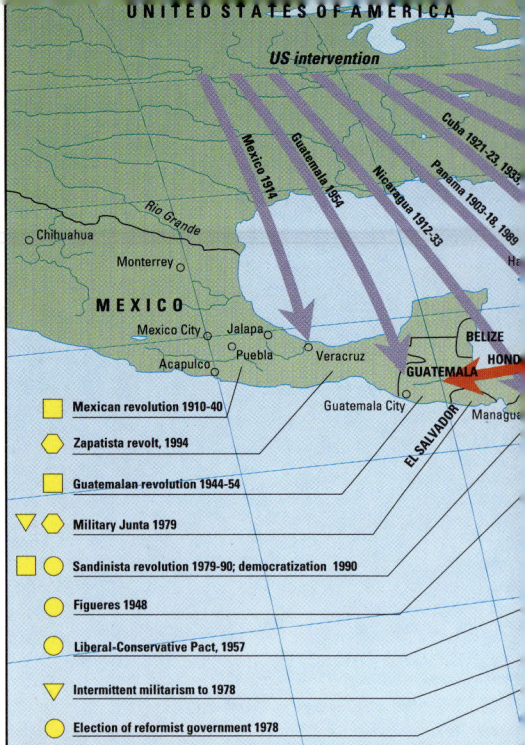

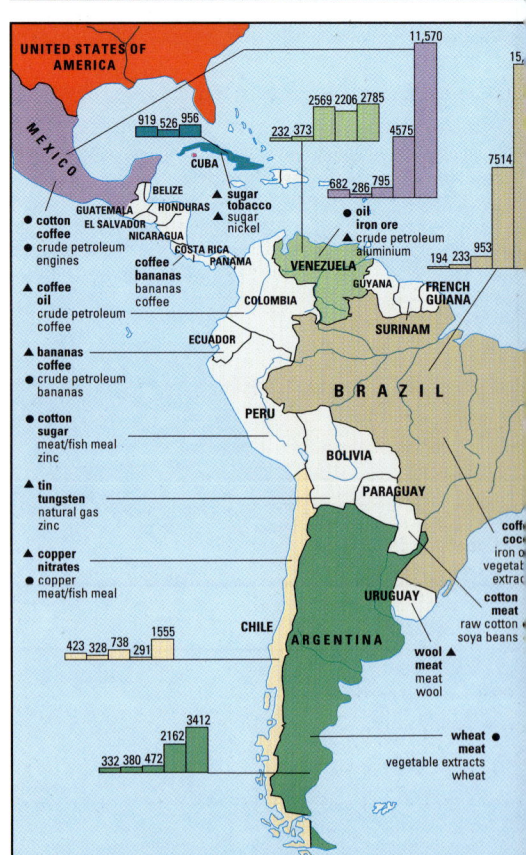

# Africa since 1945

After World War II, although some French and British liberals sympathetic to African claims for advancement initiated programmes of social improvement and political reform, these soon ran into difficulties in territories where they threatened the interests of white settler populations. Moreover, the need to exploit every asset in order to assist metropolitan recovery led to attempts to reassert colonial control. Nevertheless in the 1950s both the British and the French began to transfer responsibility to elected governments in their West African colonies.

In Muslim North Africa, longer-established nationalist movements received great stimulus from the overthrow of the Egyptian monarchy in 1952 and the subsequent rise to power of Gamal Abdel Nasser. In 1953-4 Britain agreed to withdraw its troops from the Suez Canal Zone; and in 1956 France granted independence to her protectorates of Tunisia and Morocco. But in Algeria, with a large white population, the government attempted to maintain control and incorporate the colony into metropolitan France. In 1954 the Front de Libération Nationale began a war which continued with increasing ferocity until in 1962 independence was finally granted.

At the other end of the continent, a Nationalist government dedicated to policies of racial separation ('apartheid') came to power in South Africa in 1948. Meanwhile, white settlers in East Africa also hoped to maintain their ascendancy: in Kenya, where British troops arrived to suppress the Mau-Mau insurrection directed against the settlers; and in Central Africa, where a federation of Nyasaland and Rhodesia aimed to preserve the dominance of Rhodesian whites. But in 1963 Kenya achieved independence and the Federation collapsed. Southern Rhodesia's white settlers created their own independent state in 1965, but had to accept black majority rule in 1980. Portugal retained her colonies longest, but in all of them guerrilla warfare eventually forced her ignominious withdrawal in 1974-5.

The political and economic structures of the newly independent African states remained fragile. Most possessed borders drawn by European governments in the 19th century with insufficient attention to ethnic rivalries, and almost immediately those rivalries began to tear them apart. In 1960, tribal and regional factions in Zaire (formerly the Belgian Congo) led to demands for a federal constitution at independence and, when these were refused, the army mutinied and the mineral rich province of Katanga seceded. United Nations intervention reunited the country in 1963, but two years later the army seized power. A similar pattern occurred in Nigeria, where the secession of Biafra in 1967 led to a three-year civil war which restored central control, but delivered power to the army. Elsewhere, ethnic violence caused enormous casualties – in the small state of Rwanda, Hutu-Tutsi violence left between 500,000 and 1 million dead in 1994 – while repeated droughts (compounded by government inefficiency and corruption) caused famine and massive refugee problems in many areas of East Africa. Some states found short-term relief through the exploitation of oil and other minerals, though often at the cost of diverting resources from producing food.

By the 1980s, only the Republic of South Africa maintained white supremacy in Africa. It sought to protect itself by tightening its illegal control of Namibia, by military incursions into neighbouring states, and by conceding to the impoverished labour reserves known as 'Bantustans' a spurious independence. But, under siege economically and subject to international condemnation, the apartheid system could not last. In 1990 the government freed Nelson Mandela, leader of the outlawed African National Congress, and began talks about a new political settlement. In 1994, after the first multi-racial election in South African history, Mandela peacefully gained control of the richest state in the continent.

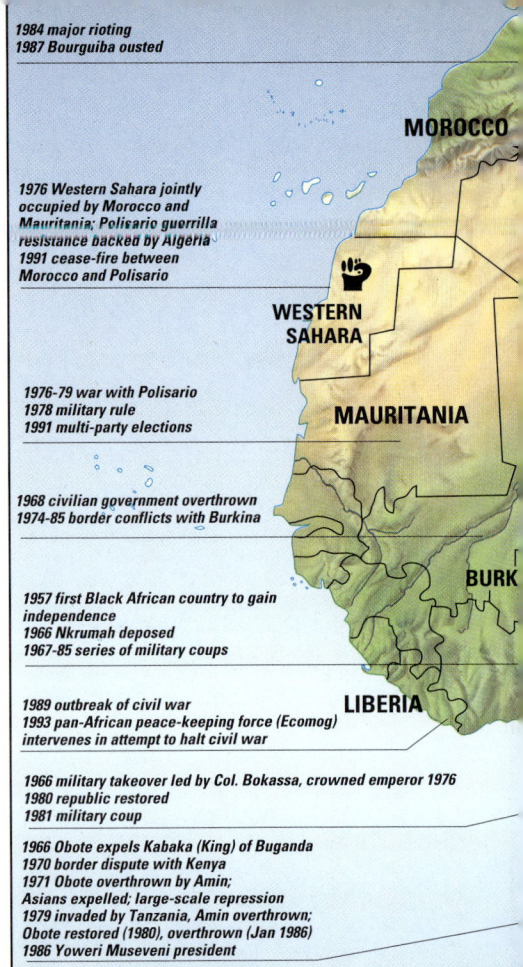

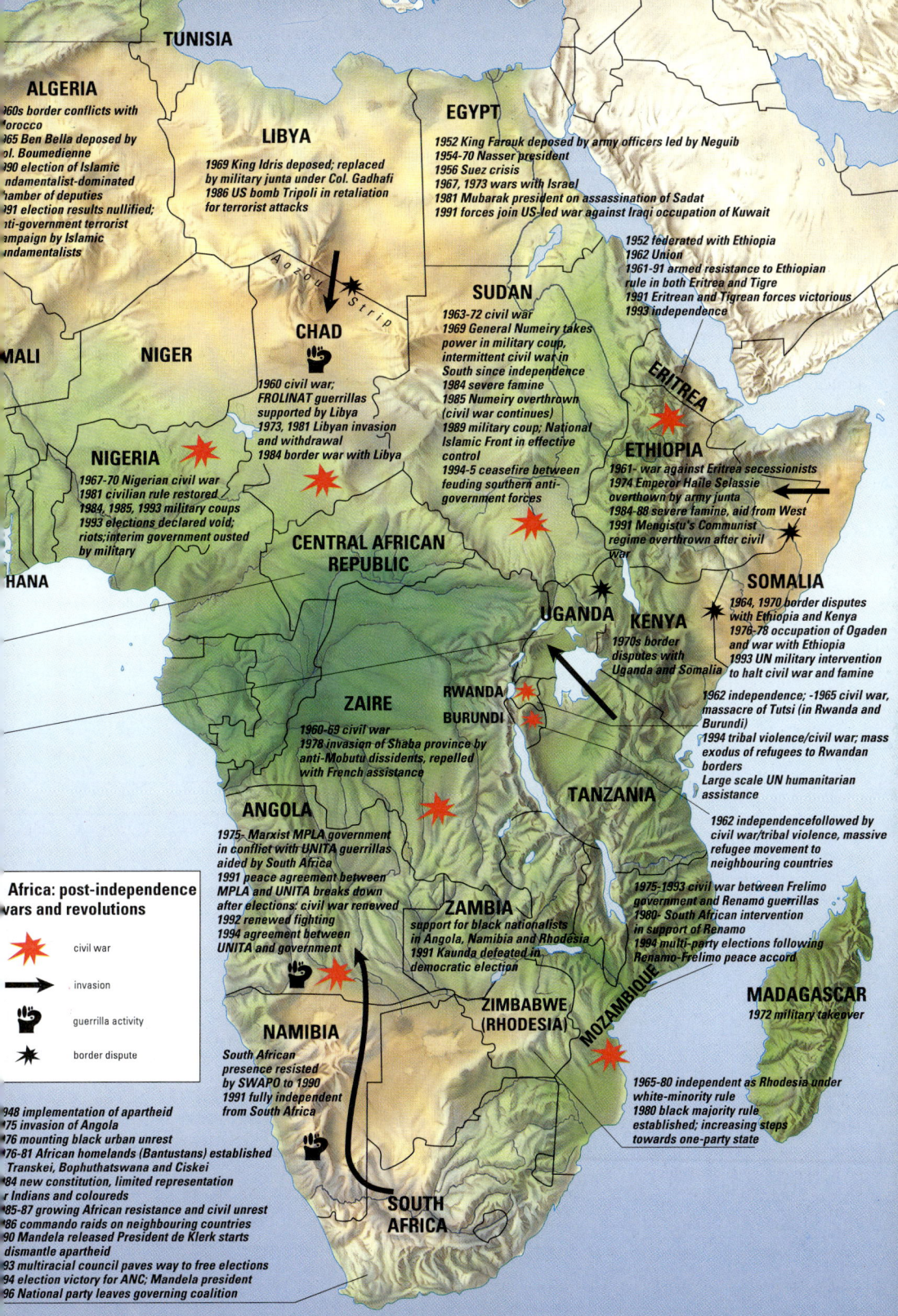

# South and South-East Asia since 1945

The history of southern Asia since independence has been dominated by three factors. First, the seizure of power by military leaders (Pakistan 1958, Indonesia 1967), with the aim – rarely successful – of abolishing corruption and stabilizing the economy; second, the resurgence of long-standing regional, tribal and religious conflicts (Naga and Sikh unrest in India; nationalist uprisings among the Mons, Shans and other 'hill people' in Thailand and Burma); finally, intervention by the Great Powers (Russia in Afghanistan; China and the United States in Vietnam).

Wars between states also characterized certain areas. The partition of the Indian subcontinent in 1947 left numerous points of friction between the new states of India and Pakistan, particularly Punjab, Kashmir and Bengal, and these erupted into war in 1965 and again in 1971 (in connection with the secession of East Pakistan to form the separate state of Bangladesh). Indian forces also expelled the Portuguese from their coastal enclaves (1961), fought China over a frontier dispute (1962), and intervened in Sri Lanka to protect the Hindu Tamil minority (1986-90). Civil wars, however, proved far more common (map 1). Malaya suffered a communist insurrection, led by ethnic Chinese, between 1948 and 1960; the Philippines experienced rebellions by both communists and Muslims from the 1960s; Cambodia was devastated by the civil war between the communist Khmer Rouge and its non-communist opponents.

The most savage conflict, however, occurred in Vietnam (map 2). After the Japanese collapse in 1945 Ho Chi Minh established a communist regime in Hanoi while the French recreated their colonial empire in the south. In 1946 armed conflict began, continuing until a humiliating defeat at Dien Bien Phu in 1954 forced the French to withdraw. Although this left Cambodia and Laos as independent states, it did not create a unified Vietnam: at the Geneva Peace Conference in 1954 Ho accepted a 'temporary' partition of the country at the 17th parallel until nationwide elections, mandated for 1956, took place. However an anti-communist regime in the south, backed by America, refused to hold elections. In 1959 Ho therefore attacked, and the US immediately provided munitions and advisers to the south, with regular troops and air strikes after 1965. Despite saturation bombing and the commitment of 500,000 US ground troops, the communists (supported by both Russia and China) held their own and in 1968 negotiations began between Hanoi and Washington. In 1973 American forces withdrew, although the US continued to supply the south on a massive scale. When the communists launched an orthodox military offensive in 1975, however, the south's army collapsed. Vietnam was now unified, under Hanoi, although its economy was ruined and its invasion of Cambodia in 1978 led to ostracism by the West.

Elsewhere in Asia, however, rapid development occurred. Following the path of Japan (page 142), Taiwan, Malaysia, Singapore, Thailand and eventually Indonesia achieved rapid rates of growth from the late 1960s. Even during the world recession of the 1980s, each experienced an annual growth rate of well over 5 per cent. Various factors were responsible: all except Singapore possessed large pools of cheap labour; all created a substantial industrial base oriented towards export markets throughout Asia, Europe and North America; all the governments sought to attract substantial foreign investment through tax incentives and infrastructural development. A major part of that investment came from Japan (map 3). Finally, political stability – Lee in Singapore; Mahathir in Malaysia; Suharto in Indonesia – underpinned the economic

*1955 supports Baluchistani separatists in Pakistan*
*Dec. 1979 invaded by USSR; Amin killed, Karmal installed as president; continued resistance by Islamic guerrillas*
*1988 USSR withdraws*
*1992 post Soviet-backed regime defeated by Islamic guerrillas*

*1958 military coup by Ayub Khan*
*1965 border clashes with India in Rann of Kutch*
*1965 war with India over Kashmir*
*1971 war with India over Bangladesh*
*1972 ceasefire lines established*
*1977 military coup by Zia ul-Haq*
*1988 democratic elections;. Benazir Bhutto prime minister (deposed 1990)*
*1993 Benazir Bhutto returns as prime minister (deposed 1996)*

**1 Post-independence wars and revolutions**
- civil war
- invasion
- guerrilla activity
- border dispute

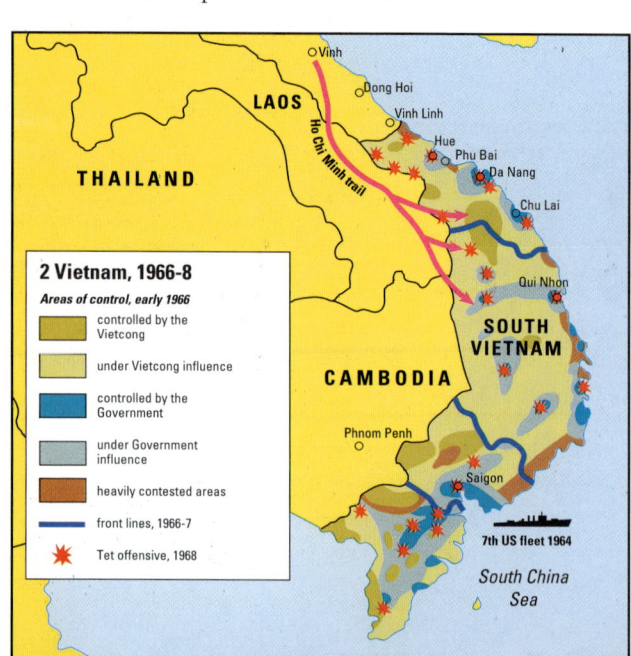

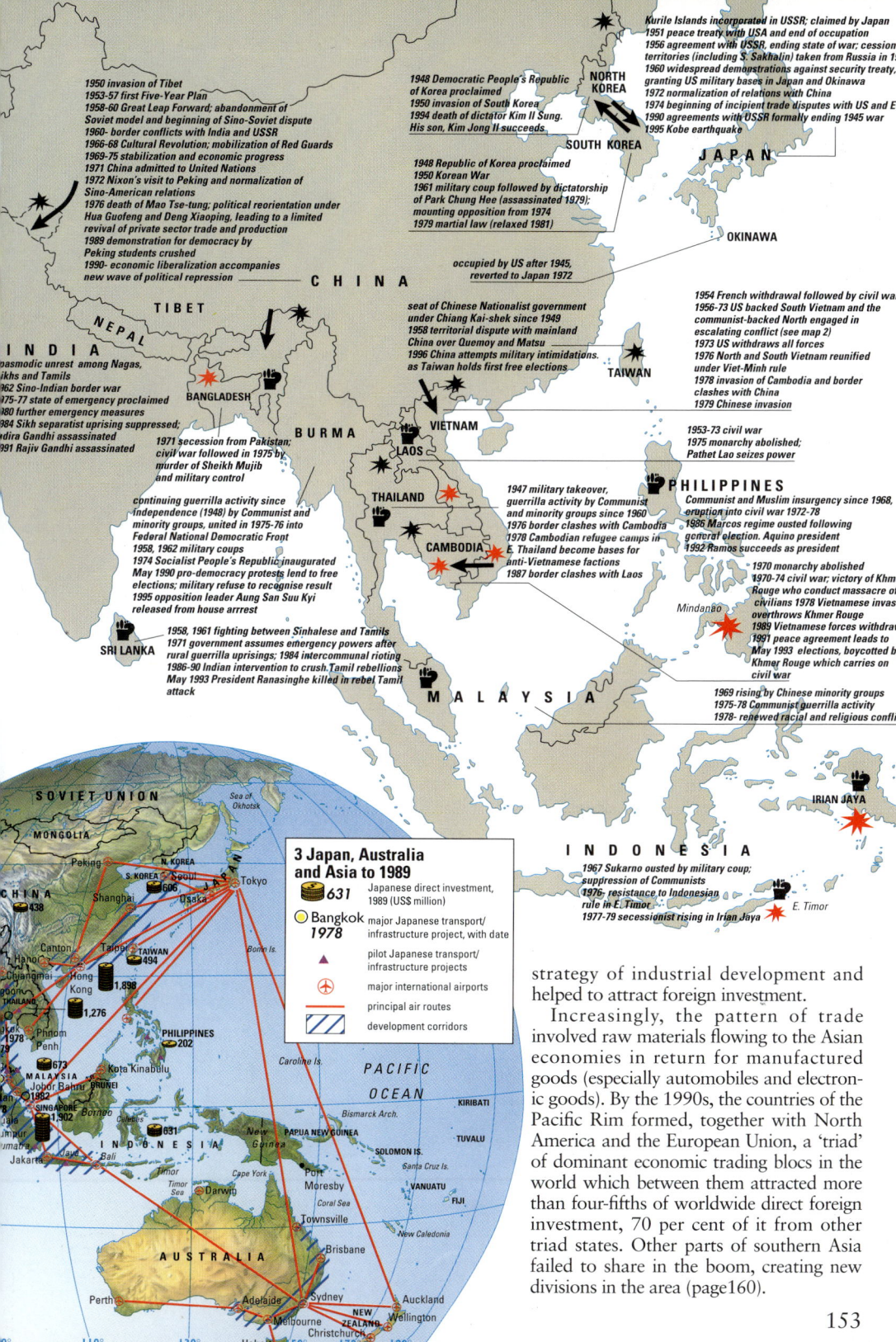

strategy of industrial development and helped to attract foreign investment.

Increasingly, the pattern of trade involved raw materials flowing to the Asian economies in return for manufactured goods (especially automobiles and electronic goods). By the 1990s, the countries of the Pacific Rim formed, together with North America and the European Union, a 'triad' of dominant economic trading blocs in the world which between them attracted more than four-fifths of worldwide direct foreign investment, 70 per cent of it from other triad states. Other parts of southern Asia failed to share in the boom, creating new divisions in the area (page 160).

# The Cold War 1947-89

The defeat of Germany, Italy and Japan and the weakening of Britain and France in World War II left the USA and USSR as the only 'superpowers'. Their ideological and political confrontation expressed itself as the Cold War. Conflict between the two had already appeared before the final victory: The Western Allies had already agreed (reluctantly) at Yalta (February 1945) to allow Soviet control of eastern Europe after the end of the war. By 1949 Stalin had developed an atomic bomb, thus ending the US monopoly of nuclear weapons. In reply, the USA built up the defence of western Europe with the formation of the North Atlantic Treaty Organization (NATO) in 1949 (page 139). In 1952 the US tested a thermo-nuclear (hydrogen) bomb; Russia followed suit in 1953.

Although it started as a conflict over central Europe, the Cold War soon developed into a global confrontation. The US saw the Korean War (1950-3: page 142) as evidence of a world-wide communist conspiracy, and American policy now became the 'containment' of Communism by a series of encircling alliances. NATO was followed by the South-East Asia Treaty Organization (SEATO) in 1954 and the Baghdad Pact (1955); the US maintained over 1400 foreign bases, including 275 bases for nuclear bombers, in 31 countries around the Soviet perimeter (map 1). As long as nuclear devices could only be delivered by aircraft, possession of these bases conferred an enormous advantage on the US. But when in the early 1960s both sides began to deploy ballistic nuclear missiles capable of being launched from land silos and submarines, the odds altered: now, in the event of war, each of the two superpowers could attack the other's cities directly (chart 3).

In October 1962, this scenario was almost put to the test when, following an unsuccessful US attempt to unseat the communist regime, the USSR established nuclear missile sites in Cuba. President Kennedy proclaimed a 'quarantine' of the island and threatened that, if the missiles were fired, the US would immediately retaliate against the USSR. The Russians then agreed to their removal (map 2). In return, Kennedy agreed to remove some US missile sites from Turkey.

This crisis, with its real threat of nuclear holocaust, proved a turning point in the Cold War. Already both monolithic blocs had begun to show signs of strain, most seriously on the Soviet side: Hungary and Poland rebelled in 1956, and from 1960 China began to quarrel openly over territory and ideology. In western Europe, France rejected American political leadership after 1958 and left NATO. A desire to limit the spread of nuclear weapons led to the conclusion of a partial test-ban treaty in 1963 and a nuclear non-proliferation treaty in 1968, but not all nuclear or potential nuclear powers signed these agreements (notably France, China and India) while others (such

1 The Soviet and American blocs, 1949-59

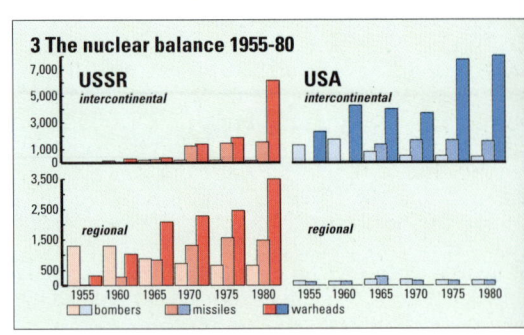

3 The nuclear balance 1955-80

as Iraq) later reneged on their commitment. The Cold War therefore continued and the superpowers created huge nuclear arsenals.

In the event, the economic and political difficulties of the USSR increased to the point where the Soviet leader Mikhail Gorbachev (1985-91) felt that only a dramatic reduction in the crushing burden of military expenditure could bring relief (page 158). First the Soviets withdrew their forces from eastern Europe (1989), then NATO and the Warsaw Pact declared that the other was no longer an enemy (1990), and finally the USSR itself began to disintegrate (1991). Further agreements on the reduction of nuclear and conventional forces soon followed, although the fate of the vast arsenal accumulated by the former USSR gave cause for concern.

# Europe since 1973

The pre-war fascist regimes of the Iberian peninsula gave way to democracy in the 1970s: Portugal in 1974, following the failure of colonial wars in Africa; Spain in 1975, following the death of General Franco. Despite an attempted right-wing coup in 1981, Spain joined NATO in 1982 and in 1986 both countries joined the European Community (EC). 1974 also saw the restoration of democracy in Greece, where a right-wing military junta had seized power in 1967, and Greece too joined the EC in 1981 (map 1).

The Community thus expanded from six members in 1957 (page 138) to nine in 1973, and twelve in 1986, and further agreements linked it with Turkey, Malta and Cyprus. The first direct elections to the European Parliament took place in 1979, and in 1985 the EC agreed an agenda and timetable for the creation of a single European market. At Maastricht in 1991 the member states agreed in principle to work towards eventual economic and monetary union and the formation of a common European foreign and security policy. All members of the rival European Free Trade Association (EFTA), except for Switzerland and Iceland, applied for membership in 1994-5, as did most of the former socialist countries of eastern Europe. In January 1995, Austria, Finland and Sweden became full members of the European Union.

Whereas the original six members had all possessed a strong industrial base, combined with a powerful agricultural workforce in 1960, by 1993 their agricultural sector had shrunk dramatically (map 2). In the 'applicant' countries, by contrast, the percentage often stood far higher (almost 50 per cent in Turkey). Furthermore, the percentage of the EC workforce engaged in industry either remained stable or declined, with the service sector employing the largest number (over 70 per cent in Britain, Belgium and the Netherlands). This development reflected the industrial depression that followed the oil crisis of 1973 (chart 3) and helped to limit the EC's foreign policy – for example, towards the civil war in the former Yugoslavia (page 158).

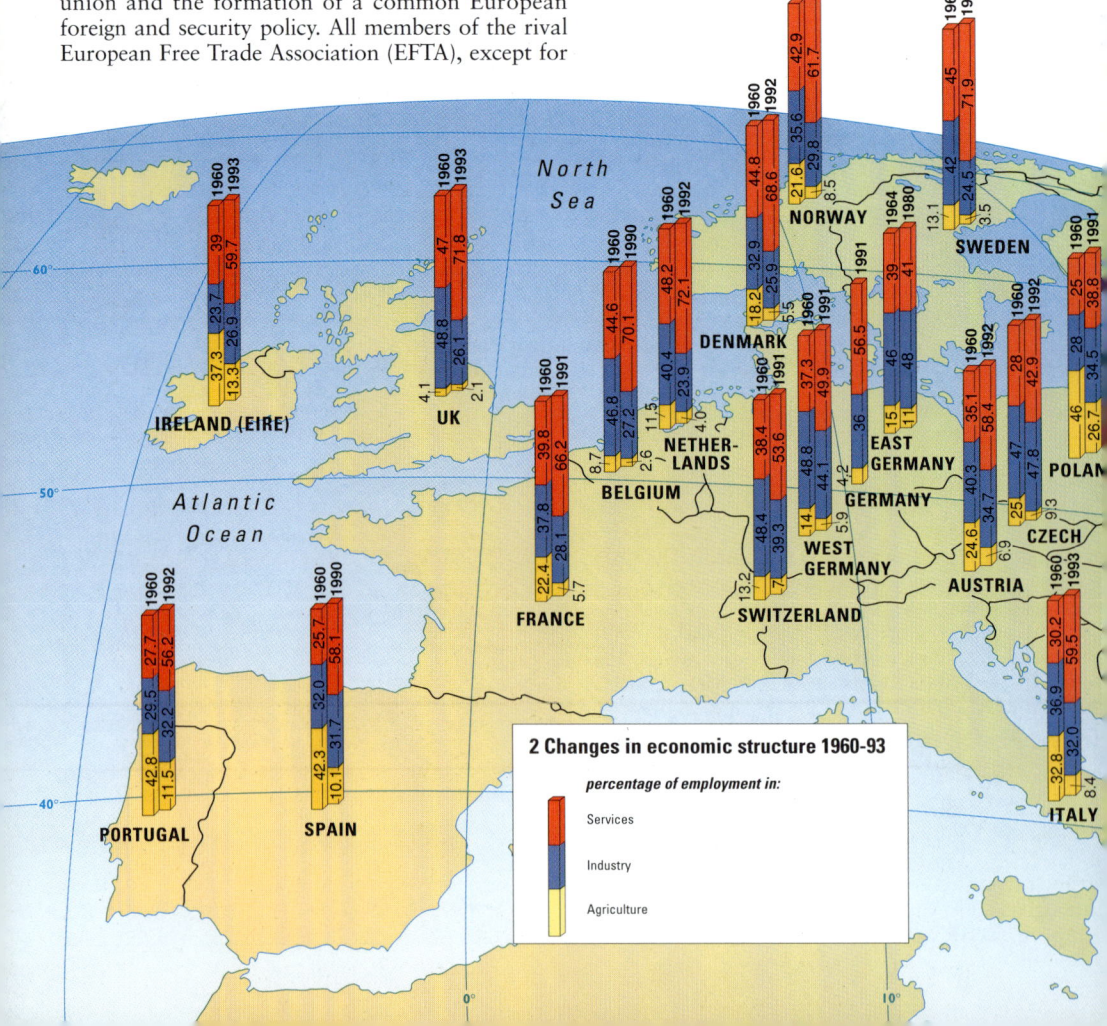

2 Changes in economic structure 1960-93

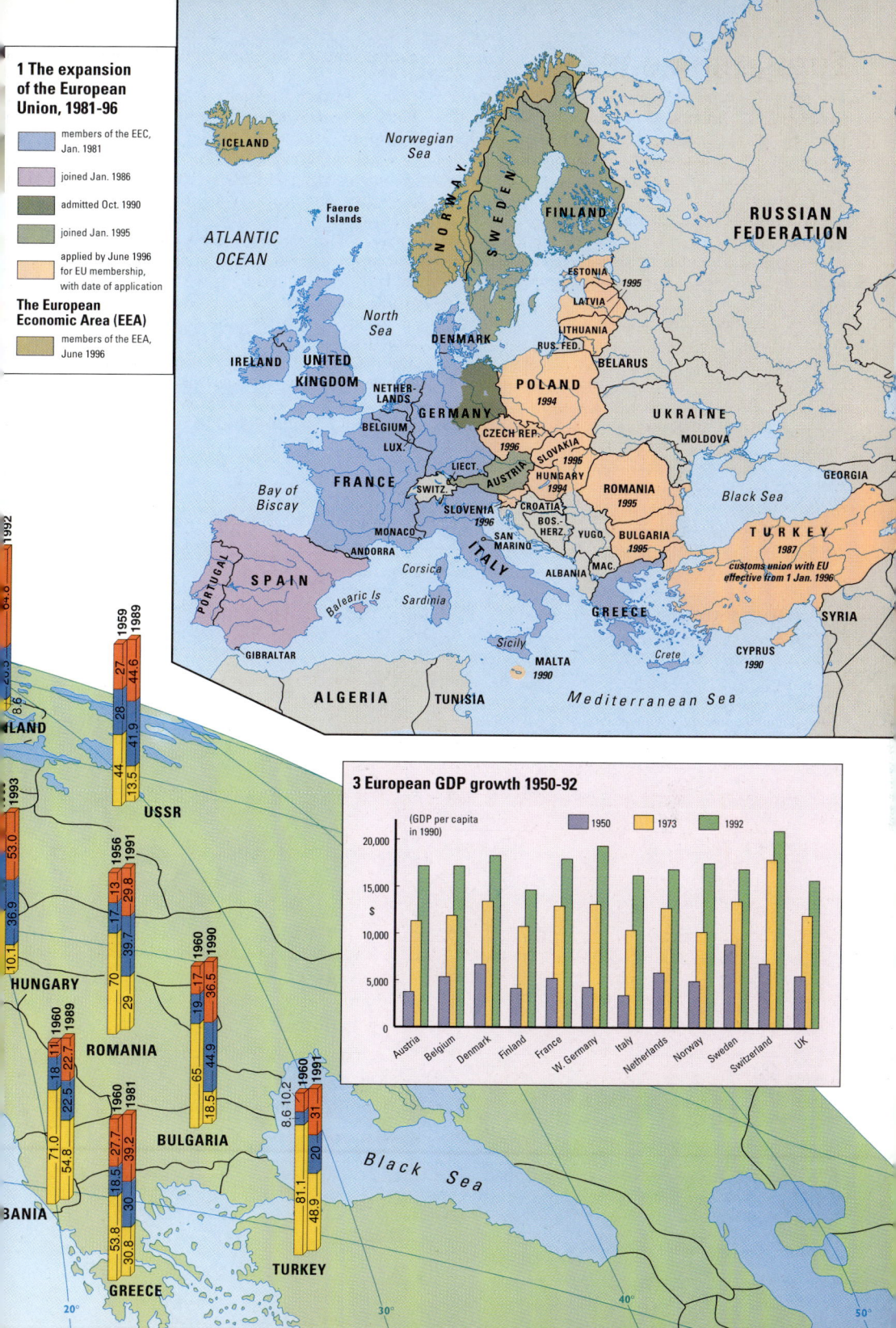

# The collapse of communism in Europe since 1989

From 1989, communism collapsed all over eastern Europe, culminating at the end of 1991 in the disintegration of the Soviet Union itself. The reasons for this startling transformation were as much economic as political. Throughout the 1970s and 1980s zero growth rates and immense external debts combined to bankrupt the communist economies of the region. Finally, unable any longer to guarantee the survival of its client states, the Soviet Union effectively abandoned them. The 'Brezhnev doctrine', formulated after the Soviet invasion to stop liberal reforms in Czechoslovakia in 1968, claimed for the Soviet Union the right to intervene in the affairs of any satellite country. But in a key speech delivered in 1987, Soviet leader Mikhail Gorbachev asserted that the 'The independence of each party, its responsibility to its people, the right to resolve questions of the country's development in a sovereign way – for us these are indisputable principles.' There could be no clearer hint to the leaders of eastern Europe – and their peoples – that they were now on their own.

The fall of communism in Europe began in August 1988 with strikes and demonstrations in Poland calling for the recognition of the free trade union Solidarity. In September 1989 a government led by Solidarity took office following partially-free elections. Shortly afterwards mass demonstrations in the German Democratic

Republic resulted in the opening of the Berlin Wall (erected by the communist government in 1961). Almost immediately a massive wave of emigration led to the collapse of the east German economy and to re-unification (3 October 1990). By 1991, free elections had been held in every country in the region, including the Soviet Union (page 140). In Czechoslovakia, tensions between Czechs and Slovaks divided the country in 1993; but everywhere except in Romania the transition to democratic rule proved relatively peaceful (map 1).

Inevitably such rapid changes created problems: political instability, as former communists sought to reassert their authority; ethnic conflicts, as age-old nationalist sentiments revived; and economic dislocations. The fall-out from these sudden events was most extreme in former Yugoslavia (map 2). The fragility of the country's unity had become increasingly clear during the 1980s. Slovenia declared its independence in 1991. A vicious seven-month war broke out when Croatia, too, declared its independence the same year: Serbian forces intervened, using as an excuse their need to protect ethnic Serbs in Croatia (12 per cent of the population).

Similar developments occurred in Bosnia-Herzegovina, where 31 per cent of the population were Serbs, 17 per cent Croats, and 44 per cent Muslims (descendants of the Slavs who converted to Islam under Ottoman rule). War broke out there in 1992 as an army of Bosnian Serbs carried out 'ethnic cleansing' – the systematic removal and sometimes extermination of rival ethnic groups – which by 1994 had caused the death of at least 100,000 and displaced half of the region's 4 million inhabitants. In 1995 a renewed Serb offensive in Bosnia provoked NATO reprisals and in November a peace-settlement was signed at Dayton, Ohio. Bosnia was partitioned into seperate ethnic republics: a predominantly Muslim state based in Sarajevo; a Serb republic with strong ambitions to unite with Serbia; and a Croat area, notionally federated with the Sarajevo government.

# The world in the 1990s

Despite unprecedented growth in prosperity after World War II, between 1960 and 1994 the economic gap separating the richest and poorest fifths of the world doubled. In part, the meagre economic performance of developing countries stemmed from rapid population growth unaccompanied by adequate increases in national income. The world population explosion slowed in the later 1980s, but long-term population increase remained a serious problem (chart 1). Improvements in health care reduced infant mortality rates and extended lifespans, except in areas where famine and disease (including AIDS) had become rife (chart 2).

In the later 1980s, the focus of economic competition between the three major trading blocs (North America, the European Union, and Japan) shifted from trade to capital. Between 1984 and 1989 the flow of foreign direct investment (FDI) rose at an annual rate of 29 per cent – three times faster than trade – to reach a total of $1500 billion.

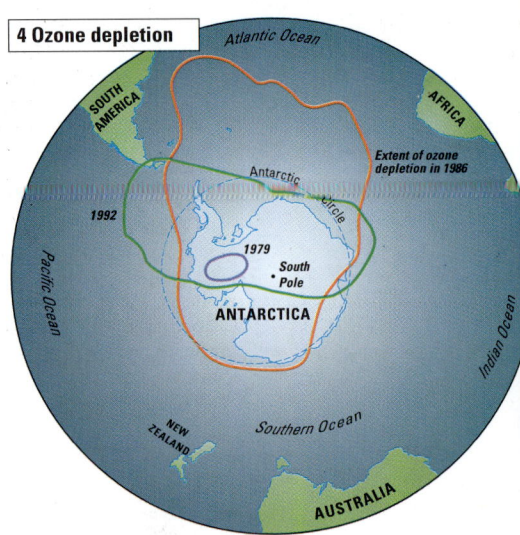

4 Ozone depletion

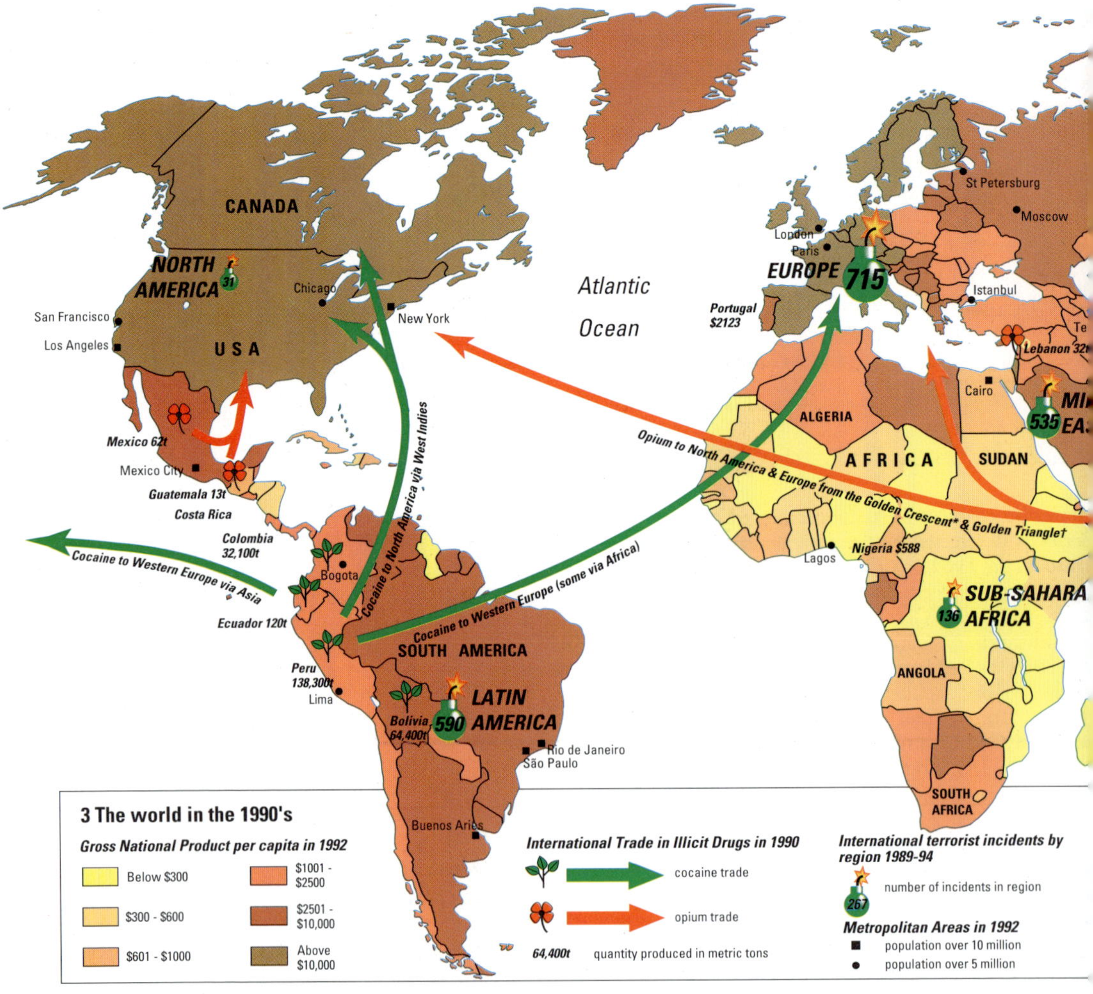

3 The world in the 1990's

**Gross National Product per capita in 1992**
- Below $300
- $300 - $600
- $601 - $1000
- $1001 - $2500
- $2501 - $10,000
- Above $10,000

**International Trade in Illicit Drugs in 1990**
- cocaine trade
- opium trade
- 64,400t quantity produced in metric tons

**International terrorist incidents by region 1989-94**
- 267 number of incidents in region

**Metropolitan Areas in 1992**
- ■ population over 10 million
- ● population over 5 million

160

Growth in world trade in goods, on the other hand, slowed from 8.5 per cent in 1988 to 3 per cent in 1991. Moreover, whereas in the earlier 1980s the proportion of world FDI in developing countries was 25 per cent, between 1985 and 1990 it shrank to a mere 17 per cent, making it increasingly difficult for those countries to finance their debts with export earnings.

However, developing countries did possess a clear competitive edge in the production and distribution of illicit drugs – opium from Asia; cocaine from South America – a $500-billion-a-year business second only to the world trade in arms. Drug production offered a vital source of hard currency and employment. Approximately 400,000 of Bolivia's 6.5 million population worked directly in the drug trade; in 1990, the gross income per acre of Peruvian coca farmers exceeded that of coffee farmers ten-fold; in 1991 Colombia alone exported an estimated 200 tons of cocaine to Europe (map 3). The UN declared the 1990s a 'decade against drugs'.

The UN also organized a conference on the Environment in Rio de Janeiro in 1992 which involved more governments (185) than any previous international gathering, and focused attention on issues such as the emission of pollution and 'greenhouse gases' (such as chlorine) that risked a potentially disastrous warming of the earth's climate by depleting the ozone layer which protects it against solar radiation (map 4). But although the economies of industrialized countries, which produced much of the existing contamination, seemed better able to adopt new, less deleterious technologies, developing countries, responsible for a growing proportion of the contamination, feared yet another expensive obstacle to their economic expansion.

Failure to tackle global problems seriously undermined confidence in the state and established institutions – whether in the former Soviet Union (page 140) or in the West, where evidence of institutionalized corruption in countries such as Japan and Italy, combined with prolonged economic recession, led some voters to favour more radical parties. But no one provided easy solutions.

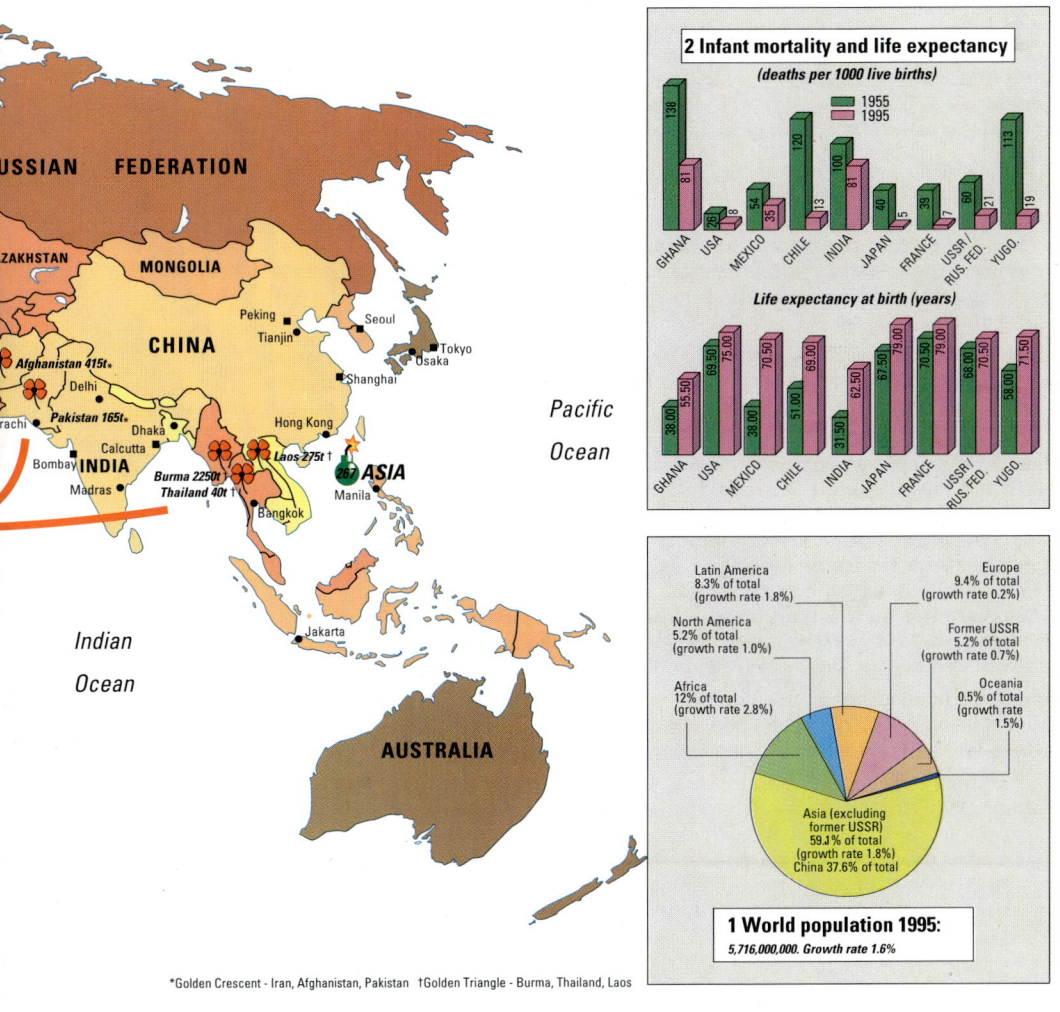

*Golden Crescent - Iran, Afghanistan, Pakistan  †Golden Triangle - Burma, Thailand, Laos

# INDEX

## 1 HISTORICAL PLACE NAMES

Geographical names vary with time and with language, and there is some difficulty in treating them consistently in an historical atlas, especially for individual maps within whose time span the same place has been known by different names. We have aimed at the simplest possible approach to the names on the maps, using the index to weld together the variations.

On the maps forms of names will be found in the following hierarchy of preference:

**a** English conventional names or spellings, in the widest sense, for all principal places and features, e.g., Moscow, Vienna, Munich (including those that today might be considered obsolete when these are appropriate to the context, e.g., Leghorn).

**b** Names that are contemporary in terms of the maps concerned. There are here three broad categories:
**i** names in the ancient world, where the forms used are classical, e.g., Latin or latinized Greek, but extending also to Persian, Sanskrit, etc.
**ii** names in the post-medieval modern world, which are given in the form (though not necessarily the spelling) current at the time of the map (e.g., St. Petersburg before 1914, not Leningrad).
**iii** modern names where the spelling generally follows that of *The Times Atlas of the World*, though in the interests of simplicity there has been a general omission of diacritics in spellings derived by transliteration from non-roman scripts, e.g., Sana rather than Ṣan'ā'.

## 2 THE INDEX

Where a place is referred to by two or more different names in the course of the atlas, there will be a corresponding number of main entries in the index. The variant names in each case are given in brackets at the beginning of the entry, their different forms and origins being distinguished by such words as *now*, *later*, *formerly* and others included in the list of abbreviations (*right*).

'Bizerta (*anc.* Hippo Zarytus)' means that the page references to that city on maps dealing with periods when it was known as Bizerta follow that entry, but the page references pertaining to it in ancient times will be found under the entry for Hippo Zarytus.

Places are located generally by reference to the country in which they lie (exceptionally by reference to island groups or sea areas), this being narrowed down where necessary by location as E(ast), C(entral), etc. The reference will normally be to the modern state in which the place now falls unless (a) there is a conventional or historical name which conveniently avoids the inevitably anachronistic ring of some modern names, e.g., Anatolia rather than Turkey, Mesopotamia rather than Iraq, or (b) the modern state is little known or not delineated on the map concerned, e.g., many places on the Africa plates can only be located as W, E, Africa, etc.

Reference is generally to page number/map number (e.g. 118/1) unless the subject is dealt with over the plate as a whole, when the references have been given sub-headings where possible, e.g., Civil War 129/4. Battles are indicted by the symbol **X**.

Though page references are generally kept in numerical order, since this corresponds for the most part with chronological order, they have been rearranged occasionally where the chronological sequence would be obviously wrong, or in the interests of grouping appropriate references under a single sub-heading.

## 3 ABBREVIATIONS

**a/c** also called
**AD** Autonomous District
**Alb.** Albanian
**anc.** ancient
**AR** Autonomous Region
**Ar.** Arabic
**a/s** also spelled
**ASSR** Autonomous Soviet Socialist Republic
**Bibl.** Biblical
**Bulg.** Bulgarian
**C** Century (when preceded by 17, 18, etc.)
**C** Central
**Cat.** Catalan
**Chin.** Chinese
**Cz.** Czech
**Dan.** Danish
**Dut.** Dutch
**E** East(ern)
**Eng.** English
**Est.** Estonian
**f/c** formerly called
**Finn.** Finnish
**form.** former(ly)
**Fr.** French
**f/s** formerly spelled
**Ger.** German
**Gr.** Greek
**Heb.** Hebrew
**Hung.** Hungarian
**Indon.** Indonesian
**Ir.** Irish
**Is.** Island
**It.** Italian
**Jap.** Japanese
**Kor.** Korean
**Lat.** Latin
**Latv.** Latvian
**Lith.** Lithuanian
**Mal.** Malay
**med.** medieval
**mod.** modern
**Mong.** Mongolian
**N** North(ern)
**n/c** now called
**Nor.** Norwegian
**n/s** now spelled
**NT** New Testament
**obs.** obsolete
**OT** Old Testament
**Pers.** Persian
**Pol.** Polish
**Port.** Portuguese
**Rom.** Romanian
**Russ.** Russian
**S** South(ern)
**s/c** sometimes called
**Som.** Somali
**Sp.** Spanish
**S.Cr.** Serbo-Croat
**SSR** Soviet Socialist Republic
**Sw.** Swedish
**Turk.** Turkish
**Ukr.** Ukrainian
**US(A)** United States (of America)
**var.** variant
**W** West(ern)
**Wel.** Welsh
**WW1** World War 1
**WW2** World War 2

**Aachen** (*Fr.* Aix-la-Chapelle *anc.* Aquisgranum) W Germany Frankish royal residence 48/1; WW1 125/1
**Abkhazia** autonomous region of Georgia 140/1
**Abyssinia** (*now* Ethiopia) 112/2
**Achaea** (*a/s* Achaia) Roman province 35/1
**Acragas** (*Lat.* Agrigentum *mod.* Agrigento) Sicily Dorian colony 30/1
**Acre** (*OT* Accho *NT* Ptolemais *Fr.* St. Jean-d'Acre *Heb.* Akko) Palestine Levantine city 20/1
**Addis Ababa** Ethiopia Italian penetration 105/1
**Aden** S Arabia early town 74/1; Ottoman Empire 102/1; taken by British 112/1; British base 145/1
**Aden Protectorate** (*successively* renamed Protectorate of South Arabia, Federation of South Arabia, People's Republic of South Yemen, People's Democratic Republic of Yemen; *now* part of United Yemen)
**Admiralty Islands** S Pacific Japanese attack 134/1
**Adowa** N Ethiopia ✗105/1
**Adrianople** (*anc.* Adrianopolis *mod.* Edirne) W Turkey Byzantine Empire 44/1; Ottoman centre 67/1; occupied by Greece 128/1
**Aegospotami** (*Turk.* Karaova Suyu) NW Turkey ✗31/2
**Aegyptus** (*mod.* Egypt) Roman province 35/1
**Afars and Issas, French Territory of** (*form.* French Somaliland *now* Republic of Djibouti)
**Afghanistan** under Abbasid sovereignty 47/2; in Safavid Empire 58/1; independent sultanate 102/1; invaded by USSR 153/1; opium trade 161/1
**Africa** early man 11/1; agricultural origins 25/1; early cultures 25/1; early empires 54/1, 55/2; slave trade 54/1, 55/2; early European voyages of discovery 72/1; European expansion and trade 74/1, 75/2; 18C European trade 97/2; European penetration 105/1; colonial empires 112/2; anti-colonial resistance 145/1; modern political developments 150/1; economy 160/1; foreign direct investment 160/1
**Africa** (*mod.* Tunisia and Libya) conversion to Christianity 32/1; Roman province 35/1; Byzantine province 44/1
**Aigun** NE China treaty port 89/2
**Ain Jalut** Palestine ✗24/1, 47/2
**Aix** (or Aix-en-Provence *anc.* Aquae Sextiae) S France archbishopric 48/1; *parlement* 77/2
**Ajnadain** Palestine ✗47/1
**Åland Islands** (*Finn.* Ahvenanmaa) SW Finland neutralized 128/1
**Alaska** state of USA purchase from Russia 108/1
**Albania** Black Death 63/1; Ottoman province 102/1; principality 119/2; annexed by Italy 129/2; Cold War 154/1; employment 156; free elections 159/1

**Albania** ancient country of Caucasus 35/1
**Albany** (*form.* Fort Orange) NE USA seized by English 81/2
**Alemannia** SW Germany part of Frankish Empire 48/1
**Aleppo** (*anc.* Beroea *a/c* Yamkhad *Fr.* Alep *Ar.* Halab) Syria Mitannian city 20/1; Byzantine Empire 44/1; centre of European trade 97/2
**Alessandria** N Italy Lombard League 51/2
**Aleutian Islands** W Alaska to USA 108/1; attacked by Japanese 134/1; retaken by Americans 135/2
**Alexandretta** (*mod.* Iskenderun) E Turkey ceded to Turkey 128/1
**Alexandria** (*Ar.* Al Iskandariyah) Egypt taken by Alexander 30/3; spread of Christianity 32/1; Roman Empire 35/1; Christian centre 41/2; Arab conquest 47/1; trade 55/2; centre of European trade 97/2
**Algeria** Ottoman province 102/1; French invasion 105/1; French colonization 104/2, 105/1, 113/1; under Vichy control 132/1; independence 145/1; political development 150/1
**Algiers** (*Fr.* Alger *Sp.* Argel *Ar.* Al Jaza'ir *anc.* Icosium) N Algeria Corsair city 55/2; Ottoman rule 66/2; Habsburg Empire 87/1; Allied landing WW2 133/2
**Alişar Hüyük** C Anatolia Hittite city 20/1
**Aljubarrota** Portugal ✗63/1
**Allenstein** (*Pol.* Olsztyn) W Poland acquired by Germany after plebiscite 128/1
**Alma-Ata** (*until 1921* Vernyy; *n/s* Almaty) C Asia industry 126/2
**Almanza** Spain ✗76/3
**Almohads** Muslim dynasty and empire of North Africa 47/2; 54/1
**Almoravids** Muslim dynasty of Morocco 47/2
**Alpes Cottiae** Roman province, France/Italy 35/1
**Alpes Maritimae** Roman province, France/Italy 35/1
**Alpes Poeninae** Roman province, France/Italy 35/1
**Alsace** (*anc.* Alsatia *Ger.* Elsass) in German Empire 51/2; acquired by French 81/2; Habsburg Empire 87/1
**Alsace-Lorraine** (*Ger.* Elsass-Lothringen) region of E France annexed by German Empire 111/2; ceded to France 128/1
**America, Central** (*a/c* Mesoamerica) agricultural origins 14/1; early peoples 22/2, 23/1; early civilizations 23/1; Aztec Empire 68/2; colonial expansion 74/1; 18C Atlantic economy 96/1; foreign direct investment 160/1
**America, North** colonization 12/2; early cultures 23/1, 69/1; early voyages of discovery 72/1; colonial expansion 81/1,2, 18C Atlantic economy 96/1; industrialization 137/2; foreign direct investment 160/1. See also Canada, United States

**America, South** colonization 12/2; agricultural origins 14/1; early peoples 23/1; early civilizations 23/1; Inca Empire 68/3; early voyages of discovery 72/1; colonial expansion 74/1, 81/1, 18C Atlantic economy 96/1; independence 107/1; modern politics 107/1; foreign direct investment 160/1
**American Samoa** S Pacific 145/1 (inset)
**Amoy** (*n/s* Xiamen) S China treaty port 89/2; Japanese influence 89/2; occupied by Japanese 117/2; 143/2
**Amphipolis** N Greece ✗31/2
**Anatolia** early agriculture 16/1; incipient urbanization 18/1; Hittite cities 20/1; Black Death 63/1; Ottoman conquest 67/1. See also Asia Minor
**Ancyra** (*mod.* Ankara *obs. Eng.* Angora) W Anatolia Roman empire 35/1; Byzantine Empire 44/1
**Andernach** (*anc.* Antunnacum) W Germany ✗51/2
**Angkor** Cambodia Buddhist site 32/1
**Angles** tribe of NW Europe, migrations 39/1
**Anglo-Egyptian Sudan** condominium 104/2; Ottoman territory under British control 112/2
**Angola** SW Africa early Portuguese trade 74/1; source of slaves 74/1; Portuguese colonization 104/2, 105/1, 112/2; independence 145/1; political development 150/1
**Angora** (*anc.* Ancyra *mod.* Ankara) W Anatolia ✗57/2
**Anguilla** island of West Indies independence 145/1 (inset)
**Anhwei** (*a/s* Anhui) province of E China Manchu expansion 88/1; economy 143/2
**Annam** N Indo-China under T'ang control 42/1; annexed by Ming 64/1; expansion and early trade 82/2
**Antarctica** 84/1; ozone depletion 160/1
**Antigua** island of West Indies colony 107/1; independence 145/1 (inset)
**Antioch** (*Lat.* Antiochia *mod.* Antakya) NW Syria Roman Empire 35/1; archbishopric 40/1; Byzantine rule 44/1
**Antipolis** (*mod.* Antibes) SE France Ionian colony 30/1
**Antung** (*now* Dandong) Manchuria treaty port 89/2
**Antwerp** (*Fr.* Anvers *Dut.* Antwerpen) Belgium town of Spanish Netherlands 86/2; WW1 125/1; WW2 133/2
**Aquileia** (*med.* Aglar) N Italy Byzantine Empire 44/1
**Aquincum** (*mod.* Budapest) Hungary Roman Empire 35/1
**Aquitaine** (*anc.* Aquitania *mod.* Guyenne) region of SW France Black Death 63/1
**Aquitania** (*mod.* Aquitaine *later* Guyenne) Roman province of Gaul 35/1; Visigothic territory conquered by Franks 48/1

**Arabia** maritime trading 18/1; spread of Judaism 32/1; centre of Islam 47/1; 18C European trade 97/2
**Arabia Petraea** Roman province of N Arabia 35/1
**Arabs** territorial losses to Byzantine Empire 44/1; independence from Ottomans 102/1; emigration from Israel 146/2
**Arachosia** (*a/c* Harauvatish) Afghanistan ancient province of Persian and Alexander's Empires 26/1
**Aragon** (*Sp.* Aragón) region of E Spain rural uprisings 63/1; Muslim minorities 84/1; Habsburg Empire 87/1
**Arakan** district of SW Burma Islamic states 60/2; British control 82/2
**Archangel** (*Russ.* Arkhangelsk) N Russia founded 79/1; industry 126/2; Allied occupation 127/1
**Arcole** N Italy ✗93/1
**Ardennes** forest Belgium/France WW1 125/1; WW2 ✗133/2
**Arelate** (*mod.* Arles) S France Roman Empire 35/1,2
**Argentina** independence from Spain 107/1; political developments 149/1; industrialization and economy 149/2; 160/1
**Arginusae** islands of the Aegean ✗31/2
**Armagnac** region of SW France annexed to France 76/1
**Armenia** (*anc.* Urartu) country of Caucasus spread of Christianity 32/1; Roman province 35/1; Muslim conquest 47/1; Ottoman Empire 102/1; independence after WW1 128/1; SSR 140/1; independence 1991 159/1
**Arras** (*anc.* Nemetocenna) N France fort 77/2; WW1 125/1
**Arretium** (*mod.* Arezzo) C Italy Etruscan city 20/1
**Artaxata** Armenia Roman Empire 35/1
**Artois** region of NE France Burgundian possession 76/1; province of France 77/2
**Ashur** (*mod.* Sharqat) Mesopotamia Assyrian Empire 20/1; Mitannian city 20/1
**Asia** early man 11/1, 12/2, 14/1; colonization by hunters 13/1; Chinese expansion 37/1; tribal movements 39/1; early voyages of discovery 72/1, 74/1; Russian expansion 79/2; 18C European trade 97/2; colonial empires 112/2; anti-colonial resistance 145/1; foreign direct investment 161/1
**Asia** (*Byzantine name* Asiana) Roman province of Anatolia 35/1
**Asia Minor** conversion to Christianity 32/1; Ottoman control 67/1. See also Anatolia
**Asir** SW Arabia Ottoman Empire 102/1
**Asoka's Empire** India 26/1
**Aspern/Essling** Austria ✗93/1

**Assyria** Empire 20/1; Roman province 35/1
**Astrakhan** S Russia occupied by Mongols 57/2; Tartar khanate 79/1; Bolshevik seizure 127/1; WW2 133/2
**Asturias** region of N Spain kingdom 48/1
**Athens** (Lat. Athenae mod. Gr. Athinai) Greece Mycenaean palace 28/2; Greek parent state 30/1; war with Sparta 31/2; invaded by Huns 39/1; Byzantine Empire 44/1; WW2 133/2
**Augusta Rauricorum** (mod. Augst) W Germany Roman Empire 35/1
**Augusta Treverorum** (mod. Trier Eng. Treves) W Germany Roman Empire 35/1
**Augusta Vindelicorum** (mod. Augsburg) S Germany Roman Empire 35/1
**Augustodunum** (mod. Autun) C France Roman Empire 35/1
**Augustów** NE Poland WW1 125/1
**Aulon** (later Avlona mod. Vlorë) Albania Dorian colony 30/1
**Austerlitz** (mod. Slavkov) Czechoslovakia ✕93/1
**Australia** (originally called New Holland) early man 11/1; before the Europeans 24/2; settlement and development 100/1; emergence of Commonwealth 113/1; WW2 135/2; Pacific trade 153/3; foreign direct investment 161
**Austrasia** the eastern Frankish Empire 48/1
**Austria** (Ger. Österreich) German settlement 51/2; acquired by Habsburgs 62/2; Black Death 63/1; attacked by Ottomans 66/2; War of the Spanish Succession 76/3; Habsburg Empire 87/1; opposition to Napoleon 93/1; annexed by Germany 129/2; Allied occupation zones 139/1; employment 156; EFTA 159/1
**Austro-Hungarian Empire** (a/c Austria-Hungary) Industrial Revolution 95/2; European alliances 118/2; world trade 1860-1913 120/3; overseas trade 121/1; WW1 125/1; dismantled 128/1
**Avignon** (anc. Avenio) S France in Great Schism 63/1; Papal enclave 77/2
**Azerbaijan** (anc. Atropatene) country of the Caucasus Mongol Empire 24/1; Muslim conquest 47/1; Ottoman conquest 58/1, 66/2; acquired by Russia 79/1, 102/1; independence after WW1 128/1; SSR 140/1; independence 1991 159/1
**Azores** (Port. Açores) islands of N Atlantic trade 74/1; Portuguese colony 112/2
**Aztec Empire** Mexico 68/2; 1492 70/1
**Babylon** Mesopotamia Sumerian city 20/1; taken by Alexander 30/3
**Badajoz** SW Spain ✕93/1
**Badr** W Arabia ✕ 47/1
**Baetica** S Spain Roman province 35/1
**Baffin Island** N Canada discovery 72/1

**Baghdad** Mesopotamia Mongol attack 24/1; Mongol conquest 57/2; under Ottoman rule 67/1; Gulf War 147/3
**Baghdad Pact** 147/1
**Bahamas** islands of N Caribbean discovery 72/1; British colony 81/1 107/1, 112/2; independence 145/1 (Inset)
**Bahrain** (f/s Bahrein Ar. Al Bahrayn) island of Persian Gulf independent sheikhdom 102/1; independence 145/1; Gulf War 147/3
**Bailén** S Spain ✕93/1
**Baku** (n/s Baki) Azerbaijan conquered by Ottomans 58/1, 66/2; industry 126/2; British occupation 127/1
**Balagansk** s/c Siberia founded 79/2
**Balearic Islands** W Mediterranean Byzantine Empire 44/1; attacked by Saracens 50/1; to Spain 76/3
**Balikpapan** E Borneo recaptured from Japanese 135/2
**Balkans** alliances 118/2; rise of nationalism 119/1
**Balkh** (anc. Bactra a/c Zariaspa) Afghanistan Mongol attack 24/1; conquest 47/1
**Baluchistan** region of NW India district of Mughal Empire 59/1; tribal agency 91/3
**Bandjarmasin** (n/s Banjarmasin) S Borneo trade centre 82/2
**Bangkok** (Thai. Krung Thep) S Thailand early trade centre 82/2; captured by Japanese 135/2; trade with Japan 153/3
**Bangladesh** (form. East Pakistan or East Bengal) 153/1
**Bantam** (form. Banten) Java early trade 60/2
**Baqubah** N Iraq oilfield 146/1
**Bar** region of NE France/W Germany Burgundian possession 76/1
**Barbados** island of West Indies British colony 107/1; independence 145/1 (inset)
**Barcelona** (anc. Barcino) NE Spain urban revolt 63/1; ✕93/1
**Basque Republic** N Spain autonomy 128/1
**Bashkir ASSR** W USSR 140/1
**Basra** (Ar. Al Başrah) Mesopotamia ✕47/1; Ottoman conquest 66/2; centre of European trade 97/2; Gulf War 146/1
**Bassano** N Italy ✕93/1
**Basutoland** (now Lesotho) S Africa British protectorate 104/2
**Batavia** (form. Sunda Kalapa, since 1949 Jakarta f/s Djakarta) Java early trade 75/2; centre of European trade 97/2; occupied by Japanese 134/1
**Batum** (n/s Batumi) Caucasus industry 126/2; British occupation 127/1
**Bautzen** E Germany ✕9m3/1
**Bavaria** (Ger. Bayern) part of Frankish Empire 51/2; Reformation 84/1; German Empire 111/2
**Bechuanaland** (now Botswana) country of S Africa British protectorate 104/2

**Beijing** (f/s Peking) N China economy 1979-92 143/2
**Belarus** (a/c Belorussia) end of Communism 159/1
**Belgian Congo** (form. Congo Free State now Zaire) colony 104/2, 112/2; independence 145/1
**Belgica** Roman province of NE France 35/1
**Belgium** (form. Spanish Netherlands or Southern Netherlands) colonial empire 112/2; world trade 1860-1913 120/3; foreign investment 1914 121/2; WW1 125/1; acquisition of Eupen and Malmédy 128/1; economic and social development 1929-39, 130/1; WW2 132/2; EEC and NATO 138/2, 154/1; employment 156
**Belgrade** (anc. Singidunum S. Cr. Beograd) C Yugoslavia Ottoman conquest 66/2; WW1 125/1; WW2 133/2
**Belize** (form. British Honduras) independence 145/1 (inset); 149/1
**Belleau Wood** NE France WW1 125/1 (inset)
**Belorussia** (n/c Belarus, f/c White Russia) independence after WW1 128/1; SSR 140/1; 1993 159/1
**Benevento** (anc. Beneventum) C Italy dukedom under Byzantine Empire 44/1
**Bengal** country of E India district of Mughal Empire 59/1; under British rule 90/1,2, 91/3
**Benghazi** (anc. Berenice Ar. Banghazi) Libya Italian occupation 105/1; WW2 132/1
**Berbers** attack Roman Africa 39/1; people of NW Africa 52/1
**Berenice** (mod. Benghazi) Libya city of Roman Empire 35/1
**Berezina** river W Russia ✕93/1
**Besançon** (anc. Vesontio) E France archbishopric 48/1; fort 77/2
**Beshbalik** W Mongolia Mongol attack 24/1
**Bessarabia** region of Romania/Russia acquired by Russia 79/1; Ottoman province 102/1; regained by Russia 127/1; lost to Romania 128/1
**Bigorre** region of SW France independent fief 76/1
**Bihać** Bosnia-Herzegovina civil war 158/2
**Bithynia** ancient country of NW Anatolia 31/1; Byzantine Empire 44/1
**Bithynia and Pontus** Anatolia Roman province 35/1
**Bizerta** (anc. Hippo Zarytus Fr. Bizerte Ar. Banzart) Tunisia under Abbasids 47/2; Habsburg Empire 87/1; WW2 133/2
**Black Death** 63/1
**Blenheim** (Ger. Blindheim) W Germany ✕(called Höchstädt by French and Germans) 76/3
**Boğazköy** (anc. Hattushash Gr. Pteria) C Anatolia Hittite city 20/1
**Bohemia** (Ger. Böhmen) W part of mod. Czechoslovakia kingdom within Holy Roman Empire 51/2; expansion 62/2; Black Death 63/1; Reformation 84/1, 86/3;

**Habsburg Empire** 87/1; Austro-Hungarian Empire 128/1
**Bolgar** (a/c Bulgar) C Russia Mongol city 24/1
**Bolivia** country of S America independence 107/1; 20C revolutions 149/1; economy 149/2
**Bombay** W India British settlement 75/2; British rule 90/2; industry 91/3; centre of European trade 97/2
**Bona** (mod. Annaba Fr. Bône) N Algeria acquired by Habsburgs 87/1
**Bonin Islands** (a/c Ogasawara Islands) N Pacific annexed by Japan 117/2; attacked by US forces 134/1
**Borneo** (Indon. Kalimantan) island of East Indies Dutch trade 82/2; Dutch and British colonization 113/1; occupied by Japanese 134/1; retaken by Allies 135/2
**Bornhöved** N Germany ✕51/2
**Bornu** Nigeria early state 55/2
**Borobudur** C Java Buddhist site 32/1
**Borodino** W Russia ✕93/1
**Bosnia** country of C Yugoslavia under Hungarian Kingdom 62/2; Black Death 63/1; vassal state of Ottoman Empire 67/1
**Bosnia-Herzegovina** (S. Cr. Bosna i Hercegovina) under Ottoman rule 102/1; part of Austria-Hungary 119/1; after WW1 128/1; independence and civil war 158/2
**Bosporan Kingdom** S Russia 35/1
**Botswana** (form. Bechuanaland) S Africa independence 145/1
**Bougainville** one of Solomon Islands, W Pacific recaptured from Japanese 135/2
**Bourbonnais** (à/c Bourbon) region of C France annexed to France 76/1
**Brandenburg** region of E Germany under Bohemian rule 62/2; Black Death 63/1; Reformation 84/1, 86/3; part of Prussia 111/2
**Brazil** discovered 72/1; early trade 74/1; Portuguese colony 81/1, 92/1; 18C Atlantic economy 96/1; independent empire 107/1; economy and political development 160/1
**Breitenfeld** E Germany ✕86/3
**Brest** (a/c Brest-Litovsk Pol. Brześć nad Bugiem) W Russia WW1 125/1
**Breton March** NW France 48/1
**Brigantes** Britain early tribe 35/1
**Brihuega** C Spain ✕76/3
**Britain** 18C Atlantic economy 96/1. See also England, United Kingdom
**Britannia Inferior** Roman province of N England 35/1
**Britannia Superior** Roman province of S England 35/1
**British Bechuanaland** S Africa 105/1
**British Cameroons** (now part of Cameroon)
**British Central Africa** (later Nyasaland) protectorate 105/1
**British Columbia** province of W Canada joins Confederation 113/1, 115/2
**British East Africa** (now Kenya) colony 105/1
**British Empire** 112/2

**British Guiana** (*now* Guyana) S America colony 107/1
**British Honduras** (*now* Belize) C America colony 107/1
**British North Borneo** (*now* Sabah)
**British Somaliland** (*now part of* Somalia) E Africa protectorate 104/2
**Brittany** (*Fr.* Bretagne) NW France on borders of Frankish Empire 48/1; Black Death 63/1; annexed to France 76/1
**Brunswick** (*Ger.* Braunschweig) N Germany urban revolt 63/1; German state 111/2; WW1 125/1
**Bukhara** city and province of C Asia Mongol attack 24/1; Muslim conquest 47/1; in Timur's empire 57/2; khanate 102/1, 108/1; industry 126/2
**Bukovina** region of Romania WW1 125/1
**Bulgaria** conversion to Christianity 40/1; Slav settlement 52/1; Black Death 63/1; under Ottoman rule 67/1, 102/1; Industrial Revolution 95/2; independence 119/1; Balkan alliances 119/2; WW1 125/1; conflict with Greece 128/1; WW2 133/2; Warsaw Pact and Comecon 138/2; employment 156; end of Communist rule 159/1. *See also* Rumelia
**Bulgars** tribe of E Europe 35/2
**Buna** SE New Guinea recaptured by Allies 135/2
**Bunce Island** Sierra Leone British settlement 55/2
**Bunker Hill** NE USA ✕99/1
**Burdigala** (*mod.* Bordeaux) SW France Roman Empire 35/1
**Burgundy** (*Fr.* Bourgogne) region of E France annexed to France 76/1; province of France 77/2
**Burkina (Faso)** *see* Upper Volta
**Burma** Mongol invasion 24/1; spread of Buddhism 60/2; early state 82/1; tributary state of Chinese Empire 88/1; under British rule 91/3, 112/2; Japanese support for independence movements 117/2; Japanese occupation 134/1; retaken by Allies 135/2; independence 145/1; political development 153/1; opium trade 161
**Bursa** (*anc.* Prusa *later* Brusa) W Anatolia centre of Ottoman state 67/1
**Burundi** (*form.* Urundi) country of C Africa native state 55/2; independence 145/1; political development 150/1. *See also* Ruanda-Urundi
**Buryat-Mongol ASSR** E USSR 140/1
**Byblos** (*mod.* Jubail) Syria Levantine city 20/1; early trade 20/1; Phoenician city 30/1
**Byzantine Empire** (*a/c* East Roman Empire) 44/1, 47/1,2, 50/1; conflict with Seljuks 47/2
**Byzantium** (*Eng.* Constantinople *mod.* Istanbul) E Thrace Dorian colony 30/1; Peloponnesian War 31/2

**Caesaraugusta** (*mod.* Zaragoza *Eng.* Saragossa) N Spain Roman Empire 35/1
**Caesarea** C Israel Roman Empire 35/1
**Caesarea** (*mod.* Cherchell) N Algeria Roman Empire 35/1
**Caesarea** (*a/c* Caesarea Cappadociae *mod.* Kayseri) C Anatolia Roman Empire 35/1; Byzantine Empire 44/1
**Cairo** (*Fr.* Le Caire *Ar.* Al Qahirah and Al Fustat – Old Cairo) Egypt Muslim conquest 47/1; early trade 55/2; Ottoman Empire 66/2
**Calcutta** E India trade 75/2; British settlement 75/2; industry 91/3; centre of European trade 97/2
**Calicut** (*a/c* Kozhikode) SW India trade 74/1; industry 91/3
**California** state of SW USA ceded by Mexico 107/1; Depression 131/2
**Callatis** Bulgaria Ionian colony 30/1
**Camarina** Sicily Dorian colony 31/2
**Cambodia** (*known formally as* Democratic Kampuchea *earlier* Khmer Republic) temple kingdoms 61/1; invaded by Siam and Vietnam 82/2; French protectorate 112/2; independence 145/1; political development 153/1
**Camden** SE USA ✕99/1
**Cameroon** (*f/s* Cameroons, Cameroun *Ger.* Kamerun) country of W Africa German colony 112/2; independence 145/1; economy 160/1
**Canada** Confederation 113/1; development 115/2; Pacific trade 152/2; NATO 154/1; economy 160/1
**Canton** (*Chin.* Guangzhou) S China Mongol base 24/1; Ming provincial capital 64/1; treaty port 89/2; centre of European trade 97/2; captured by Japanese 117/2; economy 143/3, 153/3
**Cape Bojador** NW Africa ✕55/2
**Cape Coast Castle** (*a/c* Cape Coast) Ghana centre of European trade 97/2
**Cape Colony** S Africa British colony 105/1
**Cape of Good Hope** S Africa Dutch settlement 55/2; first European voyage 72/1
**Cape Province** S Africa established by Dutch East India Co. 55/2
**Cape Town** South Africa Dutch settlement 55/2; centre of European trade 97/2
**Cape Verde Islands** W Africa Portuguese exploration 55/2; Portuguese sovereignty 112/2; independence 145/1
**Caporetto** N Italy WW1✕125/1
**Cappadocia** (*Pers.* Katpatuka) county of E Anatolia Roman province 35/1; Byzantine province 44/1
**Carales** (*mod.* Cagliari) Sardinia Roman Empire 35/1
**Carchemish** (*Turk.* Karkamiş) E Anatolia 20/1
**Caribbean** European settlement 74/1; colonial expansion 81/1; US involvement 149/1
**Carinthia** (*Ger.* Kärnten) province of S Austria medieval German Empire 51/2; acquired by Habsburgs 62/2; Habsburg Empire 87/1
**Carmania** county of E Persia 23/3, 26/1

**Carniola** (*Ger.* Krain) region of Austria/ Yugoslavia medieval Germany 51/2; acquired by Habsburgs 62/2; Habsburg Empire 87/1
**Carolina** N America British settlement 81/2
**Caroline Islands** C Pacific German sovereignty 112/2; captured by US from Japanese 135/2
**Carpathos** (*It.* Scarpanto) island of E Mediterranean colonization 28/2
**Carpi** N Italy ✕76/3
**Carthage** (*Lat.* Carthago) Tunisia Stone Age site 25/1; Phoenician colony 30/1; Byzantine reconquest 39/1; Muslim conquest 47/1
**Cassano** N Italy ✕76/3
**Castiglione** N Italy ✕93/1
**Castile** region of Spain Habsburg Empire 87/1
**Castulo** (*mod.* Cazlona) S Spain Roman Empire 35/1
**Catalonia** (*Sp.* Cataluña *Cat.* Catalunya) region of NE Spain under French rule 93/1; autonomous 128/1
**Caucasus** USSR famine 1932 126/2
**Central African Federation** (Northern Rhodesia, Southern Rhodesia, Nyasaland)
**Central African Republic** (*form.* Central African Empire *form.* Ubangi-Shari) independence 145/1; political development 150/1
**Ceos** (*mod.* Kea) island of the Aegean colonization 28/2
**Cephalonia** (*mod.* Kefallinia) island of the Ionian Byzantine Empire 45/2; Venetian territory 67/1
**Cerdagne** (*Sp.* Cerdaña) region of France and Spain Habsburg territory 77/2
**Cerigo** (*anc.* Cythera, *mod.* Kithira) island of S Greece Venetian territory 67/1
**Ceuta** (*Ar.* Sebta) Spanish enclave in N Morocco Spanish occupation 112/2
**Ceylon** (*anc.* Taprobane, Sinhala *or* Lanka *a/c* Saylan, Sarandib) 26/1; under British rule 90/1; Buddhism 91/3; independence 145/1; adopted title Republic of Sri Lanka 145/1; political developments 153/1
**Chad** (*Fr.* Tchad) country of C Africa independence from French 145/1; political development 150/1; economy 160/1
**Chagatai Empire** C Asia Mongol state 24/1
**Chahar** former province of N China 88/1; independent of Nanking 122/2
**Chalcedon** (*mod.* Kadiköy) NW Anatolia Dorian colony 30/1; centre of early Christianity 32/1
**Champa** Hindu-Buddhist kingdom of Indo-China 42/1, 60/2, 61/1
**Chandernagore** E India French settlement 75/2
**Changchun** Manchuria treaty port 89/2; economy 143/2
**Changsha** C China Han principality 36/2; treaty town 89/2; economy 143/2

**Charolais** region of E France Habsburg possession 76/1
**Château-Thierry** N France ✕93/1; WW1 125/1 (inset)
**Chechenia** (*Russ.* Chechnya) autonomous region of S Russia 159/1
**Chechen-Ingush ASSR** Caucasus 141/1
**Chekiang** (*n/s* Zhejiang) province of E China Ming economy 65/1; Manchu expansion 88/1; economy 143/2
**Cherbourg** N France French naval base 77/2; WW2 133/2
**Cherchen** Chin. C Asia silk route 37/1
**Chernigov** Ukraine bishopric 40/1; principality 53/2
**Chersonesus** Crimea Ionian colony 30/1
**Chile** 18C Atlantic economy 96/1; independence from Spain 107/1; political development 149/1; economy 149/2
**China** early man 11/1; early agriculture 16/2; centre of urban civilization 19/1; Sung Empire conquered by Mongols 24/1; Buddhism 32/1; Han expansion 36/2, 37/1; T'ang Empire 42/1; Ming Empire 65/1, 70/1; early trade 65/1; Manchu expansion 88/1; Manchu Empire 89/2; European spheres of influence 89/2; 18C European trade 97/2; Japanese occupation 117/2; Communist Party founded 122/2; WW2 135/2; economy 1979-92 143/2; Pacific trade 153/3; political development 153/1; Cold War 154/1
**Chungking** (*n/s* Chongqing) C China treaty town 89/2; capital during WW2 117/2; industry 143/2
**Chuvashi** tribe of C Russia conquered 79/1; ASSR 140/1
**Cilicia** (*Hittite name* Kizzuwadna) region of S Anatolia 31/1; Roman province 35/1; Byzantine Empire 44/1
**Cochin** region of S India Portuguese rule 74/1, 75/2; Dutch settlement 74/1; British rule 90/2
**Cochin-China** region of S Indo-China expansion into Cambodia 82/2; French control 113/1
**Cocos Islands** (*now* under Australian administration *called* Cocos-Keeling islands) Indian Ocean British control 112/2
**Colchis** ancient country of the Caucasus Ionian colonization 30/1
**Cold War** 155/1
**Cologne** (*anc.* Colonia Agrippina *Ger.* Köln) W Germany archbishopric 48/1; medieval city 51/2; WW1 125/1; WW2 133/2
**Colombia** independence from Spain 107/1; political development 149/1; economy 149/2; cocaine trade 160/1
**Colombo** Ceylon Portuguese trade 74/1; Dutch trade 75/2; capital of British colony 91/3; centre of European trade 97/2
**Colonia Agrippina** (*a/c* Colonia Agrippinesis *mod.* Köln *Eng.* Cologne) NW Germany Roman Empire 35/1

165

**Commagene** region of SE Anatolia Roman province 35/1
**Comoro Islands** E Africa spread of Islam 55/2; French colonization 112/2; independence 145/1
**Concord** NE USA ✕99/1
**Confederate States of America** 99/3
**Confederation of the Rhine** 92/2
**Congo** (form. Middle Congo or French Congo) region of Africa independence 145/1; economy 160/1
**Congo Free State** (later Belgian Congo now Zaire) 105/1, 112/2
**Constance** (anc. Constantia Ger. Konstanz) S Germany Frankish kingdom 51/2
**Constantinople** (anc. Byzantium mod. Istanbul) NW Turkey centre of early Christianity 32/1; Avar attack 39/1; patriarchate 40/1; Arab attacks 47/1; Ottoman conquest 66/1; WW1 125/1
**Coral Sea** S Pacific ✕134/1, 135/2
**Corcyra** (mod. Corfu Gr. Kerkíra) island of NW Greece Donan colony 30/1
**Córdoba** (anc. Corduba) S Spain Muslim conquest 47/1; Umayyad Caliphate and Muslim city 50/1;
**Corduba** (mod. Córdoba) S Spain Roman Empire 35/1
**Corfu** (anc. Corcyra mod. Gr. Kerkira) island of W Greece Byzantine Empire 45/3; Ottoman siege 66/2; under Venetian rule 67/1
**Corinth** (Lat. Corinthus Gr. Korinthos) C Greece parent state 30/1; Byzantine Empire 44/1
**Corinthus** (Gr. Korinthos Eng. Corinth) C Greece town of Roman Empire 35/1
**Cork** S Ireland Viking settlement 50/1
**Corregidor** C Philippines surrender to Japanese 134/1
**Corsica** island of W Mediterranean Byzantine Empire 44/1; Muslim conquest 47/1; Saracen attack 50/1; Genoese rule 87/1; annexed by France 110/1
**Corunna** (Sp. La Coruña) NW Spain ✕93/1
**Cossacks** S Russia attacked by Ottomans 79/1; anti-Bolshevik activity 127/1
**Costa Rica** country of C America independence 107/1; political development 149/1; economy 149/2; 160/1
**Crete** (Lat. Creta mod. Gr. Kriti) Byzantine Empire 44/1; Muslim conquest 47/1; Ottoman province 102/1; cession to Greece 119/1; German capture 133/2
**Crimea** (Russ. Krym) S Russia Mongol Empire 24/1; Ottoman vassal khanate 67/1; acquired by Russia 79/1
**Croatia** (S. Cr. Hrvatska) conversion to Christianity 40/1; under Hungarian Kingdom 62/2; Habsburg Empire 87/1; forms part of Yugoslavia 128/1; WW2 133/2; independence and civil war 158-159

**Croton** (mod. Crotone) S Italy Achaean colony 30/1
**Crusades** 45/2
**Ctesiphon** (a/c Tayspun) Mesopotamia Roman Empire 35/1
**Cuba** discovered 72/1; Spanish colony 74/1; 81/1; independence 107/1; US Protectorate 149/1; Cold War crisis 155/2
**Cynossema** W Anatolia ✕31/2
**Cyprus** Gr. Kypros Turk. Kibris anc. Alashiya) Greek and Phoenician colonization 30/1; Byzantine Empire 44/1; Muslim expansion 47/1; acquired by Turks 66/2; independence 145/1
**Cyrenaica** region of N Africa Roman province 35/1; Muslim conquest 47/1; Ottoman rule 55/2; Italian conquest 105/1
**Cyrene** (It. Cirene) N Libya Dorian colony 30/1; spread of Christianity and Judaism 32/1; centre of Roman province 35/1
**Cythera** (a/c Cerigo mod. Gr Kithira) island S Greece colonization 28/1; captured by Athens 31/2
**Cyzicus** NW Anatolia Ionian colony 30/1; taken by 30/3; ✕31/2
**Czechoslovakia** created 128/1; territory lost to Germany and Hungary 129/2, 133/2; Comecon and Warsaw Pact 138/3; employment 156; end of Communist rule 159/1
**Czechs** post-War migration to West 139/1
**Czernowitz** (now Russ. Chernovtsy Rom. Cernăuţi) E Austro-Hungarian Empire WW1 125/1
**Dacia** (mod. Romania) Byzantine Empire 44/1
**Dagestan ASSR** Caucasus 140/1
**Daghestan** region of Caucasus acquired by Russia 102/1
**Dahomey** (n/c Benin) country of W Africa early state 55/2; French colony 105/1, 112/2; independence 145/1
**Dairen** (n/s Dalian Russ. Dalny) Manchuria ceded to Russia and Japan 89/2; 143/2
**Dai Viet** kingdom of N Indo-China 61/1
**Dalmatia** region of E Adriatic Byzantine Empire 45/2; civil war 143/2
**Daman** (Port. Damão) NW India Portuguese settlement 91/3
**Damascus** (Fr. Damas Ar. Ash Sham or Dimashq) Syria Levantine city 20/1; Byzantine Empire 44/1; Muslim conquest 47/1; revolt against Ottoman rule 66/2; Ottoman Empire 67/1
**Damietta** (Ar. Dumyat) N Egypt Byzantine Empire 44/1
**Da Nang** (Fr. Tourane) C Indo-China Vietnamese war 152/2/3
**Danzig** (Pol. Gdańsk) N Poland Free City 128/1
**Dardanelles** (Turk. Çanakkale Boğazi anc. Hellespont) straits, NW Turkey demilitarized and remilitarized 128/1

**Dar es Salaam** E Africa occupied by the Germans 105/1
**Darfur** region of W Sudan stone age culture 25/1; early state 54/1, 55/2
**Dauphiné** region of SE France province of France 77/2
**Dego** N Italy ✕93/1
**Deira** ancient kingdom of N England 48/2
**Delaware** state of E USA settled by Swedes 81/2; British colony 99/1; Depression 131/2
**Delhi** city and region of N India district of Mughal Empire 59/1; Indian Mutiny 90/2
**Delian League** Greece 31/2
**Delium** E Greece ✕31/2
**Denain** N France ✕76/3
**Denmark** conversion to Christianity 40/1; Reformation 84/1; Industrial Revolution 95/2; war with Prussia and Austria 111/2; WW1 125/1; N Holstein acquired by plebiscite 128/1; WW2 133/2; EEC and NATO 138/2, 154/1; employment 156
**Diu** NW India 59/1; Portuguese settlement 75/1, 75/2, 112/2; centre of European trade 97/2
**Diyarbakir** SE Anatolia revolt against Ottoman rule 66/2
**Djerba** island of Tunisia ✕57/2
**Djibouti** (s/c Jibuti) NE Africa occupied by French 105/1
**Dobruja** (a/s Dobrudža) region of Romania/Bulgaria Ottoman Empire 67/1, 119/1, 128/1
**Dodecanese** (Gr. Dhodhekanisos) islands of SE Aegean occupied by Italy, ceded to Turkey 119/1
**Dominica** island of West Indies British colony 107/1; independence 145/1 (inset)
**Dominican Republic** Caribbean independence 107/1; US intervention 149/1
**Dorchester-on-Thames** S England ✕48/2
**Dorestad** (a/c Duurstede) Netherlands Viking invasion and settlement 50/1
**Douala** Cameroon W Africa German occupation 105/1
**Dresden** E Germany ✕93/1; WW1 125/1; WW2 133/2
**Dristov** Romania ✕52/1
**Dubai** (Al. Dubayy) SE Arabia 147/3
**Dublin** (Ir. Baile Atha Cliath) Ireland Scandinavian settlement and control 50/1; WW1 125/1
**Dunkirk** (Fr. Dunkerque) N France fortification 77/2; WW2 132/1
**Dura-Europos** (mod. Salahiyeh) Syria Mithraic site 32/1; Roman Empire 35/1
**Durazzo** (anc. Epidamnus later Dyrrhachium mod. Durrës) Albania WW1 125/1
**Durocortorum** (mod. Rheims) N France Roman Empire 35/1
**Dushanbe** (1929-1961 Stalinabad) Russ. C Asia industry 126/2
**Dutch East Indies** (now Indonesia) early Dutch trade 75/2; early Dutch possessions 82/2; occupied by

Japanese 134/1; independence 145/1 (inset)
**Dutch Guiana** (now Surinam) S America 79/1, 112/2
**Dutch New Guinea** (later West Irian n/c Irian Jaya) East Indies transferred to Indonesia 145/1
**Dutch Republic** (or United Provinces or Holland) in War of Spanish Succession 76/3; revolt against Spain 86/2
**Dyrrhachium** (earlier Epidamnus mod. Durrës It. Durazzo) Albania Roman Empire 35/1; Byzantine Empire 44/1
**Eastern Rumelia** region of Balkans Ottoman province 102/1; ceded to Bulgaria 119/1
**Eastern Turkestan** C Asia Chinese protectorate 88/1
**East Indies** agricultural origins 16/1; early kingdoms 61/1; early trade 82/2; 18C European trade 97/2. See also Dutch East Indies, Indonesia
**East Prussia** (Ger. Ostpreussen) region of E Germany WW2 132/1; divided between Poland and Russia 159/1
**Eckmühl/Ebersberg** S Germany ✕93/1
**Ecuador** independence 107/1, 149/1; political development 149/1; economy 149/2; cocaine trade 160/1
**Edessa** (mod. Urfa) SE Anatolia First Crusade 45/2
**Egypt** (officially Arab Republic of Egypt form. United Arab Republic Lat. Aegyptus Ar. Misr) 15/1; centre of urban civilization 18/1; ancient 20/1; Old Kingdom 21/2; early settlement 25/1; campaigns of Alexander 31/1; spread of Christianity and Judaism 32/1; Arab conquest 44/1; Byzantine Empire 44/1; Fatimid Caliphate 54/1; conquered by Turks 55/2; Ottoman province 102/1; expansion into Sudan 105/1; independence 145/1; wars with Israel 146/2; political development 150/1; Anglo-French attack (Suez War) 150/1; economy 160/1; Gulf War 147/3
**El Agheila** Libya WW2 133/2
**El Alamein** Egypt ✕WW2 133/2
**England** Scandinavian settlement 50/1; expansion of Christianity 40/1; Black Death and religious unrest 63/1; possessions in France 76/1; Reformation 84/1; WW1 124-5. See also Britain, Great Britain, United Kingdom
**Ephesus** (Turk. Efes) W Anatolia early trade 20/1; Roman Empire Byzantine Empire 44/1
**Epidamnus** (later Dyrrhachium It. Durazzo mod. Durrës) Albania Dorian colony 30/1
**Epirus** ancient country of NW Greece 30/1; Roman province 35/1; Byzantine Empire 44/1; to Greece 119/1
**Equator, Confederation of the** E Brazil 107/1

**Equatorial Guinea** (form. Spanish Guineà a/c Rio Muni) country of W Africa  independence 145/1; economy 160/1
**Eritrea**  region of NE Ethiopia  Italian rule 103; Italian colony 104/2, 129/2; political development 145/1
**Estonia**  country of the Baltic  acquired by Russia 79/1; Reformation 84/1; independence from Russia 128/1; constituted SSR 139/1, 140/1; independence 159/1
**Ethiopia**  expansion of Christianity 32/1; 16C state 55/2; Italian invasion 105/1, 129/2; independence regained 145/1; economy 160/1
**Etruscans**  ancient people of Italy 30/1
**Eupen**  E Belgium  ceded by Germany 128/1
**Europe**  early man 11/1; colonization by hunters 12/1; agricultural origins 15/1; amber trade 28/1; agricultural settlement 28/1; Hun and Avar invasions 39/1; Germanic and Slavonic invasions 39/1; expansion of Christianity 40/1; Viking, Magyar and Saracen invasions 50/1; Black Death 63/1; 19-20C alliances 118/2; WW1 124-5; post-war territorial changes 139/1; economic blocs (EEC, EFTA, Comecon) 138/2; employment 156; economic blocs from 1957 157; collapse of Communist power 159/1; foreign direct investment 160
**Eylau** (a/c Preussisch-Eylau now Bagrationovsk) E Prussia ✕93/1
**Faeroe Islands** (a/s Faroes)  Norse settlement 50/1
**Falkland Islands** (Span. Islas Malvinas) islands of S Atlantic 107/1; claimed by Argentina 145/1; war 149/1
**Fanning Island**  C Pacific  British possession 145/1 (inset)
**Faroe Islands** (a/s Faroes)  Norse settlement 50/1
**Fars** (a/c Persis, Parsa)  Persia  Muslim conquest 47/1
**Fashoda**  S Sudan  British/French confrontation 105/1
**Fatimids**  Muslim dynasty of Egypt 47/2, 54/1
**Federated Malay States** (now Malaysia) independence 145/1
**Feodosiya** (a/c Kefe, Kaffa anc. Theodosia) Crimea  acquired by Russia 79/1
**Ferghana**  region of C Asia  Chinese protectorate 42/1; Muslim expansion 47/1
**Fernando Po** (Sp. Fernando Poó form. Macias Nguema Biyogo) island of Equatorial Guinea  Dutch and Spanish settlement 55/2; Spanish colony 112/2; 145/1
**Fez** (Fr. Fès Ar. Al Fas) Morocco  early trade 55/2; occupied by French 105/1
**Fezzan** (anc. Phazania) region of C Libya  occupied by Italians 105/1
**Fihl**  Palestine ✕47/1
**Fiji**  S Pacific  Melanesian settlement 24/2; British colony 112/2; independence 145/1 (inset)

**Finland**  Reformation 84/1; WW1 125/1; independence 127/1; employment 156; EFTA 159/1
**Finns**  post-war migration from Karelia 139/1
**Flanders** (Fr. Flandre Dut. Vlaanderen) region of N Belgium  Black Death 63/1; WW1 125/1 (inset)
**Florida**  British rule 81/1, 99/1; annexed by USA 98/2; Depression 131/2; base for invasion of Cuba 155/2
**Foix**  region of S France  acquired by France 76/1
**Foochow** (a/s Fu-Chou n/s Fuzhou) SE China  treaty port 89/2
**Formosa** (n/c Taiwan)  cession to Japan 117/2; air attack by US 134/1; US bases 154/1
**Fort Amsterdam** (later New Amsterdam now New York)  Dutch post 81/2
**Fort Lamy** (now N'Djamena) C Africa  occupied by French 105/1
**Fort William** (n/c Thunder Bay) C Canada  growth 115/2
**Fouta Djallon** (a/s Futa Jallon) W Africa  early state 105/1
**France** (anc. Gaul Lat. Gallia) conversion to Christianity 32/1; Arab invasion 47/1; Viking and Saracen invasions 50/1; Scandinavian settlement 50/1; Black Death 63/1; 15C-16C reunification 76/1; War of Spanish Succession 76/3; administrative system under Louix XIV 77/2; Vauban fortresses 77/2; Industrial Revolution 95/2; 18C Atlantic economy 96/1; trade with Africa and Asia 97/2; European alliances 118/2; world trade 1860-1913 120/3; foreign investment 1914 121/2; overseas trade and investment 121/1; WW1 124-5; EEC, NATO 154/1, 156/1; economy 156, 160/1
**Franche-Comté**  region of E France  Habsburg Empire 87/1
**French Cameroons** (now part of Cameroon) W Africa  independence 145/1
**French Congo** (a/c Middle Congo now People's Republic of the Congo) W Africa  colony 105/1, 112/2
**French Equatorial Africa**  union of French colonies 104/2
**French Guiana**  S America 107/1
**French Guinea** (now Guinea) W Africa  colony 105/1
**French Indochina** (now Cambodia, Laos and Vietnam)  colonized 89/2; occupied by Japanese 117/2, 134/1; independence 145/1
**French Somaliland** (Fr. Côte Française des Somalis later French Territory of the Afars and Issas now Republic of Djibouti) NE Africa 103
**French Sudan** (now Mali) W Africa  colony 105/1
**French Territory of Afars and Issas** (Djibouti)
**French West Africa**  former union of French colonies 104/2, 112/2
**Friedland** (now Pravdinsk) E Prussia ✕93/1

**Friedlingen**  W Germany 76/3
**Fukien** (n/s Fujian) province of SE China  Ming province 65/1; Japanese influence 89/2, 117/2, under Nanking control 122/1; economy 143/2
**Gagauzia**  minority area of S Moldova 159/1
**Galatia**  country of C Anatolia  Roman province 35/1
**Galich** (mod. Galicia) region of SW Russia  Kievan principality 53/2
**Galicia** (Russ. Galich)  in Austria-Hungary during WW1 125/1
**Gallipoli** (anc. Callipolis Turk. Gelibolu) W Turkey  Ottoman centre 67/1; WW1 125/1
**Gambia**  country of W Africa  British settlement 55/2; independence 145/1
**Gandara** (a/s Gandhara) region of E Afghanistan  Indian kingdom 26/1
**Gansu** (f/s Kansu) province of NW China  economy 1979-92 143/2
**Gascony** (Fr. Gascogne) region of SW France  part of Frankish Empire 48/1; province of France 77/2
**Gaza**  Palestine  Philistine city 30/1; Levantine city 20/1; Byzantine Empire 35/1; Roman Empire 44/1
**Gaza Strip**  Palestine  autonomy 146/2
**Georgia**  state of S USA  colony 99/1; industry 114/1; population 115/3; Depression 131/2
**Georgia**  country of the Caucasus  Mongol Empire 24/1; acquired by Russia 79/1; kingdom 102/1; independent after WW1 128/1; SSR 140/1; independence 1991 159/1
**Germania Inferior**  province of Roman Empire 35/1
**Germania Superior**  province of Roman Empire 35/1
**Germantown**  E USA ✕99/1
**Germany** (Lat. Germania Ger. Deutschland now Federal Republic of Germany and German Democratic Republic) conversion to Christianity 40/1; Magyar invasion 50/1; Thirty Years' War 86/3; Reformation 84/1; fragmentation 93/1; Industrial Revolution 95/2; expansion in Africa 102/3; unification 111/2; colonial empire 112/2; 19C alliances 118/2; world trade 1860-1913 120/3; overseas trade and investment 121/1; foreign investment 1914 121/2; WW1 124-5; territorial changes after WW1 128/1; expansion 1934-41 129/2; territorial losses to Poland 138/2; Allied control zones 139/1; East and West reunited 159/1
**Germany, East** (German Democratic Republic or DDR) 138/2; Warsaw Pact 138/3, 154/1; employment 156
**Germany, West** (German Democratic Republic or FDR)  EEC 138/2; NATO 154/1; employment 156
**Germiyan**  Turkoman principality of W Anatolia 67/1
**Ghana** (form. Gold Coast) W Africa  early kingdom 25/1; independence 145/1, 150/1
**Goa**  district of W India  59/1; early trade 74/1, 75/2; Portuguese

settlement 90/1, 91/3; centre of European trade 97/2
**Golan Heights**  Syria  occupied by Israel 146/2
**Gold Coast** (now Ghana)  slave trade 96/1; early European settlement 105/1 (inset); British colony 105/1, 112/2
**Golden Horde**  Khanate of the Mongol Empire 24/1
**Goražde**  Bosnia-Herzegovina  civil war 158/2
**Gorlice**  SE Poland ✕125/1
**Goths**  invasions 39/1
**Granada**  city and region of Spain  Muslim minority 84/1; Habsburg Empire 87/1
**Great Britain**  opposition to Napoleon 92-3; trade with Africa and Asia 97/2; 19C European alliances 118/2; WW1 124-5; WW2 132-3. See also England
**Great Khan, Empire of the**  E Asia  Mongol state 24/1
**Greece** (anc. Gr. Hellas mod. Gr. Ellas)  Levantine ports 20/1; campaigns of Alexander 30/3; invaded by Visigoths 39/1; Black Death 63/1; conflict with Bulgaria and Turkey 102/1; independent kingdom 119/1; WW1 124-5; WW2 132/2; Cold War 154/1; employment 156; infant mortality and life expectancy 160
**Grenada**  island of W Indies  British colony 107/1; self-government 145/1 (inset); US invasion 149/1
**Guadalcanal**  island of Solomons, S Pacific ✕135/2
**Guadeloupe**  island of W Indies 81/1; French territory 107/1, 145/1 (inset)
**Guam**  island of W Pacific  occupied by US 115/2; occupied by Japanese 134/1; recaptured by US 135/2; US base 154/1 (inset)
**Guangdong** (f/s Kwangtung) province of S China  economy 1979-92 143/2
**Guangxi** (f/s Kwangsi) province of S China  economy 1979-92 143/2
**Guantánamo Bay**  E Cuba  US naval base 155/2
**Guatemala**  country and city of C America  founded 74/1; 18C Atlantic economy 96/1; independence 107/1; US involvement 154/1; opium trade 160
**Guiana**  region of S America  colonized by Dutch and French 81/1; 18C Atlantic economy 96/1. See also Surinam, French Guiana, Guyana
**Guinea** (form. French Guinea)  independence 145/1
**Guinea-Bissau** (form. Portuguese Guinea) W Africa  independence 145/1
**Guizhou** (f/s Kweichow) province of S China  economy 1979-92 143/2
**Gujerat** (n/s Gujarat) region of W India  district of Mughal Empire 59/1; under British rule 90/1, 90/2
**Gupta Empire**  India 27/3; destroyed by White Huns 39/1
**Gurgan** (a/s Gorgan anc. Hyrcania) city and region of N Persia  Muslim conquest 47/1

**Guyenne** (a/c Aquitaine anc. Aquitania) region of SW France French Royal domain 76/1; province of France 77/2
**Gwynedd** early Welsh principality 48/2
**Habsburg Lands** 62/2, 63/1
**Hadhramaut** region of S Arabia Muslim expansion 47/1
**Hadrumetum** (mod. Sousse) Tunisia Phoenician city 30/1
**Hafsids** Muslim dynasty of Tunisia 47/2
**Hainan** island S China Mongol attack 24/1; early soviet 122/2
**Haiphong** N Vietnam early trade 82/2; railway 89/2
**Haiti** Toussaint l'Ouverture's revolt 92/1; independence 107/1; US intervention 149/1; political development 149/1. See also Hispaniola
**Halicarnassus** (mod. Bodrum) W Anatolia Byzantine Empire 44/1
**Hamadan** (anc. Ecbatana) W Persia Mongol attack 24/1; Mongol conquest 57/2
**Hammurabi, Empire of** 20/1
**Han** NW China expansion 88/1; Empire 89/2
**Hanau** W Germany ✕93/1
**Hangchow** (a/s Hang-chou, n/s Hangzhou) C China provincial capital 65/1; captured by Kuomintang 122/1; economy 143/2
**Hankow** C China treaty town 89/2
**Hanoi** (form. Thang Long) N Vietnam Mongol attack 24/1; trade centre 82/2; Japanese occupation 117/2
**Hausa States** (a/c Hausaland) Nigeria 54/1, 55/2
**Havana** (Sp. La Habana) Cuba imperial trade 74/1
**Hawaiian Islands** (f/c Sandwich Islands) C Pacific early Polynesian settlement 24/2; annexed by US 112/2; war in the Pacific 134/1
**Hebei** (f/s Hopeh) province of N China economy 1979-92 143/2
**Hebrides** (form. Nor. Sudreyar) Scandinavian settlement 50/1
**Heilungkiang** (n/s Heilongjiang) province of NE China economy 143/2
**Hejaz** (Ar. Hijaz) region of W Arabia centre of Islam 47/1; under Abbasid sovereignty 47/2
**Henan** (s Honan) province of C China
**Heraclea Pontica** (mod. Ereğli) N Anatolia Greek colony 30/1
**Heracleopolis** Lower Egypt 20/1
**Herat** (anc. Alexandria Areion) C Persia Muslim conquest 47/1
**Herzegovina** SE Europe Ottoman vassal state 67/1; civil war 158/2
**Hesse** (Ger. Hessen) Reformation 84/1; unification with Germany 111/2
**Hibernia** (mod. Ireland) Roman Empire 35/1
**Hipponium** (mod. Vibo Valentia) S Italy Greek colony 30/1
**Hippo Regius** (Sp. Bona Fr. Bône mod. Annaba) Algeria Phoenician city 31/1; Roman Empire 35/1
**Hippo Zarytus** (mod. Bizerta) Tunisia Phoenician city 30/1

**Hiroshima** city and prefecture of W Japan 117/1; bombed by US 135/2
**Hispaniae** Roman province 35/2
**Hispaniola** (mod. Dominican Republic and Haiti) island of West Indies early exploration 72/1; early trade 74/1
**Ho Chi Minh Trail** Vietnam/Laos 152/2
**Höchstädt** W Germany ✕76/3
**Hohenlinden** S Germany ✕93/1
**Holland** Black Death 63/1; province of Dutch Republic 86/2; WW1 124-5; world trade 1860-1913 120/3; foreign investment 1914 121/2. See also Netherlands
**Hollandia** (n/c Jayapura) N New Guinea Allied landing in WW2 135/2
**Holstein** region of N Germany medieval German Empire 51/2; Reformation 84/1; in German Confederation 111/2; divided between Denmark and Germany 128/1
**Holy Roman Empire** Black Death 63/1; Thirty Years War 86/3
**Honan** (n/c Henan) region of C China Ming province 65/1; economy 143/2
**Honduras** country of C America early exploration 72/1
**Hong Kong** 89/2; acquired by Britain 113/1; trade and industry 122/2; occupied by Japanese 134/1; British colony 145/1; Pacific trade 153/3
**Hopeh** (n/s Hebei) province of N China economy 143/2
**Hubei** (f/s Hupei) province of C China economy 143/2
**Hunan** province of C China Manchu expansion 88/1; warlord control 122/1; industrial development 143/1
**Hunchun** NE China treaty port 89/2
**Hungary** Mongol invasion 24/1; conversion to Christianity 40/1; early kingdom 62/2; Black Death 63/1; Ottoman control 66/2; medieval Christian state 67/1; Reformation 84/1; Habsburg Empire 87/1; movement for independence 92/1; independence after WW1 128/1; occupation of SE Czechoslovakia 129/2; economic and socio-political development 131/3; Axis satellite 132/1; Warsaw Pact and Comecon 138/3; employment 156; end of Communist rule 159/1. See also Austro-Hungarian Empire
**Hungnam** N Korea 1950-53 war 143/1
**Huns** tribe on borders of Roman Empire 35/2; invasion of Europe 39/1
**Hupeh** (n/s Hubei) province of C China Manchu expansion 88/1; industrial development 143/1
**Iceland** Norse settlement 50/1; Reformation 84/1; independence from Denmark 128/1 (inset); NATO 138/3; economy 160/1
**Iceni** ancient tribe of Britain 35/1
**Ichang** C China treaty town 89/2

**Il-Khan Empire** Persia Mongol state 24/1
**Illyrian Provinces** Adriatic under French protection 93/1
**Illyricum** Roman province of Adriatic 35/1
**Ilva** (mod. Elba) island of W Italy Etruscan city 30/1
**Inca Empire** Peru 68/3; 1492 70/1
**Inchon** (a/c Chemulpo Jap. Jinsen) S Korea US landing in Korean war 143/1
**India** rise of civilization 18/1; early urban centres 26/1; early empires 26/1; campaigns of Alexander 30/3; centre of Buddhism and Hinduism 32/1; Mughal Empire 59/1; first seaborne European visit 72/1; trade 74/1, 75/2; growth of British power 90/1; Mutiny 90/2; 18C European trade 97/2; under British rule 113/1; Japanese offensive 135/2; independence 145/1; boundary dispute with China 153/1; economy 160/1
**Indo-China** rice farming villages 19/1; early trade routes 113/1; occupied by Japanese 117/2; 1945-75 war 154/1
**Indonesia** (form. Dutch East Indies) independence 145/1; political developments 153/1; economy 153/3, 160/1
**Indus Valley** NW India 18/1
**Inner Mongolia** N China Manchu expansion 88/1; Japanese occupation 134/1, 135/2; economy 143/2
**Ionian Islands** (anc. Heptanesus) W Greece ceded to Greece 119/1
**Iran** (f/c Persia) oilfields 146/1; Baghdad Pact 154/1; Iran-Iraq War 146/1; opium trade 161
**Iraq** (form. Mesopotamia) British mandate 102/1; independence 145/1; Baghdad Pact 154/1; Iran-Iraq War 146/1; Gulf War 147/3
**Ireland** (anc. Hibernia Ir. Eire) expansion of Christianity 40/1; Scandinavian settlement 50/1; Reformation 84/1; revolt against England 92/1; neutral in WW2 132/1; EEC 138/3; employment 156. See also Irish Free State
**Irish Free State** (created 1922, since 1937 Republic of Ireland) 128/1
**Island No 10** C USA ✕99/1
**Ismailia** E Egypt war with Israel 146/2
**Isonzo** (S. Cr. Soča) river Italy-Yugoslavia battles of WW1 125/1
**Israel** (form. part of Palestine) independence 145/1; economy 160/1; Gulf War 147/3
**Istria** region of NW Yugoslavia Byzantine Empire 44/1; conquered by Franks 48/1
**Italia** Roman province of S Italy 35/1
**Italian Somaliland** (now S part of Somalia) colony 104/2, 105/1, 113/1, 129/2
**Italy** Greek colonization 30/1; conversion to Christianity 32/1; Visigothic and Ostrogothic invasions 39/1; Black Death 63/1;

under Napoleon 93/1; Industrial Revolution 95/2; unification 110/1; colonial empire 112/2; world trade 1860-1913 120/3; WW1 125/1; S Tyrol regained 128/1; expansion 1934-39 129/2; WW2 132-3; NATO 138/3, 154/1; employment 156
**Itil** N Caspian Khazar city 53/2
**Ivory Coast** (Fr. Côte d'Ivoire) country of W Africa French colony 112/2, 105/1; independence 145/1; economy 160/1
**Iwo Jima** Japanese island of N Pacific ✕135/2; US base 154/1
**Jamestown** E USA ✕99/1
**Jammu and Kashmir** native state of British India 91/3
**Jankau** Bohemia ✕86/3
**Japan** Mongol invasion 24/1; Buddhism and Shintoism 32/1; Chinese cultural influence 42/1; invasion of Korea and China 65/1; 15-16C civil war 65/2; early trade 75/2; modern development 83/1, 112/2; expansion in Asia 117/2; WW2 134/1, 135/2; industrial products and exports 1945-90 143/3; Pacific trade 153/3; US bases 154/1
**Jassy** (Rom. Iaşi Turk. Yaş) NE Romania Ottoman attack 66/2; WW2 133/2
**Java** (Indon. Jawa) island of C Indonesia Mongol expedition 24/1; early man 26/2; spread of Buddhism and Hinduism 32/1, 60/2; Mongol expedition 61/1; early trade 82/2; occupied by Japanese 134/1
**Java Sea** naval battle of WW2 134/1
**Jena** E Germany ✕93/1
**Jericho** (Ar. Ariha) Palestine site of early village 16/1; autonomy 146/2
**Jerusalem** (anc. Hierosolyma Roman Aelia Capitolina Heb. Yerushalayim Ar. Al Quds) Israel Levantine city 20/1; Byzantine Empire 44/1; Muslim conquest 47/1; Ottoman Empire 67/1; in Arab-Israeli conflict 146/2
**Jiangsu** (f/s Kiangsu) province of E China economy 1979-92 143/2
**Jiangxi** (f/s Kiangsi) province of SE China economy 1979-92 143/2
**Jilin** (f/s Kirin) province of NE China economy 1979-92 143/2
**Joppa** (mod. Jaffa Ar. Yafa Heb. Yafo) Palestine Levantine city 20/1
**Jordan** independence 145/1; conflicts 146/2, 147/1; economy 160/1; Gulf War 147/3. See also Transjordan
**Juan-juan** (a/c Avars) tribe of N China 39/2
**Judaea** Palestine Roman province 35/1
**Jutland** Denmark ✕125/1
**Kabardino-Balkar ASSR** Caucasus 141/1
**Kabul** Afghanistan Muslim conquest 47/1; district of Mughal Empire 59/1
**Kaffa** (It. Caffa Turk. Kefe anc. Theodosia mod. Feodosiya) Crimea Ottoman conquest 66/2
**K'ai-feng** N China Mongol attack 24/1; Ming provincial capital 65/1; industry 143/1

**Kanem-Borno** early empire of NC Africa 54/1
**Kano** Nigeria Hausa city-state 54/1, 55/2; taken by British 105/1
**Kansk** S Siberia industry 126/2
**Kansu** (n/s Gansu) province of NW China 42/1; Manchu expansion 88/1; economy 143/2
**Karachaevo-Cherkess AR** Caucasus 140/1
**Karafuto** southern part of Sakhalin island of Pacific Russia acquired by Japan 117/2; reoccupied by Russia 135/2
**Karagwe** early state of Uganda 55/2
**Kara-Kalpak ASSR** C Asia 140/1
**Karakhanids** Muslim dynasty of C Asia 47/2
**Karakorum** Mongolia Mongol capital 24/1
**Karakoyunlu** district of E Anatolia 67/1
**Karaman** (anc. Laranda) S Anatolia early trade 21/2; Turkoman principality 67/1
**Karelia** region of Finland and N Russia to Russia 79/1; ASSR 140/1
**Kars** E Anatolia conquered by Ottomans 58/1; conquered by Ottomans 66/2; lost to Russia 127/1
**Kashgar** Sinkiang Mongol attack 24/1; Han expansion 37/1; early trade 42/1; Muslim risings against Chinese 88/1
**Katsina** Hausa city-state of N Nigeria 54/1, 55/2
**Katyn** Poland 132/1
**Kaunas** (form. Russ. Kovno) Lithuanian SSR WW2 133/2
**Kazakhs** Turkic people of C Asia, conquered by Russians 79/2; 140/1
**Kazakhstan** C Asia horse-based pastoralism 18/1; famine 1932 126/2; SSR 140/1
**Kazan** C Russia 1905 Revolution 109/2; Bolshevik seizure 127/1
**Kazan** Mongol khanate of C Russia conquered by Russia 79/1
**Kenya** (form. British East Africa) British colony 105/1; independence 145/1; political development 150/1; economy 160/1
**Kerbala** (Ar. Karbala) Mesopotamia ✗47/1
**Khakass AR** Central Asia 140/1
**Khalkha** Mongol tribe 65/1
**Khanbalik** (mod. Peking) N China Mongol attack 24/1
**Khania** (a/s Canea anc. Cydonia) Crete palace and city 28/2
**Khanty-Mansi AR** W Siberia 140/1
**Kharkov** Ukraine founded 79/1; 1905 Revolution 109/2; Bolshevik seizure 127/1
**Khartoum** British occupation 105/1
**Khazar Empire** S Russia 47/1
**Khiva** (a/c Khwarizm anc. Chorasmia) region of C Asia independent khanate 102/1
**Khmer** (mod. Cambodia) SE Asia kingdom under Hindu influence 42/1; temple kingdom 61/1
**Khoisan** people of S Africa 54/1, 55/2

**Khurasan** (a/s Khorasan) region of C Persia Muslim conquest 42/1, 47/1; under Abbasid sovereignty 47/2; Safavid Empire 58/1
**Khwarizm** (a/c Khiva anc. Chorasmia) region of C Asia under Abbasid sovereignty 47/2
**Kiangsi** (n/s Jiangxi) province of SE China under the Ming 65/1; Manchu expansion 88/1; Nationalist control 122/1; Soviet under Mao Tse-tung 122/2; economy 143/2
**Kiangsu** (n/s Jiangsu) province of E China Manchu expansion 88/1; economy 143/2
**Kiev** (Russ. Kiyev Ukr. Kyyiv) Ukraine Mongol attack 24/1; bishopric 40/1; Viking trade 52/1; principality 53/2; 1905 Revolution 109/2
**Kievan Russia** 50/1, 53/2
**Kirghiz** Turkic people of C Asia, destroy Uighur Empire 42/1; conquered by Russians 108/1; 140/1
**Kiribati** (f/c Gilbert Is) Pacific 145/1 (inset)
**Kirkuk** N Iraq oilfield 146/1
**Kirman** (a/s Kerman anc. Carmana) region of S Persia Muslim conquest 47/1
**Kish** N Mesopotamia Sumerian city 20/1
**Kiska** island of Aleutians, Alaska captured by Japanese 134/1; retaken by Americans 135/2
**Kiukiang** C China treaty town 89/2
**Kiungchow** S China treaty port 89/2
**Knossos** (Lat. Cnossus) Crete farming site 28/1; 28/2
**Kokand** (a/s Khokand) C Asia Muslim khanate 102/1; conquered by Russia 108/1
**Komi ASSR** W Siberia 140/1
**Komi-Permyak AR** W Siberia 140/1
**Komsomolosk-na-Amure** Russ. Far East industry 126/2
**Kongo** early kingdom of W Africa 54/1, 55/2
**Königsberg** (since 1946 Kaliningrad) W Russia Reformation 84/1; WW2 132/1, 133/2
**Konya** (anc. Iconium) S Anatolia revolt against Ottoman rule 66/2
**Korea** (anc. Koryo or Silla Jap. Chosen) spread of Buddhism 32/1; conquered by Chinese 37/1; invaded by Japan 65/1; invaded by Manchus 88/1; end of Chinese tributary status 89/2; acquired by Japan 112/1, 117/2, 122/2; WW2 134/1, 135/2; 1950-53 war 143/1
**Korea, North** militarization 154/1
**Korea, South** militarization and US bases 154/1
**Koryak AD** E USSR 140/1
**Kovno** (Pol. Kowno now Kaunas) W USSR WW1 125/1
**Kowloon** S China acquired by Britain 89/2
**Krasnoi** W Russia ✗93/1
**Krasnovodsk** Russ. C Asia on railway 108/1; Revolution 127/1
**Krasnoyarsk** S Siberia founded 79/2; railway 108/1; industry 126/2

**Krivoy Rog** S Ukraine WW2 133/2
**Kronstadt** (Russ. Kronshtadt) NW Russia 1905 Revolution 109/2; WW1 125/1
**Kumasi** Gold Coast, W Africa 105/1
**Kumbi Saleh** W Africa possible site of capital of Ghana Empire 54/1
**Kunming** W China French sphere of influence 89/2; economy 143/2
**Kuomintang China** 122/1
**Kurds** people of N Iraq, uprisings 150/1; Gulf War 147/3
**Kurile Islands** (Russ. Kurilskiye Ostrova Jap. Chishima-retto) acquired by Japan 117/2; reoccupied by USSR 135/2; disputed with USSR 153/1
**Kursk** W Russia 1905 Revolution 109/2; WW2 133/2
**Kush** early kingdom of Sudan 25/1
**Kutch** (f/s Cutch) region of W India border dispute with Pakistan 153/1
**Kuwait** country of Persian Gulf Ottoman sovereignty 58/1; independence 145/1; Gulf War 147/3
**Kwajalein** Marshall Islands, C Pacific occupied by US 135/2; US base 154/1 (inset)
**Kwangchowan** S China acquired by France 89/2
**Kwangsi** (n/s Guangxi) province of SW China under Ming 65/1; Manchu expansion 88/1; economy 143/2
**Kwangtung** (n/s Guangdong) province of S China under Ming 65/1; Manchu expansion 88/1; Kuomintang 122/1; economy 143/2
**Kwararafa** W Africa early state 54/1
**Kweichow** (n/s Guizhou) province of SW China under Ming 65/1; Manchu expansion 88/1; Kuomintang 122/1; economy 143/2
**Kyakhta** S Siberia Russian trade with China 88/1; Russian trade 97/2
**Labrador** region of NE Canada rediscovered 72/1; to Newfoundland 115/2
**Labuan** N Borneo British colony 113/1
**Lacedaemon** (a/c Sparta) S Greece Byzantine Empire 23/1
**La Fère Champenoise** NE France ✗93/1
**Lagos** Nigeria taken by British 105/1; British colony 112/2
**Lahore** NW India district of Mughal Empire 59/1; in Mughal Empire 66/2; industry in British India 91/3
**Languedoc** region of S France French Royal domain 76/1; province of France 77/2
**L'Anse aux Meadows** Newfoundland Norse colony 23/1; 69/1
**Laodicea** (mod. Denizli) W Anatolia Roman Empire 35/1
**Laodicea** (mod. Latakia Fr. Lattaquié) Syria Byzantine Empire 44/1
**Laon** N France ✗93/1
**Laos** country of SE Asia 61/1; kingdom of Luang Prabang 82/2; end of Chinese tributary status 89/2; French protectorate 112/2; independence 145/1; Pathet Lao 153/1 ; opium trade 161

**Lapita** early people of Melanesia 24/2
**La Plata** early people of S America 18C Atlantic economy 96/1
**Lapps** people of N Russia 40/1
**Larisa** (a/s Larissa Turk. Yenişehir) C Greece Byzantine Empire 44/1
**Las Navas de Tolosa** S Spain ✗47/2
**Latin Empire** 45/2
**Latvia** country of the Baltic independence from Russia 128/1; socio-political change 131/3; SSR 139/1, 140/1; annexed by Russia 159/1; independence 159/1
**Lausanne** Switzerland 1924 Conference 128/1
**Lazica** early country of the Caucasus 44/1
**Lebanon** district of Ottoman Empire 102/1; French mandate 102/1; independence 145/1; Middle East conflict 147/1; Gulf War 147/3; political disturbances 154/1; economy 160/1
**Lechfeld** S Germany ✗50/1
**Leicester** (anc. Ratae) C England Viking base 50/1
**Leipzig** (Battle of the Nations) E Germany ✗93/1
**Lemberg** (Pol. Lwów now Russ. Lvov) N Austria-Hungary E Germany WW2 133/2
**Lemnos** island of the Aegean ceded to Greece 119/1
**Leningrad** (form. and again from 1991 St. Petersburg Russ. Sankt-Peterburg between 1914 and 1923 Petrograd) NW Russia industry 126/2; WW2 132-3
**Lepanto** (mod. Gr. Navpaktos) C Greece ✗67/2
**Leptis Magna** (a/s Lepcis Magna mod. Lebda) N Libya Stone Age site 25/1; Phoenician city 30/1; Roman Empire 35/1
**Lesbos** (mod. Gr. Lesvos a/c Mitylene) island of the Aegean Greek parent state 30/1
**Lesotho** (form. Basutoland) S Africa independence 145/1; economy 160/1
**Leucas** (mod. Gr. Santa Maura) W Greece Greek colony 30/1
**Lexington** NE USA ✗99/1
**Leyte Gulf** C Philippines WW2 naval battle 135/2
**Liaoning** province of NE China economy 1979-92
**Liberia** country of W Africa independent state 104/2, 112/2; economy 160/1
**Libya** Arab conquest 47/1; under the Almohads 54/1; under Ottoman Empire 55/2; Italian colony 102/1, 104/2, 112/2; independence 145/1, political development 150/1; US base 154/1; economy 160/1
**Liegnitz** (Pol. Legnica) W Poland Mongol attack 24/1; Reformation 86/3
**Ligny** Belgium ✗93/1
**Lincoln** (anc. Lindum) E England Danish Viking base 50/1

**Lindisfarne** (a/c Holy Island) N England Viking attack 50/1
**Lindsey** early kingdom of E England 48/2
**Lindum** (mod. Lincoln) E England Roman Empire 35/1
**Lisbon** (Port. Lisboa anc. Olisipo) Portugal Muslim conquest 40/1, 47/1; colonial trade 74/1; ✕03/1
**Lithuania** country of the Baltic conversion to Christianity 40/1; early expansion 62/2; Black Death 63/1; acquired by Russia 79/1; Reformation 84/1; independence 128/1; loses Memel territory to Germany 129/2; Soviet Socialist Republic 139/1, 140/1; retaken by Russia 159/1; independence 159/1
**Livonia** region of NW Russia occupied by Teutonic Knights 62/2; conquered by Russia 79/1; Reformation 84/1
**Locarno** Switzerland 1925 Conference 128/1
**Lodi** N Italy Lombard League 51/2; ✕93/1
**Lombardy** region of N Italy Habsburg Empire 87/1; unification of Italy 110/1
**Lonato** N Italy ✕93/1
**Londinium** (mod. London) S England Roman Empire 35/1
**London** (anc. Londinium) S England Vikings 50/1; urban unrest 63/1; Industrial Revolution 95/2; WW1 125/1
**Lorraine** (Ger. Lothringen) region of NE France part of medieval German Empire 51/2; acquired by Habsburgs 76/1; Habsburg Empire 87/1; German Empire 111/2
**Louisiana** state of S USA French rule 81/1,2; purchased by USA 98/2; Spanish rule 99/1; population 115/3; Depression 131/2
**Lo-yang** (als Luoyang) N China sacked by Hsiung-nu 39/1; industry 143/1
**Luanda** Angola Portuguese settlement 55/2; early trade 74/1; centre of European trade 97/2
**Luang Prabang** SE Asia early political centre 61/1
**Lucknow** N India Indian Mutiny 90/2; industry 91/3
**Lungchow** SW China treaty port 89/2
**Lusatia** (Ger. Lausitz) region of E Germany acquired by Habsburgs 62/2; Habsburg Empire 87/1
**Lutetia** (mod. Paris) N France Roman Empire 35/1
**Lutter** W Germany ✕86/3
**Lützen** C Germany ✕86/3, 93/1
**Luxembourg** (Ger. Luxemburg) EEC and NATO 138/2
**Luzon** island of N Philippines Spanish control 74/1; US landings 135/2
**Luzzara** N Italy ✕76/3
**Lycia** country of SW Anatolia 31/1; Roman Empire 35/1
**Lydia** country of W Anatolia Byzantine Empire 44/1
**Macao** (Port. Macau) S China early Portuguese trade 74/1; Portuguese settlement 75/2; centre of European trade 97/2; Portuguese colony 89/2, 112/2, 145/1
**Macassar** (Indon. Makasar) East Indies Dutch settlement 75/2, 82/2
**Macedonia** SE Europe 31/1; Roman province 35/1; Byzantine Empire 44/1; Ottoman province 102/1; divided between Serbia, Greece and Bulgaria 119/1; Greek-Bulgarian conflict 128/1
**Madagascar** (form. Malagasy Republic) Indonesian settlement 25/1, 54/1, 3; settlement from Africa 55/2; French penetration 105/1; French colony 105/1, 112/2; independence 145/1; political development 150/1; economy 160/1
**Madeira** island of E Atlantic Portuguese territory 112/2, 145/1
**Madras** (now Tamil Nadu) state and city, S India British settlement 75/2; under British rule 90/2; trade and industry 91/3
**Madrid** C Spain captured by French 93/1; Industrial Revolution 95/2
**Magenta** N Italy ✕110/1
**Maginot Line** E France defence system 132/1
**Magna Graecia** the Greek colonies of S Italy 31/1,2
**Maine** state of NE USA British settlement 81/2; population 115/3; Depression 131/2
**Malaca** (mod. Málaga) S Spain Roman Empire 35/1
**Malacca** (Mal. Melaka) district of S Malaya early sultanate 61/1; European discovery 72/1; early trade 74/1; captured by Dutch 75/2; under Portuguese rule 82/2; centre of European trade 97/2; British possession 113/1
**Málaga** (anc. Malaca) S Spain ✕76/3
**Malatya** (anc. Melitene) E Turkey Hittite city 20/1; revolt against Ottoman rule 66/2
**Malawi** (form. Nyasaland) country of C Africa independence 145/1; political development 150/1; economy 160/1
**Malaya** spread of Islam 60/2; British control 112/2; occupied by Japanese 134/1. See also Malaysia
**Malaysia** (state formed by amalgamation of Malaya, Sarawak and Sabah) independence 145/1; economy 160/1; Pacific trade 153/2
**Maldives** islands of N Indian Ocean protectorate 112/2; independence 145/1
**Mali** (form. French Sudan) country of West Africa independence 145/1; political development 150/1; economy 160/1
**Mali Empire** early state of W Africa 54/1; 70/1
**Malindi** Kenya Muslim colony 54/1; early Portuguese trade 55/2
**Malmédy** E Belgium ceded by Germany 128/1
**Maloyaroslavets** W Russia ✕93/1
**Malplaquet** N France ✕76/3
**Malta** island of C Mediterranean British colony 112/2; WW2 133/2; independence 145/1
**Mamelukes** (a/s Mamluk) 47/2
**Manchouli** N China treaty town 89/2
**Manchukuo** (name given to Manchuria as Japanese puppet state)
**Manchuria** (called 1932-45 Manchukuo) region of NE China Manchu homeland 88/1; occupied by Russia 89/2; Russian and Japanese spheres of influence 117/2; Japanese puppet state 117/2, 122/1; 134/1; reoccupied by Russia 135/2
**Manchus** people of NE China, under the Ming 65/1; homeland expansion 88/1
**Mandalay** C Burma trade 82/2; terminus of Burma Road 117/2; occupied by Japanese 134/1; retaken 135/2
**Manhao** SW China treaty town 89/2
**Manila** C Philippines early trade 74/1; Spanish settlement 75/2; Spanish trade 97/2; captured by Japanese 134/1
**Manitoba** province of C Canada joins Confederation 113/1; economic development 115/2
**Manus Island** W Pacific Allied base 135/2
**Manzikert** E Anatolia ✕44/1
**Marcomanni** early tribe of C Europe 35/2
**Marengo** N Italy ✕93/1
**Mari** people of C Russia 53/2, 79/1; ASSR 140/1
**Marianas** (form. Ladrones) islands of W Pacific German colony 112/2; US occupation 135/2
**Marienwerder** (Pol. Kwidzyn) N Poland 1920 plebiscite 128/1
**Maritime Provinces** (Russ. Primorskiy Kray) Russ. Far East acquired from China 89/2
**Marne** river NE France ✕125/1
**Marquesas Islands** S Pacific Polynesian dispersal centre 24/2; French colony 145/1 (inset)
**Marseilles** (Fr. Marseille anc. Massilia) S France galley port 77/2
**Marshall Islands** C Pacific German colony 112/2; occupied by US 135/2
**Martinique** island of W Indies French settlement 81/1; French territory 107/1, 112/2, 145/1 (inset)
**Maryland** state of E USA colony 81/2, 99/1; population 115/3; Depression 131/2
**Massachusetts** state of NE USA British colony 99/1; population 115/3; Depression 131/2
**Massachusetts Bay** NE USA British colony 81/2
**Massawa** N Ethiopia Ottoman settlement 55/2; Italian attack 105/1
**Matsu** island SE China Nationalist outpost 154/1
**Mauretania** region of NW Africa conversion to Christianity 32/1
**Mauritania** country of NW Africa independence from France 145/1; political development 150/1; economy 160/1
**Mauritius** (Fr. Maurice) island Indian Ocean early trade 75/2; British colony 113/1
**Maya** people and civilization of C America 22/2, 23/1, 68/2
**Mecca** (Ar. Al Makkah) W Arabia birth of Islam 47/1; Ottoman Empire 66/2
**Media** (a/c Mada) ancient country of NW Persia campaigns of Alexander 30/3
**Medina** (Ar. Al Madinah) W Arabia centre of Islam 47/1; Ottoman Empire 66/2
**Mediolanum** (mod. Milano Eng. Milan) N Italy Roman Empire 35/1
**Mediterranean Sea** Greek colonization 30/1; Phoenicians 30/1; Saracen invasions 50/1
**Melanesia** region of W Pacific early settlement 24/2
**Melilla** (anc. Rusaddir) N Morocco Habsburg Empire 87/1
**Melitene** (mod. Malatya) E Anatolia spread of Mithraism 32/1; Roman Empire 35/12
**Memel Territory** (Ger. Memelgebiet or Memelland) region of SW Lithuania annexed by Germany 129/2
**Memphis** Lower Egypt city of Ancient Egypt 20/1,21/2; campaigns of Alexander 30/3; Roman Empire 35/1; Byzantine Empire 44/1
**Mengtze** (Fr. Mong-tseu) SW China treaty port 89/2
**Mercia** early kingdom of C England 48/2
**Merv** (since 1937 Mary anc. Alexandria) Russ. C Asia spread of Christianity 32/1; Muslim conquest 47/1
**Mesoamerica** classic period 22/2, 23/1
**Mesopotamia** (mod. Iraq) early agriculture 16/1; centre of urban civilization 18/1; Alexander's Empire 31/2; spread of Mithraism 32/1; Roman Empire 35/1; Muslim conquest 47/1
**Mexico** Aztec Empire 68/2; imperial trade 74/1; population 98/2; political development 107/1; independence 113/1; US intervention 149/1; Zapatista revolt 149/1; economy 160/1; opium trade 160; infant mortality and life expectancy 160
**Middle East** (a/c Near East) Cold War 147/1
**Midway** island of C Pacific WW2 ✕ 134/1; US base 135/2, 154/1 (inset)
**Milan** (It. Milano anc. Mediolanum) N Italy Lombard League 51/2
**Miletus** W Anatolia Levantine port 20/1; Mycenaean city 28/2; Greek parent state 30/1; Roman Empire 35/1; Byzantine Empire 44/1
**Mindanao** island of S Philippines Japanese occupation 134/1; retaken by US 135/2
**Mindoro** island of C Philippines US landings in WW2 135/2
**Ming Empire** China 65/1
**Mocha** (Ar. Al Mukhā) S Yemen centre of European trade 97/2

**Modena** (*anc.* Mutina) N Italy Lombard League 51/2; unification of Italy 110/1
**Moesia** region of Balkans district of Byzantine Empire 44/1
**Moesiae** late Roman province of Greece 35/2
**Moesia Inferior** Roman province of the Balkans 35/1
**Moesia Superior** Roman province of the Balkans 35/1
**Mogadishu** (*n/s* Muqdisho *It.* Mogadiscio) Somalia Muslim colony 54/1; Italian occupation 105/1
**Mohács** Hungary ✕67/2
**Moldavia** (*Turk.* Boğdan *Rom.* Moldova) region of Romania/Russia Hungarian 62/2; under Ottoman control 67/1; occupied by Russia 93/1; part of Romania 119/1; SSR 140/1; independence (Moldova) 159/1
**Moluccas** (*Indon.* Maluku *Dut.* Molukken *form.* Spice Islands) islands of E Indies Muslim expansion 60/2; early Portuguese trade 74/1; Dutch control 82/2
**Monastiraki** Crete palace site 28/2
**Mondovi** NW Italy ✕93/1
**Monemvasia** (*It.* Malvasia) S Greece Byzantine Empire 45/2; Ottoman conquest 66/2
**Mongol Empire** 24/1
**Mongolia** (*form.* Outer Mongolia) nomadic pastoralism 19/1; Mongol Empire 24/1; under Turkish Empire 39/1; Chinese incursions under Ming 65/1; Chinese protectorate 89/1; autonomy 89/2; Russian sphere of influence 112/2; limit of Japanese expansion 117/2
**Montenegro** (*S. Cr.* Crna Gora) region of S Yugoslavia under Ottoman rule 102/1; 19C alliances 118/2; independent state 119/1; WW1 125/1; forms part of Yugoslavia 128/1; WW2 133/2
**Montenotte** N Italy ✕93/1
**Montereau** N France ✕93/1
**Montmirail** N France ✕93/1
**Montreux** Switzerland 1936 conference 128/1
**Montserrat** island West Indies British colony 145/1 (inset)
**Moravia** (*Czech.* Morava *Ger.* Mähren) region of C Czechoslovakia medieval German Empire 51/2; occupied by Poland 61/1; acquired by Bohemia 62/2; Hussite influence 63/1; Reformation 84/1; Habsburg Empire 87/1; forms part of Czechoslovakia 128/1
**Mordvinian ASSR** W USSR 140/1
**Morea** (*a/c* Peloponnese) region of S Greece Byzantine Empire 45/2; conquered by Ottomans 67/1
**Morocco** (*Fr.* Maroc *Sp.* Marruecos) under Almohads 54/1; Sharifian dynasties 55/2; independent sultanate 102/1; Spanish conquest 105/1; French and Spanish protectorates 112/2; independence 145/1; conflict with Algeria 150/1; US bases 154/1; economy 160/1

**Morotai** island N Moluccas, E Indies captured by Allies 135/2
**Moscow** (*Russ.* Moskva) W Russia early bishopric 40/1; city of Vladimir-Suzdal 53/2; captured by Napoleon 93/1; Industrial Revolution 95/2; industrial development 126/2; Bolshevik seizure of power 127/1; military district 141/1
**Mossi** early states of W Africa 60-61
**Mostar** Herzegovina, Yugoslavia civil war 158/2
**Mosul** (*Ar.* Al Mawsil) Iraq Muslim conquest 47/1; Ottoman Empire 67/1; oilfield 146/1
**Mozambique** (*form.* Portuguese East Africa *Port.* Moçambique) early trade 75/2; Portuguese settlement 75/2; centre of European trade 97/2; Portuguese colony 105/1; 113/1; independence 145/1; political development 150/1; economy 160/1
**Mughal Empire** India 66/2
**Mukden** Manchuria capital of Manchuria 88/1; treaty town 89/2; Japanese occupation 117/2
**Muscat and Oman** (now Oman) SE Arabia British protectorate 102/1
**Muscovy** early principality of W Russia 66/2, 79/1
**Muslims** minority in Bosnia and Serbia 158/2
**Mwenemutapa** early state of SE Africa 55/2
**Mycenae** ancient city of S Greece 28/2
**Mysore** (*now* Karnataka) region of S India district of Mughal Empire 59/1
**Mytilene** (*a/s* Mitylene) island of Aegean ceded to Greece 119/1
**Nagasaki** W Japan early European trade 74/1, 75/2; industry 83/1; Dutch trade 97/2; bombed by US 135/2
**Nagorno-Karabakh** Caucasus 140/1; 159/1
**Namibia** (*form.* South West Africa *earlier* German South West Africa) German colony 105/1, 112/2; independence from South Africa 145/1, 150/1; economy 160/1
**Nanking** (*n/s* Nanjing) N China Ming provincial capital 65/1; treaty port 89/2; occupied by Japan 117/2; economy 143/2
**Nanning** S China treaty port 89/2
**Nantes** NW France Scandinavian settlement 50/1
**Naples, Kingdom of** Black Death 63/1; to Austria 76/3; Habsburg Empire 87/1; satellite of France 93/1; unification of Italy 110/1
**Narbonensis** (*a/c* Gallia Narbonensis) Roman province of S France 35/1
**Narbonne** (*anc.* Narbo) S France Muslim conquest 47/1
**Naroch** lake W Russia WW1A125/1
**Nations, Battle of the** (Leipzig) E Germany ✕93/1
**Naucratis** Egypt Greek colony 30/1
**Nauru** island W Pacific independence 145/1 (inset)

**Navarre** (*Sp.* Navarra) region of N Spain/SW France acquired by France 77/2; Habsburg Empire 87/1
**Navas de Tolosa** S Spain ✕47/1
**Neapolis** (*mod.* Napoli *Eng.* Naples) S Italy Greek colony 30/1, 31/2; Roman Empire 35/1
**Nehavend** (*anc.* Laodicea in Media) W Persia ✕47/1
**Nepal** tributary state of Chinese Empire 88/1; 89/2; economy 160/1
**Nerchinsk, Treaty of** 88/1
**Netherlands** (*a/c* Holland *form.* Dutch Republic United Provinces) agriculture and land reclamation 26/2; Habsburg Empire 87/1; Industrial Revolution 95/2; 18C Atlantic economy 96/1; trade with Africa and Asia 97/2; colonial power 112/2; EEC and NATO 138/2; economy 160/1. See also Belgium, Flanders, Holland
**Netherlands, Austrian** (*mod.* Belgium) revolt against Emperor 92/1
**Netherlands East Indies** (now Indonesia) occupied by Japanese 134/1. See also East Indies, Borneo, Java, Moluccas, Sumatra
**Netherlands, Spanish** (*later* Holland *or* United Provinces; *and* Belgium) Reformation 84/1; Dutch revolt 86/2
**Neustria** the Frankish lands of N France 48/1
**Nevis** island W Indies British colony 107/1; self-government with St. Christopher 145/1 (inset)
**New Amsterdam** (*earlier* Fort Amsterdam *now* New York city) colonized by Dutch 81/2
**New Britain** island Papua New Guinea early Melanesian settlement 24/2; retaken from Japanese 135/1; to New Guinea 145/1 (inset)
**New Brunswick** province of E Canada joins Confederation 113/1; 115/2
**New Caledonia** islands S Pacific early Melanesian settlement 24/2; French colony 112/2, 145/1; US base 134-5
**Newchwang** Manchuria treaty port 89/2
**New England** NE USA British settlement 81/2
**Newfoundland** province of E Canada rediscovered 72/1; British colony 81/1; British settlement 81/2; joins Dominion 115/2
**New France** French possessions in Canada 81/2
**New Galicia** Spanish colony of C Mexico 74/1
**New Granada** (*mod.* Colombia) Spanish colony 74/1, 81/1; vice-royalty in rebellion against Spain 92/1, 107/1; 18C Atlantic economy 96/1
**New Guinea** (*now part of* Papua New Guinea) early settlement 24/2; Dutch/German/British control 112/2; attacked by Japanese 134/1; retaken by Allies 135/2. See also West Irian

**New Hampshire** state of NE USA colony 81/2; 99/1; population 115/3, Depression 131/2
**New Hebrides** (*Fr.* Nouvelles Hébrides *now* Vanuatu) islands S Pacific early Melanesian settlement 24/2; British/French condominium 112/2; US base 134/1; independence 145/1 (inset)
**New Ireland** island Papua New Guinea early Melanesian settlement 24/2; occupied by Japanese 134/1
**New Jersey** state of E USA colony 81/2, 99/1; population 115/3; Depression 131/2
**New Mexico** state of SW USA ceded by Mexico 107/1; population 115/3; Depression 131/2
**New Orleans** S USA French/Spanish occupation 81/1
**New Sarai** S Russia Mongol city 24/1
**New South Wales** state of SE Australia settlement and development 100/1; statehood 113/1
**New Spain** (*mod.* Mexico, C America and Caribbean) Spanish vice-royalty 74/1; early voyages of discovery 81/1; rebellion against Spain 92/1
**New Territories** S China acquired by Britain 89/2
**New York City** (1653-64 called New Amsterdam *earlier* Fort Amsterdam) 81/2; industry 114/1; population 114/1; economic growth 137/2
**New Zealand** early Polynesian settlement 24/2; settlement and development 101/2, 113/1; pacific trade 153/3; foreign direct investment 161
**Nicaea** (*mod.* Iznik) W Anatolia Roman Empire 35/1; Byzantine Empire 45/2
**Nicaragua** country of C America early exploration 72/1; independence 107/1; US protectorate 107/1; Sandinista revolution 149/1
**Nicephorium** (*mod.* Rakka) Syria Roman Empire 35/1
**Nicobar Islands** Indian Ocean territory of British India 91/3
**Nicomedia** *mod.* Izmit) W Anatolia Roman Empire 35/1; Byzantine Empire 44/1
**Nicopolis** W Greece Byzantine Empire 45/2
**Niger** country of W Africa French colony 105/1; independence 145/1; economy 160/1
**Nigeria** country of W Africa British colony 104/1, 105/1, 112/2; independence 145/1; political development 150/1; economy 160/1
**Nineveh** Mesopotamia early farming village 16/1; 20/1; Assyrian Empire 20/1; Mitannian city 20/1
**Ningpo** (*n/s* Ningbo) E China treaty port 89/2
**Ningxia** (*f/s* Ningxia) province of N China economy 1979-92 143/2
**Nippur** C Mesopotamia Sumerian city 20/1

171

**Nish** (S. Cr. Niš anc. Naissus) E Yugoslavia Ottoman Empire 67/1; WW1 125/1
**Nishapur** (Pers. Neyshabur) W Persia Mongol conquest 57/2; Safavid conquest 66/2
**Nisibis** (mod. Nusaybin) E Anatolia Roman Empire 35/1
**Nizhniy Novgorod** (since 1932 Gorkiy) C Russia town of Vladimir-Suzdal 53/2; 1905 Revolution 109/2; Bolshevik seizure 127/1
**Nomonhan** (a/c Khalkin Gol) E Mongolia Russo-Japanese conflict 117/2
**Nördlingen** S Germany ✕86/3
**Noricum** Roman province of C Europe 35/1
**Normandy** region of N France Scandinavian settlement 50/1; French Royal domain 76/1; province of France 77/2
**Normans** in Sicily and S Italy 45/2
**North Carolina** state of E USA colony 81/2, 99/1; population 115/3; Depression 131/2
**Northern Cook Islands** (Manihiki Islands)
**Northern Ireland** religious divide and Industrial Revolution 95/2
**Northern Rhodesia** (now Zambia) British colony 104/2, 105/1, 112/2
**North Ossetian ASSR** Caucasus 140/1
**Northumbria** early kingdom of N England 48/2; Scandinavian settlement 50/1
**North Vietnam** independence 145/1. See also Vietnam, Indo-China
**North West Frontier Province** N Pakistan in Indian Empire 91/3
**Norway** conversion to Christianity 40/1; Black Death 63/1; Reformation 84/1; WW2 132/1, 133/2; NATO and EFTA 138/3, 154/1; economy 156, 160/1
**Norwich** E England Scandinavian settlement 50/1
**Notium** W Anatolia ✕31/2
**Nottingham** C England Danish Viking base 50/1
**Nova Scotia** (form. Acadia) province of E Canada ceded by France 81/2; British possession 81/1, 99/1; joins Confederation 113/1; economy 115/2
**Novgorod** (Norse Holmegaard) NW Russia bishopric 40/1; Viking trade 50/1, 54/1; industry 126/2; WW2 133/2
**Novgorod Empire** NW Russia 53/2; conquered by Muscovy 79/1
**Novgorod-Seversk** early principality of W Russia 53/2
**Novibazar, Sanjak of** Ottoman province of Yugoslavia 119/1
**Nubia** region of NE Africa early settlement 25/1; Christian kingdom 54/1
**Numidia** Roman province of N Africa 35/1
**Nupe** Nigeria early Hausa state 54/1, 55/2
**Nyasaland** (now Malawi) British protectorate 112/2

**Odessa** S Ukraine founded 79/1; 1905 Revolution 109/2; Bolshevik seizure 127/1; WW2 133/2
**Odessus** (mod. Varna) Bulgaria Greek colony 30/1; Roman Empire 35/1
**Offa's Dyke** 48/2
**Okinawa** island SW Japan captured by US 135/2; reversion to Japan 153/1; US base 154/1
**Olbia** S Russia Roman Empire 35/1
**Old Calabar** Nigeria 55/2
**Old Sarai** S Russia Mongol city 24/1
**Olmec States** C Mexico 22/2
**Oman** region of E Arabia Muslim expansion 47/1; under Abbasid sovereignty 47/2; British sphere of influence 145/1; economy 160/1; Gulf War 147/3
**Ontario** province of E Canada joins Confederation 113/1; economic development 115/2
**Oran** (Ar. Wahran) N Algeria acquired by Habsburgs 76/1; Habsburg Empire 87/1; WW2 133/2
**Orange** principality of S France 81/2
**Oregon** state of NW USA acquired by USA 98/2; population 115/3; Depression 131/2
**Orenburg** (1938-57 called Chkalov) C Russia founded 79/1; Bolshevik seizure 127/1
**Orissa** (form. Jajnagar) region of E India district of Mughal Empire 59/1; state of modern India 91/3
**Orkney** islands of NE Scotland Norwegian Viking settlement 50/1
**Orléanais** region of C France 76/1; 77/2
**Ormuz** (a/s Hormuz anc. Harmozia) S Persia Portuguese control 58/1; Portuguese base 66/2, 74/1
**Oslo** (until 1924 Kristiania a/s Christiania) Norway WW2 132/1, 133/2
**Ostrogoths** invasion of Europe 35/2
**Otford** S England ✕48/2
**Ottoman Empire** Mongol invasion 57/2; 70/1; expansion into Europe 113/1, 2; decline 102/1, 119/1; WW1 125/1
**Oudenaarde** (Fr. Audenarde) Belgium ✕76/3
**Outer Mongolia** (now Mongolia) Chinese protectorate 88/1; independence 122/2

**Pacific Ocean** early Polynesian settlement 24/2; WW2 134/1; sovereignty of islands 145/1 (inset)
**Padua** (It. Padova anc. Patavium) N Italy WW1 125/1
**Paeckche** Korea early state destroyed by T'ang 42/1
**Pagan** C Burma Mongol attack 24/1; Buddhist site 32/1; early empire 61/1
**Pakhoi** S China treaty port 89/2
**Pakistan** independence 145/1; secession of Bangladesh 153/1; boundary dispute with India 153/1; Baghdad Pact and US alliance 154/1; economy 160/1; opium trade 161

**Palatinate** (Ger. Pfalz) historical region of W Germany Reformation 84/1; German unification 111/2
**Palau** (f/s Pelew) SW Caroline Islands, W Pacific occupied by US 135/2
**Pale** Bosnia-Herzegovina Bosnian Serb capital 158/2
**Palestine** (Lat. Palaestina now Israel and Jordan) Levantine cities and ports 20/1; Byzantine Empire 44/1; Ottoman province 102/1; WW2 132/1; partition between Israel and Jordan 146/2
**Pamphylia** ancient country of southern Anatolia 30/1, 35/1, 44/1
**Panama** independence 107/1; US intervention 1989 149/1; US base 154/1; economy 160/1
**Panama Canal** opening 112/2
**Panipat** N India ✕59/1
**Panmunjom** Korea 1953 armistice 143/1
**Pannonia** C Europe Avar Kingdom 48/1
**Pannonia Inferior** Roman province of C Europe 35/1
**Pannonia Superior** Roman province of C Europe 35/1
**Panticapaeum** (mod. Kerch) Crimea Greek colony 30/1; Roman Empire 35/1
**Papal States** C Italy Black Death 63/1; Reformation 84/1; unification of Italy 110/1
**Paphlagonia** ancient country of N Anatolia 30/1; 44/1
**Paphos** (Lat. Paphus) Cyprus Greek colony 30/1
**Papua New Guinea** SW Pacific independence 145/1; economy 160/1. See also New Guinea
**Parhae** (Chin. Pohai) early Korean state 42/1
**Paris** N France parlement 77/2; ✕93/1; Industrial Revolution 95/2
**Parma** N Italy Roman Lombard League 51/2; unification of Italy 110/1
**Pasargadae** SW Persia ✕25/5
**Passchendaele** NW Belgium WW1✕ 125/1(inset)
**Pearl Harbor** Hawaii bombed by Japanese 134/1
**Pechenegs** tribe of Ukraine, 45/2, 52/1, 53/2
**Pecsaete** tribe of early England 48/2
**Pegu** early state of S Burma, Buddhist site 32/1; early trade 82/2
**Peipus, Lake** (Russ. Chudskoye Ozero Est. Peipsi Järv) W Russia ✕53/2
**Peking** (form. Mong. Khanbalik, Chin. Beijing) N China Ming capital 65/1; Japanese occupation 117/2; economy 143/2, 153/3
**Peninsular War** 93/1
**Pennsylvania** state of E USA colony 81/2, 99/1; population 115/3; Depression 131/2
**Pergamum** (Gr. Pergamon Turk. Bergama) W Anatolia Roman Empire 35/1

**Périgord** region of C France annexed to France 76/1
**Perm** (1940-57 called Molotov) C Russia founded 79/1; Bolshevik seizure 127/1; industry 126/2
**Persepolis** Persia taken by Alexander 30/3; Muslim conquest 47/1
**Persia** (now Iran) Mongol invasion 24/1; campaigns of Alexander 30/3; attacked by White Huns 39/1; under Abbasid sovereignty 47/2; Safavid Empire 58/1, 67/1, 70/1; independent kingdom 102/1
**Persian Gulf** (a/c Arabian Gulf or The Gulf) Iran-Iraq War 146/1; Gulf War 147/3
**Peru** Spanish colonization 74/1; 18C Atlantic economy 96/1; independence 107/1; cocaine trade 160; economy 160/1
**Petrograd** (before 1914 St. Petersburg since 1924 Leningrad) WW1 125/1; Russian Revolution 127/1
**Petsamo** (Russ. Pechenga) NW Russia Russian conquest from Finland 133/2
**Phazania** (mod. Fezzan) region of S Libya 35/1
**Philadelphia** E USA founded 79/1; economic growth 137/2
**Philippines** early trade 74/1; Spanish conquest 82/2; occupied by Japanese 117/2, 134/1; retaken by Americans 135/2; independence 145/1; political development 153/1; US bases 154/1; industry and economy 153/3, 160/1
**Philippine Sea** ✕135/2
**Philippopolis** (mod. Plovdiv Turk. Filibe) Bulgaria Byzantine Empire 44/1; Ottoman Empire 67/1
**Philomelium** (mod. Akşehir) C Anatolia Byzantine Empire 45/2
**Phnom Penh** Cambodia 60/2, 82/2; Vietnam war 153/3
**Phocaea** W Anatolia Greek colony 30/1
**Phoenicia** at time of Greeks 30/1
**Phoenicians** move into Africa 25/1
**Phrygia** ancient country of W Anatolia 30/1; Byzantine Empire 44/1
**Picts** early tribe of Scotland 39/1
**Piedmont** (It. Piemonte) region of N Italy 110/1
**Pigs, Bay of** Cuba CIA invasion 155/2
**Pisidia** ancient country of C Anatolia 44/1
**Podolia** region of S Ukraine acquired by Lithuania 62/2
**Poetovio** (mod. Ptuj Ger. Pettau) N Yugoslavia Roman Empire 35/1
**Pohai** (Kor. Parhae mod. Manchuria) NE China early state 42/1
**Poitiers** (anc. Limonum) C France ✕47/1, 48/1; 17C seat of intendant 77/2
**Poitou** region of W France province of France 77/2
**Pola** (mod. Pula) N Yugoslavia Roman Empire 35/1; WW1 125/1
**Poland** conversion to Christianity 40/1; union with Lithuania 62/2; Black Death 63/1; acquired by Russia 79/1; Reformation 84/1;

revolt against Russia 92/1; WW1 125/1; WW2 132/1; territorial changes 138/2, 139/1; Warsaw Pact and Comecon 138/3, 154/1; employment 156; end of Communist rule 159/1
**Polish Corridor** 128/1
**Polynesia** islands of C Pacific early settlement 24/2
**Pomerania** (*Ger.* Pommern *Pol.* Pomorze*) region of N Europe medieval German Empire 51/2; Reformation 84/1; unification of Germany 111/2
**Pomerelia** (*Ger.* Pommerellen) region of N Europe occupied by Teutonic Knights 62/2
**Pondicherry** (*Fr.* Pondichéry) SE India French settlement 75/2; French enclave 91/3
**Pontus** district of N Anatolia 30/1; Roman province 35/2; Byzantine Empire 44/1
**Portage la Prairie** (Fort La Reine)
**Port Arthur** (*Chin.* Lushun *Jap.* Ryojun) Manchuria ceded to Russia and Japan 89/2, 108/1
**Port Arthur** (*now* Thunder Bay) C Canada growth 115/2
**Port Moresby** SE New Guinea Allied base WW2 134/1, 135/2
**Port Said** N Egypt Egyptian-Israeli war 146/2
**Portugal** (*anc.* Lusitania) Muslim conquest 47/1; 18C Atlantic economy 96/1; trade with Africa and Asia 97/2; colonial empire 112/2; WW1 125/1; NATO and EFTA 138/3, 154/1; US bases 154/1; economy 156, 160/1
**Portuguese East Africa** (*now* Mozambique) 87/2, 112/2
**Portuguese Guinea** (*now* Guinea-Bissau) W Africa Portuguese colony 112/2; independence 145/1
**Portuguese Timor** E Indies annexed by Indonesia 145/1
**Posen** (*Pol.* Poznań) W Poland unification of Germany 111/2; ceded by Germany 128/1
**Posidonia** (*later* Paestum *mod.* Pesto) S Italy Greek colony 30/1
**Potidaea** N Greece Dorian colony 30/1
**Prague** (*Cz.* Praha) Czechoslovakia bishopric 40/1; Communist coup 159/1
**Pressburg** (*Cz.* Bratislava) C Czechoslovakia ✕50/1
**Preveza** C Greece ✕67/2
**Prince Edward Island** (*form.* St Jean) island of E Canada joins Dominion 115/2
**Provence** region of S France Frankish Empire 48/1; medieval German Empire 51/2; province of France 77/2
**Providence** NE USA founded 81/2
**Prusa** (*mod.* Bursa) W Anatolia Byzantine Empire 44/1
**Prussia** (*Ger.* Preussen) region of E Germany Reformation 84/1; unification of Germany 111/2
**Przemyśl** Austria-Hungary WW1 125/1
**Puerto Rico** W Indies conquered by US 107/1

**Pugachev uprising** Russia 79/1
**Punjab** region of NW India Muslim expansion 47/1, 90/1; state of British India 90/2, 91/3
**Pusan** (*Jap.* Fusan) S Korea 1950-3 war 143/1
**Puteoli** (*mod.* Pozzuoli) C Italy Roman colony 35/1
**Pylos** (*a/s* Pilos *It.* Navarino) SW Greece Levantine port 20/1; Mycenaean palace site 28/2
**Pyongyang** (*Jap.* Heijo) N Korea 1950-53 war 143/1
**Qadisiya** S Mesopotamia ✕47/1
**Qarabagh** region of Caucasus conquered by Ottomans 58/1
**Qatar** sheikhdom of Persian Gulf 102/1; Gulf War 147/3
**Qinghai** (*f/s* Tsinghai) province of N China economy 1979-92 143/2
**Quadi** Germanic tribe 35/1
**Quebec** city, E Canada capital of New France 81/2; population 115/2
**Quebec** province, E Canada joins Confederation 113/2; economic development 115/2
**Quelimane** Mozambique Portuguese settlement 105/1
**Quemoy** island SE China Nationalist outpost 153/1, 154/1
**Quentovic** (*a/s* Quentowic) N France Vikings 50/1
**Qui Nhon** S Vietnam war 152/2
**Rabaul** Papua New Guinea Japanese base in WW2 135/2
**Ragusa** (*now* Dubrovnik) W Yugoslavia Mongol attack 24/1; Byzantine Empire 44/1; Ottoman vassal republic 67/1; Reformation 84/1
**Rai** (*anc.* Rhagae *Bibl.* Rages *Gr.* Europus) N Persia Mongol attack 24/1; Muslim conquest 47/1
**Ramillies** Belgium ✕76/3
**Ramla** Palestine ✕47/1
**Rangoon** (*anc.* Dagon) Burma Buddhist site 32/1; early trade centre 82/2; occupied by Japanese 134/1; retaken by British 135/2
**Rann of Kutch** region of W India boundary disputes with Pakistan 153/1
**Rapallo** N Italy 1922 Conference 128/1
**Ras al Khaimah** (*Ar.* Ra's al Khaymah) SE Arabia emirate 147/3
**Ratisbon** (*Ger.* Regensburg) S Germany ✕93/1
**Reformation** 84/1, 86/3
**Regensburg** (*anc.* Castra Regina *obs. Eng.* Ratisbon) S Germany bishopric 40/1; Frankish royal residence 48/1
**Reggio** (*a/c* Reggio di Calabria *anc.* Rhegium) S Italy Ottoman siege 66/2
**Réunion** (*form.* Bourbon) island Indian Ocean French colony 112/2
**Rhaetia** (*mod.* Switzerland) Roman province 35/1
**Rhegium** (*mod.* Reggio di Calabria) N Italy Greek colony 30/1, 31/2
**Rheims** (*Fr.* Reims *anc.* Durocortorum *later* Remi) N France archbishopric 48/1; sacked by Vandals 50/1; ✕93/1; WW1 125/1; WW2 133/2

**Rhine, Confederation of the** Napoleonic creation 93/1
**Rhineland** (*Ger.* Rheinland) region of W Germany remilitarized 128/1, 129/2
**Rhode Island** state of NE USA colony 81/2; population 115/3; Depression 131/2
**Rhodes** (*mod. Gr.* Rodhos *Lat.* Rhodus *It.* Rodi) Aegean Greek state 30/1; ✕47/1; Ottoman conquest 66/2; under Knights of St John 67/1. See also Dodecanese
**Rhodesia** (*form.* Southern Rhodesia *now* Zimbabwe) British colony 112/2; independence (UDI) 145/1
**Rhodus** (*mod. Gr.* Rhodes *Eng.* Rhodes) island SE Aegean Roman Empire 35/1
**Riga** Latvia, NW USSR short-lived Communist control 127/1; WW2 133/2
**Rio Barbate** Spain ✕47/1
**Rio Muni** (*a/c* Spanish Guinea *now* Equatorial Guinea) W Africa Spanish colony 104/2
**Rivoli** N Italy ✕93/1
**Riyadh** (*Ar.* Ar Riyāḍ) C Saudi Arabia Gulf War 147/3
**Rocroi** NE France ✕86/3
**Rodez** region of S France 76/1
**Romagna** region of N Italy unification of Italy 110/1
**Roman Empire** 34-5
**Romania** Industrial Revolution 95/2; independence 102/1; interwar alliances 118/2; on break-up of Ottoman Empire 119/1; WW1 125/1; acquisition of Transylvania 128/1; Warsaw Pact and Comecon 138/3; employment 156; end of Communist rule 156, 159/1. See also Moldavia, Wallachia
**Rome** (*anc.* Roma *It.* Roma) C Italy arrival of Christianity 32/1; Roman Empire 34-5; sacked by Vandals and Visigoths 39/1; Magyar raid 50/1; papal patrimony 51/2; under French rule 93/1; annexed by Italy 110/1; WW2 133/2
**Roncesvalles** N Spain ✕48/1
**Rouen** (*anc.* Rotomagus) N France archbishopric 48/1; Scandinavian settlement 50/1; urban revolt 63/1; *parlement* 87/1
**Royale, Ile** (*now* Cape Breton Island) E Canada French settlement 81/2
**Ruanda-Urundi** (*now* Rwanda and Burundi) C Africa Belgian colony 112/2
**Ruapekapeka** N Island, New Zealand ✕101/2
**Ruhr** region of NW Germany Industrial Revolution 95/2; occupied by French 128/1
**Rumelia** (*mod.* Bulgaria) Ottoman vassal state 67/1
**Rupert's Land** region of N Canada Hudson's Bay Company 81/1; British possession 81/2
**Russia** (in Europe) conversion to Christianity 40/1; Kievan Russia 53/2; Viking trade 52/1; Black Death 63/1; expansion 79/2; opposition to Napoleon 93/1; Industrial Revolution

95/2; 1905 Revolution 109/2; 19C European alliances 118/2; world trade 1860-1913 120/3; foreign investment 1914 121/2; WW1 125/1; development 1926-40 126/2; Revolution 127/1; Allied intervention 127/1. See also USSR and Russian Federation
**Russia** (in Asia) expansion 79/2; acquisition of Maritime Province from China 89/2; 19C spheres of influence 112/2
**Russian Federation** free elections 159/1
**Ruthenia** region of SW Ukraine acquired by Poland-Lithuania 62/2; incorporated into Czechoslovakia 128/1 occupied by Hungary 129/2
**Rwanda** (*form.* Ruanda) early state of C Africa 55/2; independence 145/1; political development 150/1; economy 160/1
**Ryazan** C Russia early bishopric 40/1; town of Murom-Ryazan 53/2; acquired by Muscovy 79/1; industry 124/2
**Ryukyu Islands** (*f/c* Loochoo Islands) E China Sea acquired by Japan 117/2
**Saar** (*Ger.* Saarland *Fr.* Sarre) district of W Germany Industrial Revolution 95/2; League of Nations mandate and plebiscite 128/1
**Sabrata** (*a/c* Abrotonum) Libya Punic city 30/1; Roman Empire 35/1
**Sadowa** (*a/c* Königgrätz) Bohemia ✕111/2
**Sahara** region of N Africa trade routes 55/2
**Sahel** region of W Africa early settlement 25/1
**Saigon** (*n/c* Ho Chi Minh) S Vietnam early trade centre 82/2; Japanese base WW2 134/1; war 152/2
**St. Christopher and Nevis** W Indies British colony 107/1; 145/1 (inset)
**Saint-Domingue** (*now* Haiti) French colony 81/1
**St. Petersburg** (1914-24 Petrograd 1925-91 Leningrad) W Russia founded 79/1; acquired by Muscovy 79/1; Industrial Revolution 95/2
**Saipan** island Marianas. C Pacific Japanese base in WW2 134-5/1,2
**Sakhalin** (*Jap.* Karafuto) island Russ. Far East north acquired by Russia 108/1; south acquired by Japan 117/2; south reoccupied by Russia 135/2; claimed by Japan 153/1
**Salamanca** N Spain ✕93/1
**Salamantica** (*a/c* Helmantica *mod.* Salamanca) N Spain Roman Empire 35/1
**Salamis** (*later* Constantia) Cyprus Greek colony 30/1; Roman Empire 35/1
**Salisbury** (*n/c* Harare) S Rhodesia 105/1
**Salonae** (*a/s* Salona) Albania Roman Empire 35/1; Byzantine Empire 44/1
**Salonika** (*a/s* Salonica *a/c* Thessalonica *Gr.* Thessaloniki *Turk.* Selanik) N Greece bishopric 40/1; occupied by Ottomans 67/1; WW1 125/1

173

**Samara** (1935-91 Kuybyshev) C Russia founded 79/1; on railway to east 108/1; Bolshevik seizure 127/1
**Samarkand** (anc. Maracanda) C Asia Mongol attack 24/1; Muslim conquest 47/1; Timur's Empire 57/2; Soviet Union 126/2
**Samoa** islands S Pacific early settlement 70/2; German colony 112/2. See also Western Samoa
**Samogitia** (Lith. Žemaitija) region of NW Russia occupied by Lithuania 37/1, 62/2
**San Agostín** (now St. Augustine) SE USA Spanish fort 74/1
**Sandinista revolt** Nicaragua 149/1
**San Francisco** (form. San Francisco de Asís) W USA Spanish settlement 81/1; economic growth 137/2
**Santa Cruz** (n/c Ndeni) Solomon Islands WW2 ✕135/2
**Santa Fé de Bogotá** (n/c Bogotá) Colombia Spanish capital of New Granada 74/1
**Santo Domingo** (now Dominican Republic) W Indies Spanish colony 74/1; 81/1
**Santuao** E China treaty port 89/2
**São Tomé and Príncipe** islands W Africa united as independent republic 145/1
**Saracens** invasion of S Europe 50/1
**Saragossa** (anc. Caesaraugusta mod. Zaragoza) N Spain bishopric 40/1; ✕93/1; captured by French 93/1
**Sarajevo** C Yugoslavia captured by Ottomans 67/1; Ottoman administrative centre 67/1; WW1 125/1; WW2 133/2; civil war 158/2
**Saratoga** NE USA ✕99/1
**Sardinia** (It. Sardegna) island W Mediterranean Muslim conquest 47/1; Byzantine Empire 44/1; Muslim conquest 47/1; Saracen attacks 50/1; Habsburg Empire 87/1; Kingdom of 110/1
**Sardis** (a/s Sardes) W Anatolia Roman Empire 35/1; Byzantine Empire 44/1
**Sarkel** S Russia ✕52/1
**Sarmatians** (Lat. Sarmatae) tribe of Caucasus and S Russia 30/1, 35/1
**Sarmizegetusa** Romania Roman Empire 35/1
**Sasanian Empire** Western Asia 27/3
**Saudi Arabia** Gulf War 147/3
**Savoy** (Fr. Savoie It. Savoia) region of France/Italy medieval state 51/2; Calvinism 84/1; Habsburg Empire 87/1; ceded to France 110/1
**Saxon March** 48/1
**Saxony** region of N Germany Frankish Empire 48/1; Black Death 63/1; Reformation 84/1
**Scandinavia** (anc. Scandia) Viking invasions of Europe 50/1; world trade 1860-1913 120/3. See also Denmark, Sweden, Norway
**Scapa Flow** N Scotland WW1 125/1
**Schleswig-Holstein** region of N Germany unification of Germany 111/2
**Scotland** (anc. Caledonia) Scandinavian settlement 50/1;

Black Death 63/1; Reformation 84/1
**Scupi** (mod. Skoplje Mac. Skopje Turk. Üsküb) Byzantine Empire 44/1
**Scythians** ancient tribe of S Russia 30/1
**Sebastopol** (Russ. Sevastopol) Crimea. S Russia 1905 Revolution 109/2; WW1 125/1
**Sodan** N France ✕111/2, WW2 132/1
**Seleucia** (a/c Seleucia Tracheotis) SE Anatolia Byzantine Empire 44/1
**Selinus** (mod. Selinunte) Sicily Greek colony 30/1, 31/2
**Seljuks** Turkish Muslim dynasty of Middle East 45/2, 47/2
**Senegal** W Africa French colony 105/1, 112/2; independence 145/1; economy 160/1
**Senegambia** region of W Africa source of slaves 55/2; slave trade 96/1
**Seoul** (Jap. Keijo) S Korea Korean war 143/1; population 160/1
**Septimania** ancient region of S France, part of Frankish Empire 48/1
**Serbia** (now part of Yugoslavia) country of SE Europe conversion to Christianity 40/1; Byzantine Empire 45/2; empire under Stephen Dushan 62/2; Black Death 63/1; Ottoman province 67/1; Industrial Revolution 95/2; independence 102/1, 119/1; WW1 125/1; forms part of Yugoslavia 128/1; WW2 133/2
**Serdica** (a/s Sardica mod. Sofia) Bulgaria Roman Empire 35/1; Byzantine Empire 44/1
**Sevastopol** (Eng. Sebastopol med. Turk. Akhtiar) Crimea acquired by Muscovy 79/1
**Seville** (Sp. Sevilla anc. Hispalis) S Spain Emirate of Cordoba 50/1
**Shaanxi** (f/s Shensi) province of N China economy 1979-92 143/2
**Shanghai** E China treaty port 89/2; occupied by Japanese 117/2; Nationalist control 122/2; industry 122/2; economy 143/2, 153/3
**Shansi** (f/s Shanxi) province of N China Ming province 65/1; Manchu expansion 88/1; economy 143/2
**Shan State(s)** Burma part of India 91/3
**Shandong** (f/s Shantung) province of E China economy 1979-92 143/2
**Shantou** (f/s Swatow) S China special economic zone 143/2
**Shantung** (n/s Shandong) province of E China under Ming 65/1; Manchu expansion 88/1; Japanese influence 122/1; economy 143/2
**Shanxi** (f/s Shansi) province of N China economy 1979-92 143/2
**Shensi** (n/s Shaanxi) province of N China under Ming 65/1; Manchu expansion 88/1; economy 143/2
**Shenzhen** S China special economic zone 143/2
**Shetland** (form. Hjaltland) NE Scotland Norwegian settlement 50/1
**Shias** Muslim minority of S Iraq 147/3
**Siam** (now Thailand) spread of Buddhism 32/1, 60/2; conquests 82/2; under Japanese influence

117/2; occupied by Japanese 134/1
**Sian** (n/s Xi'an) China Ming provincial capital 64/1
**Siberia** Russian expansion 79/2
**Sichuan** (f/s Szechwan) province of W China economy 1979-92 143/2
**Sicily** (Lat. and It. Sicilia) island C Mediterranean Greek colonization 30/1, Byzantine Empire 44/1; Saracen raids 50/1; German attacks 51/2; to Savoy 76/3; Habsburg Empire 87/1; Kingdom of the Two Sicilies annexed to Piedmont/Sardinia 110/1; WW2 133/2
**Sidon** (mod. Saïda Ar. Sayda) Lebanon Assyrian Empire 20/1; Levantine city 20/1; Phoenician city 30/1; taken by Alexander 30/3
**Sierra Leone** country of W Africa slave trade 96/1; British settlement 105/1; British colony 112/2, 113/1; independence 145/1; economy 160/1
**Sikkim** country of Himalayas British protectorate 89/2 dependency of India 91/3; annexed to India 145/1
**Silesia** (Ger. Schlesien Pol. Śląsk) region of Germany/Poland medieval German Empire 51/2; acquired by Habsburgs 62/2; Habsburg Empire 87/1; unification of Germany 111/2; divided between Germany and Poland 128/1
**Silla** (Eng. Korea Kor. Koryo) occupied by T'ang 42/1
**Singapore** (earlier Tumasik) S Malaya early trade 82/2; occupied by Japanese 134/1; independence 145/1; Pacific trade 152/2; economy 153/3, 160/1
**Sinkiang** (n/s Xinjiang) province of NW China part of Han Empire 88/1; cession of territory to Russia 89/2; economy 143/2
**Sinope** (mod. Sinop) N Anatolia Greek colony 30/1; Roman Empire 35/1; Byzantine Empire 44/1
**Slovakia** forms part of Czechoslovakia 128/1; occupied by Hungary in WW2 132/1
**Slovenia** in Yugoslavia 128/1; independence 159/1
**Smolensk** W Russia bishopric 40/1; principality 53/2; acquired by Napoleon 93/1; Bolshevik seizure 127/1; industry 126/2
**Smyrna** (mod. Izmir) W Anatolia Roman Empire 35/1; Byzantine Empire 67/1; Ottoman Empire 67/1; centre of European trade 97/2
**Socotra** island Arabian Sea British control 103; acquired by Britain 112/2
**Sofala** Mozambique Portuguese settlement 55/2; early trade 75/2
**Sofia** (anc. Serdica a/s Sardica med. Sredets) Bulgaria Ottoman control 67/1; WW2 133/2
**Sogdiana** (a/c Sogdia, Suguda) ancient region of C Asia Chinese protectorate 42/1
**Solferino** N Italy ✕110/1
**Solomon Islands** SW Pacific British protectorate 113/1 (inset); occupied by Japanese 134/1; retaken by Allies

135/2; independence 145/1 (inset)
**Somalia** (form. British and Italian Somaliland) independence 145/1; political development 150/1; economy 160/1
**Somaliland** divided between British, Italians and French 103
**Somme** river NE France WW1 offensive 125/1 (inset)
**Songhay** (a/s Songhai) early empire of W Africa 55/2; 70/1
**Soochow** E China treaty port 89/2; industry 122/2
**Sopron** (Ger. Ödenburg) Hungary to Hungary after plebiscite 128/1
**Sorbs** Slavic tribe of C Europe 48/1
**South Africa** Union 112/2; Republic 145/1; political development 150/1
**South Carolina** state of SE USA colony 81/2, 99/1; population 115/3; Depression 131/2
**South-East Asia** early civilizations 26/2; Mongol attacks 61/1; post 1945 conflicts 151/1, 154/1
**Southern Rhodesia** now Zimbabwe f/c Rhodesia) British colony 105/1, 112/2
**South Ossetian AR** Caucasus 140/1
**South Tyrol** (Ger. Südtirol It. Alto Adige) region of Austro-Hungarian Empire acquired by Italy 128/1
**South Vietnam** independence 145/1; war 152/2. See also Vietnam, Indo-China
**South Yemen** (also called People's Democratic Republic of Yemen form. Federation of South Arabia earlier Protectorate of South Arabia earlier Aden Protectorate) independence 145/1; union with north Yemen 145/1; political development 150/1; economy 160/1
**Spa** Belgium 1920 Conference 128/1
**Spain** (anc. Hispania) early invasions 39/1; conversion to Christianity 40/1; Muslim conquest 47/1; Umayyad caliphate 47/2; Reformation 84/1; War of the Spanish Succession 76/3; colonial empire 92/1; opposition to Napoleon 93/1; Industrial Revolution 95/2; 18C Atlantic economy 96/1; 19C alliances 118/2; world trade 1860-1913 120/3; US bases 154/1; economy 156, 160/1
**Spanish Guinea** (now Equatorial Guinea) W Africa colony 113/1
**Spanish March** 48/1
**Spanish Sahara** (a/c Western Sahara includes Rio de Oro) NW Africa 102; Spanish colony 105/1; partition between Morocco and Mauritania 145/1, 150/1; economy 160/1
**Spanish Succession, War of the** 76/3
**Sparta** (a/c Lacedaemon) S Greece Mycenaean palace site 28/2; Peloponnesian War 31/2; Roman Empire 35/1
**Spartalos** N Greece ✕31/2
**Sphacteria** S Greece ✕31/2
**Srebrenica** NE Herzegovina UN safe area 158/2
**Srinagar** N India capital of Kashmir 91/3

rivijaya E Indies early empire 61/1
talingrad (until 1925 Tsaritsyn since 1961 Volgograd) S Russia WW2 132-3
tresa N Italy 1935 Conference 128/1
tyria (Ger. Steiermark) province of E Austria acquired by Habsburgs 2/2; Habsburg Empire 87/1
udan (form. Anglo-Egyptian Sudan) ritish control 102/1; Mahdist state 05/1; Anglo-Egyptian condominium 105/1; independence 145/1, 50/1; economy 160/1
udetenland C Europe German nnexation 129/2
uez Canal N Egypt Egyptian-raeli war 146/2; Anglo-French tack 150/1
uifen NE China treaty port 89/2
ukhothai C Thailand Buddhist site 2/1; major political centre 61/1
umatra (Indon. Sumatera) E Indies read of Buddhism 32/1; Dutch ossession 112/2; occupied by apanese 134/1
umerians ancient people of esopotamia 21/2
ung Empire China Mongol conuest 24/1
intel N Germany ✕48/1
urabaya (Dut. Soerabaja) Java ading centre 82/2; occupied by apanese 134/1
wakopmund SW Africa German ettlement 105/1
watow (n/s Shantou) S China eaty port 89/2; Japanese occupaon 117/2; 143/2
waziland country of SE Africa ritish protectorate 113/1; independence 145/1; economy 160/1
weden conversion to Christianity 0/1; Viking expansion 50/1; Black eath 63/1; Reformation 84/1; dustrial Revolution 95/2; EFTA 38/3; economy 156, 160/1
witzerland Reformation 84/1; dustrial Revolution 95/2; neutral WW2 132/1; EFTA 138/3; economy 156, 160/1; infant mortality and e expectancy 160
ydney SE Australia founded 100/1; llied base in WW2 135/2
yracusa (a/s Syracusae mod. Siracusa Eng. Syracuse) Sicily Greek olony 30/1; Roman Empire 35/1; yzantine Empire 44/1
yria Mitannian cities 20/1; Arab onquest 47/1; Ottoman province 02/1; WW2 132/1; independence 45/1; Gulf War 147/3
zechwan (n/s Sichuan) province of China under Ming 65/1; Manchu xpansion 88/1; Nationalist control 22/1; economy 143/2
zemao SW China treaty town 89/2
agliacozzo C Italy ✕51/2
aiwan (a/c Formosa) Mesolithic tes 16/2; early settlements 16/2; ontested by Dutch and Spanish 2/2; rising of aboriginals 88/1; cquired by Japan 89/2, 122/1, 7/2; seat of Chinese Nationalist overnment 153/1; Japanese vestment 153/3

Taiyuan (a/s T'ai-yüan) N China T'ang city 42/1; Ming provincial capital 65/1; French railway 89/2
Tajiks people of C Asia 140/1
Talas river C Asia ✕47/1
Talavera C Spain ✕93/1
Tamanrasset S Algeria Saharan trade 55/2; French occupation 105/1
Tamsui N Taiwan treaty port 89/2
Tana S Russia Mongol conquest 57/2
Tanais S Russia Greek colony 30/1
Tananarive (n/s Antananarivo) Madagascar centre of Merina kingdom 105/1
Tanganyika (form. German East Africa now part of Tanzania) independence 145/1; political development 150/1
Tangier (a/c Tangiers Fr. Tanger Sp. Tánger Ar. Tanjah anc. Tingis) Morocco centre of European trade 97/2; international control 105/1
Tannenberg (Pol. Stębark) E Prussia ✕WW1 125/1
Tannu Tuva (now Tuvinskaya ASSR) C Asia Russian protectorate 89/2
Tanzania (formed by amalgamation of Tanganyika and Zanzibar) 150/1; infant mortality and life expectancy 160. See also German East Africa
Tarawa Gilbert Islands, S Pacific ✕135/2
Tarentum (mod. Taranto) S Italy Greek colony 30/1
Tarim Basin C Asia occupied by China 42/1, 88/1
Tarnopol (now Russ. Ternopol) E Austria-Hungary WW1 125/1; WW2 133/2
Tarquinii (later Corneto mod. Tarquinia) C Italy Etruscan city 30/1
Tarraco (mod. Tarragona) NE Spain Greek colony 30/1, 35/1
Tarraconensis Roman province of N Spain 35/1
Tarsus S Anatolia early trade 20/1; Assyrian Empire 20/1; Hittite city 20/1; Roman Empire 35/1; Byzantine Empire 44/1
Tartars (a/s Tatars) Turkic people of E Russia 79/2, 140/2
Tashkent Russ. C Asia Mongol conquest 57/2; industry 126/2
Tasmania (until 1856 Van Diemen's Land) island state of SE Australia settlement and development 100/1 (inset)
Tatar ASSR (n/c Tatarstan) W USSR 141/1, 159/1
Tengyueh SW China treaty town 89/2
Tenochtitlán Mexico Aztec capital 68/2
Teotihuacán early culture of C America 22/2
Tertry N France ✕48/1
Teschen (Cz. Těšín, Český Těšín Pol. Cieszyn) city and district divided between Poland and Czechoslovakia 128/1; Czech part retaken by Poland 129/2
Tete Mozambique Portuguese settlement 55/2
Teutonic Order Baltic 53/2
Texas state of S USA independent

107/1; population 115/3; Depression 131/2
Thailand (f/c Siam) Theravada Buddhism 60/2; political developments 153/1; US bases 154/1; economy 153/3, 160/1; opium trade 161. See also Siam
Thebes (mod. Gr. Thivai) C Greece Mycenaean palace 28/2
Thebes (Lat. Thebae earlier Diospolis Magna) Upper Egypt 20/1; Roman Empire 35/1
Theodosia (mod. Feodosiya) Crimea Greek colony 30/1
Thera (mod. Thira a/c Santorini) island of S Aegean Greek parent state 30/1
Thessalonica (a/c Salonika Gr. Thessaloniki) N Greece Roman Empire 35/1; Byzantine Empire 44/1
Thessaly (Gr. Thessalia) region of C Greece centre of Byzantine Empire 44/1; ceded to Greece 119/1
Theveste (mod. Tebessa) Algeria Roman Empire 35/1
Thirteen Colonies N America 81/1, 92/1
Thrace (anc. Thracia) region of SE Europe divided between Bulgaria and Turkey 119/1; East occupied by Greece 128/1
Thracia (Eng. Thrace) SE Europe Roman province 35/1; Byzantine Empire 44/1
Thuringia (Thüringen) region of E Germany medieval German Empire 48/1; German unification 111/2
Tiahuanaco Empire C Andes site 23/1
Tianjin (f/s Tientsin) NE China economy 1979-92 143/2
Tibet (anc. Bhota Chin. Xizang) C Asia spread of Buddhism 32/1; early expansion 39/1; unified kingdom 42/1; Chinese protectorate 88/1; British sphere of influence 89/2; economy 143/2; absorbed by China 145/1
Tientsin (n/s Tianjin) NE China treaty port 89/2; Japanese occupation 117/2; economy 143/2
Tiflis (n/c Tbilisi) Caucasus Mongol attack 24/1; Muslim conquest 47/1; Mongol conquest 57/2; Ottoman conquest 58/1; urban growth 141/1
Timbuktu (Fr. Tombouctou) W Africa occupied by French 105/1
Timor island of E Indies early Portuguese colony 75/2; Dutch/Portuguese control 112/2; occupied by Japanese in WW2 134/1
Timur's Empire Persia 57/2
Tingis (mod. Tangier) Morocco Roman Empire 35/1
Tingitana NW Africa region of Roman Empire 35/1
Tinian island Marianas, C Pacific occupied by US in WW2 135/2
Tippu Tib's Domain E Africa 105/1
Tirana Albania Ottoman Empire 102/1
Tobruk (Ar. Tubruq) N Libya WW2 132/1
Togo (form. Togoland) country of W Africa independence 145/1; economy 160/1
Togoland W Africa German colony 105/1, 112/2

Tokyo (form. Edo) C Japan industrialization 83/1; trade 153/3
Toledo (anc. Toletum) C Spain Muslim conquest 47/1
Toletum (mod. Toledo) C Spain Roman Empire 35/1
Tomi (now Constanta) Romania Greek Colony 30/1; Roman Empire 35/1
Tonga island kingdom of S Pacific early settlement 24/2; British protectorate 112/2; independence 145/1 (inset)
Tongking (Fr. Tonkin) region of N Indo-China Hindu-Buddhist state 82/2; tributary state of China 88/1
Toulouse (anc. Tolosa) S France Muslim conquest 47/1; parlement 81/2
Tours (anc. Caesarodunum later Turones) C France archbishopric 48/1; seat of intendant 77/2
Trafalgar S Spain ✕93/1
Transjordan country of N Arabia Ottoman province 102/1; British mandate 132/1
Transkei region of SE Africa independent Bantustan 150/1
Transnistria Russian-speaking region of E Moldova 159/1
Transoxiana ancient region of C Asia Muslim conquest 47/1
Transylvania region of Hungary/Romania part of Austro-Hungarian Empire 119/1
Trapezus (mod. Trabzon Eng. Trebizond) NE Anatolia Greek colony 30/1; Roman Empire 35/1
Trebizond (Turk. Trabzon anc. Trapezus) NE Anatolia Byzantine Empire 44/1
Trebizond, Empire of NE Anatolia 67/1
Trier (Eng. Treves Fr. Trèves anc. Augusta Treverorum) W Germany archbishopric 48/1
Trieste (anc. Tergeste S. Cr. Trst) WW1 125/1; WW2 133/2
Trinidad island of W Indies British colony 107/1; independence 145/1
Triple Alliance 118/2
Tripoli (Ar. Tarabulus al Gharb anc. Oea) N Libya trans-Saharan trade 55/2; Muslim conquest 66/2; centre of European trade 97/2; Italian occupation 105/1
Tripoli (Ar. Tarabulus ash Sham anc. Tripolis) Syria Roman Empire 35/1; Byzantine Empire 44/1
Tripolitania N Africa district of Byzantine Empire 44/1; under Almohads 54/1; Italian occupation 105/1
Troy (Lat. Ilium Gr. Troas) NW Anatolia 28/2
Trucial Coast (later Trucial Oman, Trucial States now United Arab Emirates) E Arabia British control 102/1
Truk Caroline Islands, C Pacific Japanese base in WW2 134/1, 135/2
Tsaritsyn (1925-61 Stalingrad now Volgograd) S Russia founded 79/1; urban growth 141/1; Bolshevik seizure 127/1

175

**Tsinghai** (n/s Qinghai) province of NW China incorporated into Manchu (Ch'ing) Empire 88/1; economy 142/1
**Tsingtao** (Chin Ch'ing-tao, n/s Qingdao) E China German treaty port 89/2; Japanese occupation 134/1; economy 143/2
**Tukharistan** region of C Asia Chinese protectorate 42/1
**Tunis** (anc. Tunes) N Africa Ottoman conquest 55/2, 66/2; Habsburg Empire 87/1; centre of European trade 97/2; French occupation 105/1
**Tunisia** under the Almohads 54/1; autonomy under Ottoman Empire 102/1; French protectorate 105/1; under Vichy control 132/1; WW2 132-3; independence 145/1; economy 160/1
**Turkestan** region of C Asia walled cities 18/1; spread of Buddhism 32/1; during T'ang Empire 42/1; Chinese protectorate 88/1
**Turkey** on break-up of Ottoman Empire 102/1; Greek occupation of west 128/1; neutral in WW2 132/1; Baghdad Pact and NATO 147/1, 154/1; employment 156; opium trade 161; Gulf War 147/3. See also Anatolia, Asia Minor, Ottoman Empire
**Turkmen SSR** C Asia 140/1
**Tuscany** (It. Toscana) region of N Italy medieval German Empire 51/2; unification of Italy 110/1
**Tuzla** Bosnia-Herzegovina civil war 158/2
**Two Sicilies** kingdom 110/1
**Tyre** (anc. Tyrus Ar. Sur) Lebanon Levantine city 20/1; early trade 20/1; Phoenician city 30/1; taken by Alexander 30/3
**Tyrol** (Ger. Tirol It. Tirolo) region of W Austria medieval German Empire 51/2; Habsburg Empire 87/1; peasant revolt 92/1; South Tyrol to Italy 128/1
**Uganda** British protectorate 105/1, 112/2; independence 145/1; political development 150/1; economy 160/1
**Ugarit** (mod. Ras Shamra) ancient city of Syria Mitannian city 20/1
**Uighurs** Turkic tribe of C Asia 42/1
**Ukraine** region of SW USSR famine 1932 126/2; post-WW1 independence 128/1; SSR 140/1; independence 1991 159
**Ulm** S Germany ✗93/1
**Umayyads** Muslim dynasty, Caliphate 47/1, 48/1
**United Arab Emirates** (form. Trucial States earlier Trucial Oman, Trucial Coast) federation of sheikhdoms, Persian Gulf creation 145/1; Gulf War 147/3
**United Arab Republic** name given to union of Egypt and Syria 1958-61, retained by Egypt after dissolution until 1972
**United Kingdom** Industrial Revolution 95/2; world trade 1860-1913 120/3; foreign investment 1914 121/2; NATO and EEC 138/2, 154/1; economy 156, 160/1. See also

England, Scotland, Wales, Great Britain
**United States** War of Independence 99/1; industrialization 114/1; population 115/3; world trade 1860-1913 120/3; foreign investment 1914 121/2; WW2 in Asia and Pacific 134-5; involvement in Latin America 149/1; civil rights and urban unrest 1960-68 137/2
**Upper Volta** (Fr. Haute-Volta n/c Burkina) country of W Africa independence 145/1; economy 160/1
**Urga** (mod. Ulan-Bator Mong. Ulaanbaatar) Mongolia seat of Lamaistic patriarch 88/1
**Uruguay** part of Brazil 107/1; independence 107/1; political development 149/1; industry and economy 149/2; 160/1
**U.S.S.R.** collectivization and population movements 1923-39/labour camps 1932 126/2; famine 1932 126/2; fighting against Japan 135/2; Warsaw Pact Comecon 138/3, 154/1; nationalities 140/2; constituent republics 141/1; Cold War 154/1; military districts and bases 141/2; employment 156; territorial gains after WW2 159/1; dissolved 159/1
**Utah** state of W USA ceded by Mexico 107/1; population 115/3
**Utica** Tunisia Stone Age site 25/1; Punic city 30/1
**Uzbek SSR** C Asia 140/1
**Valencia** (anc. Valentia) E Spain bishopric 40/1; Muslim minority 84/1; ✗93/1
**Valona** (anc. Avlona Turk. Avlonya now Alb. Vlorë) S Adriatic Ottoman town 66/2
**Vandals** Germanic tribe, invasion of Europe and N Africa 39/1
**Varangians** Russia Viking raiders 52/1
**Varna** (anc. Odessus 1949-57 Stalin) E Bulgaria ✗67/1
**Venezuela** 18C Atlantic economy 96/1; independence 107/1; political development 149/1; economy 149/2, 160/1
**Venice** (It. Venezia anc. Venetia) Reformation 84/1; Black Death 63/1; WW1 125/1
**Vichy** France satellite state of Germany in WW2 132/1
**Vietnam** unification of north and south 153/1; 1945-75 war 152/2; economy 160/1. See also North Vietnam, South Vietnam, Indo-China
**Viipuri** (Sw. Viborg Russ. Vyborg) SE Finland captured by Russia 132/1
**Vijaya** (mod. Binh Dinh) S Indo-China capital of Champa Kingdom 61/1
**Villaviciosa** Spain ✗76/3
**Vilna** (Pol. Wilno Russ. Vilno Lith. Vilnius) Lithuania/Poland WW1 125/1; Polish seizure 128/1
**Vimeiro** Portugal ✗93/1
**Virginia** state of E USA colony 81/2; population 115/3; Depression 131/2
**Visigoths** Germanic invaders of Europe 39/1

**Vitez** Bosnia-Herzegovina civil war 158/2
**Vitoria** N Spain ✗93/1
**Vittorio Veneto** N Italy WW1✗125/1
**Vladimir-Suzdal** early principality of C Russia 53/2
**Vladimir-Volynsk** early principality of W Russia 53/2
**Volga Bulgars** early people of C Russia 52/1; 53/2
**Volhynia** region of W Ukraine acquired by Lithuania 62/2
**Volsinii** (a/c Velsuna med. Urbs Vetus mod. Orvieto) C Italy Etruscan city 30/1
**Volturno** S Italy ✗110/1
**Vukovar** E Croatia occupied by Serbs 158/2
**Wagram** Austria ✗93/1
**Waitangi Treaty** New Zealand 101/2
**Wake Island** C Pacific attacked by Japanese in WW2 134/1; US base 154/1 (inset)
**Wales** (Lat. Cambria Wel. Cymru) Scandinavian settlement 50/1; Black Death 63/1; Reformation 84/1
**Wallachia** (Turk. Eflâk) region of Romania under Hungarian suzerainty 62/2; under Ottoman control 67/1; occupied by Russia 93/1, 119/1; part of Romania 119/1
**Wallis and Futuna Islands** C Pacific French colony 145/1 (inset)
**Walvis Bay** SW Africa occupied by British 105/1
**Warsaw** (Pol. Warszawa Ger. Warschau) C Poland Grand Duchy under French protection 93/1; WW1 125/1
**Warsaw Pact** 138/2
**Waterford** S Ireland Scandinavian settlement 50/1
**Waterloo** Belgium ✗93/1
**Weihaiwei** N China treaty port 89/2
**Wenchow** (n/s Wenzhou) E China treaty port 89/2; 143/2
**Wessex** early kingdom of S England 48/2
**Western Sahara** see Spanish Sahara
**Western Samoa** S Pacific German colony 112/2; independence 145/1 (inset)
**West Indies** Spanish colonial trade 74/1. See also Caribbean
**Westphalia** (Ger. Westfalen) region of NW Germany satellite kingdom of Napoleon 93/1; unification of Germany 111/2
**White Horde** Mongol group of C Asia 57/2
**White Mountain** (Cz. Bílá Hora) Bohemia ✗86/3
**Whydah** (mod. Ouidah) Dahomey, W Africa early Dutch, French and English settlement 55/2
**Wilno** (Eng. Vilna Lith. Vilnius) W Russia transferred from Lithuania to Poland 128/1
**Wittenberg** E Germany Reformation 84/1
**Wittstock** N Germany ✗86/3
**World War I** 125/1
**World War II** 132-3
**Wuhu** E China treaty port 89/2
**Württemberg** region of S Germany Reformation 84/1; unification of

Germany 111/2
**Wusung** E China treaty port 89/2
**Xiamen** (f/c Amoy) S China special economic zone 143/2
**Xinjiang** (f/s Sinkiang) province of NW China economy 1979-92 143/2
**Yakut ASSR** E USSR 140/1
**Yamalo-Nenets AR** N Siberia 140/1
**Yarmuk** river Israel ✗47/1
**Yaroslavl** W Russia acquired by Muscovy 79/1
**Yekaterinburg** (1924-91 Sverdlovsk) W Siberia founded 79/1; railway to east 108/1; Tsar shot 127/1
**Yemen** (a/c Yemen Arab Republic) spread of Islam 47/1; Ottoman sovereignty 66/2, 102/1; union with South Yemen 145/1; Gulf War 147/3
**Yenan** N China destination of Long March 122/1
**York** (anc. Eburacum) N England bishopric 40/1, 3; Norse kingdom 50/1
**Yorktown** E USA ✗99/1
**Yoruba States** W Africa 54/1, 105/1
**Ypres** (Dut. Ieper) S Belgium centre of urban revolt 63/1; WW1 125/1 (inset)
**Yucatán** region of E Mexico early Indian state 22/2; modern province 107/1
**Yugoslavia** created after WW1 128/1; Cold War 154/1; Comecon 138/3; civil war 158/2. See also Serbia, Croatia, Montenegro, Herzegovina, Dalmatia, Slovenia, Bosnia, Macedonia
**Yunnan** (a/s Yün-nan) province of SW China under the Ming 65/1; Manchu expansion 88/1; Muslim rebellion 89/2; Chinese advance against Japanese forces 135/2; economy 143/2
**Zaire** (form. Belgian Congo earlier Congo Free State) C Africa independence 145/1; political development 150/1; economy 160/1
**Zambia** (form. Northern Rhodesia) independence 145/1; political development 150/1; economy 160/1
**Zante** (anc. Zacynthus mod. Gr. Zakinthos) SW Greece Venetian possession 67/1
**Zanzibar** island E Africa Muslim colony 54/1; early trade 75/2; Portuguese settlement 75/2; occupied by British 105/1; British protectorate 112/2; union with Tanganyika 145/1
**Zapotec** early civilization of C America 22/2
**Zeelandia** Formosa Dutch settlement 75/2
**Zeila** (Som. Saylac) Somalia Muslim colony 54/1
**Zhejiang** (f/s Chekiang) province of E China economy 1979-92 143/2
**Zhuhai** S China special economic zone 143/2
**Zimbabwe** C Africa early kingdom 54/1; modern political development 150/1; economy 160/1. See also Rhodesia
**Zurich** (Ger. Zürich) Switzerland Reformation 84/1; ✗93/1